THE COMP
IDIO
GUIDE

Astrology Dictionary

by Arlene Tognetti and Stephanie Jourdan, Ph.D.,
with Cathy Jewell

ALPHA
A member of Penguin Group (USA) Inc.

This book is dedicated to everyone who is curious about astrology, and who wants to know more.

ALPHA BOOKS

Published by the Penguin Group

Penguin Group (USA) Inc., 375 Hudson Street, New York, New York 10014, USA

Penguin Group (Canada), 90 Eglinton Avenue East, Suite 700, Toronto, Ontario M4P 2Y3, Canada (a division of Pearson Penguin Canada Inc.)

Penguin Books Ltd., 80 Strand, London WC2R 0RL, England

Penguin Ireland, 25 St. Stephen's Green, Dublin 2, Ireland (a division of Penguin Books Ltd.)

Penguin Group (Australia), 250 Camberwell Road, Camberwell, Victoria 3124, Australia (a division of Pearson Australia Group Pty. Ltd.)

Penguin Books India Pvt. Ltd., 11 Community Centre, Panchsheel Park, New Delhi—110 017, India

Penguin Group (NZ), 67 Apollo Drive, Rosedale, North Shore, Auckland 1311, New Zealand (a division of Pearson New Zealand Ltd.)

Penguin Books (South Africa) (Pty.) Ltd., 24 Sturdee Avenue, Rosebank, Johannesburg 2196, South Africa

Penguin Books Ltd., Registered Offices: 80 Strand, London WC2R 0RL, England

Copyright © 2010 by Amaranth

International Standard Book Number: 978-1-59257-987-7
Library of Congress Catalog Card Number: 2010926627

12 11 10   8 7 6 5 4 3 2 1

Interpretation of the printing code: The rightmost number of the first series of numbers is the year of the book's printing; the rightmost number of the second series of numbers is the number of the book's printing. For example, a printing code of 10-1 shows that the first printing occurred in 2010.

Printed in the United States of America

Note: This publication contains the opinions and ideas of its authors. It is intended to provide helpful and informative material on the subject matter covered. It is sold with the understanding that the authors, book producer, and publisher are not engaged in rendering professional services in the book. If the reader requires personal assistance or advice, a competent professional should be consulted.

The authors, book producer, and publisher specifically disclaim any responsibility for any liability, loss, or risk, personal or otherwise, which is incurred as a consequence, directly or indirectly, of the use and application of any of the contents of this book.

Most Alpha books are available at special quantity discounts for bulk purchases for sales promotions, premiums, fund-raising, or educational use. Special books, or book excerpts, can also be created to fit specific needs.

For details, write: Special Markets, Alpha Books, 375 Hudson Street, New York, NY 10014.

Publisher: *Marie Butler-Knight*
Associate Publisher: *Mike Sanders*
Senior Managing Editor: *Billy Fields*
Executive Editor: *Randy Ladenheim-Gil*
Book Producer: *Lee Ann Chearneyi/Amaranth@ LuminAreStudio*
Development Editor: *Lynn Northrup*

Senior Production Editor: *Janette Lynn*
Copy Editor: *Cate Schwenk*
Cover Designer: *Rebecca Batchelor*
Book Designers: *William Thomas, Rebecca Batchelor*
Layout: *Rebecca Batchelor*
Proofreader: *John Etchison*

Contents

Introduction

The planet Uranus rules astrology. We love that because Uranus rules wandering and seeking and discovery by chance ... the sort of discoveries that change *everything*. And expect a variety of viewpoints amongst authors. There are several camps: astrology as pure science; astrology as intuitive art; astrology as a psychological tool; and those that believe it incorporates science, art, and therapy. As a group, astrologers embody the Aquarian characteristics of being very unique and individual while avidly participating in group consciousness, while also being open-minded, light-hearted, and (sometimes) kooky. *Welcome home!*

Astrology lovers are passionate students of this ancient way of reading the heavens—and we know you are no exception. You use astrology to reveal intimate truths about your self, your future, and your most important dreams and desires. And however much you learn about astrology, you want to know *more*, so that you can dig deeper into the meanings you see in your birth chart, or even cast charts and read them for friends and family. Now that getting your birth chart is as simple as entering a few personal details (your birth date, birth place, and birth time) in a computer program or online, you're only a couple of clicks away from having your chart done—but you still have to be able to read and understand it!

How to Use This Dictionary

More and more people like you are getting their charts done ... and wanting to know how to interpret the astrological symbols they find in the chart wheel. What does it all mean? In *The Complete Idiot's Guide Astrology Dictionary*, you'll get hundreds of entries on everything about astrology A to Z—*everything* you want to know to read your chart and make interpretations, all in one easy-to-reference place, at your fingertips. Readers learn all the astrological terms and topics that professional astrologers use and consider important. So reading and using this dictionary is the equivalent of taking a class with a professional astrologer ... only *better!*

A New Astrology Dictionary for a New Generation

With the expert advice of two professional astrologers, Arlene Tognetti and Stephanie Jourdan, Ph.D., the definitions and interpretations in this dictionary represent the most current meanings of astrological terms—as well as how professional astrologers interpret them for their clients. This is no dusty, dog-eared, outdated tome from the flower-power 1970s filled with convoluted, esoteric definitions no one could understand (much less use). This is an astrological dictionary for the on-demand digital age—with innovative, smart, fun information today's New Age tech-savvy, networking users will find fresh, relevant, and revealing. With your birth chart in hand (or not), you can use this astrology dictionary to learn more about what *you* want to know—when and how *you* want to know it.

Today's generation of astrology lovers have the benefit of exploring their birth charts in ways previous generations couldn't do without going to a professional astrologer—casting a chart back then was a time-consuming, meticulous process better left to the experts! Now, you don't have to learn how to *cast* a chart (or pay someone to do it) … you can skip directly to learning how to understand and *interpret* a chart. Everything you need to know is here, in this dictionary.

Astrology A to Z

Entries in *The Complete Idiot's Guide Astrology Dictionary* may be divided into two parts. The first part gives you the definitive meaning of the term or topic; then, after the Star icon (⭐), in the second part of each entry, you'll get interpretations that you can apply to learn more about yourself … or whoever's chart you're reading. So you not only get the definition, you learn how to use it to make astrological interpretations. In some cases, you learn more about how the term or topic applies to humanity, as well.

Entries in this book follow dictionary order for alphabetization. However, in charts, tables, and boxes, we use zodiac order to cycle through the signs and ephemeris order to cycle through the planets.

Know Your Astro Themes

At the end of each entry in the dictionary, users will find a series of icons that designate Astro Themes. By looking at the icons, you'll be able to see at a glance what areas of astrology the term or topic impacts most importantly. Astro Themes include:

- Aspects, look for the symbol △.

- Birth Charts, look for the symbol **BC**.

- Compatibility, look for the symbol ☯.

- Houses, look for the symbol 🏠.

- Planets, look for the symbol ○.

- Retrogrades, look for the symbol ℞.

- Signs, look for the symbol ☼.

- Zodiac, look for the symbol **Z**.

Memorize the Astro Themes and use them to help you build connections. You'll gain valuable insights into how each dictionary entry fits into astrology as a whole.

Key Astrology Graphics

At the back of the dictionary, you'll find an Astrology at a Glance appendix that collects key astrology graphics, such as the zodiac wheel, the house wheel, and the natural planets and natural signs in their houses.

Acknowledgments

From Arlene: I would like to acknowledge two of my several Master Teachers in Astrology, Dorothy B. Hughes and Bruce Hammerslaugh, who encouraged me to keep investigating and studying, and most of all, to help others with my gifts and tools.

And Thank YOU, Cathy Jewell and Lee Ann Chearneyi of Amaranth, for your support, teamwork extraordinaire, and patience in the process of creating this twenty-first-century dictionary!

From Stephanie: Michael Chearney, dear friend, thank you so much. I am so grateful to my dear family for loving astrology and its pantheon as much as I do. Our after-dinner discussions warm my heart.

This has been a delightful project because of Lee Ann Chearneyi of Amaranth and my fellow writers.

Trademarks

above the Earth   **1.** When a planet is located above the horizon, namely anywhere between the ascendant and descendant via the midheaven, it is above the Earth. **2.** If a planet is found in the seventh, eighth, ninth, tenth, eleventh, or twelfth houses, it is above the Earth. **3.** The planets that appear above the horizon on a birth chart are those that were visible in the sky at the time of birth.

✦ **1.** What planets were above the Earth at your birth? If the majority of planets in your birth chart are above the horizon line, this will relate a human behavior of extroversion. You may appear or behave more outgoing and externally driven, meaning that you react more to what's going on in the world around you than to what's going on internally, or even things happening outside your home and family life. Career and nonfamily groups may be very influential for you. Houses above the horizon relate to areas such as career, partnerships (including marital and business partnerships), court, joint ventures/strategic alliances, religion, travel, colleges, publishing, social events, encounters with new people, funerals, social networks, town councils, community service, world trade, organizations and associations, public dealings, and public reputation. **2.** Individuals with most planets above the Earth usually appear to be more assertive or aggressive, and may also seem very confident. Relationships with others are very important. **3.** In a perfectly balanced birth chart, the planets are evenly distributed above and below the horizon, which brings balance to all areas of your life. Count how many planets you have above the Earth and how many planets you have below the Earth to see where your nature lies and what areas of life are a focus for you. See also *ascendant, below the Earth, birth chart, descendant, horizon, house, midheaven (Medium Coeli).* **BC** 🏠 ◯

adept   A birth chart without any planets or the ascendant in one of the elements. ✦ **1.** If you do not have any planets or your ascendant in the element of air, you are an air adept. A chart devoid of water is a water adept. No earth ascendant or planet is an earth adept. No fire is a fire adept. To be an adept in one of the elements indicates that you have mastered the nature of that element in past lifetimes and are inclined toward that element. The temptation to follow that element has been removed in this lifetime. **2.** An adept has highly evolved traits, skills, or expressions in the element that is missing from their birth chart, presumably because those abilities have already been mastered. Adepts are able to pass the energy of their mastered elements to other people, but not to themselves unless they have made the other elements conscious as well in their own lives. See also *astrologer/ist, elements.* ☯ **Z**

Age of Aquarius   **1.** One of the twelve astrological ages, named for the signs of the zodiac. Each age lasts about 2,150 years. The astrological ages move backward in the zodiacal sky. **2.** The age of Pisces began at the time of Jesus' birth and lasted for the next 2,000 years or so. Following the age of Pisces, and the sign preceding Pisces in the zodiac, is the Age of Aquarius. **3.** Astrologers do not agree as to how long each age lasts, or when, specifically, it starts. The Age of Aquarius may have started in or at the time of the Convergence in 1989, but others say 1970 was the magic date, and still others say this new age will not begin until 2021.

✦ **1.** Aquarius is a humanistic sign. It wants to help others, in a big picture kind of way. Everyone needs the basics, for example, and Aquarius wants to make that happen, to make a better future, in which everyone has food, housing, clean water, and access to health care. Pisces is more concerned with helping people right now to have better lives, and to alleviate the suffering they see. Pisces wants everyone to be content in life and to be spiritually connected. This is compatible with what Aquarius wants, but Pisces looks at things from a more personal level—the small picture—and is not so concerned with the future. In the shift from Pisces to Aquarius, we begin to look beyond ourselves. **2.** Because Aquarius looks to the future and has a love of technical and futuristic gadgets, the Age of Aquarius likely started with the advent of the Internet and the widespread use of computers and electronic devices that enhance social connections. **3.** When it's good, Aquarius is a great humani-tarian, inventing and changing things to make life better in the future. Aquarians think outside the box, so they have no difficulty imagining ways to make things better. Aquarius can be destructive, giving in to a desire to demolish something to replace it with a new idea. Aquarius may also act out negatively and violently, with an anti-establishment attitude that can lead to protest and destruction, without making any productive change. In this way, Aquarius acts like the Hindu goddess Shiva—as she destroys with one hand, she creates with the other. See also *Aquarius, astrologer/ist, planetary cycles.*

☼ Z

air, element **1.** One of the four astrological elements. The other elements are earth, fire, and water. A masculine (yang) element, air stands for intellect, media, and matters to do with communication and observation. **2.** The twelve astrological signs are divided equally among the four elements. The three air signs are Gemini, Libra, and Aquarius. **3.** The twelve houses are also equally divided among the elements. The three air houses are the third, seventh, and eleventh. These houses correspond to the three air signs and are called the houses of relationships, because they deal with siblings, marriage and other partnerships, and friendships, respectively. Planets found in these houses/signs are known as air planets.

✦ **1.** To find out whether or not you have air planets in your birth chart, you need to figure out what signs the planets in your chart are in. See how many planets are in the earth signs of Gemini, Libra, or Aquarius which rule the third, seventh, and eleventh houses. **2.** People ruled by air signs tend to value quick thinking and are better at multitasking and flights of fancy than other people are. If most of your friends would describe you by the way you think, then you may have a lot of planets in air signs in your birth chart; check and see. **3.** People with lots of air planets in their birth charts, or planets in the air signs of Gemini, Libra, or Aquarius, tend to develop intellectual relationships and communicate more with people. If you have lots of air planets in your birth chart, you may feel a need to communicate all of your thoughts and ideas with others to feel connected to the earth plane. **4.** What if there aren't many air planets in your birth chart? You might sometimes have difficulty with communication—maybe you don't best express yourself with words. You might be misunderstood, and you likely do not have the intellectual approach common in those ruled by air planets. You might be a more emotional person. If your planets aren't in air signs, where are they? Figure that out, and see what it means for you. When you don't have many planets in a particular element, it often just means that the houses associated with that element will not be the focus of your life. See also *adept, air sign, Aquarius, earth sign, elements, eleventh house, fire sign, Gemini, Libra, seventh house, third house, water sign.* **BC** ☯ 🏠 ○ ☼

air sign   **1.** Gemini, Libra, and Aquarius are the three air signs, or the air triplicity. Air signs are logical and rational. They are thinkers and are mentally sharp, but may also be visionary, and are always thinking of the possibilities in life. **2.** The air signs are focused on innovation on the earth plane.

✷ **1.** If your Sun sign is Gemini, Libra, or Aquarius, your mind and thoughts are your main focus. If you're an air sign, you are likely intellectual, studious, observational, inquisitive, and quick-witted. You're more rational than emotional, and you may be a good public speaker. You're very social. Logic is your friend, and you're no airhead. You're an objective observer, though some might consider you detached. Air signs are thinking all the time, and are very brain focused. As an air sign, you don't mean to get lost in your thoughts, but you really enjoy their company. You make quick decisions; it can seem like you're doing nothing, but really you're hard at work, in your head. Once you decide to do something, you take fast action. Part of the action for you is thinking and talking. A long conversation with someone can also lead to very fast action. Once you've processed everything, you follow through, with no second-guessing. You might be dissatisfied with the outcome, in which case, you'll rethink it and jump back in! Air signs sometimes look like airheads, but there's a lot going on others can't see. **2.** All the air signs have a masculine or yang energy. Like air itself, air signs are sometimes turbulent, sometimes calm. Air fluctuates from stillness to a calm breeze to a strong wind, so though the energy is masculine, air signs cover the entire energetic spectrum. If you're an air sign—Gemini, Libra, or Aquarius—your energy can go back and forth, and your behavior can change very quickly. Like the changing jet stream, you can shift from quiet to energetic in the time it takes you to breathe in. In combination with all the other information in a

A

birth chart this provides a very personalized reading of an individual.
3. If you're an air sign, how do you mix with the other elements?
Briefly, here's a look at your elemental compatibility: An air and earth
combination is mind over matter! Air is in the heaven, and earth is
on the ground—they are far apart, and it will take work to keep them
together—but opposites sometimes do attract. Air and air: it may be
difficult to get your head out of the clouds, but you think alike, so you
can process a lot together quickly, and your methods are the same.
You talk together and then you're ready to act. Air and water: what
a mix—bubbly champagne! It can be disconcerting, but it's also delicious. You may find you don't have a taste for the mix. Air and fire: the
oxygen in air is fuel for fire, and air finds fire energizing. These relationships tend to work best when fire leads, and if the air sign allows
this, it's a good combination. These energies can feed each other if the
combination is good. Air is flexible, and feeds fire to move ahead and
manifest its relationship. Fire encourages enthusiasm in air. See also
air, element; Aquarius; elements; Gemini; Libra; yang. ☼

Akashic Record   **1.** The causal plane library of all data pertinent to
each and every soul—human, animal, vegetable, or mineral—as well
as the universe itself. **2.** The Akashic Record is *etheric* and nonexistent
in the physical plane. **3.** Akashic is a Sanskrit word that means etheric.
4. The Akashic Record can be accessed psychically by humans or
effortlessly by disincarnate entities, including the deceased who have
not yet reincarnated and souls who have never chosen to incarnate.
✦ It's very important to work only with psychics and mediums who
know what they're doing, because any random spirit looking for a bit
of fun can look at your Akashic Record and give you key details about
your life when you are getting a psychic reading.

angels   Ancient Christian and Judaic writings associate astrological
signs or planets with specific angels. Four of the seven archangels
each rule an element. See also *elements.* ◯ ☼ **z**

Angels and their Associations

Michael	Fire Signs
Uriel	Earth Signs
Raphael	Air Signs
Gabriel	Water Signs

angle **1.** There are four main angles in the birth chart: ascendant (ASC), descendant (DEC), midheaven (or Medium Coeli, MC), and nadir (or Imum Coeli, IC). The ascendant and descendant are connected along a line called the horizon on a birth chart. The midheaven and nadir connect along a vertical line called the meridian on a birth chart. These are the most important points in a chart; powerful drive and motivational energy is located at these angles. **2.** Planets in angles are the strongest and most significant in a birth chart and will influence an individual's personality. See also *ascendant, birth chart, descendant, midheaven (Medium Coeli), nadir (Imum Coeli).* **BC Z**

angular house **1.** The first, fourth, seventh, and tenth houses in the birth chart. Angular houses are those following the four angles in a birth chart and are the strongest of the twelve houses. As with angles, planets in these houses are very powerful. **2.** These houses correlate to the cardinal signs: Aries, Cancer, Libra, and Capricorn. **3.** The first house (ascendant, east angle) represents the self and personality. **4.** The fourth house (IC, nadir, north angle) represents home and family. **5.** The seventh house (descendant, west angle) represents partnerships and marriage or significant others. **6.** The tenth house (MC, midheaven, south angle) represents the public self and career or public standing. ✲ **1.** The angular houses represent your strongest influences, and planets in these houses in your birth chart have a powerful impact. **2.** Look at your birth chart and make a note of the signs on your ascendant (cusp of first house), your IC or nadir (cusp of fourth house), your descendant (cusp of seventh house), and your MC or midheaven (cusp of your tenth house). Make a list of the ruling planets of these four signs. Now make a note of any planets that are within 10 degrees of these angles in your birth chart. Notice which planets have positive aspects such as sextile, trine, or conjunction in your chart; these planets naturally help you the most to get what you want. Notice which planets are challenged by aspects such as squares or oppositions; these planets relate to the traumatic experiences that have happened that need to be healed. See also *angle, birth chart, cardinal (quality), house.* △ 🐾 ◯ ☼

antiscion **1.** When two planets mirror each other in that they sit opposite each other by degrees on either side of the Cancer-Capricorn axis, they are called *antiscion.* For example, 20 degrees Taurus is antiscion 10 degrees Leo. Both points are equidistant from 0 degrees

A

Cancer and Capricorn. **2.** Pairs of signs that mirror each other to form antiscions are Aries/Virgo, Taurus/Leo, Gemini/Cancer, Libra/Pisces, Scorpio/Aquarius, and Sagittarius/Capricorn. **3.** In the birth chart, this creates a mild opposition within the upper or lower hemisphere. Each of the paired planets wants attention. ✧ **1.** If you have an antiscion in your lower hemisphere, the planet in the first quadrant wants you to take personal action and the planet in the second quadrant wants you to experience its energy in your interactions with others, especially family, children, co-workers, or employees. **2.** If you have an antiscion in your upper hemisphere, you may feel a pull between your third quadrant planet, which wants you to express your more latent or repressed qualities, and your fourth quadrant planet, which wants you to find your purpose in the world. See also *contrascion, fertility, hemisphere.*

Apollo finger   In mythology, Apollo is the god of the Sun. In palmistry, the third finger or ring finger of each hand relates to the person's Sun sign. ✧ Your individuality relates to your Sun sign, so this finger carries information on your ego and your soul. See also *Jupiter finger.* ☯ **Z**

April 20 to May 21   Birth dates for the Sun sign Taurus. The position of the Sun during these dates correlates with an astrological Sun sign. Those born between April 20 and May 21 have Taurus as their Sun sign. See also *Taurus.* ☉

Aquarius   **1.** The eleventh sign of the zodiac. **2.** Those born between January 21 and February 19 have Aquarius as their Sun sign. Also called the water bearer, Aquarius is a yang, or masculine, fixed air sign. The ruling planet for Aquarius is Uranus, named for the ancient Greek god of the sky. Uranus is a planet of the unconventional and unexpected—this sign values freedom. **3.** The glyph for Aquarius is waves ♒—and the symbol is the water bearer, a person bringing water to the Earth. The water bearer is nourishing the Earth with water—proving Aquarius to be a more emotional sign than the other air signs. This relates to the giving aspect of the Aquarian personality. **4.** Aquarius is the natural ruler of the eleventh house, the house of hope and friendship, both of which are strong traits of Aquarians. **5.** Other associations for Aquarius are the color blue and the gem amethyst.

✦ **1.** The body parts associated with Aquarius are the ankles, the circulatory system, and the nervous system. Aquarians should protect their ankles when playing sports—and be careful in high heels! Aquarians should do whatever is needed to protect their sometimes fragile nervous systems from undue stress and strain. Airy Aquarians would do well to stay grounded to the Earth by walking to keep the blood flowing. **2.** When your Sun sign is Aquarius, you're independent—Aquarians value their freedom more than anything else. You may appear emotionally distanced, but you're a true friend, loyal and giving. As an air sign, you're a thinker, but Uranus makes you an intuitive and innovative thinker. You may be innovative in other ways—perhaps even eccentric. Aquarius is a sign with an offbeat sensibility: you definitely march to your own drummer. Sometimes this leads you straight into trouble—you like finding new ways to do things, which may necessitate breaking a few rules. **3.** Aquarius is the sign of altruism and humanitarianism. Aquarians care about the world and its future. Aquarius is a fixed sign, however, which means it's sometimes stubborn. Take stock of your actions and be sure you aren't behaving out of stubbornness or boredom. Drama queens can take advantage of your open, friendly nature and corner you at a party or use up all of your research time. **4.** What subjects and what careers might appeal to Aquarians? Aquarians are big idea people, but they're also humanitarians. Combining passion about humanitarian causes with a love of science, Aquarians make leaders in areas of science and technology, particularly when it's going to benefit others. Aquarians do especially well in complex fields, like quantum physics or aeronautical engineering—your love for futuristic technology makes you the perfect designer for the next form of space travel. You would also do well in television, especially in some off-beat situation comedy or forum for young scientists. You may be an inventor, and computer science is also a good field for you, in information technology (IT) or web design. You would also make a good counselor or astrologer. Other subject areas you tend to enjoy are history, creative writing—for film, especially—and areas that are outside the box (like you), such as holistic medicine. **5.** *Watch out for:* Don't be different just to stand out. Be yourself. Aquarians have a tendency toward radicalism or taking ideas to extremes; make sure to put your energy to good use. Public protest is good when it's for a good cause, but perhaps not every cause needs this response. You are a thinker, but remember that the thoughts and ideas of others count, too. **6.** *I'm not an Aquarius, but my best friend is:* your Aquarius best friend is loyal and very interesting—no one thinks like this bff does. Your water bearer friend also tends to tell the truth no matter what, so don't come here looking for some sympathy about your botched design—if your concept is a mess, Aquarius will tell you so. Your Aquarian best friend is also very independent, so don't take it personally if this person seems to disappear like quicksilver from your life. Your friend likely needs some alone time—lure your friend back with a tantalizing new idea. See also *Age of Aquarius, Aquarius ascendant, Aquarius descendent.* ☼

Aquarius/Aquarius   1. Aquarius is an air sign ruled by Uranus, so two Aquarians together make for an intellectually stimulating bond. When two Aquarians get together, their relationship is one of communication. **2.** When partners of the same sign come together, karmic opportunities and challenges manifest. For this pair, the possibilities include learning to communicate with each other with a new vocabulary or language … or, it could mean becoming lost in flights of intellect untethered to the real world of experience. ✦ **1.** Aquarius/Aquarius enjoys sharing a wide range of unusual views and talking about everything under the sun. Their conversation needs no particular direction, but they will feed off each other's intellect, and enjoy debating and discussing many intelligent, unusual subjects. **2.** Aquarians harmonize with other Aquarians, so long as their belief systems are alike. Because Aquarius is a fixed sign, Aquarians tend to be stubborn, and when two Aquarians' belief systems differ, they may both spend a lot of time trying to argue their positions. Because Aquarians are independent, these two may spend lots of time apart, but neither will mind—they'll enjoy their time apart as much as they enjoy their time together. **3.** This pairing is particularly good as co-workers or friends. As a parent, Aquarius does better once the offspring has their own opinions, sense of independence, and friends. Aquarian children can be very Peter Pan-like. This combination is also great in marriage or domestic partnership, as both want the same kind of casual commitment and businesslike functioning. See also *Aquarius.* ☯ ☼

Aquarius/Aries   1. The energy of these two signs, Aquarius air and
Aries fire, works well together. Both signs value spontaneous conversation and independent thinking. **2.** Aries appreciates Aquarius's
imaginative, independent streak, and Aquarius likes Aries' energy
and strength. ✦ **1.** Aquarius wakes Aries up to a whole world of
new possibilities and Aries gets Aquarius organized so Aquarius
can make changes more effectively. **2.** For this pairing to work well,
Aquarius must be willing to let Aries take the lead. It's easier when
both like playing cat and mouse games. Aquarius plays hard-to-get
and Aries is thrilled by the hunt. Some Aquarius/Aries couples thrive
on this dynamic. **3.** Aquarius/Aries is a lively and spirited union that
works well as friends and lovers, if the balance is right. If Aquarius
feels bullied by Aries, airy Aquarius might retreat up into the clouds.
See also *Aquarius, Aries.* ☯ ☼

Aquarius ascendant   Also called Aquarius rising. The rising sign
is Aquarius; Aquarius is the sign on the cusp of the first house in the
birth chart and the sign on the eastern horizon at the moment of
birth.

✦ **1.** When your rising sign is Aquarius, Aquarius is the mask you
are comfortable presenting to the world. You may be a Taurus with
a Scorpio Moon, but your Aquarian traits are those that will be first
visible to others. **2.** Your rising sign also represents the sign you are
here to master in this life. The Aquarian traits of freedom, the desire
to develop your own independent thinking, to think outside the box,
and to present yourself in a compassionate, humanitarian way are
on the list of things you're here to do. Those with Aquarius as their
rising sign are unusual in their ideas, visionary and futuristic in their
approach, and concerned and compassionate in their community.
The Aquarius rising has a need for freedom, movement, and travel,
yet they love their home base and need a nest, castle, or tent to be
their base of operations. **3.** If Aquarius is your rising sign, you'll be
known by others as futuristic, entrepreneurial, inventive, and creative.
You may speak in terms of the future, as well. You want to make
changes to society to make the future better. You appear independent and stubborn. You are strong-willed, and you also have strong
convictions and a strong constitution. You appear to be always
thinking outside the box, and don't need to follow a traditional code
of behavior. You are cordial, and can be talkative and communicative.

You're also very open-minded. Aquarius rising has an adventurous spirit, and gets bored with routine. This rising sign needs a goal to maintain discipline. Communicating and developing new ideas keep the Aquarius rising engaged in life. Their best partnerships are with their intellectual equal. See also *Aquarius, Aquarius descendant, ascendant.* **BC** ☼

Aquarius/Cancer   1. Aquarius the air sign has several things in common with Cancer the water sign. Family and the home front is where these two signs will understand each other and relate well. **2.** When Aquarius/Cancer get together, making sure the home base and family members are secure and well taken care of are the focus. ✦ **1.** Aquarius can respect Cancer's need for privacy and Cancer can respect Aquarius's need to help the community. But Aquarius doesn't understand Cancer's possessive nature and Cancer is sometimes hurt by Aquarius's need for freedom and independence. Cancer may feel abandoned by Aquarius, and Aquarius may not stick around to explain things. **2.** Cancer tends to mother and Aquarius loves being childlike. Problems arise when Cancer gets locked into an adult role and Aquarius into a child role, unless Cancer is the actual parent. **3.** As long as both are committed to keeping channels of communication open, the Aquarius/Cancer combination can thrive both personally and professionally. See also *Aquarius, Cancer.* ☯ ☼

Aquarius/Capricorn   1. These are neighboring signs in the zodiac (Capricorn is the sign preceding Aquarius), a mix of air and earth. Capricorn's influence on airy Aquarius is to slow it down a bit, because Capricorn is an earth sign. **2.** When Aquarius/Capricorn get together, there is a tendency to work on business or projects, and whatever they are working on together, they take it very seriously. ✦ **1.** Aquarius can pull Capricorn out of their normal way of thinking and behaving, while Capricorn provides Aquarius with the structure and self-discipline to accomplish whatever goal they set. Capricorn's ability to manifest an idea into a physical reality is amazing, and Aquarius admires this. **2.** If too dominant, Capricorn may structure and discipline Aquarius to the point that Aquarius feels like their freedom is at risk—a really big problem for Aquarians, who need their spontaneity. **3.** When Aquarius and Capricorn share mutual respect, these two make good friends, good business partners, and they offer each other a good support system for achieving their goals. An Aquarius/Capricorn marriage can work well, so long as each understands the other's need for alone time. See also *Aquarius, Capricorn.* ☯ ☼

Aquarius descendant   1. The descending sign is Aquarius; Aquarius is the sign on the cusp of the seventh house in the birth chart. **2.** The seventh house is the house of partnerships and marriage or significant others. ✴ **1.** When your descending sign is Aquarius, Aquarius describes how you relate to others in partnership. This can be a romantic partner, a business partner, a partner on a project, or even a specific relationship with a friend or family member. No matter what your Sun sign is, your descendant will tell you a lot about yourself in these kinds of relationships. Having boyfriend trouble? Look no further than your seventh house. **2.** Aquarius descendant presents as the Aquarius Sun sign, with independence as key. Those with Aquarius descendant want freedom in all partnerships. They do not want to be pinned down. Ever heard the phrase "commitment phobic"? That's Aquarius descendant. Even in a marriage or a business partnership, they need their freedom and individuality. In any cooperative relationship, really, at work, or in personal life, it's hard to pin down the Aquarius descendant. They take an easygoing, nonjudgmental approach in all partnerships. They have a strong desire to cooperate with a partner to achieve concrete goals. They will rebel against traditional partnership rules—they don't like to be told what to do or how to do it in any kind of partnership—and may seek out nontraditional relationships. **3.** When Aquarius is your descendant, you may be very loyal and also faithful, but you need to be trusted with your freedom. If your partner can give you the freedom to express yourself as an individual within the relationship, you'll be more willing to commit. See also *Aquarius, Aquarius ascendant, descendant.* **BC** ☼

Aquarius/Gemini   1. The Aquarius/Gemini pairing is pretty close to perfect. These two air signs communicate well together and think alike. **2.** This pair talks about everything from trivia to world events to their ideas for solving their own—and the world's—problems. Aquarius and Gemini may have different solutions, but they will enjoy debating them together endlessly. ✴ **1.** Aquarius/Gemini like expressing differences of opinion, and aren't emotionally attached to the outcome. Once the debate is finished, these two move on to the next debate. As intellectual equals, partners in this combination learn a lot just being around each other. **2.** Aquarius/Gemini don't have to live together, or even in the same time zone, but when they pick up the phone, the conversation from last week continues as if no time has passed. **3.** Through Aquarius, Gemini's social circle starts expanding beyond childhood friends and siblings and starts to incorporate thinkers that are changing the world. In return, Gemini helps Aquarius see how temporary problems are and that life is happier with committed relationships. **4.** Aquarius/Gemini is a good combination for friendship or for a teacher-student, parent-child, or husband-wife pairing. See also *Aquarius, Gemini.* ☯ ☼

Aquarius/Leo   1. These signs, Aquarius and Leo, are opposite each other in the zodiac. The air sign Aquarius feeds the fire sign Leo. Air and fire are elements that are basically compatible. **2.** In this pairing, Aquarius is not bothered by Leo's need to be center stage, and Leo isn't bothered by Aquarius's need for physical and mental freedom. ✵ **1.** Mutual respect and good intellectual rapport is the norm for this Aquarius/Leo combination, though Leo's physical nature can be at odds with Aquarius's more intellectual style. **2.** Leo feels inspired by Aquarius to turn creative projects into political statements. In return, Leo thrills Aquarius by turning Aquarius's ideas into three-dimensional existence, such as a song, a teleplay, a website, or the artwork for a humanitarian cause. **3.** This pairing is excellent for business partners and lovers that turn into life-long friends. Aquarius and Leo offer mutual support and remain compatible as long as they allow each other space for personal and business growth. See also *Aquarius, Leo.* ☯ ☼

Aquarius/Libra   1. Like the Aquarius/Gemini combination, Aquarius and Libra are both air signs, with a deep intellectual compatibility. **2.** Aquarius and Libra share a sense of fairness and curiosity for design. ✵ **1.** Aquarius/Libra enjoys the joys of partnering, sharing a natural ability to understand each other's needs. Each has a special awareness of what the other needs in terms of security, privacy, and love. **2.** Romantically, these two flirt and text like crazy. Eventually, Aquarius comes to realize that freedom and marriage might actually dovetail. They crave equality, and if Aquarius and Libra are fair and just with each other, this is a perfect partnership.

3. Libra loves Aquarius's mind and feels proud to be Aquarius's relative, employee, friend, or partner. The pairing might make for better lovers than marriage partners, but a good marriage is possible. See also *Aquarius, Libra.* ☯ ☼

Aquarius/Pisces   1. Aquarius and Pisces are both humanistic signs, and the mix of air and water can be invigorating. **2.** Pisces is an emotional water sign, sensitive and compassionate to the needs of others, both the individual and the community. The Aquarian humanitarianism is geared more toward the group—they want things to be better for everyone, and are less likely to take note of their next-door neighbor's personal difficulties. ✧ **1.** Each of these signs, Aquarius and Pisces, recognizes and understands in the other the need to be of service. Aquarius is forward-thinking, not just because they think outside the box, but also because they think and plan for the future. But Pisces tends to spend more time in the here and now. They don't want to plan for how to fix problems in the future—they see a problem and want to fix it now. **2.** Pisces will drop everything and respond emotionally and immediately, while Aquarius is still thinking out the possible solutions and the likely impact of each one on future circumstances. Pisces is emotional and Aquarius is intellectual, and this is the fundamental difference between water and air. **3.** If they share beliefs—social beliefs, morals, spiritual beliefs—Pisces and Aquarius get along wonderfully. Without that common thread, Pisces feels lonely and Aquarius feels overwhelmed in attempting to figure out Pisces' moods. But in the long term, and especially in romantic relationships, Aquarius may not be able to meet Pisces' emotional needs, which may feel stifling to the freedom-loving Aquarius. See also *Aquarius, Pisces.* ☯ ☼

Aquarius rising   See *Aquarius ascendant.*

Aquarius/Sagittarius   1. The water bearer and the archer is another air-fire combination, but Aquarius and Sagittarius are the two most independent signs of the zodiac—in that way, they have a lot in common. **2.** Sagittarians like to be spontaneous and free, and Aquarians value freedom very highly, almost above all else (even family). ✧ **1.** As long as they are willing to appreciate these qualities in each other, Aquarius and Sagittarius see eye to eye. But if one of them thinks the other's freedom is threatening, or that their own freedom is being challenged, the relationship will falter.

2. Sagittarius, the fire sign, is fueled by Aquarius's airy intellectual and future-thinking ways, because Sagittarians are always shooting for the heavens. Sagittarius is hopeful and looks to the future with optimism, which encourages the future—thinking of Aquarius. Sagittarius is a philosopher, and loves to banter and debate with the cerebral Aquarius. **3.** The Aquarius/Sagittarius pairing is a fulfilling intellectual partnership—these two can write or teach well together, for example, and they might make a good stand-up comedy team, bringing their banter to the stage. But marriage might be a bit more challenging; Aquarius is too enterprising and Sagittarius too adventuring to agree to any partnership that feels constraining. See also *Aquarius, Sagittarius.* ☯ ☼

Aquarius/Scorpio   1. This is a challenging combination of air and water; as much as Aquarius values freedom, Scorpio values control. **2.** It's virtually impossible for both members of this Aquarius/ Scorpio partnership to get what they need the most in a relationship. ✸ **1.** Both signs want to control their personal freedom and their personal environment—which could make for some interesting arguments between Aquarius and Scorpio about what color to paint the bedroom! **2.** If this Aquarius/Scorpio pair shares beliefs, and are compatible that way (they support the same political party, for example, and they have the same religious beliefs and worldview), they can get along. But mix these two signs when they don't share such beliefs, and arguments may start that never end. The chemistry may be contentious and each sign will attempt to dominate (and change) the other. **3.** Scorpio is a very strong, committed sign, and Aquarius can be very stubborn, so it's difficult to sway either of these signs when their minds are made up. **4.** The Aquarius/Scorpio relationship proves challenging, except under the best of conditions and circumstances. Whether friends, domestic partners, co-workers, or family members, patience and good intent are required (and may not be enough to carry you, despite your good efforts). See also *Aquarius, Scorpio.* ☯ ☼

Aquarius/Taurus   1. This can be an easygoing combination, with some work. These are both fixed signs: Aquarius is an air sign, and Taurus is earth. **2.** Taurus is methodical, can be slow-moving toward goals, but always completes them. Aquarius is also good at completing goals, but wants to do it at the speed of light. ✸ **1.** To Aquarius, a Taurean's earthbound pace can feel like plodding along, which will frustrate airy Aquarius. Taurus, on the other hand, may find it difficult to understand Aquarius's need for change and innovation, because Taurus likes routine and the security of home life. **2.** Earth and air are very far apart, and it can be difficult for this Aquarius/Taurus pair to see each other's points of view. Their comfort zones are also far apart, and if they can maintain those while in partnership, they'll get along. **3.** Each partner on a project may have to work independently on their contribution, which Aquarius and Taurus bring together in the end. This pairing could be best friends, but it might not be marriage material (again, that distance). The partners in this relationship have to be willing to respect each others' individual way of thinking and doing things. See also *Aquarius, Taurus*. ☯ ☼

Aquarius/Virgo   **1.** Aquarius and Virgo are an air and earth mix with the potential for a good union. Both resonate to sacred patterns and sophisticated, elegant thinking. **2.** Aquarius is an innovative thinker and likes to move quickly on ideas, and Virgo likes to create, but is also a thinker and planner. ✧ **1.** If both Aquarius and Virgo partners are neat and tidy (or are both not so neat and tidy), they'll get along even better—this is a sign of their inner workings, and if you mix them up, they'll likely drive each other crazy. **2.** If compatible, Aquarius and Virgo make great friends; they look out for each other and are very supportive. They also make a good father/son or mother/daughter combination. As for marriage, though, Aquarius has an easier time committing to Aries, Gemini, Libra, and Sagittarius mates. Sorry Virgo! See also *Aquarius, Virgo*. ☯ ☼

archetype   Archetypes in astrology consider the symbolic meaning of the planets and the myths and symbols associated with the Sun signs and the planets. An archetypal astrologer looks at the chart as a story in process and helps clients to identify personal myths. Archetypal astrologers are often well versed in Jungian philosophy and teachings and employ dream therapy and guided visualization as part of sessions. See also *tarot and astrology*. ☯ **Z**

Aries   **1.** The first sign of the zodiac. **2.** Those born between March 21 and April 20 have Aries as their Sun sign. Also called the ram, Aries is a yang, or masculine, cardinal fire sign. The ruling planet of Aries is Mars, named for the Roman god of war (the Greek called this god Ares). Mars is all about power and energy—both of which Aries have in spades. As a fire sign, Aries has a hot temper. **3.** The glyph for Aries is the horns of the ram ♈ and the symbol is the ram. **4.** Aries is the natural ruler of the first house, the house of physical self, personality, and early childhood. **5.** Other associations for Aries are the color red—fiery!—and the diamond, not only a beautiful and valuable stone, but also nearly indestructible, as the hardest known natural material on Earth.

✧ **1.** The body part associated with Aries is the head. If you're an Aries, you tend to dive in to most situations—head first! This can leave you with some bumps and bruises on the noggin. Aries is also susceptible to head injuries and migraines. **2.** Aries are headstrong and powerful. When your Sun sign is Aries, you're likely running something—are you in charge of your school's canned food drive? The star of the spring play? The president of the debate club? Aries is active and competitive. If you play a sport, you play to win! You're full of energy and like to be outside, biking, hiking, running. You're competitive in school, too, and tend to do well. You're no wallflower, and speak out in class, sharing the answer—and your opinion—freely. Because you're so outgoing, you have a lot of friends who are, too. You're social, and like friends who can keep up with you. You're a risk-taker, and enjoy trying new things. You're likely to take any challenge. You tend to be impatient, and don't like having to figure out people who aren't straightforward, like you are. Your favorite people are energetic and creative, and very independent. You're an attention getter, and others have to work to keep up with you and to keep your attention. **3.** As a cardinal sign and the first sign in the zodiac, Aries is a sign of beginnings, and also leadership. **4.** What subjects and careers might appeal to Aries? Areas of study that support creative freedom tend to be favorites for Aries. You enjoy the arts, and subjects like dance or theater allow you freedom of expression and freedom of movement. You also enjoy work that keeps you moving, physically—preferably not a desk job. You're independent, and can work alone or in a group. You'll find success working in sales, travel, or IT, or in more creative areas such as architecture, design, or engineering. Service work such as teaching or environmentalism also suits you—and can potentially keep you out of a stuffy office. **5.** *Watch out for:* the Aries take-charge attitude. Yes, Aries are great leaders, but they sometimes bulldoze right over others' ideas with their energy. Be careful not to let your selfish side win out, and learn to work with others. Also, remember that you can be honest and kind at the same time. You sometimes have a hard time actually feeling your feelings—it's easier to consider them. Aries have a hard time with patience. You like starting new things, but may lose interest before they're finished. Your adventurous and courageous nature can quickly translate into recklessness. **6.** *I'm not an Aries, but my best friend is:* if you want a friend who is honest, smart, courageous, full of pranks, and willing to be the first to sign up for anything daring, this is the friend for you. Aries enjoys a challenge. This is a great companion for boxing, wingman for flirting, for kicking you in the butt to get you out of your rut, and looking out for your family or pets when you are out of town. Is your mom an Aries? An Aries mom is likely very energetic and fun, but may also be ambitious, not just for herself, but for you. Aries friends are the same in this as Aries moms: they may have a tendency to push you to be your best, and you should understand that though they do this out of love, if you aren't comfortable with it, you'll have to learn to stand up for yourself and make your own way. See also *Aries ascendant, Aries descendent.* ☼

Aries/Aquarius   See *Aquarius/Aries.*

Aries/Aries   **1.** Enthusiastic and headstrong, the Aries same-sign pairing is fire squared. **2.** When partners of the same sign come together, both the strengths and the challenges of the sign can manifest in the relationship. Aries partners may be experiencing a karmic destiny to push ahead, but need to be careful that the push does not degenerate into mere pushiness or impulsive action with no thoughtful base. ✧ **1.** Aries partners can become great inventors or creators together, but they both want to be in charge, which will lead inexorably to conflict. **2.** As lovers, the Aries duo is the couple who starts fights with each other so they can have hot make-up sex … lots of screaming, before and after. **3.** An Aries parent and child relationship can be really difficult. The Aries parent may feel she had it tough so why shouldn't her child. A more evolved Aries parent seizes the opportunity to be the role model for his child that he always wanted. Look to the other family Sun signs surrounding an

Aries/Aries pair to add calming and balancing energy. An Aries duo makes for a stormy partnership, whether as friends, co-workers, or as family. See also *Aries*. ☯ ☼

Aries ascendant   Also called Aries rising. The rising sign is Aries; Aries is the sign on the cusp of the first house in the birth chart and the sign on the eastern horizon at the moment of birth. ✷ **1.** When your rising sign is Aries, you present Aries characteristics to the world. This may be true no matter what your Sun sign is, because your ascendant is your outward presentation. **2.** Aries ascendant presents as the Sun sign's symbol, the ram, charging into things with energy. You will appear enthusiastic, dynamic and adventurous. Aries rising signs are very outgoing and excited about new adventures. If Aries is your ascendant, you appear to be independent, feisty, and self-reliant. **3.** If Aries is your rising sign, you like to be challenged every day. If there is nothing to learn, make, do, fight, or dominate, Aries rising feels frustrated. They have a lot of energy and dance in their chairs while sitting at their keyboards. Aries rising is also blessed with a very strong constitution. They are the human polar bears that go swimming in the ocean in wintertime. Aries rising has strong instincts and can survive anywhere. As children, they do what they want and can be challenging to discipline as they fight back. Most Aries rising excel at communications because they write as fast as they talk. Aries can be gruff and all-business by day, but at night they are romantics and homebodies. See also *Aries, Aries descendant, ascendant*. **BC** ☼

Aries/Cancer   **1.** Aries the fire sign and Cancer the water sign are at odds, even on the most basic focus in life. **2.** Cancer wants to adapt, connect, and bond, while Aries wants to be free to do their own thing! ✷ **1.** As a water sign, Cancer feels everything and may be easily hurt by Aries' detached attitude and sharp tongue. Aries' idea of advice is to just "buck up" and move on. Aries can see beyond the emotions that Cancer tends to get mired in, but they still don't want to go there, and they may look for the quickest way out of the relationship. **2.** The place of mutual understanding between Aries and Cancer may be that they both feel strongly about offering help when help is needed. **3.** Aries and Cancer may work better as friends or co-workers than as romantic partners. When they share beliefs, they can work well together to complete a common goal; otherwise, this relationship may be plagued with resentment and misunderstanding. See also *Aries, Cancer.* ☯ ☼

Aries/Capricorn **1.** Aries is a fire sign, while Capricorn is an earth sign. You might think that fire and earth wouldn't understand each other, but cautious and methodical Capricorn is motivated by the enthusiasm of impulsive, let-down-your-hair Aries. **2.** When they are open to each other, Aries and Capricorn can find balance. ✦ **1.** Capricorn brings Aries down to a more practical level, while Aries lifts Capricorn out of their natural seriousness. **2.** The Capricorn/Aries pair often is so busy trying to figure out how to make something work that they are able to find common ground to build on; if they can do this, then the pair may accomplish more than would meet the eye given their different styles. **3.** Aries and Capricorn are complementary in business and as co-workers. Marriage between these signs might be difficult, with neither partner finding full satisfaction. See also *Aries, Capricorn.* ☯ ☼

Aries descendant **1.** The descending sign is Aries; Aries is the sign on the cusp of the seventh house in the birth chart. **2.** The seventh house is the house of partnerships and marriage or significant others. ✦ **1.** When your descending sign is Aries, Aries describes how you relate to others in partnership. This can be a romantic partner, a business partner, a partner on a project, or even a desire for cooperation toward a committed situation or relationship. No matter what your Sun sign is, your descendant will tell you a lot about yourself in these kinds of relationships. Having roommate trouble? Look no further than your seventh house. **2.** Aries descendant seeks out people who are independent, energetic, aggressive, and sexual, and who like a little adventure in their relationships. The Aries descendent is always interested in a good challenge when it comes to relationships. Aries wants to catch someone worth winning, available or not. **3.** Aries descendant tends to avoid confrontation and anger in their own expression, so they attract it in relationships. This typically happens when the Aries descendant picks a partner who can fight their fights for them. See also *Aries, Aries ascendant, descendant.* **BC** ☼

Aries/Gemini **1.** Aries is a fire sign and Gemini is an air sign—these signs are very compatible, with airy Gemini feeding Aries' fire. Fire and air are one of the most compatible pairings for any form of partnership, including marriage. **2.** The Aries/Gemini pair communicates well, and on any subject! ✦ **1.** Aries and Gemini both love to talk, and they also both love to get out there and try new things. Gemini has an intellectual and creative mind, while Aries likes to be the builder, bringing Gemini's ideas to fruition. **2.** Aries and Gemini have a good, basic understanding of each other's needs, and they handle life in compatible ways. **3.** The Aries/Gemini combination works well as siblings, friends, lovers, and business partners. The only exception might be when Aries is the teacher and Gemini is the student who questions Aries authority a bit too much. See also *Aries, Gemini.* ☯ ☼

Aries/Leo   **1.** These signs combine fire and fire; Aries and Leo are very compatible, and are often very attracted to each other, but this much fire may be hazardous! **2.** Leo is a director, and needs someone to direct; Leo will try to be the leader in any relationship. But Aries is pioneering, independent, self-directed, and has lots of self-esteem. ✦ **1.** Aries likes to be out in the world on their own, and may not take Leo's lead. These signs will have great energy when collaborating—again, all that fire! **2.** Aries and Leo will encourage each other to grow and to try new things. This duo is fiery and passionate, sometimes even volatile. To outsiders, they may seem not to get along, but they like arguments, and find arguing a healthy expression. After a big blowout, they don't hold grudges. They simply move on, and their relationship deepens. **3.** For this pairing to function well in the workplace, Aries has to let Leo be the boss (or let Leo think they're the boss). When this happens, Aries/Leo can be a good marriage combination, too. See also *Aries, Leo.* ☯ ☼

Aries/Libra   **1.** Aries and Libra are fire and air signs, compatible elements. They are opposite each other in zodiac, and opposites often attract. **2.** Libra is a giver, and understands Aries. Aries profits from the balance and steadiness Libra can provide. ✦ **1.** This pair can be a good match if Libra is willing to give up some control, and let Aries have his or her freedom. Libra likes consistency and security, and will have to adjust to Aries' impulsivity. **2.** Libra helps Aries with completion and follow-through, which is not an Aries trait; Aries tends to get bored before finishing a project. **3.** Libra holds her partners to their word and expects responsibility from those around her. Aries helps lighten Libra up and brings energy to the partnership. Libra is serious when committed, and stays the course, while Aries prefers to leave the beaten path. **4.** When they accept each other and each others' influence, without one trying to change the other, Aries and Libra can have a very fulfilling partnership, in business, friendship, or marriage. See also *Aries, Libra*. ☯ ☼

Aries/Pisces   1. Aries is a fire sign and Pisces is water, which tends to drown out fire. Aries like to get things done, and the Aries urge to action may pack too much power for reflective Pisces. **2.** Aries jumps into things, while Pisces needs an emotional attachment before acting. ✵ **1.** Pisces might accuse Aries of being distracted: Aries jumps around (like fire), while Pisces is enriched by focusing on one thing, which bores Aries. **2.** Aries may hurt Pisces' feelings—usually unintentionally—because Pisces needs an emotional commitment, which is not a high priority for Aries, for whom curiosity is a key driver. Pisces is committed, and sticks to what he or she believes with devotion. Aries changes devotions, which Pisces cannot fathom! **3.** Aries and Pisces is not the most compatible pairing for marriage or business, unless the relationship is pushing creative boundaries; but these two are fine friends. See also *Aries, Pisces*. ☯ ☼

Aries rising   See *Aries ascendant*.

Aries/Sagittarius   1. Put two fire signs together, and sparks will fly—even when their flames burn a bit differently. **2.** Aries gets out and gets things done, while Sagittarius is easygoing, and tends to think more than Aries. ✵ **1.** Sagittarius has a more philosophical view of life, they observe more, remember their experiences, and learn from their past, applying their knowledge in their lives. Aries is adventurous and keeps trying new things, without considering how disastrously things turned out previously in a similar situation. **2.** Aries and Sagittarius can be compatible, because both love to travel, build something, or just be creative. Sagittarius brings out the visionary in Aries, and Aries brings out the more inventive or entrepreneurial side of Sagittarius. **3.** Both are progressive and look to the future, so Aries and Sagittarius aren't at odds about their goal, but they will have a different view of how to reach it. Aries and Sagittarius are usually supportive of each other's goals, and they understand each other. They won't have expectations of each other, so there isn't disappointment in unmet expectations. Neither has a need to control the other. **4.** Aries/Sagittarius can be good as friends, as well as business or marriage/relationship partners. See also *Aries, Sagittarius.* 🌓 ☼

Aries/Scorpio   1. The Aries/Scorpio duo is a combination of fire and water. Sometimes this pair will get along, sometimes they won't. Both of these signs are ruled by Mars, the god of war and of getting your goals. **2.** The Aries/Scorpio relationship will be intense and passionate. �֎ **1.** Aries and Scorpio love a good debate, and make great problem-solvers together—picture them as partners in the FBI, for example. When they work well together they really work well together, but sometimes these two just don't get along. **2.** Scorpio is one of the more self-sufficient water signs, but they like to get beneath the surface: they do not abide secrets. Aries understands this, but it's in the Aries nature to sometimes just act. Aries doesn't like waiting around while Scorpio thinks things through, prepares, and gets a plan going. Scorpio needs to size things up before making a move, and might blame or resent Aries' impulsivity when things don't go as planned. **3.** Both signs are intense when pursuing a goal, but this intensity can make cohabitation between Aries and Scorpio tricky. Aries and Scorpio both like to be in control of their environments, which may make decorating difficult! Scorpio brings out Aries' passion, and can help them with decisiveness, while Aries brings their enthusiasm to Scorpio, who can get mired down in their research and planning. The Aries/Scorpio pairing is best for a business partnership, for co-workers, or for friendship. See also *Aries, Scorpio.* 🌓 ☼

Aries/Taurus   1. These Aries fire and Taurus earth signs are neighbors in the zodiac. **2.** When together, Aries gets Taurus energized and moving, and Taurus grounds Aries and helps with follow-through. ✖ **1.** Aries is attracted to Taurus's grounded nature, and is good at lightening up Taurus, getting them to try new things. Aries respects individuality and can go about their business, letting Taurus think. Taurus gets Aries to focus and settle—a little. **2.** Taurus always finishes what they start, taking their time and processing things, while Aries multitasks, gets bored, and then moves on to something else. For this pairing to work, Aries has to back off and let Taurus go through their process at their own pace. **3.** Of all fire and earth combinations, Aries and Taurus get along the best. They have mutual respect, and need to give each other space, which these two naturally do. Taurus is not threatened when Aries flits off, and in fact, enjoys the alone time. This combination is good for marriage and committed relationships, co-workers, boss-employee relationships, and friendships. See also *Aries, Taurus.* ☯ ☼

Aries/Virgo   1. This is a fire and earth combination; Aries brings the combustibility of new beginnings to the Virgo grounding of ritual and love of natural patterns. **2.** While Virgo needs a plan, Aries hates a plan. ✴ **1.** Virgo usually wants to know everything a partner does, in order to analyze it. Aries, however, doesn't readily give out the details. If these two give each other the space to be who they are, they'll be okay. Their methods of doing things are very different, and they will have to work around that. **2.** Virgo wants Aries to have a plan, which Aries thinks isn't needed. Much as Virgo might try, Aries can't be controlled. **3.** Aries likes discipline, but they have to be free-spirited. Virgo may never seem so restrictive as they are around Aries. Aries' impulsive nature brings this organized, planning side out in Virgo. **4.** The Aries/Virgo pair may debate, and they may disagree, but they will communicate their differences to each other, so there will not be deception in the relationship. Aries and Virgo simply process things differently: one's a thinker and planner and one's an actor and doer. They may be incompatible because of this. The best relationship for this pairing is friendship or business. Picture Aries as the visionary COO with Virgo as their detail-oriented CFO. See also *Aries, Virgo.* ☯ ☼

ascendant   1. Also known as the rising sign, the sign and degree on the cusp of the first house, the eastern horizon of the chart, at the exact time and place of birth. **2.** On a birth chart, the ascendant line is the left side of the horizon line (the right side is the descendant). Were the chart a clock, the ascendant would be at the nine o'clock position.

✴ **1.** Your ascendant is the sign rising on the eastern horizon the minute you were born. Each sign rises in the course of a 24-hour day, for about two hours. So your rising sign could be the same as your Sun sign, but this is only likely if you're born around sunrise, because the Sun sign is the first sign on the horizon each day. When your Sun sign and rising sign are the same, you are very congruent

A

in that your true self is pretty much what people see … *what you see is what you get.* Your inner dialogue matches what you are communicating to others. You have to be more aware, though, that other people are not as honest and straightforward as you are. **2.** If your Sun sign and your rising sign are different, the you others see may not be the real you. Your ascendant or rising sign is on the cusp of the first house, the house of personality and physical self. This represents the outward you—what you present to others, and what they see. For this reason, it's sometimes called a mask. It's your game face. It's also how you see the world. You may feel that your ascendant feels truer to your personality than your Sun sign, especially if you are female. Your sense of style, how you communicate—these are all aspects of the ascendant. **3.** Your rising sign also represents the sign you are here to master in this life, and what you need to learn. Look to your rising sign for clues to where you can best put your efforts in this lifetime to learn and grow. **4.** The ascendant or rising sign also marks areas of strength for you. This is because the ascendant is the collection of traits and behaviors that your subconscious mind believed would enable you to survive most readily. The subconscious mind, ruled by the Moon, observes all of the reactions to your behaviors from the time you were born and identifies which of your behavioral reactions meet your needs; some believe that this process actually starts in the womb. The Moon then signals your Mars to promote the most advantageous behaviors and traits, thus ensuring your survival as a physical being. The Moon is looking for what gets you fed, protected, and listened to. As you realize the behaviors that are designed to reach these goals may no longer be needed because you are beyond basic survival, you outgrow your ascendant and start to shed the mask your rising sign represents. You become more like your Sun sign. **5.** Planets within 10 degrees of your ascendant on your birth chart, especially those within the first house, are more easily expressed than the other planets, unless challenging aspects (such as a square or opposition) hamper their expression. These planets are more active in your personality and they activate the other houses whose signs they rule. You will tend to favor your first house and those other houses with signs on their cusps that are ruled by the planets on your ascendant. See also *birth chart, descendant, horizon.* △ **BC** 🏠 ○ ☼

ascending   See *descending*.

aspect grid   1. A table representing the aspects between planets in a birth chart. **2.** The aspect grid is a triangular-shaped series of boxes with the planets listed along two sides. The information in the boxes indicates the relationship between pairs of planets. These planetary relationships will also appear as lines within the center of a birth chart. These lines are usually keyed. The line may have a symbol on it that represents its aspect, such as an opposition, quincunx, trine, square, semi-sextile, or conjunction. Or the lines may appear as different colors, such as blue for harmonious aspects and red for challenging aspects. Many computer programs reflect the aspects as thick or thin according to the tightness of the orb. Oftentimes, broken lines are used for quincunxes and sextiles to easily distinguish them from trines and squares. See also *aspects between planets, birth chart.* △ **BC** ◯

aspects between planets   1. Angles between the planets. The birth chart is a circle, which is 360 degrees. Aspects indicate the distance, in degrees, between the planets in a birth chart. Aspects are in place at the time of birth, and remain in place. **2.** Planets with certain angles between them are said to be in aspect to each other. Particular aspects indicate the relationship between the planets involved; some relationships are beneficial, while others are challenging. In general, aspects show how the parts of the psyche (the soul) function in or out of harmony as a whole. Think of the planets as a cast of characters in the movie that is a human life. The planets that have soft or easy angles between them are like the cast members who always get along with the protagonist and keep the general plot unfolding. Nearly every movie has characters who are in harmony with the protagonist, along with characters who keep getting into trouble and creating conflict for the protagonist. The planets that are without aspects are like characters that make cameo appearances; those planets have to wait until a progressed planet or transiting planet makes an angle with them to have an impact on the protagonist. **3.** There are five major aspects (conjunction, sextile, trine, square, and opposition) and four minor ones (quincunx, semi-sextile, semi-square, and sesquisquadrate). See also *angle, conjunction, opposition, quincunx, sextile, semi-sextile, semi-square, sesquisquadrate, square, trine.*

asteroids   1. Discovered in the 1800s, this relatively new addition to astrology consists of planetoids that orbit the Sun between Mars and Jupiter. **2.** Asteroids appear in birth and other astrological charts much as planets do, and exist in aspect to planets. However, most astrologers do not consider the energy of asteroids to be as stable as that of planets. Astrologers use asteroids to help illuminate what's going on in the astrological houses when interpreting birth charts for clients. **3.** The first four asteroids, Ceres, Pallas Athene, Vesta, and Juno, activated feminine consciousness in humanity. Since antiquity, femininity was limited to only the Moon and Venus. Interestingly, the first asteroid ephemeris was published when the women's liberation movement commenced. No longer was the feminine only considered to be of value as a mother or a mate. Thanks to the inclusion of these Greek goddess myths, men and women started to openly explore the value of the feminine in the masculine realms and vice versa. New careers opened to both genders and it became acceptable for men to be present at the birth of their children and to raise them as well. The discovery of the feminine as seen in the asteroids has led to an increase in intuition, compassion, and connection between science and spirituality all over the world. **4.** Ceres, the first discovered asteroid, is now considered a dwarf planet, like Pluto. It is named after the Greek goddess of agriculture. **5.** Pallas Athene, the second asteroid discovered, is often called Pallas, and is named after the Greek goddess of war and wisdom. **6.** Juno, the third asteroid discovered, is named for the Roman goddess of marriage. **7.** Vesta is named for the Roman virgin goddess of the hearth. **8.** Chiron, also known as the wounded healer, is a "centaur" asteroid (astronomically a comet labeled a planetoid) found between Saturn and Uranus. Of all the asteroids, Chiron has the most stable orbit and is usually considered by astrologers with the planets when interpreting basic astrological birth charts. See also *Ceres, Chiron, Juno, Pallas, Vesta.* ◯

asteroid transits   There are thousands of asteroids orbiting the Sun. They form a belt between Mars and Jupiter. Ceres, ruler of Mother Earth and unconditional love, was the first to be discovered, on January 1, 1801. All of the asteroid transits activate feminine dynamics in both sexes. See also *asteroids.* ◯**Z**

astrologer/ist   **1.** A person who analyzes the position of the planets at the time and place of one's birth, creating a birth chart; one who uses birth chart information to provide insights into personality and facets of life such as relationships, health, and place of work or residence. **2.** Astrologers study astrological information, looking at relationships and correlations in the data making up birth charts, as well as progressed and other charts. **3.** Astrologers are ruled by the planet Uranus, the sign of Aquarius, and the eleventh house. See also *astrology, birth chart, business astrology.* **BC ☯ Z**

astrological calendar   **1.** A 365-day (or 366-day for leap year) calendar of the appearance of the Sun's ecliptic through the zodiac. **2.** Though everyone knows now that the Earth orbits the Sun, and not the other way around, geocentric or Earth-centered astrology works with the solar system as though the Earth is the center of the universe. This is how humans experience life, after all, as though they are the center of the universe. **3.** The astrological calendar ends and begins when the Sun enters the sign of Aries at the zero-degree, zero-minute position. ✦ You can use an astrological calendar to look for favorable planetary transits day by day, and gain insights into good timing for specific activities and endeavors. See also *geocentric.*

astrological symbols   Glyphs and symbols used to represent astrological Sun signs, planets, luminaries, asteroids, aspects, nodes, and angles. A birth chart will indicate all information with these symbols. See also *birth chart, glyph.* **BC Z**

astrology   The study of the positions and aspects of the planets, Sun and Moon (the luminaries), and asteroids based on the idea that these bodies and their relationships influence people and events on Earth. See also *astrologer/ist.* **BC Z**

astronomical order of the planets   The order of planets by distance in our solar system: Sun, Mercury, Venus, (Earth), Moon, Mars, Jupiter, Saturn, Uranus, Neptune, and Pluto. Most astrologers will refer to ephemeris order when listing planets for astrological interpretations. See also *ephemeris order of the planets.* ○

astronomy   1. The scientific study of the universe and all its entities, including planets, stars, and galaxies. Astronomy deals with the position, size, motion, composition, energy, and evolution of celestial objects. For centuries, people have studied the night sky, looking for clues about the nature of the world we live in. **2.** Thanks to the tireless efforts of astronomers, new planets and effects are discovered, stimulating new levels of consciousness in humanity and providing more completion to astrology. The day will come when every sign has its own rulers, both masculine and feminine. See also *astrology.* **Z**

astrophysiognomy   See *planetary physiques.*

August 22 to September 22   Birth dates for the Sun sign Virgo. The position of the Sun during these dates correlates with an astrological Sun sign. Those born between August 22 and September 22 have Virgo as their Sun sign. See also *Virgo.* ☼

axis   1. The astrological chart is divided into twelve segments called *houses.* Each of the six lines that divide the chart into the twelve houses is called an axis. **2.** The horizontal axis that creates the southern and northern hemispheres in the chart establishes the ascendant and descendant. **3.** The vertical axis that creates the eastern and western hemispheres in the chart establishes the midheaven and the nadir. **4.** Each axis relates to the two houses it supports, which are opposites. See also *ascendant, birth chart, descendant, house, midheaven (Medium Coeli), nadir (Imum Coeli).*

Axis Chart

1st/7th axis	Independence vs. relationship
2nd/8th axis	Attachment vs. detachment
3rd/9th axis	Speaking vs. listening
4th/10th axis	Personal vs. public
5th/11th axis	Human creation vs. divine intervention
6th/12th axis	Effort vs. surrender

B

Babylon   **1.** This Mesopotamian city is the present-day location of Baghdad. In ancient times it was the world center of commerce and also the center for culture and science. **2.** The Tower of Babel, devoted to astrology, was built in Babylon. The Babylonians created tables for the phases of the Moon and learned to predict eclipses. They also compiled The Illumination of Bel around 2100 to 1900 B.C., a work on astrology. The Babylonians divided their year into twelve parts and gave each part an astrological name. Astrologers were often referred to as Babylonians because Babylonians were so renowned for their astrological acumen. See also *astrology, Moon phases.* ◯

balsamic Moon   **1.** This is the phase when the Moon is fewer than 45 degrees behind the natal Sun in the birth chart. It's the last Moon phase, preceding the new Moon (also called the dark Moon, the witches' Moon, or the wishing Moon). **2.** There are eight lunar phases, and of these, the balsamic Moon is the final phase, the last three days of the lunar cycle preceding a new Moon.

✦ **1.** In the astrological birth chart, a balsamic Moon reflects your soul's desire to make unresolved past life emotional trauma conscious so that it can be claimed and understood. **2.** If you were born under a balsamic Moon, you are probably more psychic and emotional than your new Moon counterparts. You're also more inwardly focused. **3.** For humanity, this final Moon phase, when the Moon goes from crescent to dark, is a time for introspection, as well as rest and recuperation. You may find your old emotional baggage unpacks itself on your bed and invites you to sleep with it so that you can come out of denial and own your emotional issues. During the balsamic Moon you are here to finish up a cycle and complete a karmic need, not to start things. You probably don't like crowds or the limelight—you enjoy

your privacy, and might like to work alone. You might be a night owl.
You find it satisfying when you complete things, and feel a strong
urge to finish a big task. You will work steadfastly toward this task,
and when it's done, you'll go off and hibernate for a while. You also
encourage other people to start the process of germinating new projects, meditating upon their recent accomplishments, and pondering
what exciting goal might emerge next. **4.** Moon phases are also used
in forms of divination such as fortune telling and tarot card reading.
Because lunar astrology focuses upon the relationship between the
Sun and the Moon, it is easy to remember that lunar astrology uses
Moon phases to explain the dynamics of relationships. We tend to
think of the Moon as constantly fluctuating, but actually, the Moon
doesn't change. Only the Sun's light upon the Moon changes. See
also *dark Moon, Moon phases.* ◯

barren planets   **1.** Mars and Saturn are so masculine in nature
that they can interfere with a woman's fertility. **2.** Some astrologers
include the Sun as a barren planet, in addition to Mars and Saturn.
The Sun is part of the masculine principle and also very hot; heat
interferes with fertility. **3.** The South Node of the Moon rules loss
of energy and can also indicate barrenness. As a moving point, the
South Node is treated as a planet.

✦ **1.** When located on the cusp of the fifth or eleventh houses, barren planets may cause infertility or issues with physical limitations
or predispositions with your fertility, your health, your psyche, and
your lifestyle. **2.** If Mars is located in your fifth house, you have a
lot of creative drive and need an outlet for its expression. Without
this outlet, Mars energy builds up in your upper back, causing back
pain. (The fifth house rules the upper back.) Mars in the fifth house
can also mean your first baby will be born prematurely or born
before you are ready. If you have Mars in your fifth house and have
your heart set on having a baby at an ideal time in your life, be sure
to seek out lots of opportunities to be creative. Mars likes working
with metal, tools, rock, and granite. Creative welding and sculpting are good choices. Acupuncture is an excellent way to mitigate
problematic Mars energy. Why? Because it uses sharp, pointy, metal
to pierce your body. Mars loves sharp, pointy, metal tools and it
loves cutting and piercing. Mars also rules tattoos. A well-chosen
tattoo on your upper back can disperse some of that Mars energy.

3. Saturn in the fifth house can mean having children when you are older than other parents. It can also mean that your creative energy should be channeled into the entertainment industry or into work with children rather than having children. Saturn rules bones, and regular chiropractic adjustments can do wonders for fertility for you if you have Saturn in the fifth house. **4.** The eleventh house is about spontaneous, unplanned pregnancy. Mars in your eleventh house means the sperm are out of control and need guidance. Visualizing a magnet on the egg that is super-attractive to the sperm can help with this. Saturn can block when you're too serious about the whole process, but it can also manifest when you lighten up and invite the assistance of divine intervention. **5.** If your South Node is in your fourth house of pregnancy, it indicates a loss of energy around the pregnancy, which can result in miscarriage. You may have spent many past lifetimes caring for children and your soul growth now lies in the pursuit of career success, fame, and other tenth house goals. Pregnancy will be easier when your natal South Node is trined by your progressed Moon or by the ruler of your fourth house. See also *barren signs, eleventh house, fifth house, Mars, masculine principle, Saturn, South Node, Sun, trine.* 🏠 ◯ △

barren signs 1. Gemini, Leo, and Virgo. Gemini rules movement, which makes it difficult for the fertilized egg to implant in the uterine lining. Leo rules children, but when it comes to conception, it may bring on too much heat. Virgo resists invasion as a way of maintaining pure and perfect health. Sperm are seen as invaders. **2.** When on the cusp of the fifth or eleventh house, these planets may indicate difficulty conceiving children or a lack of children in the life of the person whose birth chart is being interpreted. It can also mean fewer children than desired. The fifth house rules children. The eleventh house rules the conception of new ideas, so along with the fourth house, it also rules conception. **3.** The barren signs are also referenced in gardening, and indicate periods useful to weed. See also *barren planets, Chiron, eleventh house, fertile signs, fertility, fifth house, gardening, Gemini, Leo, Virgo.* ☼

beholding signs 1. These are pairs of signs that are either both in the northern hemisphere or both in the southern hemisphere. **2.** Beholding signs share the same distance from the horizon line, which really means they are the same distance from the tropics.

3. Aries and Virgo are beholding signs, as are Taurus and Leo, Gemini and Cancer, Libra and Pisces, Scorpio and Aquarius, and Sagittarius and Capricorn. See also *horizon*. ☼

below the Earth   1. When a planet is located below the horizon, it is said to be below the Earth. **2.** If a planet is found in the first, second, third, fourth, fifth, or sixth house, it is below the Earth. **3.** The planets that appear below the horizon on a birth chart are those that were not visible in the sky at the time of birth. ✦ **1.** What planets were below the Earth at your birth? If the majority of planets are below the horizon line on your birth chart, including the South Node of the Moon and your chart's ruler (the planet that rules your rising sign), introversion is the likely result. This is further enforced if Chiron (the planetoid) is in the upper hemisphere. You may appear shy and be internally driven, or more influenced by what's happening inside you than what's going on in the world around you. You also may seem to be more passive than aggressive, and may behave in self-contained and self-conscious ways. You may also be service oriented. Family, home, and security (financial and personal) are very important to you. You are likely a caretaker in your family, as the third, fourth, fifth, and sixth houses relate to siblings, parents, children, and other personal responsibilities. Relationships of early childhood and family are also important in your life. **2.** In a perfectly balanced birth chart, the planets are evenly distributed above and below the horizon, indicating a balance of these areas in your life. See also *above the Earth, birth chart, Chiron, horizon*. **BC** 🏠

**benefic   **See *beneficial*.

beneficial   1. Also called benefic, meaning positive or favorable. **2.** Certain aspects are considered beneficial in a birth chart. Major aspects that are beneficial include sextile (60 degrees) and trine (120 degrees). A trine is the most beneficial of these. **3.** Minor aspects that are beneficial include semi-sextile (30 degrees), quintile (72 degrees), and biquintile (144 degrees). **4.** Certain planets are considered more beneficial than others in astrology. Jupiter is known as the greater benefic; Venus as the lesser benefic. Before the discovery of Neptune, Jupiter ruled the sign of Pisces. Jupiter is connected to Neptune through their dual rulership of Pisces. Neptune is also a benefic, as is the Sun and the Moon. Mercury is neutral. It can be

B

beneficial or unfortunate, depending upon the sign it is in and its relationship to the ruler of that sign. **5.** Beneficial planets play a supportive and constructive role in the birth chart

✦ **1.** If you have beneficial aspects or planets in your birth chart, what does this mean? If you have benefic planets in their home signs or in their exalted signs, you will feel their support in all areas of your life. Depending upon the strength of the malefics (some aspects and planets are also known as malefic, or harmful) in your chart, life just might be easier for you. You learn from your mistakes quickly and can identify and change your self-defeating patterns. If you have benefics in their signs of detriment or fall, you may feel like you're always swimming upstream, working hard for each dollar or every lesson. You may be overwhelmed by some trauma you experienced and find yourself unable to move forward. However, if the benefic is well-aspected to other planets, especially the planet that rules the sign it is in, then the hardship may be strongly mitigated. **2.** An absence of beneficial aspects or planets does not indicate a negative (malefic) effect; this depends on what else you have going on in your birth chart—you have to look at the big picture! See also *aspects between planets, detriment, exalted, home signs, Jupiter, malefic, Mercury, Moon, quintile, sextile, trine, Venus.* △ ☯ ○

besieged   **1.** When a benefic planet, such as Jupiter or Venus, is positioned closely between a pair of malefic planets such as Mars and Saturn in the birth chart, it is referred to as besieged by those malefics. **2.** The besieged benefic loses much of its beneficial effect. See also *beneficial, malefic.* **BC** ○

bff astrology   **1.** This is the area of astrology that interprets the astrological compatibility of best friends forever (bff). **2.** Beneficially aspected natal Moons create best friends—especially for women. The Moon relates to emotions, and compatible Moon signs forge a strong bond. ✦ **1.** If you want to find out how compatible you are with your bff (or a potential bff), find out what your natal Moons are—this is the sign the Moon was in at your birth. **2.** It's unlikely that you'll have a long-lasting friendship with someone if your natal Moons aren't compatible. Looking at the relationship between your natal Moons will help you see the challenges you might face in the relationship, as well. **3.** When you feel immediately comfortable with another person, you are experiencing the harmony of two natal Moons in a beneficial aspect. The Moon is intuition, and you may feel a familiarity with someone, or an instant trust and closeness that you can't explain. This is the relationship of your natal Moon to the other person's—it's a Moon connection. See also *birth chart, Moon, Moon in the signs.* **BC** ☯ ○

birth certificate   **1.** This is also called a certificate of live birth. **2.** A record of birth information, including date, location, and, often, time of birth. **3.** Many hospitals have a practice of keeping a long form of the birth certificate and issuing a short-form birth certificate to the parents. The short form often doesn't include the time of birth, but the hospital will often release the long form when it's requested.

✦ **1.** Don't have a copy of your birth certificate? You don't need one to do your astrological birth chart; it's just a good place to look for the information you need. If you want a notarized, official copy of your birth certificate, and you know where you were born, you can usually order a copy from that state's Division of Vital Records. A quick online search will tell you where to look. (See the Centers for Disease Control and Prevention [CDC] site: www.cdc.gov/nchs/w2w.htm.) **2.** What if you have no idea what time or even where you were born? Focus on what signs your natal planets were in when you were born and what aspects they have with each other instead of what houses they are in. Your natal chart can be created using 12:00 p.m. for your birth time and the city where you grew up. Then look at your chart and note any planets that are at 29 or 0 degrees, because they may have changed signs that day. You can ask an astrologer to check whether any of those planets did indeed change signs that day, and if so, think about what that planet represents and ask yourself how you more naturally give it expression. For instance, if Mercury moved from 29 degrees Cancer to 0 degrees Leo on your birthday, you can ask yourself whether you are more Cancer-like or Leo-like in the way you communicate and express yourself. If you were born with Mercury in Cancer, you tend to express yourself in a more subdued, cautious, nurturing, and sensitive manner. If you were born with Mercury in Leo, you tend to be dramatic, over-the-top, entertaining, and bold. **3.** If you're wondering if someone's birth certificate is accurate or forged, doing an astrological birth chart based on the birth information the suspect birth certificate contains may reveal essential truths. By interpreting the birth chart, you may see instantly whether the chart matches the person's personality and so gain clues surrounding authenticity. **4.** It is often easier to narrow the window of possible birth time by working with the personal planets, especially those near the house cusps. You can find the most likely house for Mercury by asking people what they think and talk about most, and where they do their daily work. The kind of vehicle they drive can also provide clues, because Mercury rules cars. Venus is about what we attract and are attracted to, so ask where they like to be, what they like to shop for, the gifts they give, and the kinds of compliments they receive. Mars is about our direction in life and what we question. See also *birth date, birth place, birth time, noon birth chart, rectification.* **BC**

birth chart   1. Also called a natal chart, this is a chart of the placement of the planets at the exact date, time, and location of a person's birth. **2.** Birth charts are very specific, and accurate information is essential to the creation of an astrological birth chart; the more specific the information, the more personalized the birth chart will be.

✦ **1.** Information needed to cast your chart includes your exact date of birth, the name of the town or city where you were born, and your time of birth. Your natal chart shows the life your soul has chosen to experience in this lifetime. Those experiences unfold as planets evolve in their relationship with the Sun, which triggers opportunities and challenges in you. **2.** Why create your birth chart? There is a lot more to who you are than your Sun sign can tell you. Each of the planets in your chart rules an aspect of your psyche. Knowing what sign each planet is in and the house where it lives helps you understand yourself in ways you can't see objectively. Learning about the planets, their characteristics, and their behavioral effects can help you tap into your deeper resources and transform negative behaviors into behavioral strengths. **3.** It looks like the planets are frozen in place on your birth chart, but, of course, they keep on keeping on. This is why many people get regular astrological readings. The four main charts an astrologer uses in addition to your birth chart are the solar progressed chart, the solar arc chart, the transits, and the solar return chart. **4.** You can do your own birth chart—it's very simple using the websites and computer programs available now. The problem arises with what to do with the chart once you have it. It's great to be able to create your own birth chart, but how do you interpret the information on it? There are many websites that offer natal reports that describe who you are based on what signs and houses your planets are in, along with your rising sign. There are also dynamic charts, which are reports about how transiting planets are activating your natal planets. These are great starting points for learning about your birth chart, but they don't weigh which planet is likely to exert more influence on you; that is still the work of a trained astrologer. To get the most nuance and resonance, consult your astrologer to guide you through more sophisticated relationships and interpretations found in your charts. See also *aspects between planets, birth date, birth place, birth time, composite chart, solar arc chart, solar progressed chart, solar return, transits.* **BC**

birth date   **1.** Exact date of birth, for use in creating an astrological birth chart, including month, day, and year. The date of birth is essential information in the creation of an accurate birth chart. **2.** Date of birth reveals the Sun sign, but from day to day, there are lots of changes in the sky—if the date is off by a day, the Sun sign might be different! The Sun appears to travel 1 degree each day, moving through one astrological sign each month. **3.** Knowing the exact time of birth is critical to knowing the rising sign, because the degree of the ascendant changes every four minutes. There are 30 degrees within each sign, so the ascendant sign changes every two hours. **4.** Each zodiac sign is divided into three parts of 10 degrees called decans. The first third of the sign also carries the energy of the first sign of that element. For instance, 5 degrees Leo also carries the energy of the first fire sign of Aries. The second third (the next 10 degrees) of the sign is the second sign of the element and the third part of the sign (the final 10 degrees) is the third sign of the element. Every degree of each sign has a slightly different energy than all the other degrees of that sign. See also *birth chart, decan, geocentric, Sabian symbols, Sun sign.* **BC**

B

Your date of birth reveals not only what sign the Sun was in at your birth, but also what signs the other planets were in:

- Your **Sun** sign tells you about your basic character.
- Your **Moon** sign is your emotional expression.
- Your **Mercury** sign is how you communicate and think.
- Want to know about your relationships in general? Look at your **Venus** sign.
- The sign your **Mars** is in reveals how you take action.
- Your **Jupiter** sign reveals your philosophy.
- Through your **Saturn** sign, you can learn about the obstacles you will encounter, including your fears and self-imposed limitations.
- What makes you a unique individual? You can find the answer in your **Uranus** sign.
- Your **Neptune** sign is all about your dreams, delusions, spirituality, and visions.
- Your **Pluto** sign is your means of expressing your power, sexuality, and ability to transform.

birth moment   See *birth time*.

birth place   **1.** Exact location of birth, using latitude and longitude, for use in creating a birth chart. **2.** Latitude refers to the horizontal division of the Earth into degrees, with the equator as the starting point. Latitude indicates how far north or south of the equator a location is. **3.** Longitude uses the Greenwich Meridian as the starting point; birth location is noted in degrees east or west of this point. **4.** The more exact this information, the more accurate information in a birth chart will be.

✧ **1.** Often, the place of birth is given on a birth certificate; most computer programs will only ask you for the city, state, and country. **2.** You don't likely have latitude and longitude information for your birth place at your fingertips, but that's okay—you don't need it. Today's computer programs quickly calculate the latitude and longitude of any location. If you want to find the latitude and longitude of your birth place (in degrees and minutes), type the name of your city of birth, along with the words latitude and longitude, into a search engine. **3.** Many countries and U.S. states use the same names for towns and cities—you might be born in Hollywood, California, or

Hollywood, Florida. Be sure to note the name of the county that you were born in, as well as your zip code. **4.** The Earth's axis is currently tilted about **23.44** degrees. This doesn't affect the time that it takes for signs to pass over the equator very much, but it makes a big impact on how long each sign takes to ascend on the eastern horizon. The western signs of Capricorn through Gemini take fewer than two hours to ascend in the northern hemisphere and the eastern signs of Cancer through Sagittarius take longer than two hours. The closer your birth place is to a polar region, the greater the difference in the length of time to ascend. (The reverse is true in the southern hemisphere.) Above the Arctic Circle, ever-increasing portions of the ecliptic are swallowed up by the horizon, so certain signs are never able to ascend. People born in this region either have absent houses in their birth charts or no houses at all. Of course, their lives are as full as yours, but you wouldn't know it from their birth charts. This is not a reflection upon people born at the North Pole, but simply the problem that accompanies any system that divides a sphere. In this case, it's the system of houses. When you stand at the North Pole, every direction is south. The house system breaks down in the same way a compass ceases to function on either pole. Arctic charts must be interpreted using the planets and signs only. The bottom line is that your place of birth can really affect your birth chart! See also *birth chart, Sun sign.* **BC**

birth time   **1.** Also called the birth moment. The exact time of birth, meaning the time of an infant's first breath, for use in creating a birth chart. Birth time should include hour and minute of birth, as well as A.M. or P.M. **2.** Hospital procedure for time-keeping varies. In some, clocks reset automatically via satellite to keep the time accurate. Often, hospital staff set the clocks. Birth time might be recorded down to the second, but it might also be rounded up or down, or it might not be recorded until a while after the birth takes place. This is often the case for home births.

✴ **1.** Many people do not know what time of day they were born; a good first place to check is your birth certificate. As these do not always give an exact time of birth, you might also check with a parent or grandparent—if someone kept a baby book for you, it will likely include your time of birth, along with other fascinating facts, such as the date you got your first tooth and when you took your first steps. **2.** Note that time of birth in creating a birth chart is based on Equivalent Greenwich Mean Time (EGMT, also known as Zulu Time or Universal Time). You may need to convert the time from the time zone in which you were born. This is a very simple calculation, but one you must remember to do—unless you are using a computerized program for calculating birth charts. Then the computer will do this step for you. Most astrologers use computer programs that will figure out the correct time based on your location and the birth time at that location. If your birth time was recorded in military time and the number is greater than 12, just subtract 12 from the number. For example, if your birth time is 19:32, subtract 12 from 19. Now you know that you were born at 7:32 P.M. **3.** If your recorded birth time is an exact hour or half hour, this can be a sign that the time wasn't accurately recorded. You might want to have your chart rectified by an astrologer, especially if the astrological readings you have received are not quite accurate. **4.** Why is the specific time so important? Not only can your Sun sign change, but the position of the planets will shift, and your rising sign will be different if your birth time is off by a matter of minutes. The chart shifts 1 degree every four minutes. Every degree of every sign has a characteristic associated with it. Knowing your exact time enables you to benefit from the insights that correspond to that degree. **5.** Without an accurate birth time, you can still create a birth chart, but it will not be as accurate or personalized, and therefore it may not be as meaningful to you or as useful in your life. See also *birth chart, birth place, Sun sign.* **BC**

What if you don't know what time you were born? This is a common problem in the creation of birth charts. You can always use noon as your birth time. However, now there are excellent software programs that can determine your birth time with a surprising rate of accuracy. To run such a program, your astrologer needs dates of experiences that are associated with the first, fourth, seventh, and tenth houses. If you are unsure of your birth time because you were adopted at birth, or for any other reason, keep records (with dates and times, whenever possible) of the events in your life that specifically affect your identity, such as leadership, people moving in or out of your home, your relationship with your parents, marriage, pregnancy, partnerships (including business partners), fame, success, and important points on your career path. When you have recorded at least 15 of these events, an astrologer can rectify your chart to determine the minute you were born.

bi-wheel chart   A bi-wheel chart offers a view of two wheels compared to each other. Each wheel is a chart unto itself, but in a bi-wheel, the inner chart's ascendant is used as the anchor for both charts. ✦ If you want to know how one partner is affected by another partner, but you only have one partner's time of birth, you can run a bi-wheel. The chart with the known time of birth should be used for the inner wheel. Noon can be used for the chart with the unknown time of birth, which is selected as the outer wheel. The produced chart shows the chart with the known time in the center with its usual ascendant and the other chart follows suit with the same degree placed at the ascendant, enabling you to compare how the outer chart's planets aspect and impact the inner chart. See also *birth chart, transiting planets.* **BC** ☯ **Z**

black hole   1. The name for the gravitational pull that results from the collapse of a decaying star. **2.** The pull of a black hole is inescapable. **3.** Called a black hole because all light that hits it is absorbed. **4.** At the center of the Milky Way is an area known as the Galactic Center, at a location called Sagittarius A*, which is believed to be a supermassive black hole (scientists hypothesize that black holes are at the center of every galaxy). While there may be hundreds of black holes in the Milky Way, Sagittarius A* is seen as most influential in astrology. **5.** Black holes are ruled by the crone goddess Hecate. The word crone is derived from the name Chronus, which is the Greek name for Saturn. Chronos is the god of time and boundaries. Hecate is a blend of Mercury, the Moon, and Saturn. She and Mercury both rule magic, crossroads, and trivia, and Hecate stands at the junction of three choices, three options, or three paths. ✦ Hecate guarded the boundaries between the earthly world and the spirit world. A black hole is considered the birth canal leading from this dimension into the next, and Hecate is the midwife to those pulled into the black hole. If you have a black hole in your birth chart, Hecate reassures you that life never ends and is also never really out of control. Your higher self is always supervising and at the same time respectful of the choices you make as a free agent. See also *Chronos (Kronos).* **BC** ◯

black Moon   1. Also called the dark Moon, dead Moon, or Lilith. (Don't confuse it with the asteroid Lilith!). Often referred to as a second Moon, though it actually is not. **2.** It is a point on the elliptic that the Moon travels, an area of apogee in the Moon's elliptical orbit of the Earth, and the Moon's farthest point from the Earth in this orbit, which is an area of empty focus in the orbit. **3.** Because there is no solar reflection, the Moon isn't visible from the Earth during this time of about three days; the Moon is hidden from view. ✦ **1.** In astrology, the black Moon, Lilith, is interpreted as hidden areas of the self, possibly areas you refuse to see or areas you are not aware of. The black Moon also represents feelings of shame, guilt, and envy, emotions you may try to hide from others. She also rules secrets and secret sexual relationships. Once the repressed energy is made conscious, Lilith becomes a source of power. **2.** A little background on Lilith: she was Adam's first wife before Eve. She was Adam's equal, and refused to submit to him. Instead, she rebelled and ran away. When God demanded her return, she refused and Eve was created. Lilith eventually returned as the serpent that tempted Eve to eat of the tree of knowledge. **3.** Lilith is often blamed for miscarriages. **4.** How can you find out if there's a black Moon on your birth chart? You'll see the symbol, or glyph, of a black Moon flipped sitting atop a cross: black Moon ☾. Your astrologer will include the black Moon glyph in the set of displayed heavenly points before casting your chart. See also *birth chart, Lilith, Moon.* ◯

What does your black Moon mean? That depends on what sign it's in. Let's cycle through the zodiac:

- **A black Moon in Aries** can cause you to be overly defensive of your opinions and positions because of your desperate need to be right.

- **If your black Moon is in Taurus**, you might need a lot of proof of love, usually in the form of compliments and gifts.

- **A black Moon in Gemini** might make you into a schemer for your benefit.

- **If your black Moon is in Cancer,** you might have a strong need to mother that causes you to obsess about children—yours and other people's.

- **If your black Moon is in Leo,** you might create drama to punish loved ones.

- **Your black Moon in Virgo** can cause you to criticize your beloved until he or she "breaks."

- **A black Moon in Libra** could lead you to break up marriages (yours or someone else's) or to sue people.

- **If your black Moon is in Scorpio**, you may try to tempt others away from their partners or spouses.
- **A Sagittarius black Moon** might influence you to con others out of their money.
- **If your black Moon is in Capricorn,** you tend to make others feel ashamed or unable to meet your standards.
- **If your black Moon is in Aquarius,** you might value intellect over the heart.
- **If your black Moon is in Pisces**, you might psychically spy on others, especially your lover.

business astrology   A business astrologer can interpret a birth chart and the current cycles of the planets to reveal good times to make a career change, buy a house, or sign a contract with a new client, for example. ✧ The sign on the cusp of your sixth house tells you what jobs and skills easily come your way. This house also tells you what to look for in employees. The sign on the cusp of your tenth house tells you what kind of employers will best support your success. Additionally, the sign on the cusp of your twelfth house offers you clues about what to name your business. See also *Capricorn, second house, sixth house, Taurus, tenth house.* **BC** 🌓 🏠

cadent house **1.** The third, sixth, ninth, and twelfth houses in the birth chart. The cadent houses immediately follow the succedent houses in the zodiac. *Cadere* means to fall away, and these houses are described as falling away from the angular and succedent houses. **2.** Cadent houses correlate to the mutable astrological signs: Gemini, Virgo, Sagittarius, and Pisces. **3.** The third house relates to expression, knowledge, grammar and secondary school, siblings, environment, neighbors, daily travel, and communication. **4.** The sixth house is the house of day-to-day personal responsibilities, including those in the workplace, pets, physical health, and service to others. **5.** The ninth house corresponds to religion, courts of law, spectator sports, and publishing, as well as higher education and travel. **6.** The twelfth house is the house of the collective unconscious, charity, karma, mental health, addictions, music, dance, movies, dreams, and the inner life.

✦ Like the associated signs, planets in these houses tend to be changeable in their effects. The effect of any planet in a cadent house is weakened or more passive than it would be in the angular houses. So Venus in your third house is not as influential as it would be in your fourth house. If the planet is in the sign that it rules, it will not be as weakened in a cadent house, because the sign adds the most strength to the planet rather than the house. See also *angular house, Gemini, house, ninth house, Pisces, Sagittarius, sixth house, succedent house, third house, twelfth house, Virgo.*

calculating a birth chart **1.** This is the process of inputting specific information about an individual to create a personalized birth chart. **2.** The necessary information includes full date of birth, specific time of birth (including minutes), and location of birth (the latitude and longitude). **3.** Today most astrologers utilize birth chart software that, after the required information is entered, creates the birth chart quickly and accurately. **4.** Calculating a birth chart manually is a lot more complicated and time consuming than using a computer program. Briefly, here are the steps: first, the astrologer fills out a calculation form with the client's name and all of the required information. Then the astrologer checks to see whether daylight savings time or war time was in effect at the time and place of birth. Birth time is rewritten as a 24-hour clock time (also known as military time), then converted into Equivalent Greenwich Mean Time (EGMT), and rewritten in decimal form. The astrologer notes the amount of time from midnight to the time the client was born in Greenwich time. This is the EGMT interval, which is divided by 24 (hours) to render the constant multiplier (tricky math!). The astrologer checks an ephemeris and fills in a table called the longitude calculation box with the degrees and minutes for the locations of all of the planets at the client's birth time (with an adjustment to EGMT). Then the astrologer lists all the planetary locations for the day after the client's birth. By subtracting the birth date's locations from the next day's locations, the astrologer can calculate the daily motion of each planet. The degrees of each location is changed into minutes (60 minutes per degree) and multiplied by the constant multiplier. Then those numbers are changed back into degrees and minutes. Next the astrologer fills in the declination box in the same way. Finally, the astrologer has all the information needed to plot the planets onto the client's blank chart. Whew!

✦ Computer software is usually used to complete your birth chart after you give the astrologer all the information needed—thank goodness. The software handles all of the tricky mathematical calculations in a matter of seconds. See also *birth chart, birth date, birth place, birth time, computer programs.* **BC**

Cancer   **1.** The fourth sign of the zodiac. **2.** Those born between June 22 and July 23 have Cancer as their Sun sign. Cancer is a feminine, or yin, cardinal water sign. The ruling planet for Cancer is the Moon, which governs emotions and intuition. **3.** The glyph for Cancer is two claws of a crab ♋, and the symbol is the crab. Cancer may have a tough outer shell, but it's there to protect an emotional and sensitive core. **4.** Cancer is the natural ruler of the fourth house of home and family, as well as the subconscious mind, patterns, behaviors, and life foundations. **5.** Other associations for Cancer are the colors sea green and silver—the colors of the ocean and the Moon—and the pearl.

✧ **1.** The body parts associated with Cancer are the breasts and the stomach. You love to eat—but beware of using food as an emotional crutch. You are susceptible to digestion problems, especially when you're stressed out or nervous. When you're in a foreign country, you might want to remember not to drink the water! **2.** When your Sun sign is Cancer, you're funny and fun to be with. You may use humor to keep others at a distance, to protect yourself. You may not appear to be, but you're extremely sensitive. You're very loyal and are happiest with your family. You are very protective of those you love, including your friends, and tend to mother them a bit. You're the friend others come to when they need taking care of. You look like you have it all together, but you might feel insecure—you're always feeling more than you can express. You have a great memory and a love for history—family history, ancient history, you name it. You keep photos and mementos, and you keep people, too. Cancer doesn't let go of friends or family very easily. You are tenacious in other ways, too—you usually reach your goals, though like a crab, you may scuttle toward them in a less than straight line. Your memory and intuition make you a great judge of people. You are also good at making—and holding on to—money. **3.** Cancer is a cardinal water sign, and this sign expresses leadership in the emotional arena, through family leadership, for example. Cancer is family oriented, and very emotionally attached to family. You are sensitive nurturers who relate to life through their emotions. **4.** What subjects and careers might appeal to Cancer? Cancer might like to study cooking, history, psychology or some form of health care. Helping others is one of the best career choices for Cancer. This might mean caretaking, nursing, social work, or teaching. Cancer makes good psychologists; you'd do well running a nursery school (and you also tend to make great parents, too). Cancer is great at managing people in ways that bring out their best potential and highest good. For Cancer, co-workers are like extended family. Cancer is emotionally involved in work, no matter what it is. If Cancer finds it difficult to become emotionally connected to work or your co-workers, you will be dissatisfied. **5.** *Watch out for:* you might overuse that hard crab shell exterior—remember to let others in … and be careful about pricking with those sharp claws. Cancer crab claws can be expert, efficient organizers, but can also scuttle you, too. Because you love family life, you might be something of a homebody. Try not to be a stick in the mud—get out there and try new things. You're very sensitive; sometimes maybe too sensitive. An emotional slight can be very traumatic to you, and you have to be careful not to indulge your tendency to wallow in those negative emotions, or to let your crabby, insecure side take over. You tend to retreat rather than confront during a conflict, to keep things peaceful. **6.** *I'm not a Cancer, but my best friend is:* Your Cancer best friend is kind and nurturing—they want to make sure you're okay. Sometimes they might seem overly concerned about your well-being, and you might need a little breathing room. Be careful of Cancer's feelings, and tell them how you feel, but do it very gently, or they will retreat from you. Tread gently. Cancer does not handle confrontation or conflict very well. Really, they want to be treated as they treat you, with plenty of caring concern. See also *Cancer ascendant, Cancer descendant.* ☼

Cancer/Aquarius   See *Aquarius/Cancer.*

Cancer/Aries   See *Aries/Cancer.*

Cancer ascendant   Also called Cancer rising. The rising sign on the birth chart is Cancer; Cancer is the sign on the cusp of the first house in the birth chart and the sign on the eastern horizon at the moment of birth. ✦ **1.** When your rising sign is Cancer, this sign reveals the face you show to others—it's your mask, or your public persona. You use Cancer traits on the surface of your life and this is what others can easily see in you. **2.** Your rising sign also represents the sign you are here to master in this life. Cancer rising is destined to work with family, family issues, and the emotional life of family. This may be hard work. They may have a love/hate family relationship, but family is very important to Cancer ascendant, even if there's loads of conflict. Cancer rising wants family harmony, but they may not get it. Their karmic duty is working openly with family issues, no matter what the response is from other family members. Cancer rising is also devoted to creating a harmonious family life for themselves outside their family of origin. **3.** If Cancer is your rising sign, you are very emotional and sensitive, but you might hide this beneath a less than approachable exterior (that crab shell). Others may see you as moody, and you do have a tendency to feel things deeply and dwell on those feelings. When you put those feelings to work for you, you are very sensitive to others' feelings, and this can make you a wonderful, nurturing friend. See also *ascendant, Cancer, Cancer descendant.* **BC** ☼

C

Cancer/Cancer **1.** When two Cancers come together, both partners are water signs ruled by the Moon. **2.** When partners of the same sign combine, they often accentuate both the strongest and most challenging characteristics of the sign. For Cancers, this means obsession with family, in both good and not so good ways. This pair may be exhibiting a karmic desire to create or restore nurturing relationships. ✵ **1.** Cancer/Cancer pairings can work out very well. **2.** Cancer partners understand each other's needs, and don't want to hurt each other's feelings. They can read each other's body language well, and tell when there is an unspoken problem, or when one of them is just feeling moody. This pair is on an even keel most of the time. Each respects the other's need for privacy and quiet time, and they have a deep understanding of each other's emotional needs. **3.** Cancer is very compatible with other Cancers, and they attract each other—even in groups, or extended families. The Cancer/Cancer pairing makes good friends, neighbors, and marriage or domestic partners, as well as other family relationships, such as mother/child or grandfather/grandchild. See also *Cancer.* ☯ ☼

Cancer/Capricorn **1.** This is a water and earth pairing, and it can get muddy when Cancer and Capricorn mix. **2.** These two signs are opposites, but opposites do attract. ✵ **1.** Do you like the mud? Cancer and Capricorn together are like the energy of well-irrigated, fertile soil in a raised bed. **2.** Cancer gives Capricorn emotional balance along with a home base, while Capricorn gives Cancer a practical point of view. In the best of circumstances, when Cancer gets moody or overwhelmed, Capricorn can help ground them and bring them back to balance. **3.** Cancer and Capricorn make a good student-teacher pair, and are good friends, business partners, and marriage or domestic partners. See also *Cancer, Capricorn.* ☯ ☼

Cancer descendant **1.** The descending sign is Cancer, so Cancer is the sign on the cusp of the seventh house in the birth chart. **2.** The seventh house deals with partnerships of all kinds, including marriage and significant others.

✤ **1.** When your descending sign is Cancer, you relate to others in partnership in ways that a Cancer relates. No matter what your Sun sign, your descendant sign will tell you a lot about yourself in partnership kinds of relationships. Is your neighbor driving you crazy with demands about your fence-line shrubbery? Take a look at your descendant to help you figure out why you interact—and react—the way you do. **2.** How does a Cancer descendant behave in partnerships? The Cancer descendant is ruled by the Moon, so it's very emotional. Cancer is a water sign, so people with a Cancer descendant are emotionally attached to any partner. When they deal with people, they try to do it in a personal way. They are emotional and sensitive, and for them, any partner is like a family member— their emotional bond is that strong. All partnerships are deep and serious for the Cancer descendant, and they will seek out this type of partnership. Cancer on the descendant makes the native feel that any partnership they have should be part of their inner circle—like family. They will, for example, hold their partner very close to them, and might not want the details of their relationships revealed to the public. They are private, devoted, and protective of their partner. Cancer descendant is also very attached to partners—it's generally a bad idea to accuse someone with a Cancer descendant of not being loyal or strong. Even when a relationship is difficult or when arguing with a partner, Cancer descendant remains bonded—they are not going to bail on someone they love. See also *Cancer, Cancer ascendant, descendant.* **BC** ☼

Cancer/Gemini **1.** This water sign and air sign mix together to make champagne! **2.** Cancer and Gemini get along well intellectu- ally and can talk about lots of things. ✤ **1.** Cancer gives Gemini emotional nourishment and support, while Gemini gives Cancer humor and intellectual support. These two can talk about family, work, home, travel—you name it. **2.** Cancer and Gemini get along well and are neighborly and cooperative—this relationship is gener- ally harmonious. On the downside, Cancer's feelings might be hurt by Gemini's talking—Gemini likes to talk about everything, while Cancer likes to keep some things very private. If Gemini divulges Cancer's secrets, there could be trouble for this pair. Cancer really values privacy, and could get angry about any perceived overexposure. **3.** When Gemini understands Cancer's needs, these two make good business partners and co-workers, great friends, and good marriage or domestic partners. See also *Cancer, Gemini.* ☯ ☼

Cancer/Leo   1. These two neighbors in the zodiac are water and fire. **2.** What Cancer and Leo have in common is that both are loyal and devoted to family. ✴ **1.** Cancers are emotionally centered and tend to withdraw into their shell when they feel threatened; Leo, on the other hand, works things out by talking about them. **2.** Cancer can be moody and withdrawn, and Leo doesn't understand this—Leo is an extrovert. These two share a desire to maintain their home life in peace, but Leo likes a more demonstrative partner. Cancer is often too cautious and guarded for Leo. **3.** Leo is willing to go out on a limb for Cancer, but Cancer is afraid to take such risks. Cancer's need for security constrains a Cancer/Leo pair—they like to stay within their comfort zone. Long-term, Cancer might feel that Leo pushes them to do things they aren't comfortable with. Cancer is cautious about exposing themselves; within their comfort zone, they speak freely, but outside their comfort zone, they withdraw. **4.** This Cancer/Leo pairing can make good friends or co-workers. The success of a Cancer/Leo marriage or domestic partnership is more difficult to predict. A closer look at this pair's birth charts might reveal specific compatibility issues. See also *Cancer, Leo.* ☯ ☼

Cancer/Libra   1. This water sign and air sign result in fizz; it's bubbly at first, but falls flat quickly. **2.** Both Cancer and Libra are cardinal signs. ✴ **1.** Libra will respect Cancer's need for privacy, and Cancer will respect Libra's easygoing nature and need for balance. These two have mutual respect for each other's values. But Libra can be in love with love—they are idealistic, and look at things through rose-colored glasses. **2.** Cancer either feels something or they don't, and they don't want to try anything that might jeopardize their emotional security. Libra has a tendency to go off in another world, which may not feel safe to Cancer. Cancer doesn't give their heart away until they are certain of the person they are giving it to, and this may not be Libra. **3.** A Cancer/Libra pairing can produce good work together, writing, teaching, or completing a project. They make good friends and co-workers, and have potential for a productive employee/boss relationship, as well as siblings. The Cancer/Libra pairing may be difficult as husband and wife or domestic partners, though. See also *Cancer, Libra.* ☯ ☼

C

Cancer/Pisces   **1.** Water and water—what could flow better? These two, Cancer and Pisces, understand each other. **2.** Cancer and Pisces are both emotionally committed and devoted in partnership and share a commitment to the spirit and heart of family. ✨ **1.** Cancer allows Pisces their imaginative and creative time, and can rest assured that Pisces won't stray far. Pisces is very sensitive, and is usually sensitive to Cancer's needs. **2.** Cancer/Pisces is an emotional combination, filled with compassion and empathy. If these two don't like each other, the relationship will be emotionally charged, and their dislike will be intense. There's not a lot of thinking between these two; they both know how they feel. These two may cling to each other. **3.** If they allow each other their privacy, Cancer/Pisces will get along well, and can make good friends, have a great student-teacher relationship, or make good marriage or domestic partners. See also *Cancer, Pisces*. ☯ ☼

Cancer rising   See *Cancer ascendant*.

Cancer/Sagittarius   **1.** A water sign and a fire sign—sometimes this mix of elements makes for a steamy combination, and some-times the water douses the flame. **2.** Cancer is ruled by the Moon, while Jupiter rules Sagittarius.

✨ **1.** Sagittarius is very gregarious and outgoing—sometimes too outgoing for Cancer. Cancer likes what they know; they enjoy domestic life, and don't necessarily want to be out in the world trying new things all the time. But Sagittarius likes to be out and about and they are enthusiastic about … everything! **2.** Cancer can't understand Sagittarius's need for freedom, and may feel hurt and abandoned by it. Cancer also might feel worn out by Sagittarius's abundant energy. These differences between the two can threaten Cancer's emotional security, and you know what happens when a crab feels threatened? They may try to pinch you, but they're more likely to scuttle away as quickly as they can. The crab wears a protec-tive shell for a reason! **3.** When Cancer and Sagittarius disagree, this fire sign can get the water boiling—Cancer may get angry and resentful toward their Sagittarius partner. Likewise, Cancer can put out Sagittarius's fire with their emotional demands. Sagittarius may get bored if they spend too much time in a routine. Sagittarius craves spontaneity and adventure. **4.** When Cancer has a lot of Leo in their birth chart, this energy will balance out better, and Cancer will get along well with Sagittarius. Otherwise, this partnership may not be for the long term. Cancer and Sagittarius can be friends or co-workers, but may not have a truly deep relationship. This pairing is not common for marriage or domestic partnerships. See also *Cancer, Sagittarius.* ☯ ☼

Cancer/Scorpio   **1.** These two water signs attract each other and can find each other in a crowd. **2.** Scorpio's intense emotional energy goes well with Cancer's need for emotional support. ✦ **1.** Cancer and Scorpio may have a deep, emotionally intense relationship. If Scorpio is too controlling, Cancer will pull away: they don't want to be controlled. Cancer might seem passive to Scorpio, but they are more easygoing and private. **2.** In general, there is a mutual bond between Cancer and Scorpio—some reason why the two are drawn to each other with such passion and devoted energy. **3.** The Cancer/Scorpio pair makes good friends (especially childhood friends), co-workers, and siblings. As for marriage—it might work, or it might not. A look at the particulars of the charts will help assess the potential for this relationship. See also *Cancer, Scorpio.* ☯ ☼

Cancer/Taurus   **1.** Water and earth are excellent together in this pairing; these two signs share similar goals. **2.** The earth sign Taurus understands Cancer's need for security and emotional nourishment as well as their devotion to home life. Likewise, Cancer understands Taurus's need for security and stability and can provide it. ✦ **1.** Cancer and Taurus can be lifelong friends and are often united by a common creative interest, such as writing or painting. Perhaps these two were college roommates who become friends for life, or served together in the armed forces. **2.** Once this relationship takes root, it will grow and stabilize, creating benefits potentially for the long-term. If Cancer and Taurus part, they will remain fondly in each other's memories. **3.** The Cancer/Taurus signs are good neighbors, and this pairing is good for all kinds of partnerships, from family to business to romance. Cancer and Taurus make good friends and business partners, form a solid parent/child bond, and make good marriage or domestic partners. See also *Cancer, Taurus.* ☯ ☼

Cancer/Virgo   **1.** Water and earth mix well in the Cancer/Virgo pairing; water's sacred powers are well understood and put to use by the meticulous service of Virgo. **2.** Cancer is a nurturer, and wants to help Virgo reach their goals and expand their horizons. Virgo is

more analytical than Cancer, and brings practicality to the relationship. ✧ **1.** Cancer sometimes gets overly emotional, and Virgo can help Cancer separate thought from emotion. Cancer sometimes gets so caught up in the emotions of a situation that it becomes magnified until it doesn't matter what the facts of the situation are. Cancer can become emotionally invested in a situation as they feel it, but Virgo is far too rational for such behavior. **2.** Virgo needs to empathize and be patient (rather than dismiss Cancer's emotionality as irrational), so Virgo will be great at balancing Cancer's emotional responses. Virgo can talk Cancer down from their heightened emotional ledge. **3.** If Virgo is too analytical, Cancer's feelings might get hurt. Virgo might go so far as to be dismissive of Cancer's emotional understanding of the world—that will be a deal-breaker for this pair. **4.** The Cancer/Virgo pairing makes good neighbors and friends, and is a beneficial teacher-student combination. See also *Cancer; Virgo.*
☯ ☼

Capricorn **1.** The tenth sign of the zodiac. **2.** Those born between December 22 and January 21 have Capricorn as their Sun sign. Capricorn is a feminine, or yin, cardinal earth sign. The ruling planet for Capricorn is Saturn, named for the Roman god of agriculture and the harvest. Saturn is all about discipline, limitations, and responsibility. **3.** The glyph for Capricorn is the V-shaped beard of the goat ♑, and the symbol is the goat, the sea-goat. Capricorn is rock steady. **4.** Capricorn is the natural ruler of the tenth house of career, public image, and social responsibilities. These are all important to Capricorn, which is ambitious and responsible by nature. **5.** Other associations for Capricorn are the colors dark green and brown—earth colors—and the gemstone garnet.

✧ **1.** The body parts associated with Capricorn are the teeth, bones, knees, and other joints. You're prone to cavities, so be sure to brush and floss daily. Get plenty of calcium to keep your teeth and bones strong. Also, avoid exercise that's hard on the joints; try swimming or yoga instead. Arthritis and other joint problems are a concern, so don't overstress them—do joint-friendly activities, and watch your weight (excess weight is very hard on your joints). **2.** When your Sun sign is Capricorn, you're serious and realistic. To others, you may seem unapproachable and cold, but really you're just serious and self-sufficient. You're also ambitious and have great stamina.

Capricorn will endure through any challenge to reach a goal. And if you're a Capricorn, you're a goal-setter, realistically planning your method for achieving that goal, and then following through your plan, even if it takes years. You might complain about the process or the time/effort invested, but you will get it done. You're a great planner, organized and detail-oriented. Saturn's influence of limitations makes you realistic. You don't just look at the bright side, and you aren't likely to be fooled into thinking something is better than it actually is. You realize that there is both an upside and a downside, and it's best to know everything about both so that you can make an informed decision. You have great leadership potential, and are very driven. If you say you're going to make your first million before age 30, you'll do it! **3.** As a cardinal earth sign, Capricorn is stoic, serious, and responsible. Capricorn is steadfast. Everything is serious to you, and you aren't often described as lighthearted. Capricorn has a strong work ethic and tends toward leadership in business or community. Capricorn often leads via your chosen career and make very good CEOs. You might just be the best leader in the zodiac. Moreover, Capricorn leads with an eye on the big picture. You aren't selfish leaders, but want to bring everyone with you when achieving goals—Capricorn wants everyone to do well. On the downside, this tenacious drive can make Capricorn harsh taskmasters. You also want others to be as serious as you are, and most of the time, that's just not possible. **4.** What subjects and careers might appeal to Capricorn? Capricorn will do well in corporate careers in business, finance, real estate, investments, government, and public service. You are often administrators or directors in the companies where you work. You can establish a business and are very good at earning and managing money. Capricorn is very resourceful. You like to study and often want to learn about everything, and will study all subjects with equal intensity. You also like history, which is part of strategizing for Capricorn. Capricorn does things for the long haul, so whatever you are learning now could be useful for some project or situation down the road. Capricorn is also streetwise, and can learn by watching and observing. You like to learn by experience, which is very helpful for business success. **5.** *Watch out for:* your serious nature means that you sometimes overlook what's important to others. You don't always have to point out what's wrong with someone else's idea, and you also don't have to obsess over every detail of a plan or project—be willing to make a mistake, or to let others make theirs. You are your own toughest critic—try and go a little easier on yourself. Likewise, cut others some slack once in a while—not everyone has your single-mindedness and stamina. Your self-sufficiency and disciplined nature can make you seem unfeeling and rigid, when you really just have amazing self-control. It's not always necessary to utilize that gift, especially with friends and family. Trust others with your feelings and your insecurities. You're cautious and conservative, and this may look like gloom and doom to others. Try to let your spontaneous side romp in a pasture now and then, without planning the field trip in advance! **6.** *I'm not a Capricorn, but my best friend is:* your Capricorn best friend can handle just about anything you might have to tell them. Be open—they aren't easily shocked. In general, it takes a lot to get a Capricorn mad. Your Capricorn friend will expect you to do your best—always—and you may find yourself working harder and becoming better because of them. They will be proud of you for striving, but won't abide procrastination or, heaven forbid, a complete lack of goal setting. You need some motivation and ambition to be Capricorn's friend. Even a made-up plan or goal can be used to get them off your back for a little while! See also *Capricorn ascendant, Capricorn descendant.* ☼

Capricorn/Aquarius   See *Aquarius/Capricorn.*

Capricorn/Aries   See *Aries/Capricorn.*

Capricorn ascendant   Also called Capricorn rising. The rising sign is Capricorn, so Capricorn is the sign on the cusp of the first house in the birth chart and the sign on the eastern horizon at the moment of birth. ✦ **1.** When your rising sign is Capricorn, that's the way you appear to others and Capricorn is the image you present with intent to the world. **2.** Capricorn ascendant is serious and focused, and will develop a strong character in this lifetime. Capricorn rising is here to work on and learn about business and the material world, including money and other resources. They will likely have financial ups and downs as they learn the lessons they need, and may find themselves without money at some point—their job is to learn how to get it! This lifetime will be an experience of poverty and prosperity for Capricorn rising, materially, emotionally, and spiritually. They will also be learning how to follow through and get a plan for just about anything. This rising sign is studious and hard-working. They are thoughtful and productive, and have a strong constitution. In combination, these traits will lead Capricorn rising to eventual victory in any battle. **3.** If Capricorn is your rising sign, you will appear determined, strong-willed, focused, and steadfast. You might even be described as tenacious. You'd likely do well in the military, because you follow hierarchy well and are organized and orderly. You don't like to see chaos—yours or someone else's. To others, you may appear to have no passion, or to be too serious. You just don't wear your heart on your sleeve. You tend to be cautious and maybe even a little guarded—you need to know what, or who, you're dealing with before you can really show yourself. See also *ascendant, Capricorn, Capricorn descendant.* **BC** ☼

Capricorn/Cancer See *Cancer/Capricorn.*

Capricorn/Capricorn **1.** This earth sign is ruled by Saturn, the planet of order and structure, so Capricorns get along with others of the same Sun sign. **2.** When partners of the same sign come together, both the strengths and the challenges of the sign can manifest in the relationship. Capricorn partners may be experiencing a karmic destiny to build, but need to be careful not to build material things at the expense of nurturing emotional intimacy.

✧ **1.** Capricorn is great at business, so two Capricorns together make fantastic business partners—they want to succeed in business and career, and to have a strong reputation in society. These two share an intellectual understanding of the world that they each find attractive in the other. Capricorn is a deep thinker, and looks for common ground with others. These two will boost each other up. They recognize that life has ups and downs, and they don't expect an easy road, but they will support each other on their entire journey together. **2.** If both people in a Capricorn pair are both feeling down at the same time, they may need a third party to help pull them out of it. Because they like intimate relationships that function like a business, these two tend to climb to the top of the social and financial heap, and may appear to be a model successful couple. Under that appearance, they may be exhausted. They might forget to have fun together or to spend quality time with their children. **3.** Double Capricorn marriages flourish in Hollywood because each partner gets all the drama, emotional expression, and fun that they need through their work. **4.** This pairing is good as friends, teacher/student, and especially as business partners or co-workers. These two would be perfect partners in a new business—they would both strive to make the business a success. See also *Capricorn*. ☼

Capricorn descendant   1. The descending sign is Capricorn; Capricorn is the sign on the cusp of the seventh house in the birth chart. **2.** The seventh house is the house of partnerships and marriage or significant others.

✴ **1.** When your descending sign is Capricorn, you relate to others in partnership through Capricorn, whether the partnership is romantic, business-related, or involves work on a creative project. Look at how Capricorn behaves with others to see how you will experience partnership. **2.** Capricorn descendant is serious and focused, practical and resourceful. If Capricorn is your descendant, you are cautious about attracting someone, and may even appear suspicious of any possible partners. This descendant is very particular about partnerships—you won't open up to just anyone, and will remain guarded until you feel secure in the relationship, whether it's a business partnership, a friendship, or a romantic relationship. Capricorn descendant should look for partners who take life seriously. Someone who is good at business will share a bond with Capricorn, who will likely have numerous business relationships. This descendant works hard, and needs a partner who also works hard and is primarily goal-oriented. Capricorn descendant also appreciates financial stability or success in a domestic partner. Capricorn descendant negotiates well, and needs someone who also does this—they like a partner they can debate with and work things out with. **3.** Capricorn descendant sees relationships like contracts, and is likely to want the details of a marriage or other partnership negotiated and agreed upon before entering into such a union. They may not need a prenup, but they will want full disclosure from their partners in every relationship. Capricorn descendant can't negotiate in full faith without all the details, and it may take quite some time before they feel they have all the details and can process them fully. They don't fear commitment … exactly, they just need to be sure. They do not jump right in to any relationship, but once they have the details and decide to commit, it's for life—or at least that's how they see it.

Their commitment to a partnership, once made, is deep and all-encompassing, and their loyalty to a partner is virtually unshakeable. See also *Capricorn, Capricorn ascendant, descendant.* **BC** ☼

Capricorn/Gemini   1. Capricorn is a cardinal earth sign—practical and steadfast, consistent, hardworking, and persevering. Gemini is a mutable air sign, always thinking fast and with a flexible mind. **2.** Gemini tends to skim quickly along the surface of things, which doesn't suit serious Capricorn. These two signs are not very compatible—Gemini likes to move way too fast for Capricorn, which is way too slow for Gemini. ✦ **1.** In the workplace, Capricorn and Gemini might do well, as long as they have different tasks to perform. They'll frustrate each other if they have to work too closely together. But Gemini could be a salesperson, while Capricorn manages business back at the office. Earth and air can get along so long as the air sign takes on the more public and communicative role, and the earth sign handles the more organizational and methodical work. Capricorn has management and executive skills, but may do best when not working with the public. **2.** Often the mercurial nature of Gemini frustrates the goal-oriented nature of Capricorn, who may lose track of all the light-footed twists and turns of Gemini thinking. Mutual exhaustion can be the result, and not a happy expression of it usually, sadly. **3.** The Capricorn and Gemini pairing is not the best match as close friends or for marriage or domestic partnerships. See also *Capricorn, Gemini.* ☯ ☼

Capricorn/Leo   1. The Capricorn and Leo pairing combines earth and fire. In this pairing, the elements vie for nurturing predominance—which element can grow the best result? **2.** Capricorn and Leo are signs that both have executive and leadership abilities, and each could spur the other on to reach greater heights in business. ✦ **1.** There is friction between these two signs, and the Capricorn/Leo relationship might end in a power struggle. These signs are both independent, and may not see the point of working together. **2.** Leo likes lots of attention, and can be a flashy showoff. Leo is good at getting things done and is great at leading others to achieve a goal. Capricorn is more quiet and serious—they work more behind the scenes and tend to be more introspective than Leo. This pair might bruise each other's egos in a close relationship. Then again, they might relish their relationship as competitors. **3.** Capricorn

C

and Leo make good business partners and co-workers, with Leo out front and Capricorn as the backroom organizer and facilitator. These two signs are not the best marriage or domestic partners, and are not often seen as close friends, but can be good neighbors. See also *Capricorn, Leo.* ☯ ☼

Capricorn/Libra   **1.** Capricorn is a cardinal earth sign, and Libra is a cardinal air sign. Capricorn loves making things. Libra loves talking, relating, and communicating. **2.** These two work well together—they can encourage and inspire each other to grow. ✦ **1.** Capricorn and Libra make a good team on projects. Libra might get bored waiting for Capricorn, who works at a slower pace. Capricorn's serious and cool nature might inadvertently hurt Libra's feelings, because Libra needs a lot of love and attention. **2.** Libra can breathe life into Capricorn by constantly presenting new ideas, whether viable or not, forcing Capricorn out of set ways. **3.** The Capricorn and Libra pairing can work well as friends and co-workers, but it may not be the best for marriage or domestic partnerships where more patience may be required for success. See also *Capricorn, Libra.* ☯ ☼

Capricorn/Pisces   **1.** An earth and water mix, the Capricorn/Pisces pairing produces a solid friendship. **2.** Capricorn has the ability to build the dreams of Pisces in the material world. ✦ **1.** Pisces can inspire Capricorn to reach great heights, but Capricorn's emotional inconsistency may inadvertently hurt Pisces. Pisces always wants to delve under the surface, where Capricorn might feel the situation is good enough to implement without any further analysis. **2.** Pisces' intuition can be a foil to Capricorn earthiness; mostly with good result. **3.** Capricorn and Pisces make good friends, neighbors, or co-workers. This pairing is also good for the parent/child or teacher/student relationship. As for marriage or domestic partnership, Pisces may have to sacrifice some of their emotional needs in this relationship—Capricorn can provide stability, though, and this is important to Pisces. See also *Capricorn, Pisces.* ☯ ☼

Capricorn rising   See *Capricorn ascendant.*

Capricorn/Sagittarius   These neighboring signs combine earth and fire. They are friendly and cordial, working best in neighborly relationships. ✦ **1.** Sagittarius admires Capricorn's tenacity and

C

perseverance. Capricorn can help Sagittarius with focus in a work partnership. **2.** Sagittarius can find the admirable Capricorn traits of hard-working determination stifling when Capricorn tries to employ them on Sagittarius. Freedom is important to Sagittarius, but it might seem like irresponsibility to steadfast Capricorn, whose patience is tried by Sagittarius. **3.** Sagittarius is easily bored and likes to try new things. Again, this may seem like flightiness to Capricorn. These two can work well together if they learn to respect their differences, but otherwise, they may not get along at all. **4.** Capricorn/Sagittarius relationships work best when they aren't too deep or serious. They might not make the best marriage or domestic partners or even business partners (though might be more successful in business when Sagittarius is the free-wheeling entrepreneurial boss and Capricorn the loyal employee). Too much togetherness for Capricorn and Sagittarius brings out their differences and results in tension. This pairing is good as friends, co-workers, or neighbors, though, when their dynamic is wisely expressed. See also *Capricorn, Sagittarius.* ☯ ☼

Capricorn/Scorpio   **1.** Capricorn/Scorpio is an earth and water mix—they grow a garden well. Scorpio brings the nurturing passion and intense focus to Capricorn's putting down roots. **2.** These two are generally very harmonious; what one sign lacks in emotion the other supplies in tenacity. ✧ **1.** These signs respect each other's goals and needs, and there is a good flow of energy between them—no one feels threatened in this relationship. **2.** Capricorn and Scorpio are both strong-willed, and share an intense drive to get things done. Scorpio can nudge Capricorn along, while Capricorn makes Scorpio shine! These two are passionate about accomplishing their goals. **3.** Capricorn/Scorpio get things done faster together than they do working alone. **4.** The Capricorn/Scorpio pairing is good for a parent/child, teacher/student, or employer/employee relationship. They make good friends, co-workers, and business partners, as well as good marriage or domestic partners. See also *Capricorn, Scorpio.* ☯ ☼

Capricorn/Taurus   **1.** These two earth signs are a great combination—Taurus is Capricorn's best match in the zodiac. **2.** Taurus gives to Capricorn an emotional groundedness; Capricorn gives to Taurus a drive to do more. ✧ **1.** Capricorn and Taurus process events and situations in the same way, and have a deep understanding and appreciation for each other. They are steadfast and take their time with things, and are consistent with and loyal to each other. **2.** Where other sign pairings might produce competition or imbalance of some kind, Capricorn and Taurus complement and strengthen, digging deeper into the Earth and discovering the profound joys of a well-tended life. **3.** The Capricorn/Taurus pairing makes great friends, co-workers, business partners, and marriage or domestic partners. They are also good as siblings or in a parent/child relationship. See also *Capricorn, Taurus.* ☯ ☼

Capricorn/Virgo   **1.** This earth and earth combination is second only to the Capricorn/Taurus combination for compatibility. These two are both serious and organized, and they understand each other very well. **2.** Virgo is disciplined and analytical—traits Capricorn admires. Virgo appreciates Capricorn's goal-oriented work ethic. ✷ **1.** Capricorn and Virgo share mutual respect and can debate together without hurt feelings. When these two enter a relationship, they are in it for the long haul, and their relationship is rock steady. **2.** Virgo's love of sacred patterns is a joy to Capricorn, who wants nothing but to build in profound union. **3.** The Capricorn/Virgo pair is usually compatible in every combination. They make excellent friends, neighbors, co-workers, and business partners. They work well on projects together, especially when money is involved. Family relationships are generally good between Capricorn and Virgo, and they are also excellent marriage or domestic partners. See also *Capricorn, Virgo.* ☯ ☼

cardinal cross   See *grand cross.*

cardinal (quality)   **1.** One of the three qualities used to classify the astrological signs. (The others are fixed and mutable.) **2.** Cardinal signs are Aries, Cancer, Libra, and Capricorn, representing each of the four elements: earth, fire, water, and air. **3.** The cardinal signs are the first in each season. As such, cardinal signs represent beginnings. They are about direction and energy expended toward a direction. Each sign represents a point on a compass: Aries is east, Cancer is north, Libra is west, and Capricorn is south. Cardinal signs are the active go-getters in the zodiac.

✳ **1.** If you're a cardinal sign, you might like to start things, or maybe you're the first to step up and volunteer when help is needed. You might not be big on the finish, but people are likely to see you as ambitious, because you get out there and get things going. Some might call you pushy, but really you just have a lot of energy that wants to move out of you. You are a force of nature. **2.** You may have lots of planets in cardinal signs in your birth chart, and if this is the case, you might be inclined to take on too much. Lots of planets in Aries? You like to make things, so choose crafts and projects that can be completed in a weekend. Plenty of planets in Cancer? Set a limit on how many collections you want to have at any one time and then stick to the rules—sell off an old collection when you hit your limit. And remember, a new collection is always out there, waiting for you. Do you have more than one planet in Libra? Watch your tendency to compromise. Compromise is good, but you don't always have to be the one to make it. Compromise too often and you'll lose yourself. More than your share of Capricorn planets? Be clear with colleagues about your role at work: you can get the business going and make key decisions, but your colleagues will need to be in charge of the day-to-day routine. **3.** Of the four cardinal signs, Aries is the most active—Aries is the first sign of the zodiac, so this sign initiates everything. Aries brings a fresh face to the workplace and makes an excellent leader. Cardinal Aries energy stimulates enthusiasm—everyone benefits from the Aries "can do" attitude. If you have lots of planets in Aries, and are wondering whether you overwhelm people, get in their personal space, interrupt, or reveal too much information too soon, you probably do. But your friends will forgive you, because you are a lot of fun! See also *Aries, Cancer, Capricorn, fixed, Libra, mutable (quality).* ◯ ☼

cardinal points **1.** In astrology, the first degree of each of the cardinal signs in a birth chart. The cardinal signs are Aries, Cancer, Libra, and Capricorn. **2.** Also the name for the four angles marking the horizon and meridian. These four angles are the ascendant, descendant, nadir, and midheaven, the most important points in a birth chart. ✳ The four cardinal points help define your personality or ego, your genealogical roots and familial behavior patterns, your shadow or alter ego, and your public persona and the impact you'll have on the world in this lifetime. See also *Aries, ascendant, Cancer, Capricorn, cardinal, descendant, Libra, midheaven (Medium Coeli), nadir (Ilum Coeli).* **BC** ☯

cardinal signs   See *cardinal (quality).*

celestial equator   **1.** The Earth's equator projected outward on to the imaginary celestial sphere used in astrology. **2.** The Sun does not orbit the celestial equator. The Earth's axis is tilted, and the Sun follows this equator. The Sun crosses the celestial equator twice in each calendar year, marking the two equinoxes. The furthest points are the cardinal points of the solstices. See also *cardinal points, celestial sphere, equinox, solstice, zodiac.* **BC**

celestial sphere   **1.** The name for the imaginary circle of the heavens with the Earth in the center. **2.** The Earth-centered (geocentric) sphere of the universe used in astrology. **3.** Also called the heavenly sphere. **4.** Planets and heavenly bodies were also called celestial spheres in the geocentric model of the universe. See also *celestial equator, celestial music, Copernicus, Nicolaus; geocentric, heliocentric, zodiac.* **BC**

centaur   **1.** The name for about thirty comets called planetoids found orbiting the Sun between Jupiter and Neptune. All of the centaurs' orbits cross the paths of certain outer planets in our solar system. They all have unstable orbits, meaning that their orbital paths change as they are influenced by the larger outer planets' orbital resonances. **2.** Chiron, half-asteroid, half-comet, was the first discovered centaur. Chiron bridges old methods of healing with new technology. **3.** Greek mythology depicts the race of centaurs as untamed and unruly, like the orbits of the centaurs. **4.** The only centaurs included in astrology are Chiron, Pholus, and Nessus. The centaurs are considered crucial links between pairs of outer planets. Chiron is viewed as an opportunity for healing mental, emotional, and physical wounds. See also *Chiron.* ◯

Ceres   **1.** The first discovered asteroid, seen in 1801 by Guiseppe Piazzi. Now considered a dwarf planet, like Pluto, it is the smallest dwarf planet in the solar system. **2.** Ceres is named for the Roman goddess of growing plants and of motherly love. In Greek mythology she is called Demeter. **3.** Ceres resonates with the feminine signs of Taurus, Cancer, and Virgo. ✦ **1.** Most astrological software includes the old and new asteroids. In your birth chart, Ceres can show you how you offer and receive unconditional love and nurturing. **2.** Ceres is an especially important asteroid for women who make the needs of their families or career a priority over their own personal needs. See also *asteroids, birth chart, feminine principle.* ◯

C

In what sign do you have Ceres in your birth chart?

- **Ceres in Aries** likes to nurture others by inspiring them and offering opportunities for self-appreciation through spontaneity.
- **In Taurus, Ceres** sings to her loved ones and gives to herself by enjoying sensuous experiences.
- **Ceres in Gemini** communicates her love and takes care of herself by indulging her curiosity.
- **Ceres in Cancer** cooks with love as a way of giving, and feels nurtured while gardening or saving money for something special.
- **Ceres in Leo** shows love through generosity and invites compliments and appreciation for self-nurturing.
- **Ceres in Virgo** offers service as love and feels nurtured when she takes the time to prepare healthful food.
- **Ceres in Libra** delights in pleasing a partner, making their desires her greatest joy. She gives herself love by taking time to be artistic.
- **A Scorpio Ceres** loves others by healing them and connecting to their pain. She nurtures herself by cleaning out closets to make space for new clothes.
- **A Sagittarius Ceres** offers sage advice as love and feels self-love when exercising out in nature.
- **Ceres in Capricorn** works hard to demonstrate love and caring for others and feels loved when recognized.
- **Ceres in Aquarius** accepts what's strange or unique in others as a way of loving them and encourages herself to be a free butterfly as a way of caring for herself.
- **Ceres in Pisces** writes poetry to give to others and reads it aloud to nurture herself.

In what house do you have Ceres in your birth chart?

Ceres ♀	Keywords
First house Ceres	Your independence is your way of loving others so as not to burden them.
Second house Ceres	Flowers, cards, and gifts all spell unconditional love.
Third house Ceres	Let your partners know that whether it's meaningful to them or not, you feel loved when you hear the words.
Fourth house Ceres	You run the risk of martyrdom unless you learn to include yourself in all the nurturing you dole out so generously.
Fifth house Ceres	You always make time to attend everyone's games, recitals, and performances. Invite others to attend your victories, too.
Sixth house Ceres	Cleaning up is how you show you care. Hiring a maid or springing for a custom closet raises your own self-esteem.
Seventh house Ceres	You love your partner unconditionally, like an ideal mother or father. Accept this and find someone who also loves this way.
Eighth house Ceres	Changing your loved ones is how you show them you care. It's fair, because you also welcome constructive criticism.
Ninth house Ceres	Foreigners find you to be the ultimate host because you genuinely embrace other cultures and religions. Reward yourself with an exotic yet educational trip.

2. If your chart doesn't have any squares, a life coach might help nudge you along. Angles of 150 degrees require an adjustment from you so that both planets involved have enough expression in your life. Angles of 180 degrees are made up of two charts that are opposite each other. Most people tend to give expression to one of these planets and ignore the other. The repressed energy of the ignored planet builds up and seeks expression. If you don't give it expression, it will attract a situation into your life that challenges you, and forces change. It does this by cueing your unconscious behaviors to involve you with people or situations that will create a crisis, requiring you to access that forgotten part of you, revive it, and put it to use. Pretty tricky! It may not feel so great while you're in the middle of the crisis, but it's a good thing in the end. **3.** For any challenging planetary combinations, look at the planets' energies in the signs they express themselves through, as well as what house they occupy in your chart—they tend to show up in this area of your life. Consider how those planets could blend more harmoniously with the others. See also *angle, aspects between planets, square.* △ **BC** ○

Chinese astrology **1.** Also called Eastern astrology. Chinese astrology combines the five elements of wood, fire, earth, water, and metal and their yin or yang energy with the twelve Chinese zodiac symbols: the rat, ox, tiger, rabbit, dragon, snake, horse, sheep (ram or goat), monkey, rooster, dog, and boar. **2.** The Chinese astrology system is a sixty-year cycle of combinations of these elements and signs. See also *astrology, Hindu astrology, yang, yin.* **BC**

Chiron **1.** A large comet labeled a planetoid discovered by Charles Kowal in 1977 and named for the wise centaur of Greek mythology. **2.** When Chiron's orbit is nearest the Sun, it's just inside the orbit of Saturn. At its farthest, it's just inside the orbit of Uranus. Chiron's unstable orbit is thought to link Saturn with Uranus. Saturn rules the old ways and Uranus rules the new. **3.** Chiron was called the wounded healer for his teaching and healing skills. In Greek myth, he was the centaur son of Saturn and Philyra. The name Chiron comes from the Greek word *chiral*, which means "polarization." Chiron is half civilized (his human upper body) and half wild (his wild-horse lower body). He expresses not only physical polarization, but also the struggle between mind and spirit. Chiron struggles between the monster he believes himself to be and the divine creature he wishes he were. In the myth, he was shot in the leg with an arrow dipped in the deadly blood of the hydra by his former student, Hercules. He suffered ceaselessly from the poisoned wound, but as an immortal, could not die. Chiron was the greatest healer on Earth, but he could not heal himself because he was consumed with self-hatred and self-blame. Eventually, he gave up his immortality and became the constellation of Sagittarius, his wound healed. Chiron teaches that healing occurs only after blame and self-hatred are released.

✦ Most astrology computer software programs include Chiron (the planetoid) along with the other planets in your birth chart. The glyph for Chiron is ⚷. Chiron is the key to healing all mental, emotional, and physical disturbances in your birth chart. Where is Chiron in your birth chart, and in what sign? Chiron's location can tell you about the wounds you have and how to go about healing them. See also *planets*. ◯

In what sign do you have Chiron in your birth chart?

- **Chiron in Aries** propels you into somewhat extreme circumstances that force you to recognize who you are and what you want. Your last life may have been as the opposite gender.

- **Chiron in Taurus** activates beauty and money issues so that you will recognize your own innate value. You may have lost everything material in your last lifetime.

- **Chiron in Gemini** can show up as an obsessive/compulsive tendency until you learn to focus on ideas that make you happy. You bridge book-learning to achieve innate wisdom. This can also indicate a former life where you were mute.

- **Chiron in Cancer** prevents nurturing until you learn to give it to yourself first. You may have been homeless in a recent past lifetime.

- **Chiron in Leo** deprives you of fun until you learn to create your own reality. Your creative talents were most likely seen as a hindrance in a former life.

- **Chiron in Virgo** heightens your sensitivity to criticism, especially your own. Learn to forgive your mistakes and accept yourself as perfect for where you are now on your evolutionary path in the same way you can accept babies as perfect even though they can't walk or talk yet. It is likely that your survival depended upon you executing your job perfectly in a previous lifetime.

- **Chiron in Libra** has you so worried that you'll never find your soul mate you come across as desperate, which only attracts who you don't want. Ask yourself why you want to get married and then find ways to put those qualities into your life. Becoming what you want to marry magnetically pulls in your mate. Chances are good that you and your true love were painfully separated from each other in a recent past life.

- **Chiron in Scorpio** manifests as betrayal. Think about those relationships and how you made the relationship more powerful than living your own truth. This is how you betrayed yourself. Know that you can experience loyalty as you release your attachment to how you have been hurt … your soul is ready to be done with this pattern. You may have been severely betrayed by those in power in a past life.

- **Chiron in Sagittarius** brings you the experiences you need to become a philosopher. Practice the adage of live and let live. You may have been a victim of genocide in a past life.

- **Chiron in Capricorn** is often experienced as an abandonment complex. Take time to acknowledge your own accomplishments and achievements. This behavior will inspire others to openly acknowledge and reward you. You may have past life recollections as a slave.

- **Chiron in Aquarius** makes you feel out of sync or different from everyone else. It's hard for you to just hang out and fit in. As you learn to be yourself, you find your place as the group's lovable oddball or eccentric. You were likely ostracized by society for your unusual gifts or intelligence in a past life, such as a channel or a savant.

- **Chiron in Pisces** creates the wounded artist whose life inspires greatness in the average person. You may worry that there is no ultimate force in the universe to protect you. Get a blank, lined book and write down every supernatural thing that happens to you. By the end of a year you will be astounded by the evidence you have collected that there is an all-knowing intelligence that guides you. You were probably slain as part of a religious sacrifice in a past lifetime. Consider past life therapy; it can bring peace.

C

In what house do you have Chiron in your birth chart?

Chiron ⚷	Keywords
First house Chiron	A holistic teacher who ignites a new generation.
Second house Chiron	Heals through micro-lending, giving great support however small.
Third house Chiron	School does not support learning style.
Fourth house Chiron	Early home environment was not supportive.
Fifth house Chiron	Creative expression judged and shut down in childhood.
Sixth house Chiron	Doesn't feel okay to make mistakes.
Seventh house Chiron	Can't imagine marrying an equal.
Eighth house Chiron	Struggles to unite with others.
Ninth house Chiron	Disappointed by religion.
Tenth house Chiron	Fame is illusive, but highly desired.
Eleventh house Chiron	Always searching for a feeling of community.
Twelfth house Chiron	The filmmaker who shows the world that, despite our differences, everyone seeks unconditional love.

Chiron transits   With the most stable orbit among the asteroids and planetoids, Chiron transits are carefully observed by astrologers. ✴ As Chiron transits your chart, you may experience the following: a delivery of new insights and resolution to old problems; a rekindling of old emotional trauma that can be resolved through your enlarged experience and maturity; physical pain that draws your attention to a part of your body that is holding stuck trauma; opportunities to teach; a situation or physical ailment that can only be healed by recognizing the beauty of being human; an introduction to holistic healing that helps you with a chronic condition; or a newfound understanding that enables you to be a renegade within an established or conservative system. See also *Chiron.* ◯ **Z**

Chronos (Kronos) The Greek name for Saturn, the god of agriculture and harvest and father of Zeus, who is Jupiter in Roman mythology. See also *Jupiter, Saturn.* ◯

colors Each of the twelve astrological signs is associated with a particular color or colors. The color(s) correspond to the vibrational frequencies of the planets and are translated into their respective signs. ✦ What color is associated with your Sun sign? If you're an energetic Aries, your color is fiery red or burnt umber. Taurus as the cow maiden likes meadow green and as the bull prefers red-orange. Gemini enjoys cheery yellow. The water sign Cancer loves cool sea green, sea blue, and silver. Leo the lion likes the gold and orange of the summer Sun. Virgo appreciates yellow-green and classic navy blue and gray. Libra is soothed by pastel blue and lavender. Passionate Scorpio craves crimson, black, and deep blue-green. Adventurous Sagittarius loves the violet of the sky after a perfect sunset. The earth sign Capricorn feels at home in dark green and brown. Airy Aquarius appreciates the electric blue of a bold, cloudless sky and a clear, pale yellow. Intuitive Pisces loves the ocean's colors, turquoise and pale green, as well as pale blue and red-violet once in a while. See also *gems.* ☯

compatibility In astrology, this is how well people are likely to get along based on the characteristics of their Sun signs and the details of their birth charts. ✦ **1.** The placement of your Sun in a particular sign will react differently with different people's Sun placements, because the elements of the signs may or may not be compatible. The sign and house placement bring out different characteristics in one another. You might sense this by how you feel and behave with different people. You might feel more your true self with some Sun signs, and with others, you may hide behind the mask of your ascendant. **2.** Rising signs (or ascendants) and other factors, such as Moon signs, are also influential in determining compatibility. See also *composite chart, Moon, relationship astrology, synastry.* **BC** ☯

composite chart **1.** This is the name for an astrological chart that combines the information from two people's birth charts. **2.** This is a modern technique used in relationship astrology, called synastry, to assess a relationship between two people—the chart is essentially an astrological chart for the relationship itself, and does not simply indicate the compatibility of the two people. **3.** A composite chart is calculated by finding the mean distance between each pair of same planets in the birth charts. ✴ Want to know the strengths and weaknesses in your relationship with a friend, family member, or business associate? A composite chart holds the key. An astrologer can create one of these using the information from your birth chart, along with information from the other person's birth chart. You'll discover how your planets combine to produce likely and unlikely outcomes. A composite chart uses the midpoint between the same planets in the two birth charts to create a combined placement for each planet. The composite chart shows the nature of the relationship itself, and is ideal for all kinds of partnerships. See also *birth chart, compatibility, relationship astrology, synastry.* **BC** ☯

computer programs   **1.** Contemporary astrologers use a variety of computer programs to create birth, progressed, solar return, prenatal, and lunar phase charts as well as maps for their clients. **2.** Once personal information, including specific time and date of birth and birth location, is entered, the computer program will create a surprising variety of informative charts. ✴ Compared to the old-fashioned methods of creating birth charts, the computerized systems are revolutionary. Not only are they incredibly fast and much less tedious, they also eliminate that catch-all, human error. If you were creating a birth chart by hand, you'd need an ephemeris, table of houses, atlas, and other resources to look up the necessary information to correlate with your birth facts. See also *birth chart, calculating a birth chart, ephemeris.* **BC**

conjunction   **1.** This is one of the major aspects and the most powerful aspect in astrology. **2.** The glyph for conjunction is ☌. On a birth chart, planets are said to be in conjunction when two or more occupy the same degree or are within 10 degrees of each other. This means that, at the time of birth, these planets appeared to be in the same location in the sky. **3.** The tighter the orb, or distance between the planets, the more powerful the conjunction. ✴ **1.** Do you have a conjunction in your birth chart? Look for the symbol: ☌. The planets involved will determine the meaning of the conjunction, but the relationship of the planets tends to be intense and unified. Are the planets compatible? Or are they at odds? **2.** The house the conjunction appears in will tell you where this planetary action takes place in your life. **3.** The sign the conjunction appears in influences how the conjunction affects you. **4.** Because they can be up to 10 degrees apart, it is possible that the planets in conjunction are in different signs. This will significantly affect the relationship between the planets in conjunction. A conjunction is more positive and powerful when each of the planets is enhanced by the sign it is in, and it's less effective—or even problematic—when one or both of the planets is in a sign to its detriment. If you have two planets in the same sign where they are both enhanced within a few degrees of each other, you will have an incredible edge in life. See also *aspect grid, aspects between planets.* △ ☯ ◯

constellation   The various arrangements of stars in the night sky. The twelve signs of the zodiac are named for these groupings, though they no longer refer directly to the constellations. Mathematician/astronomer Ptolemy described the zodiac in the second century. These days, astronomy students use the constellations as mnemonics—if that's Virgo, the bright star must be Spica. In 1929, the International Astronomical Union adopted the boundaries of the 88 constellations recognized today. The twelve constellations named for the signs of the zodiac are the ring through which the Sun seems to pass every year as seen from the Earth's orbit. The constellations don't align with the dates for the Sun signs any longer (see sidereal zodiac for more on this), but Western astrology still uses the names. See also *sidereal zodiac, zodiac.* ☼

contrascion   **1.** When two planets mirror each other, meaning that they sit opposite each other by degrees on either side of the Aries/Libra axis, they are called contrascion. **2.** Pairs of contrascion signs are Aries/Pisces, Taurus/Aquarius, Gemini/Capricorn, Libra/Virgo, Scorpio/Leo, and Sagittarius/Cancer. ✦ **1.** If you have a contrascion in your left hemisphere, the planet in your first quadrant wants you to take personal action and the planet in your fourth quadrant wants your actions to have more social impact. **2.** If you have a contrascion in your right hemisphere, you will feel the conflict between your second quadrant, which wants you to be aware of what is happening in your relationships, and your third quadrant, which wants you to connect more deeply with some part of yourself you neglect. See also *antiscion, fertility.*

Copernicus, Nicolaus   1. Polish astronomer (1473–1543) who first formulated the theory of a sun-centered (heliocentric) universe. **2.** Before Copernicus, the general belief was that the Earth was at the center of the universe (the term for this is geocentric). Astrology operates on this pre-Copernican system; because it focuses on the effects of the planets on beings who live on Earth (that's us), the idea that the Earth is the fixed point works well. **3.** Copernicus was a visionary—in a time when most people were comfortable with the idea that the Earth was the center of our universe, he kept looking for facts to prove his theory, that the Sun was actually the center, and the Earth rotated around it. Copernicus was an Aquarius, born on February 19. He exemplifies the airy, innovative thinker. See also *astrology, astronomy, geocentric, heliocentric, Sun.* ◯

co-ruler   1. Multiple planets in two signs in one house are called co-rulers of that house. **2.** Co-ruled signs include Scorpio, ruled by Pluto and Mars; Aries, ruled by Mars and the Sun; Aquarius, ruled by Uranus and Saturn; and Pisces, ruled by Neptune and Jupiter. **3.** Aside from Aries, signs that are ruled by outer planets that weren't discovered when astrology was first innovated are assigned an ancient ruler and a modern ruler. Ancient astrologers didn't know about Uranus, Neptune, or Pluto, so some of the known planets did double-duty until these other planets were discovered. The ancient rulers are usually discounted in modern astrology, but professional astrologers tend to keep them in mind because they might explain events that would otherwise not show up in the chart. See also *ruler.* ◯☼

**crescent Moon   **The second stage of the Moon's cycle, when the Moon is 45 to 90 degrees in front of the Sun. ✦ Do you have a crescent Moon in your birth chart? Depending upon the sign and house it's in, your Moon needs you to reach beyond your habits and usual behaviors so that you can feel and sense what really makes you happy—as opposed to what your family thinks you should want to be happy. See also *Moon, Moon phases.* ◯

cusp   1. The point at the beginning or end of a Sun sign is called the cusp; this is also the period at the beginning or end of one of the houses. **2.** The cusp of a Sun sign is the point on a birth chart where a new sign begins.

C

✧ **1.** Minutes and degrees matter in astrology, and a specific birth chart will be very accurate about your Sun sign. Think of the cusp as the (imaginary) dividing line between the signs. Someone born very close to the beginning of a sign or at the end of the preceding sign is said to be "on the cusp." This person may feel more like one sign than the other—if you were born on the cusp of Aquarius, you may feel more like a Capricorn. You will have elements of both in your personality, but one sign or the other is likely to be dominant, or more influential. **2.** Your Sun sign rules your character, your personality. It's who you are. If you're born on the cusp, it doesn't mean you have a split personality, it just means you have more of a mix of influences working within you. You can probably look at the traits of the two signs you're straddling and figure out which one really feels the most like you, but you may be happier finding ways to give both of the signs expressions in your life. **3.** Planets in the first third of the sign (the first 10 degrees) are in the first decan of the sign (each sign has three decans). The planets near the cusp of the sign have the qualities of the sign they are in along with the first sign of that element. If your Mercury was at 4 degrees Sagittarius, it would express Sagittarius as well as Aries. If it was at 4 degrees Aries, it would just be Aries. **4.** Just as you can imagine lines separating the zodiac on a birth chart, most natal charts have lines actually separating the houses. As with the signs, planets that appear on the cusp of a house are those near the beginning of a house. What does it mean if you have a planet on the cusp of a house? When one of your natal planets is early, meaning it has just crossed the cusp into the next house, it expresses maximum energy. The later it appears in the house, the farther into the house it moves, the more dissipated its energy becomes. The most energized cusp planets are those in the angular cardinal houses. See also *angular house, birth chart, cardinal (quality), decan, house.* **BC** 🏠

dark Moon   See *black Moon*.

Davison relationship chart   **1.** An astrological chart for a relationship created by English astrologer Ronald C. Davison (1914–1985). **2.** Similar to a composite chart, Davison's chart uses a midpoint between two people's birth information (place, date, and time) to create a new chart that symbolizes the relationship between the two people. ✦ You might use a Davison relationship chart to look at a relationship you're having difficulty with or one you want to develop further. A Davison relationship horoscope reflects the relationship as its own entity. Unlike a composite chart, which is not a true horoscope because the locations are not combined, a Davison relationship chart can be progressed and returned. It can be used for predictions and even locational astrology. A Davison relationship horoscope shows you the opportunities and challenges the relationship will experience. See also *composite chart, progressions, relationship astrology, relocation astrology, return, synastry.* **BC** 🌓

decan   **1.** This is also called a decanate and is a 10-degree division of each astrological sign. Each sign has three decans (there are 30 degrees total in each sign); there are 36 decans in the entire zodiac, which is a full 360 degree circle. Each decan corresponds to about 10 calendar days, so the Sun moves through about 1 degree of the zodiac each day. **2.** Each decan has a planetary ruler called a subruler that works with the planetary ruler of the sign. ✦ A decan is used to interpret particular characteristics of the astrological signs. If you know what your Sun sign is, you can also determine which decan of the sign you were born in. For example, you're an Aries no matter which decan of Aries you were born in, but based on the subruler, more nuanced and personalized information can be learned about your Sun sign. See also *cusp, house, ruler, subruler; Sun sign.* ◯ ☼

Decans by the Zodiac Signs	Subruler	Characteristic
First decan of Aries March 21 to March 30	Mars	Dominant personality and aggressive
Second decan of Aries March 31 to April 9	Sun	Fun-loving, bold leader
Third decan of Aries April 10 to April 19	Jupiter	Larger-than-life presence
First decan of Taurus April 20 to April 29	Venus	Buys the best for less
Second decan of Taurus April 30 to May 9	Mercury	Full of money-making ideas
Third decan of Taurus May 10 to May 20	Saturn	Amasses a fortune over time
First decan of Gemini May 21 to May 31	Mercury	Can imitate any accent
Second decan of Gemini June 1 to June 10	Venus	Very eloquent
Third decan of Gemini June 11 to June 20	Uranus	Inventive thinker
First decan of Cancer June 21 to July 1	Moon	security conscious
Second decan of Cancer July 2 to July 11	Pluto	Has very few regrets
Third decan of Cancer July 12 to July 22	Neptune	Unconditionally loving
First decan of Leo July 23 to August 1	Sun	Amazing with children
Second decan of Leo August 2 to August 11	Jupiter	International star quality
Third decan of Leo August 12 to August 22	Mars	Very exciting life
First decan of Virgo August 23 to September 1	Mercury	Brilliant and efficient mind
Second decan of Virgo September 2 to September 11	Saturn	Builds a service empire
Third decan of Virgo September 12 to September 22	Venus	Finds value and beauty in a simple life

Decans by the Zodiac Signs	Subruler	Characteristic
First decan of Libra September 23 to October 2	Venus	Partner is the priority
Second decan of Libra October 3 to October 12	Uranus	Needs an unconventional relationship
Third decan of Libra October 13 to October 22	Mercury	Analyzes both sides of situations to find balance and justice
First decan of Scorpio October 23 to November 1	Pluto	Deep desire to connect to others
Second decan of Scorpio November 2 to November 11	Neptune	Profoundly psychic
Third decan of Scorpio November 12 to November 21	Moon	Emotional intensity
First decan of Sagittarius November 22 to December 1	Jupiter	Naturally in the right place at the right time
Second decan of Sagittarius December 2 to December 11	Mars	Pioneering scholar
Third decan of Sagittarius December 12 to December 21	Sun	Mentor to the stars
First decan of Capricorn December 22 to December 31	Saturn	Natural architect and logician
Second decan of Capricorn January 1 to January 10	Venus	Generates big profits through ethical business conduct
Third decan of Capricorn January 11 to January 20	Mercury	Focused on practical results
First decan of Aquarius January 21 to January 30	Uranus	Misunderstood genius
Second decan of Aquarius January 31 to February 9	Mercury	Herald of the future
Third decan of Aquarius February 10 to February 19	Venus	Cultural and societal trendsetter

D

continues

continued

Decans by the Zodiac Signs	Subruler	Characteristic
First decan of Pisces February 20 to February 29	Neptune	Compassion that knows no limits
Second decan of Pisces March 1 to March 10	Moon	Sensitive nurturer
Third decan of Pisces March 11 to March 20	Pluto	Divine poetry birthed from torment

decanate   See *decan*.

December 22 to January 21   Birth dates for the Sun sign Capricorn. The position of the Sun during these dates correlates with an astrological Sun sign. Those born between December 22 and January 21 have Capricorn as their Sun sign. See also *Capricorn*. ☉

declination   The angular distances from the planets to the equator, which changes every moment as the planet travels its path on the ecliptic. See also *aspects between planets, ecliptic, planets*. ◯

degrees   **1.** A measurement used for arcs and angles. There are 360 degrees in a circle, so an astrological birth chart is 360 degrees. **2.** Each of twelve signs or houses in a birth chart is 30 degrees; the signs are divided into three parts of 10 degrees each called a decan. **3.** One degree contains 60 minutes, and each minute is 60 seconds of longitude. **4.** Every degree on the birth chart has a particular meaning or interpretation based on Sabian symbols, a system developed in the 1920s. The Sabian symbols are archetypal images that add an interpretive layer to the birth chart. ✧ **1.** Because Sabian symbols are so specific (one symbol for each degree), the symbols are not often used by most astrologers in present-day astrological consultations with querents. **2.** Degrees are mathematically calculated to figure out planetary aspects, or angles between planets in a birth chart. Aspects indicate how people will behave in different areas of life. An astrologer needs to know the degrees of the planets to understand the aspects and get clues that can help them interpret behavior. Happily, these days computer programs take care of most of the complicated math involved in determining planetary aspects.

Aspects are very important and astrologers look carefully at aspects when interpreting birth charts. See also *aspects between planets, decan, planets, querent, Sabian symbols.* △ **BC** ◯

descendant **1.** This is the sign and degree on the cusp of the seventh house, the western horizon of the birth chart, at the exact time and place of birth. **2.** On a birth chart, the descendant line is the right side of the horizon line (the left side is the ascendant), the western cardinal point or three o'clock position, if the chart were a clock.

✦ **1.** Your descendant is on the cusp of the seventh house of partnerships, marriage, committed relationships, and all forms of contracts or contractual agreements. The seventh house also rules your maternal grandmother, your second child, and your first child's school, car, and neighbors. The descendant is the line only—the cusp—so it starts the seventh house. What reveals the nuances of your descendant is what resides inside your seventh house. Planets in the seventh house add depth and interpretation to the descendant. The planets there will describe what you want in a partnership as well as what you need and what you likely attract in partnerships. **2.** The beginning of the seventh house used to be thought of as the house of open enemies or open confrontation, meaning obvious enemies (the twelfth house relates to hidden enemies), or even your opposite. In the way that the first house is the ascendant—you— the house opposite it in the birth chart, the seventh house, is the descendant—your opposite. Remember that opposites attract! You may attract your opposite so you have the opportunity to evolve— you will grow in such relationships, which take you outside your comfort zone and force you to adapt or change. You can't evolve in isolation; you have to connect, and even with those you don't feel compatible with. Open confrontation will make you stronger, even if the relationship doesn't last. **3.** If you have planets on your descendant, you may be unaware of their energies within you because they live in your alter ego or shadow self. The ruler of your descendant is the planet that rules the sign on the cusp of your seventh house. The energies—the planets—on your descendant and the ruler of your descendant will attract individuals into your life who mirror those hidden energies and characteristics. You may fall in love with the person who best displays these characteristics because that person helps you become comfortable with the rejected parts of yourself. Want to know what behaviors you have repressed? Think about all of the partners in your life, past and present, and make a mental list of their common characteristics. What traits do they share that you do not have? These are likely the traits you have repressed. See also *ascendant, birth chart, horizon, seventh house, shadow self.* **BC** 🌓 🏠 ☼

descending   **1.** Planets are said to be descending when they are between the cusp of the tenth house and the cusp of the fourth house. **2.** Descending planets have a weakened influence.

�֎ **1.** What if all of the planets in your birth chart are descending? If all of your planets are located in the eastern hemisphere, or the left side of your chart, the qualities of Mars are more emphasized in you. You are bold, independent, self-sufficient, strong-willed, dynamic, and an excellent decision maker. You may prefer to stay single or be self-employed. You are a natural leader and self-starter who likes to be in charge. The best relationships and careers for you are those that support your independence, risk taking, leadership, and high energy. You tend to make things happen rather than wait to respond—which means you are sometimes impulsive, but you get things done! **2.** What if you don't have any descending planets? Then all of your planets are ascending and are located in the western hemisphere, or the right side of your chart. The qualities of Venus are stronger in you, making you very accommodating and adaptable. You do best in relationships and flourish on a team. You have your own opinions, but you're always open to seeing the perspective of someone else. As a result, you work well as a subordinate. You may be unhappy if you cannot respect your boss, spouse, or co-workers. You may not be aware of it, but you tend to communicate in such a refined, subtle manner that other people sometimes miss the point of what you are saying. You tend to wait for things to happen and then decide how to respond. If you're unhappy with your life, choose to create your own destiny, and change it. See also *cusp, fourth house, Mars, tenth house, Venus.* **BC** 🏠 ◯

destiny   **1.** Destiny is that which is fated. **2.** In metaphysics, there is both destiny and free will, both of which are necessary in life for growth. ✖ **1.** Astrology connects destiny to your natal chart, your beginning, birth. Your chart at birth is unique, revealing the placement of the heavens at the time and place of your birth, and has a unique destiny that is the story of your soul's journey. The planets, especially the Sun, Moon, and Saturn, the rulers of your chart's axis, communicate your myth to you through archetypal images that assist you in comprehending your true nature. **2.** Your birth chart will show events you are destined to go through. You can't change the set course of destiny—you came from it and are born into it—but you always have free will. Using conscious will and awareness, you can change the circumstances of your destiny. These two factors—destiny and free will—work together in your life. See also *archetype, birth chart, fate, free will, karma, tarot and astrology.* **BC** ☯

D

detriment   **1.** One of the essential dignities, or power designations, of the planets. **2.** A planet is weaker and in its detriment when it is in the sign opposite the sign it rules. **3.** A planet in its detriment will have low energy. **4.** The opposite of detriment is rulership or home—when a planet is in its home sign, it is very comfortable, and its energy flows well. See also *dignities, exalted, fall, home signs, planets.* **BC** ○ ☼

Planet	Sign(s) of Detriment	Keywords
Sun	Aquarius	Creativity that aims for shock appeal
Moon	Capricorn	Seeks external approval
Mercury	Sagittarius and Pisces	Tendency to speak rather than listen or prefer to hear what's pleasant
Venus	Aries and Scorpio	Obsessive shopper or seducer
Mars	Libra	Avoids confrontation
Jupiter	Gemini	Overthinks situations
Saturn	Cancer	Overly strict or too many rules
Uranus	Leo	Wants to stay a child
Neptune	Virgo	Worries awake and asleep
Pluto	Taurus	Self-sabotage

direct   **1.** Also called direct energy. The motion of a planet on its normal elliptic (circular orbit of the Sun), in its normal orbit (as opposed to retrograde motion). **2.** When it's direct, a planet is interpreted as giving energy in its normal fashion. The planet's energy is more conscious, yang, consistent, and balanced, exhibiting its fullest potential. ✦ **1.** In your birth chart, a planet in direct motion lets you access your fullest potential. Direct planets give you access to your talents and abilities with ease. Retrograde planets have less direct energy, and may indicate a more difficult course or delays. The Sun and the Earth always move in a direct fashion. **2.** Direct energy and its forward motion make you feel like you're moving ahead at a normal pace and you will reach your goal. You will be more self-aware and self-assured with direct planets in your chart. See also *energy, retrograde planets, yang.* **BC** ◯ ℞

disseminating Moon   The phase of the Moon that follows the full Moon. Here, the energy of the full Moon is beginning to release. See *Moon phases.*

divisional chart   Vedic astrology, which is the Hindu system, uses sixteen divisional charts called vargas. See also *chakras and astrology, sidereal zodiac, Vedic astrology.* **BC**

earth, element   **1.** One of the four astrological elements. The other elements are air, fire, and water. A feminine (yin) element, earth stands for stability. **2.** The twelve astrological signs are divided equally among the four elements. The three earth signs are Taurus, Virgo, and Capricorn. **3.** The twelve houses are also equally divided among the elements. The three earth houses are those that correspond with the earth signs, the second, sixth, and tenth. These houses relate to self-esteem and possessions, health and service, and career and reputation. Planets found in these houses/signs are known as earth planets.

✦ **1.** To find out whether or not you have earth planets in your birth chart, you need to figure out what signs the planets in your chart are in. See how many planets are in the earth signs of Taurus, Virgo, or Capricorn, which rule the second, sixth, and tenth houses. **2.** People ruled by earth signs need proof before they can believe something. They need a physical experience to make something tangible. If you are realistic, and enjoy engaging in a logical process for an outcome, you may have lots of earth planets in your chart—check and see. **3.** If you have lots of earth planets in your birth chart, you are likely goal-oriented, patient, and strong-willed. You may have physical stamina, though you don't necessarily like physical exercise. You may really enjoy spending time with Mother Earth, gardening, rock collecting, even rock climbing. Your friends know you as reliable and patient, but you can also be stubborn and a little set in your ways. **4.** What if you have a shortage of earth planets in your birth chart? If you have few earth planets in your birth chart—or even none at all—you may lack some of the qualities of the earth element. Rather than being an industrious goal-setter, you may be indecisive and impatient. Check your birth chart to figure out the role this element plays for you, and also to see what element your planets are in—this will tell you a lot more than the missing earth planets will. If you find that you do not have any planets in earth, you are considered an earth adept. This means that you have mastered the earth element in prior incarnations, and it is missing from your chart for a reason: you might be tempted to make this lifetime all about earthly concerns if you had an avenue for its expression. Earth adepts need to focus on the other elements in this lifetime. See also *adept, air sign, Capricorn, earth sign, element, fire sign, second house, sixth house, Taurus, tenth house, Virgo, water sign.* **BC** 🜨 🏠 ◯ ☼

Earth, planet   1. The home planet, also called Mother Earth. **2.** Astrology is geocentric: the universe is viewed as though the Earth were its center. The other planets, and heavenly bodies, are seen in their relation to Earth. **3.** Astronomy is heliocentric, or Sun-centered. This view, pioneered by sixteenth-century Polish mathematician and astronomer Nicolaus Copernicus, presents the Sun as the center of the universe, and Earth is viewed in relation to the Sun. **4.** Earth is also one of the four astrological elements. ✴ **1.** As sentient beings, all humanity lives in relation to the Earth; how cultures and individuals view this relationship is crucial to human survival on the planet. **2.** Twentieth-century astronomer Carl Sagan also thought deeply about Earth's (and so humanity's) place in the universe, and the possibility that other evolved, sentient beings may inhabit the universe as well. **3.** In studying astrological birth charts, we celebrate the unique placement of the Earth and heavens at the time of each human birth. Astrology, then, is a contemplation of each person's relationship to planet Earth, and the heavens above. Collectively, astrology becomes the study of the human evolution of the Earth. See also *astrology; astronomy; Copernicus, Nicolaus; earth, element; earth sign; elements; geocentric; heliocentric; Sagan, Carl.* **BC** ◯

earth sign   1. Taurus, Virgo, and Capricorn are the three earth signs, or the earth triplicity. Earth signs are solid and disciplined. They are very loyal and practical, and like to keep their feet firmly on the ground. **2.** These signs were historically described as cold, dry, or barren. Today, they are seen as practical, realistic, and resourceful. These signs are focused on serving in a practical way on the earth plane.

E

✦ **1.** If your Sun sign is Taurus, Virgo, or Capricorn, stability is your main focus. If you're an earth sign, you are likely practical and focused. Earth signs love routine and tend to stick with one, even when it's not working for them. The first earth sign in the zodiac is Taurus, a fixed earth sign that is strong, loyal, and sometimes stubborn. Taurus wants everyone to get along. This sign likes to be forewarned of change so they can prepare for it. Taurus is fixed, which can mean stuck: Taurus really doesn't like to break from settled patterns. Virgo is the mutable earth sign. This sign is pretty adaptable, and likes change, which is movement toward better things. Virgo may go into public service, because they want to improve things. Capricorn is the cardinal earth sign. This sign makes good managers and business leaders. Details aren't as important as the big picture for Capricorn, but they are committed to getting things done, and are generally work rather than service oriented. Capricorn takes a serious approach to whatever they do—even when it's not a task they like, they will complete it, and they like having a goal to work toward. **2.** All the earth signs have a feminine or yin energy. Like Earth itself, earth signs are firm and stable. If you're an earth sign—Taurus, Virgo, or Capricorn—your energy is calming and stabilizing. Yin energy is open and receiving; earth accepts the deep roots that allow life to grow. **3.** If you're an earth sign, how do you mix with signs in the other elements? Here's a brief look at your elemental compatibility: Earth and earth together are as happy as mountainbikers reveling in muddy trails. Earth partners share the same values, sensibilities, and ideas about what constitutes happiness. An earth and air combination is mind over matter. Air is in the heaven, and earth is on the ground—they are far apart, and it will take work to keep them together—but opposites sometimes do attract. Earth and fire have a symbiotic relationship: earth provides the hearth and the organic material for a nice steady flame. Water combines with earth to grow a garden; water can turn a desert into an oasis. See also *Capricorn; earth, element; Taurus; Virgo; yin.* ☼

eastern hemisphere   See *hemisphere.*

eclipse, lunar   **1.** Occurs when the Sun, Earth, and Moon align, with the Earth in the middle, blocking the light of the Sun from illuminating the Moon. If the Moon is completely hidden in the shadow of the Earth, the eclipse is total, and the Moon will appear dark.

2. A lunar eclipse marks a period of internal, emotional, or psychic change. An internal shift might be expressed, or there may be an awakening or awareness of previously hidden feelings. Change during this time can be personally dramatic. **3.** The eclipse comes from the east, and its impact lasts one month for every hour of the eclipse. **4.** There can be zero to three lunar eclipses each calendar year.

✦ **1.** Were you born during a lunar eclipse? If so, your Sun sits opposite your Moon. Your Sun and Moon have different agendas for you. You will have to learn about these two sides of yourself and find ways to give them equal expression in your life. Otherwise, you will always feel pulled in two directions. **2.** A lunar eclipse in your birth chart gives you some special skills and gifts. You have the ability to step back and look at your behaviors and patterns and make conscious decisions about what you want to change. You can also vividly imagine what it is like to walk in someone else's shoes. **3.** Your lunar eclipse also gives you a tendency toward self-doubt. It can cause you to second-guess yourself a lot. If you can accept this, and recognize it for what it is (it's not you, it's your lunar eclipse!), you can work around it. Without this awareness, a lunar eclipse can be very draining, because your energy is moving in two directions at once. You can harness these back-and-forth energies through exercise that incorporates that same dynamic, such as doing yoga's Sun and Moon Salutations. Metaphysical studies can be a big help to you emotionally because it will teach you that everything you need to feel happy already exists within you. See also *eclipse, solar.* **BC** ◯

eclipse, solar   **1.** Occurs when the Moon passes between the Sun and the Earth during its orbit, and all three are aligned in the same part of the sky, forming a conjunction near one of the Nodes; the Moon blocks the Sun, resulting in a period of "lights out" on some part of Earth. **2.** A solar eclipse marks a period of external shift. Solar eclipses initiate a new cycle and may indicate that change is in the air—dramatic change that will last. **3.** A solar eclipse comes from the west, and its impact lasts a year for every hour of the eclipse. **4.** There are at least two solar eclipses every calendar year, and it's possible to have as many as five. Solar eclipses occur more often than lunar eclipses because the Earth and the Moon are not on the same plane as the Earth orbits the Sun; they have to be on the same plane for an eclipse. The Moon is about 5 degrees above or below the Earth. Lunar eclipses range from zero to three in a calendar year.

E

✦ **1.** What kinds of dramatic, external shifts might happen during a solar eclipse? The Sun is associated with men, so there could be a change in male leadership. Male leaders might be removed from power or they might leave political office. There could be a shift to a new type of leadership. **2.** A total solar eclipse is visible, and may manifest in a material way on Earth. Mother Nature is affected by the Sun and the Moon, and changes in the patterns of the Sun and Moon may mark changes in the weather on Earth, including earthquakes, floods, or wind shifts. **3.** Were you born during a solar eclipse? If so, study the meaning of the Nodes in your chart, because they will be especially active for you. You are naturally avant-garde and a bit of a revolutionary. See also *eclipse, lunar; Nodes (North, South)*. **BC** ◯

ecliptic   1. The path the Sun appears to take in the heavens in a calendar year. **2.** In traditional astrology, which is Earth-centered, the Sun travels around the Earth on a path that carries it through each of the twelve signs of the zodiac. The ecliptic is the path the Sun appears to take when seen from the Earth. See also *astrology, Earth, heliocentric*. ◯

education   1. In a birth chart, the ninth house, the planet that rules the sign on its cusp, and the planets and aspects found there can be interpreted regarding higher education. The ninth house's natural ruler, Jupiter, and associated sign, Sagittarius, also rule college. **2.** The third house, Mercury, and Gemini rule primary and secondary education or preschool through high school. See also *Gemini, Jupiter, ninth house, Mercury, third house, Sagittarius*. ☯ 🏠 ◯ ☼

eighth house   1. In astrology, the eighth house is the house of rebirth and transformation. Psychic development and birth are also found in this house. **2.** The eighth house also represents shared resources and inheritance or gifts of money. Joint ventures, soul mates, secrets, surgery, investments, a partner's assets, banking, retirement funds, insurance, and taxes are all in the eighth house.

✦ **1.** The eighth house is also called the house of death and regeneration, but this isn't usually meant literally. Death is usually interpreted as an ending or a transformation. What kind of transformation? It can be physical, emotional, mental, or spiritual. Puberty, or the death of childhood, is a physical transformation, as is pregnancy or menopause for women and hair loss or changes in virility for men. Emotional transformation happens in therapy and is the death of denial. Mental transformation is usually gradual and is the death of the ego. Spiritual transformation can be a religious baptism, an initiation into a secret society, a surrendering of independence into the unity of sexual ecstasy, or the discovery of a passion for art or music. **2.** Everyone has some psychic ability, including intuition. The development and use of your psychic abilities relates to your eighth house. Professional psychics often have Mercury (job), Venus (income), or Saturn (career) posited here. **3.** The eighth house also indicates how you interact with others with your money. If you're seeking a loan, or otherwise working with investments, information on that is found here. **4.** The eighth house is naturally associated with Scorpio, and is ruled by Mars and Pluto. **5.** What does it mean if you have lots of planets—or very few—in the eighth house? If the eighth house is a strong house for you, you might be headed toward a career as a healer, shaman, surgeon, ob/gyn, coroner, dictator, proctologist, insurer, sex therapist, pirate, nuclear scientist, snake charmer, or tax specialist. The eighth house is a power house that welcomes intense experience. It likes to see what others do not get to see, which is why planets there are drawn to surgery, shamanism, and murder investigation. See also *house, planetary ruler.*

elements   **1.** Method of categorizing the twelve astrological signs. The four astrological elements are earth, air, fire, and water. **2.** The houses and signs are divided among the four elements. The earth signs Taurus, Virgo, and Capricorn rule the second, sixth, and tenth houses. The air signs Gemini, Libra, and Aquarius rule the third, seventh, and eleventh houses. The fire signs Aries, Leo, and Sagittarius rule the first, fifth, and ninth houses. The water signs Cancer, Scorpio, and Pisces rule the fourth, eighth, and twelfth houses. **3.** Associations of each element are as follows. Earth signs are practical, dependable, and willful. Air signs are intellectual, communicative, and quick-witted. Fire signs are energetic, enthusiastic, and spontaneous. Water signs are emotional, imaginative, and sensitive. **4.** Celtic practitioners consider spirit to be a fifth element, uniting all earth, air, fire, and water together in the Wheel of Being.

✦ Is one of the four elements dominant in your birth chart? Figure this out by looking at your chart to see where the planets are. Note the sign each planet is in and then figure out which elements the signs are affiliated with. How many planets do you have in each of the elements? Maybe your chart is evenly spread out among the elements, or maybe one element is missing from your chart completely. If you have a majority of planets in one element, you are probably most like that element, and its characteristics will resonate with you. See also *air, air sign, earth, earth sign, fire, fire sign, planets, water, water sign.* **BC** 🏠 ○ ☼

elevation   **1.** Planets that are closer to the top of the birth chart, or closer to the midheaven, are elevated. The closer a planet is to the midheaven, the more elevated it is said to be. **2.** Planets near the ninth and tenth houses (the cusp of the tenth house is the midheaven) are elevated. **3.** Elevated planets are powerful, and have a strong emphasis in the birth chart. **4.** Elevation by latitude refers to the planet that is most northerly or southerly. ✦ **1.** If you have elevated planets in your birth chart, you will find that these planets in effect rule your chart. They may also be said to color your life's purpose. **2.** If the customary chart ruler, the ruler of the sign on the ascendant, is poorly aspected, then the most elevated planet will rule the chart in its place. See also *above the Earth, midheaven (Medium Coeli), ninth house, tenth house.* **BC** 🏠

eleventh house   **1.** In astrology, the eleventh house is the house of friends, and is also called the house of hopes, wishes, and dreams. **2.** The eleventh house represents friends, society, the fourth child, husband's children from a prior marriage, sons- and daughters-in-law, acquaintances, memberships, and groups, brotherhoods, fraternities, sororities, clubs, as well as goals, objectives, business income, plane flights, and adoption.

✦ **1.** The eleventh house is your house of collective groups, including your friends and peers. This house represents your network, the people you collect around you who share some of your beliefs. If you're in a book club or on a soccer team, the people in these activities with you share your interest in books or soccer, right? These are the people who act as your support system, helping you achieve your goals in life—whether those goals are improving your fluency in French or mastering a new position on the team. These support groups help you grow or help your friends or associates grow. Maybe you serve on a nonprofit board—that falls here, too, in the eleventh house. **2.** Your hopes, wishes, dreams, and goals for this life are also in the eleventh house. This is what you would wish for, and where you want to go or grow in this lifetime. Are you likely to have groups of people in your life that will help you fulfill these dreams? That depends in part on what you have going on in the eleventh house. **3.** The eleventh house is naturally associated with Aquarius, and is ruled by Uranus, co-ruled by Saturn. **4.** What does it mean if you have lots of planets—or very few—in this house? You tend to be naturally outgoing, social, friendly, and blessed with a diversity of friends and a large circle of acquaintances. You may be attracted to work in television or the Internet. You have probably been on safari—or it's one of your goals. Unless it's gotten old, flying thrills you as much as the trip itself. You are very open-minded and have friends in high and low places; you don't discriminate. You especially appreciate people who are unusual, authentic, and slightly eccentric. Good planets and activity in the eleventh house mean good support from your peers and other groups. You are someone with collective power behind you to push you forward. This can help you win elected office, for example, or be chosen as a leader in business. A strong eleventh house means you'll have direction toward those hopes and dreams of yours. If you don't manage the eleventh house well, you may go around in circles, never getting where you want to go. See also *house, planetary ruler.*

empty house When one of the twelve houses in the birth chart has no planets in it, the house is called an empty house. ✦ **1.** If you have an empty house in your birth chart, this doesn't mean nothing is happening in that house; rather, you just don't have to go there and work on it a lot. Your time and energy won't be as focused on a house with no planets in it. Maybe the area of life covered in this house comes naturally to you. For example, if your fifth house of family is empty, this doesn't mean that you won't have children—you could have children, but you don't need to. There's not a struggle ahead for you in that area of your life. Maybe this is something you worked out in an earlier life—you're done with that for now. **2.** An empty house is not a negative thing! On the contrary, it may mean you already have fulfillment in that area of your life. That empty fifth house can indicate no need, or destiny, to have children, but we all have free will—and you must use your free will to decide if you want something in your life, or not. An empty house implies choice in your life, rather than necessity. You've mastered that house—congratulations! See also *full house*. **BC** 🏠

energy   1. In astrology, energy refers to planetary energy. Planets have energy maintaining their orbit, and this energy is translated into behavior by astrologers. **2.** The energy of the twelve Sun signs is characterized as direct or indirect, and may also be related as external and internal or masculine and feminine. Yang energy is direct, while yin energy is indirect. Each sign is either yang or yin. **3.** Planetary energy is related to the four elements: earth, air, fire, and water. Of these, the most energetic is fire, which exudes energy, power, and drama. The least energetic is water. See also *air, element; direct; earth, element; feminine principle; fire, element; indirect; masculine principle; water, element; yang, yin.* ◯

E

ephemeris   1. A planetary table that locates the planets (and other astronomical objects) in the sky at noon and midnight each day (Greenwich Mean Time). **2.** Used by astrologers to figure out what sign the planets are in as well as what degree. **3.** Today astrologers use an electronic ephemeris that changes daily. See also *degrees.* ◯ ☼

ephemeris order of the planets   Astrologers consider the planets in ephemeris order, rather than in astronomical order. The ephemeris order is Sun, Moon, Mercury, Venus, Mars, Jupiter, Saturn, Uranus, Neptune, and Pluto. See also *astronomical order of the planets.* **BC** ◯ **Z**

equinox   1. On the first day of spring, the Sun enters Aries, beginning the zodiacal calendar, and the new year of the zodiac. The first degree of Aries, the vernal equinox, is the beginning of new growth out of the energy that has been dormant since the onset of Capricorn. **2.** On the first day of fall, the Sun enters Libra. Spring and summer growth culminates and the harvest cycle concludes when the Sun enters Libra. This is the time of year to review, to look back at the harvest of the previous season and evaluate. The fall equinox also brings a time for sharing the rewards of the previous season.

✹ Equinoxes are interpreted from the viewpoint of astrologers living in the northern hemisphere, where astrology was birthed. In the same way that astrology sees the Earth as the center of the universe, the northern hemisphere was viewed as the Earth. The southern hemisphere can be seen as the shadow or alter ego for the northern hemisphere. Your shadow holds the energy reserves that your personality draws on. Perhaps the southern hemisphere holds the energy reserves for the rest of the world. See also *Aries, Libra, shadow self.* ☼

Eris   1. A newly discovered dwarf planet that is likely to assume the role as ruler of Libra in astrology, relieving Venus of its double duty for both Taurus and Libra. **2.** In Greek mythology, Eris, a glorious goddess, is sister to Ares, the god of war who bears the Latin name Mars. We now have a sister planet for Mars, which conveniently holds the polarity in the seventh house. The discovery of Libra's true ruler will liberate Librans throughout the world and restore their connection to power. See also *Libra, Mars, planetary ruler, planets, Taurus.* ◯ ☼

essential dignities   1. The two essential dignities that serve as designations of power a planet possesses according to the sign it's in, its degree, or its proximity to other planets, the angles, or points in a chart. **2.** The essential dignities are rulership/detriment and exaltation/fall. Rulership is also referred to as home or domicile. See also *detriment, fall, home signs, planetary rulership.* ◯ ☼

evening sky, planets in   1. Physically, the planets appearing in the evening sky change based on the planetary rotations. **2.** Astrologically, the planets in the evening sky are those in the fifth, sixth, and seventh houses (5 P.M. to 8 P.M.). ✹ Evening sky planets focus on your need to work with others, the cooperative areas of your life. Children, co-workers, and partnerships are found in the fifth, sixth, and seventh houses. Planets in the evening sky of your birth chart indicate that you can't do the work you need to do in these areas alone; you need help. See also *fifth house, planets, sixth house, seventh house.* 🏠 ◯

exact   **1.** Reference to a planetary aspect in a birth chart. An exact aspect occurs when a planet is touching another planet to the same degree. **2.** Also called a conjunction, which is a power point on a birth chart. The very specific connection connotes power; the planets appear to be on top of each other in the chart, and their power is combined. ✦ **1.** Exact aspects relate to destiny in the birth chart. To develop a particular area of your future, you must go to that house for a closer look at what the planets in exact aspect reveal. You may feel drawn or even compelled to this area, and may want to focus a lot of your energy there. This could be something you're really good at—or something you become really good at because you get lots of practice. Other areas of your life may be a disaster, but this one may work like magic. **2.** People with exact aspects tend to be focused on the area where the aspect is located, and often end up being specialists in those areas. They aren't big picture people or multitaskers—but they are experts in their fields. See also *aspects between planets, conjunction.* △ **BC** ○

E

exalted   **1.** One of the essential dignities of the original seven planets. **2.** Planets are said to be exalted when they are in the sign that gives them great strength. **3.** An exalted planet has exaggerated power. **4.** The opposite of exaltation is fall—when a planet is in fall, it is very weakened. Fall is different than detriment, just as exalted is different than rulership. ✦ **1.** The Sun is exalted in Aries, so if your Sun is in Aries, though it's not the Sun's home sign, the Sun is happy because Aries provides lots of opportunities to express all that creativity. Aries is all about making things and is a highly energetic sign. Aries also likes to be first, to stand out and be noticed, which perfectly suits the radiant energy of the Sun. **2.** When the Sun is in its home sign of Leo, it is comfortable and at ease, but Aries is different enough to allow the Sun to expand its influence into new areas. This is the way all of the exalted planets work. **3.** Because there is no consistent rule that enables you to determine exaltation, you will need to memorize which sign exalts which planet. **4.** Check your chart to see if you have any exalted planets shining there. See also *detriment, dignities, fall, home signs, planets.* **BC** ○ ☼

Planet	Sign(s) of Exaltation	Keywords
Sun	Aries	Creative daring
Moon	Taurus	Constructive behaviors
Mercury	Virgo	Solution focused
Venus	Pisces	Unconditionally loving
Mars	Capricorn	Dignified competitor
Jupiter	Cancer	Scholar with great memory
Saturn	Libra	Responsible partner
Uranus	Scorpio	Powerful free agent
Neptune	Cancer	Visionary with an understanding of the past
Pluto	Aries, Leo, Virgo	Right use of power

F

fall **1.** One of the essential dignities of the planets; when a planet is in its fall sign, it is weakened and debilitated. **2.** Planets are happy in signs that enhance their nature and unhappy in signs that contradict their nature. The essential dignities point to signs that empower or weaken a planet. Rulership and exaltation enhance and detriment and fall weaken. (Rulership and detriment go together and exaltation and fall go together.) **3.** Ancient astrologers specified a sign for each of the seven original planets that is better for that planet than its home sign: its exaltation sign. The sign opposite the sign of exaltation is the sign of fall from power, now simply known as fall. **4.** In its fall sign, a planet will have less energy, or less focused energy, than it will have when it is exalted. **5.** The opposite of fall is exaltation—when a planet is exalted, it is very powerful. ✷ Do you have a planet in its fall sign in your birth chart? What will this mean? Well, for example, the Sun is exalted in Aries, but falls in Libra. The Sun is all about creative energy, so when it's in Aries, the creative energy of the Sun gets to make something. Aries is action. Libra, on the other hand, is reaction. The Sun is right at home with action, but less comfortable being the reactor. This is why the Sun is fallen in Libra. See also *detriment, exalted, home signs.* **BC** ◯ ☼

Planet	Sign(s) of Fall	Keywords
Sun	Libra	Indecisive leader
Moon	Scorpio	Disabling sensitivity
Mercury	Pisces	Confused by empathy
Venus	Virgo	Sensuality inhibited
Mars	Cancer	Passive-aggressive
Jupiter	Capricorn	Skeptical when opportunity knocks
Saturn	Aries	Impulse interferes with success
Uranus	Taurus	Bites the hand that feeds
Neptune	Capricorn	Disappointed by lack of protection from parents, employers, and government
Pluto	Libra, Aquarius, Pisces	Underachiever

family   1. In astrology, the fourth and fifth houses of the birth chart relate to family and children in general. 2. The fourth house rules mother, paternal cousins, and—in a woman's chart—children. The fifth house rules the father, second sibling, and—in a man's chart—children. 3. Particular family relationships are located in different houses of the birth chart. Maternal grandfather, paternal grandmother, and fifth-born child are in the first house. The third house rules siblings in general as well as the sixth-born child. The sixth house rules maternal aunts and uncles, and the seventh house rules spouse, third sibling, second child, maternal grandmother, and paternal grandfather. The ninth house is the location for fourth sibling, third child, and brothers- and sisters-in-law or spouse's siblings. The tenth house rules father and maternal cousins and the eleventh house rules fifth sibling and fourth-born child. Paternal aunts and uncles are in the twelfth house.

✧ **1.** How you create your own home/foundation is seen in the fourth house of your birth chart. This house describes your family of origin and how you relate to your parents. Traditionally, your mother and how you relate to her is seen in the fourth house. How you were parented also appears in this house. In addition, the fourth house indicates how you will create your own home and how you will parent your children. **2.** The fifth house represents children, your own as well as other people's children. Your relationship to kids in your life is found here, as well as how you relate to them. This house can give you information about your children, including how many you might have. If you have fertility issues, an astrologer will look at your fifth house. **3.** In the birth chart, the Moon also represents connection to family and the ability to conceive. See also *fertility, fifth house, fourth house, Moon.* BC

F

fate See *destiny.*

fathers and fathering For issues regarding fatherhood, look to the Sun, Jupiter, and Saturn, as well as the tenth house. BC

February 19 to March 21 Birth dates for the Sun sign Pisces. The position of the Sun during these dates correlates with an astrological Sun sign. Those born between February 19 and March 21 have Pisces as their Sun sign. See also *Pisces.*

feminine principle **1.** Yin is the feminine energy; this energy receives. Receiving energy traditionally is associated with women and the ability to conceive. **2.** Feminine energy is nurturing, soothing, sensitive to others, caring, and concerned. Water and earth signs have feminine energy. **3.** The feminine signs are Taurus, Cancer, Virgo, Scorpio, Capricorn, and Pisces. ✧ Feminine energy is less aggressive than masculine (yang) energy. It's less active: how you react to things can be influenced by this energy, making you more nurturing, compassionate, and possibly passive, rather than aggressive. Feminine signs are generally creative and protective. If your Sun sign is feminine, you may also desire peace. See also *earth sign, energy, masculine principle, water sign, yin.*

fertile signs   **1.** Cancer, Scorpio, and Pisces, the water signs, are
also called fertile signs. **2.** Planets on the cusp of the fourth, fifth,
or eleventh houses may indicate likely conception of children or
the presence of children in the life of the charted person. **3.** This is
also referenced in gardening; fertile signs indicate periods useful for
sowing seeds, planting, or fertilizing the garden. ✦ **1.** If Cancer
appears on the cusp of the fourth, fifth, or eleventh house in your
birth chart, this indicates that this house is very receptive to conception, because the fourth house rules pregnancy, the fifth house
rules creation, including procreation, and the eleventh house rules
conception. **2.** If Scorpio is on the cusp of your fifth or eleventh
house, that house wants to unify with another to create for the
purpose of giving birth. **3.** Do you have Pisces on the cusp of your
fourth, fifth, or eleventh house? If so, that house wants to make the
dream of a child come true. **4.** The Moon, Venus, the North Node,
Jupiter, Uranus, Neptune, or Pluto in your fourth, fifth, or eleventh
house will generate energy conducive to conception and a healthy
pregnancy. See also *barren signs, Cancer, eleventh house, fifth house,
fourth house, gardening, Pisces, Scorpio.* 🏠 ☼

fertility   **1.** In astrology, the fifth house is the house of procreation
and children and the eleventh house rules conception. **2.** The natal
Moon also shows fertility and ability to conceive. ✦ **1.** Your aspects
will tell you about your ability to conceive. To look for the possibility
of pregnancy in a birth chart, your astrologer will check to see what
signs are on the cusp of the fourth and fifth houses in your chart if
you're a woman, and what sign is on the cusp of the fifth house of
your chart if you're a man. **2.** To look deeper into fertility, find the
planet that rules the sign on the fourth house cusp for women, and
the fifth house cusp for men. If a barren sign is on the cusp, you'll
need the energy of more planets to help you conceive. This may
mean you have to wait until progressed planets can help things along
or until transiting planets move into helpful positions in your birth
chart. To find these helpful progressed or transiting planets, you may
want to seek the expertise of a fertility astrologer. **3.** A specialized
fertility astrologer can spot issues on your birth chart and offer sug-
gestions. More often than not, the issue is one of timing. The soul of
the baby may be waiting for the right time to enter the Earth plane.
See also *aspects between planets, fifth house, fourth house, progressions,
solar return, transits.* △ **BC** ☯ 🏠

fifth house   **1.** In astrology, the fifth house is the house of creative self-expression. **2.** The fifth house is the house of children, birth, and new beginnings.

✦ **1.** Will you have children? Your children and your relationship to them are covered in the fifth house. How you relate to children in your life in general is also found here. Did you ever baby sit? Do you have younger siblings? How were these experiences for you? Maybe you've had little interaction with kids, or maybe you have been a caretaker for younger siblings—you can look to your birth chart to find out if you have work to do in this area of your life. **2.** The artist in you—any artistic skills and abilities you have—will show up in the fifth house. Planets in this house affect your abilities and what you will do in artistic areas in your life, including visual art, dance, music, design, theater, entertainment—all forms of artistic self-expression—as well as how you enjoy the arts. **3.** Speculation, risk-taking, and gambling are all fifth house topics. If you have a strong fifth house, you are likely more of a risk-taker. You may be a physical risk-taker—a mountain climber, race car driver, or daredevil. You could be an emotional risk-taker, or take risks in business, as an entrepreneur or in the stock market—think Donald Trump. You will have strong passion about the areas where you take risks, creative or otherwise. **4.** The fifth house is naturally associated with Leo, and is ruled by the Sun. **5.** What you're passionate about manifesting in this lifetime is represented in your fifth house. Where's your bliss, and how do you express passion in your life? It might be through business, children, music, or something else entirely. The planets you have in this house will help define your bliss source for you, and if you have no planets in your fifth house, its natural ruler, Leo, provides this insight. See also *house, planetary ruler.* 🏠

financial astrology   See *business astrology.*

fire, element   **1.** One of the four astrological elements. A masculine (yang) element, fire stands for action. The other elements are earth, air, and water. **2.** The twelve astrological signs are divided equally among the four elements. The three fire signs are Aries, Leo, and Sagittarius. **3.** The twelve houses are also equally divided among the elements. The three fire houses are the first, fifth, and ninth. These houses correspond to the three fire signs and relate to

F

the physical self and personality; creativity, romance, and children; and social areas. Planets found in these houses/signs are called fire planets.

✦ **1.** Are there a lot of fire planets in your birth chart? Look at your chart and figure out what signs the planets are in. Remember that Aries, Leo, and Sagittarius are the fire signs. **2.** People ruled by fire signs are energetic and passionate. They have a lot of enthusiasm and focus. Think of fire as a life-giving force necessary for life—the fire element has that kind of power and focus. It can also be destructive, but out of destruction comes new life. **3.** If you have lots of fire planets in your birth chart, you are likely an active, spontaneous person. You may leap before you look, and you're likely extroverted. **4.** If you check your birth chart and find that you have only one fire planet, or maybe none at all, it can mean you are not terribly aggressive or self-focused. You may be an idea person who has a more difficult time acting on those ideas. Look at your chart and see where your planets are—maybe you have lots of air planets or water planets. This will tell you more about yourself than the absence of fire planets in your chart, which may simply mean you aren't focused on those areas in this lifetime. **5.** No fire planets in your birth chart means that you are a fire adept: you've mastered the fire element in a past lifetime. In this lifetime, you need to learn the essence of the other elements instead of falling back into the all-consuming fire you know so well. See also *adept, air sign, Aries, earth sign, elements, fire sign, Leo, Sagittarius, water sign.* **BC** ☯ ☼ ◯

fire sign   1. Aries, Leo, and Sagittarius are the three fire signs, or the fire triplicity. Fire signs are active and energetic. **2.** Fire signs are visionary and idealistic, looking to the future.

✦ **1.** If your Sun sign is Aries, Leo, or Sagittarius, action is your main focus. Aries, the first astrological sign of the zodiac, is also the first fire sign. Aries is the initiator and marks new beginnings. This fire sign is a self-starter. Aries likes to be her own boss, and doesn't necessarily want to lead others. Leo, the second fire sign (ruling the fifth house), is proud and generous, enthusiastic, and sometimes egocentric. Leos are attention seekers—the roar of a lion always gets attention—but Leos also make generous, kind leaders. Leo likes to be the boss and is good at it. If you're a Sagittarius, you are likely outspoken, enthusiastic, and something of a philosopher of life. Sagittarius is always looking to the future, and shooting for the stars in everything they do. You like to help other people shine—you don't need to be the center of attention (as long as you're the locus of attention). It's just as gratifying for you to be a cheerleader, spurring others to success. **2.** All the fire signs have a masculine or yang energy. Yang energy is active; it seeks. Fire signs can be aggressive. If you're a fire sign—Aries, Leo, or Sagittarius—your energy is very active. You're a doer, and you bring passion to everything you touch. **3.** If you're a fire sign, how do you mix with the other elements? Briefly, here's a look at your elemental compatibility. Fire and earth: this combination requires loads of mutual respect. Both know what they want, but fire can be impatient. Earth enjoys manifesting fire's desires, but also fears being taken for granted. Fire and air: the oxygen in air is fuel for fire, and air finds fire energizing. These relationships tend to work best when fire leads, and air allows this. Air is flexible, and inspires fire to move ahead and manifest a relationship. Fire encourages enthusiasm in air. Fire and fire: this pair keeps love alive for a lifetime. Together, they can face anything and create a big life that is full of fun, travel, daring, and happiness. Fire and water: this duo sizzles—that is, so long as water stays positive and fire apologizes for coming on too strong. Water brings a fluid intuitive creative sensibility that matches (but also challenges) fire's bright and elegant all-consuming flame. See also *Aries; element; fire, element; Leo; Sagittarius; yang.* ☼

first house   **1.** In astrology, the first house is the house of self, the theater of personal experience, and public image. **2.** The first house represents the self, self-identity, how you project yourself to the public. This house includes the ascendant, or rising sign. ✦ **1.** The first house is all about how you appear to others and how you project yourself to others, or how you view yourself and how others view you. What's your self-image like? How about your personality and disposition? Your astrological mask is in the first house—that's your public persona, or what you let others see. How you identify yourself in the world and how you present yourself to others is the first house of your birth chart. **2.** Your physical body and your health and vitality are also in the first house. **3.** The first house is naturally associated with Aries, and is ruled by Mars. **4.** What does it mean if you have lots of planets—or very few—in this house? Lots of planets indicate that the areas relating to this house—namely the self—will be very important to you in this lifetime. If you don't have much going on in the first house, you may be less self-assured. You may also simply not have any need for focus in this area of your life. If you're having difficulties in your life with areas covered by the first house, look not only in the first house but in its opposite, the seventh house, as well, to find clues for improving your self image. See also *ascendant, house.*

first quarter Moon   **1.** Phase when the Moon is 90 to 135 degrees ahead of the Sun in the birth chart, and half of the Moon appears illuminated in the sky. **2.** Of the eight lunar phases, the first quarter Moon is the third phase, following the new Moon and the crescent Moon, and occurring about one week after the new Moon. ⭐ A first quarter Moon in your birth chart will enable you to recognize what you have outgrown, allowing you to release old baggage, embrace change, and take action toward a more positive use of your inner and outer resources. See also *Moon phases.* ◯

fixed   **1.** One of the three qualities of classification for the astro-logical signs (the others are cardinal and mutable) that influence behavior. **2.** Fixed signs are Taurus, Leo, Scorpio, and Aquarius, representing each of the elements, earth, fire, water, and air. **3.** The fixed signs are the second in each season. As such, fixed signs repre-sent the grounded center. They are stable, consistent, and reliable.

⭐ **1.** If you're a fixed sign, you are persistent. Once you make up your mind to do something, you do it. You may even become fixated on accomplishing a goal you've set for yourself. This is great—you finish what you start, and get things done. It can lead you to become stubborn, or to be obsessive about your goal. You might also be very set in your ways—you like routine and stick to it, like you do your goals. Again, this is great—unless the behaviors or beliefs you've set-tled on don't actually serve your life in a positive way. It's difficult to lure you from a self-destructive path. You might also be inflexible—you want things the way you want them, when you want them, and aren't prone to compromise. You persevere in relationships as well, and are loyal and devoted to those you love. **2.** You may have lots of planets in fixed signs, and if this is the case, you may be stubborn to the point that you frustrate even yourself. Do you have lots of planets in Taurus? If so, you stay focused on the good life and don't let up until your bank account shows seven figures! An abundance of planets in Leo gives you the ability to create anything—your heart will show you the way. You are happiest and healthiest when you do what you love. Loads of planets in Scorpio? You understand that energy originates in the darkness, and this intrigues you. Your Scorpio planets tap into ancient knowing that can't be seen, heard, or touched by others. If you have more than two planets in Aquarius, you are a staunch humanitarian, more than a little rebellious, and always original. **3.** Of the four fixed signs, Taurus is the most stable and Aquarius is the least concentrated. See also *Aquarius, cardinal (quality), Leo, mutable, Scorpio, Taurus.* BC ☯ ◯ ☼

fixed cross   See *grand cross.*

flexed   This is a contemporary term for mutual signs. See also *mutual signs.* ☯ ☼

flower essences   Yang signs of the zodiac correspond to the warming and stimulating floral essential oils, and yin signs correspond to the cooling and soothing essences. See also *yang, yin.* ☯ Z

forecast   **1.** An older term used for reading astrological trends of planetary alignment for an individual. **2.** To predict, based on a birth chart, or using the natal chart to predict cycles and trends in a person's life for the time of the reading to six months to one year in the future. Timing is important in doing a forecast—astrological planetary cycles are viewed to predict trends. **3.** Horoscopes are general daily forecasts for each astrological sign. **4.** The farmer's almanac uses planetary cycles to make weather predictions. ✦ Whatever the forecast, you choose your future. See also *birth chart, destiny, free will.* BC ☯

fortified   **1.** Term used to describe a planet whose only aspects are positive, or a planet that is elevated or positioned in its ruling (home) or exalted sign. Positive aspects include conjunction, sextile, and trine. **2.** Opposite of impeded. See also *aspects between planets, exalted, planetary ruler.* △ ◯ ☼

Fortuna   See *Part of Fortune.*

fourth house   1. In astrology, the fourth house is the house of home and family, particularly parents—especially mother, stepmother, and mother-in-law, or the parent, stepparent, or parent-in-law that is the same gender as the native. **2.** The fourth house represents home, property, and family, particularly the family of origin. Early childhood experiences and experiences with the family home are found in this house. **3.** The fourth house also rules ancestry, heredity, and heritage. **4.** Private life and seclusion, including secluded pieces of property, are found in the fourth house. **5.** Endings, including the conditions surrounding death, are fourth house concerns. **6.** Fame awarded after death is covered in the fourth house. **7.** The parent who most influenced inner development in childhood is in the fourth house. **8.** An individual's character roots are in the fourth house.

✦ **1.** Your parents and your genetic background, as well as your family background and domestic life, are found in the fourth house. Look at the planets in the fourth house to figure out the dynamics of your relationship to your mom and dad, especially the parent who was more physically present and/or influential in your home. The fourth house planets also show your domestic relationship with your stepparents or adopted parents and parents-in-law if you have these relationships. **2.** The fourth house is the house of roots, or where you came from. This includes the home you grew up in as well as the roots of your adult life, and the home you create for yourself as an adult. Your adult home is influenced by your childhood home, and the example set for you in childhood by parents or other caregivers, such as a live-in nanny. These individuals are your role models, and they influence the foundation you create for yourself. This can also include grandparents, if that's who raised you or was most influential in your household. The location and physical environment where you were born and raised—a farm, a suburb, a city—and how that environment affected your upbringing are revealed in the fourth house. **3.** Property is also covered in the fourth house. This means real estate, land, and other tangible property. If you own a home or hope to, that's in the fourth house. Worried about losing your house? Check here. Something in opposition here can show a change in your home. Any change of residence is indicated in the fourth house, too. So if you're wondering if you should take that job across the country, look at your fourth house. **4.** The fourth house is naturally associated with Cancer, and is ruled by the Moon. **5.** Do you have lots going on in your fourth house, or nothing much at all? Lots of planets in this house can indicate a focus on family and creating a nurturing, cozy home. No planets in this house may mean that you find security and comfort in a more public life and easily adopt other families as your own. You may have such "adopted families" all over the world. See also *family, house, planetary ruler.*

F

free will   1. The ability for every person to choose her or his own path, free will co-exists beside destiny and both are essential in life for growth. **2.** Saturn, a balsamic Moon, and the South Node of the Moon represent destiny, while Uranus and the North Node of the Moon represent free will, and they operate together to reveal a person's path in life. ✦ It can be the more difficult choice to leave destiny and make a new path for yourself—you can find out, or you may come back to that destined path somewhere down the road. Remember that destiny might offer you an opportunity you hadn't planned on—ask yourself lots of questions before you decide where you want to go in this life. But wherever you go, your choice is your free will. See also *destiny, karma, North Node.* **BC**

full house   1. When one of the twelve houses in the birth chart has three to five planets in it, the house is called a full house. **2.** Also called a stellium. ✦ **1.** If you have a full house in your birth chart, this house (or houses) will have a dominant influence in your life and may determine your focus in this life. You will put effort into the areas of your life this house influences, and you'll also successfully attain the goals related to that house. You might be fixated on the areas relating to your full house, focusing all of your energy there. **2.** What you'll learn about in this life, your destiny, and what you will complete are all centered on your full house. You will be drawn to the areas represented by this house, maybe even obsessed with them. Know this: you'll attain any goals in this area in your lifetime. See also *empty house, stellium.* **BC**

full Moon   1. The appearance of the Moon when the Sun and Moon are 180 degrees away from each other. In this position, which occurs every 28 to 30 days, a full Moon is seen in the sky from the Earth. **2.** A full Moon represents the completion of a cycle. The lunar cycle culminates with the full Moon. ✦ **1.** During a full Moon, you may have an awareness of truth and clarity. This is a time in the Moon's cycle when you may be more intuitive and spiritually aware, as well as emotionally insightful. Your behavior during a full Moon may be enlightened and overly aware. **2.** If you were born on a full Moon, you are very emotionally sensitive and intuitive, and are easily moved by human emotion. You may be very in tune with the energy and the emotional responses of those around you. You have an ability to see through situations to the truth. The downside of a full Moon birth is emotional overreaction or the experience of great emotional ups and downs. Full Moon people are kind and sensitive, but may also be indecisive, and are easily confused when lots of emotion is involved. You make better decisions when there's no emotional attachment; otherwise you may find it difficult to make choices. See also *Moon, Moon phases.* ◯

Gabriel   **1.** The archangel Gabriel rules the feminine in both women and men. He is the foreteller of important births, such as John the Baptist and Jesus Christ. **2.** Gabriel is associated with the qualities of the sign of Cancer and its ruler, the Moon. **3.** Gabriel's horn is likened to the uterus because of its shape; in astrology, the Moon rules the uterus. **4.** Gabriel rules intuition, cycles, pregnancy, predictions, and protection. See also *Cancer, intuition, Moon.* ☼ ◯

gardening   **1.** Astrology is used to determine the best times for planting and harvesting. **2.** Planting in the Moon signs: water signs (Cancer, Scorpio, and Pisces) are good for planting because of their relationship to water. Planting when the Moon is in these so-called fertile signs is especially beneficial. The exception is root vegetables such as carrots, beets, yams, and ginger, which are best planted when the Moon is in an earth sign (Taurus, Virgo, and Capricorn). ✧ It's never a good idea to work on your treasured plants during an eclipse, but it is a fantastic time to weed. Eclipses are states of change, so weeding out the garden is a perfect way to lay the groundwork for new growth, and to allow big changes to manifest in your garden. If your garden is a container garden, or indoor garden, use the energy of the eclipse to do house-cleaning to clear and prepare the space for the plantings you want to see on that shelf or patio area. See also *barren signs, fertile signs, Moon phases, water sign.* ◯ ☼

Gemini   **1.** The third sign of the zodiac. **2.** Those born between May 21 and June 22 have Gemini as their Sun sign. Also called the twins, Gemini is a yang, or masculine, mutable air sign. The ruling planet for Gemini is Mercury, named for the very quick Roman messenger of the gods. Mercury is a planet of communication, expression, and thinking. **3.** The glyph for Gemini is ♊, which looks like a Roman numeral II, and the symbol is twins. The twins represent pairs of things, people, places, and situations. That's why Gemini rules your arms and your legs. The twins also rule opposites and dualities, such as your internal masculine and feminine, your external expression and inner voice, and when you feel pulled in two directions. **4.** Gemini is the natural ruler of the third house, the house of knowledge, communication, neighbors, vehicles, and siblings. **5.** Other associations for Gemini are the color yellow and the gem agate.

✦ **1.** The body parts associated with Gemini are the limbs in general, and more specifically, the fingers, hands, wrists, arms, shoulders, collar bones, thymus gland, nerves, and lungs. If you're a Gemini, you may have graceful hands, and are susceptible to lung ailments such as asthma. **2.** If your Sun sign is Gemini, you're all about communication: talking, speaking, writing—all forms of com- munication. It's important for Gemini to be able to relate to others intellectually—Gemini has great mental agility. If you're a Gemini, you have good observational skills and a well-developed sense of curiosity. Your Gemini mind is very inquisitive, and you're a quick thinker, sharp and witty. You like to talk out a subject, debating it thoroughly. You learn quickly, and after you've mastered a subject, you're ready to move on to something new. You have a tendency to get bored if you have to repeat yourself. Gemini is mutable, making people with this Sun sign flexible and adaptable, with the ability to turn on a dime both intellectually and emotionally. Mercurial—that's Gemini. You may seem bubbly, even airheaded, and as an air sign, you are likely thinking lofty thoughts. To your friends, you will be a fun and funny companion, and you have lots of friends from different groups—to match your varied interests. **3.** Gemini is the sign of great thinkers and comedic personalities. **4.** What subjects and careers might appeal to Gemini? If you're a Gemini, you have a thirst for knowledge that can't be quenched. You always want to learn more, need to know more, and are a constant student. You also have amazing recall—you can repeat verbatim a conversation you had six months ago! (How annoying!) You retain lots of information, and are good with trivia and history, seemingly pulling facts out of thin air when you need them. Careers you might be attracted to include teaching, writing, and work in media, including advertising, TV, radio, photography, promotion/publicity, and publishing. **5.** *Watch out for:* Your dual nature can give you a tendency to vacillate. You may not make decisions quickly, or you may be indecisive or change your mind as you go. You may not be consistent in your decisions. You also get bored when you aren't intellectually stimulated, and when you get bored, you move on. This can make you look superficial to colleagues, so concentrate on fostering the persona of a quick-moving, nimble thinker in pursuit of the big idea. Your ability to select information based on what is most important to your future is a gift, but it means that you may not study what's on the test, or give a rote presentation. **6.** *I'm not a Gemini, but my best friend is:* Your Gemini best friend is a talker—let them talk! If they aren't talking, that's a certain indicator that something is wrong. To find out what's bothering them, just say, "Talk to me!" Be careful not to misconstrue a Gemini's multi-tasking as a sign of disinterest in you or a lack of commitment to your friendship; your Gemini friend is busy finding new avenues for you to explore together. Embrace the curiosity and ever-moving Gemini facility to see and ponder everything. If a Gemini loves you, you can be sure they will count the ways, to your mutual delight. See also *Gemini ascendant, Gemini descendant, third house.* ☿

Gemini/Aquarius   See *Aquarius/Gemini.*

Gemini/Aries   See *Aries/Gemini.*

Gemini ascendant   Also called Gemini rising. The rising sign is Gemini; Gemini is the sign on the cusp of the first house in the birth chart and the sign on the eastern horizon at the moment of birth.

✦ **1.** If your rising sign is Gemini, Gemini is the mask you are comfortable presenting to the world. You may be a Cancer with a Taurus Moon, but your Gemini traits are those that will be first visible to others—to others, you appear like Gemini. **2.** Your rising sign also represents the sign you are here to master in this life. If you have Gemini rising, you love words, math, rational thought, games, puzzles, and clear deductive reasoning. In this life, you may be learning to speak your feelings in a kind but factual manner, regardless of the repercussions. Any inclination toward gossip is being replaced by words of inspiration and a focus on the positive. **3.** If you're a

Gemini ascendant, you have an inquiring mind—you always want to know what's going on, and you want to know now! You can't be put off for a few days when you ask for something—you need that answer. If you have to wait, you are likely to look elsewhere for the information or move on to something new. If you ask a Gemini rising to get information, they will do it in a hurry, and they will provide lots of details. Gemini rising is more meticulous than the Gemini Sun sign. Gemini ascendant is a perennial student, always learning and growing. You don't like to be restricted in one place or one subject—you prefer to move around. You enjoy public speaking and doing presentations. You need an intellectual equal as a partner, and need people in your life who are as communicative as you are. In relationships, you often seek people who value freedom, such as Sagittarius (the opposite of Gemini on the zodiac). You are very good at listening to others and communicating back to them, and are clever and adaptable. **4.** Throw a Gemini rising into a city or town they don't know, and they love it—they are the perfect partner for adventure travel. Fresh air is relaxing for air signs, and the more space around them, the better they feel. You like to be physically active, to help your body keep up with your mind. **5.** You may appear to be unattached, or not devoted, because you don't like to be stuck in one place. You need an open-minded partner (in life or business) who is willing to be spontaneous. This rising sign is as loyal as any other, but you need spontaneity and intellectual challenge to keep you interested. In your home and work environments, you like to break up routine with different activities, including conversation, errands, even meetings. You are mentally stimulated by people who want to communicate ideas in some way. If the Sun is in a water or earth sign, then Gemini rising can be happy communicating at home by e-mail. See also *ascendant, Gemini, Gemini descendant.* **BC** ☼

Gemini/Cancer   See *Cancer/Gemini.*

Gemini/Capricorn   See *Capricorn/Gemini.*

Gemini descendant   **1.** The descending sign is Gemini; Gemini is the sign on the cusp of the seventh house in the birth chart. **2.** The seventh house is the house of partnerships and marriage or significant others.

✦ **1.** If your descending sign is Gemini, Gemini describes how you relate to others in partnership, whether it's a romantic partner, a roommate, a business partner, a partner on a project, or even a specific relationship with a friend or family member. (This means Sagittarius is your rising sign.) No matter what your Sun sign is, your descendant will tell you a lot about yourself in these kinds of relationships. Having difficulties with someone in partnership? Look no further than your seventh house. **2.** Gemini descendant likes partners that present as the Gemini Sun sign, with independence as a key trait. You attract partners who are intellectual, studious, talkative, and always interesting conversationalists. You enjoy spending time with people who are interested in new ideas or concepts, and like partners who are observant and want to learn. Gemini descendant is interested in education, and in continuing to learn throughout life. They need intellectual stimulus and information, and school can provide this. You need people around you who can keep up with you, communicate on your level, challenge you and your beliefs, and try to get you to intellectually stimulate yourself, to read more, and maybe take classes. Gemini can be a difficult descendant sign to have—you'll be forced to do lots of work! You may not want to be pushed so much, and this could cause conflict. You have definite opinions, and you like to instigate conversation. You are willing to press for information and answers. Gemini descendant needs communication—it's how they experience the world. You are very direct and to the point, but usually have a good sense of humor. Your insights and opinions are interesting and exciting; there's never a dull moment with Gemini descendant. See also *descendant, Gemini, Gemini ascendant.* **BC** ☼

G

Gemini/Gemini **1.** Gemini/Gemini is a full partnership—twins paired up equals four people, each with their own personality, in the relationship! Gemini attracts Gemini because of a shared love of communication. Gemini/Gemini can talk for hours and hours together, and never get tired of the conversation. **2.** For a Gemini, communication—talking, writing, even yelling—is exciting. So talking is central to the Gemini/Gemini relationship; these same-sign partners could be working through karmic issues related to how communication is done, as well as learning lessons in the staying power of ideas to heal or hurt.

✦ **1.** With four people in the conversation (instead of two), there are no awkward silences in a Gemini/Gemini pairing, and there's an abundance of topics of conversation. These partners are masters of social networking and communicate easily in almost any situation or on any kind of platform—e-mail, letter, phone, one-on-one, you name it. Even in a heated dispute, these two are just communicating, and they won't hold any grudges. Being shut down from communicating is a big problem for Gemini, but that's not a problem in this pairing. These two will try to show each other up in debate and go to any length to restore or continue talking to each other. **2.** Gemini/Gemini doubles the power of this mutable sign, and each partner understands the other's need for change and love for travel. These two will be flexible with each other. This relationship has an intellectual foundation. Gemini/Gemini gets each other's senses of humor, and they don't take things too seriously. This is a very compatible pairing for most relationships, including, student/teacher, workmates, parent/child, or a marriage/domestic partnership. See also *Gemini.* ☽ ☼

Gemini/Leo   1. Gemini/Leo is an air and fire mix, and it's one of the best combinations. Leo is fed by Gemini (air feeds fire). **2.** Leo loves attention, and Gemini gives Leo plenty of it—through communication. Gemini seeks Leo's opinion and wants to talk to Leo about everything. ✦ **1.** As long as Gemini is willing to be a sidekick to Leo's superhero, these two will get along very well. Gemini is super flexible, and won't be threatened by Leo's need to be the focus, or to have things their way. Gemini can work with Leo's needs and can lighten Leo up a bit—Leo is a fixed sign. **2.** Leo likes Gemini's inquisitive mind, and admires a strong intellect. Together, they are voracious and hold a great capacity to learn much together. **3.** Leo as a teacher and Gemini as the student is a great pairing. A Leo parent and Gemini child are also very compatible, as is the Leo boss and Gemini employee. This is a good marriage/domestic partnership pairing, no matter which partner is which Sun sign. See also *Gemini, Leo.* ☽ ☼

Gemini/Libra   1. Gemini and Libra are two air signs attracted to each other and are very compatible. Gemini appreciates Libra's optimism. Libra also has an artistic, creative mind and is stimulated by Gemini's ability to see many possibilities. **2.** Gemini/Libra sees beauty and love in the world, and both signs learn from this.

⭐ **1.** Libra is about balance—they will think things through. Gemini likes to change things up and will throw new ideas at Libra. This is stimulating for both partners in this pairing. They communicate well, understand each other, and can give each other space without difficulty or hurt feelings. **2.** Gemini/Libra is an easygoing pairing; these two travel well together. **3.** Gemini/Libra is a good combination for the parent/child, teacher/student, boss/employee, co-worker, and business partner relationship. These signs make a great friendship. Both are natural flirts and are happiest flirting with each other. As life partners, Gemini's need for communication works well with Libra's need to know everything going on in the relationship. See also *Gemini, Libra.* ☯ ☼

G

Gemini/Pisces   **1.** Gemini/Pisces is an air and water mix. Gemini is intellectual air sign that typically tries to avoid any kind of routine. Gemini is always asking questions of Pisces: why this, why that, what do you think? Pisces doesn't like this intense mental scrutiny, which can feel overwhelming. **2.** Gemini is the twins and Pisces is two fish in different directions—there is a lot of movement going on in the Gemini/Pisces relationship.

⭐ **1.** Generally, Pisces is very emotional and sensitive, and Gemini flits about from place to place quickly. The fish is respectful of people's energy and tries to go with the flow surrounding them, while the twins challenge people's attention spans and concentration with endless ideas and maneuvering. Gemini and Pisces have different styles for communicating their intellectual passions. **2.** Gemini likes to argue, and Pisces can be hurt by excessive arguments and yelling. Pisces is a good listener, and Gemini does love to talk, but the twins also want a stimulating conversation partner. Intuitive Pisces processes the world and expresses ideas emotionally; the fish take their time to make decisions about people or situations. Gemini doesn't have the patience for this—they make quick decisions, without fully processing. **3.** To Pisces, Gemini seems to be flitting across the surface of the water, and Pisces needs to be submerged—they think Gemini isn't serious or deep, and might even accuse Gemini of being superficial and insensitive (if Pisces were the accusing type, which they aren't!). Gemini doesn't want to slow down or be brought down

to the ground by too much emotion—they won't be controlled.
4. The Gemini/Pisces partnership is not the most compatible pairing in any situation—it takes too much work for Pisces to try and make this relationship successful. An exhausted Pisces is likely to declare Gemini the de facto "winner" and swim away, relieved to escape the twins' incessant love of chatter. Gemini/Pisces can be good as buddies, and have fun together, but this isn't a great combination for any serious relationship. Gemini and Pisces make okay siblings, but this isn't a good pairing for business, friendship, or lasting marriage/domestic partnership. See also *Gemini, Pisces.* ☯ ☼

Gemini rising   See *Gemini ascendant.*

Gemini/Sagittarius   **1.** Air and fire combine in the Gemini and Sagittarius pairing. These two have a strong attraction—they are opposites on the zodiac. **2.** Sagittarius loves adventure and travel, and really likes new experiences. Sagittarius also has a strong urge to learn, grow, and explore. With Gemini/Sagittarius, this pairing exhibits enthusiasm and has an ability to adapt, as well, because both are mutable signs.

✦ **1.** Sagittarius is something of a philosopher about life; they may need to be pressed into actually experiencing things, and Gemini is good at applying this pressure. Sagittarius likes to think about what they're going to do before they do it, and doesn't like to feel rushed into things. Gemini has the quick response of an air sign: Gemini wants to do things now. Sagittarius might say that in the future, they'd like to travel to some exotic place, and Gemini would respond, "Let's go this weekend!" **2.** Gemini might throw out ten ideas, and Sagittarius will need to sort methodically through all of the ideas to pick the best one to focus on. Gemini doesn't care to sort or focus—they'll try them all, and in no particular order, and might not follow through on any of them. This is a challenge to Sagittarius, who wants to follow through. **3.** There is a strong intellectual and emotional attraction between Gemini and Sagittarius. They want many of the same things—travel, education—but they have different ideas of how and when to get them. They vary greatly on the execution of their ideas, and this can cause conflict. **4.** This pairing can get along very well, as long as they can make some agreement on the pace of the relationship. This is true of any pairing of Gemini/ Sagittarius—they will conflict on pacing in the workplace, in business partnerships, in friendships, and romantic or marriage partnerships, too. This pairing will slug it out forever, or become feisty ex's. See also *Gemini, Sagittarius.* ☯ ☼

Gemini/Scorpio   1. The Gemini and Scorpio air and water combination is not the best mix. The two signs share passion, but do not share the means of expressing it at all. **2.** Gemini enjoys being out in the world, talking to anyone and everyone about everything; Gemini are open with others, unconcerned about talking to strangers, and good at public speaking. Scorpio, on the other hand, is very private, and Gemini's talkativeness and sharing might appear to Scorpio like a breach of trust.

G

✴ **1.** Scorpio doesn't want Gemini sharing their business with everyone they meet; it doesn't matter if what's shared is personal and private or something innocuous. Scorpio doesn't want Gemini to share their dinner plans, at least not without Scorpio's okay. And let's face it, Gemini is not asking anyone's permission to talk. Scorpio will not be pushed into overexposure or oversharing. **2.** Scorpio's comfort zone is private smoldering passions, and Gemini lives outside this zone. Gemini's oversharing is insensitive and can seem deliberately hurtful to Scorpio. If Gemini actually exposes one of Scorpio's secrets, Scorpio will get angry. Mistrust and misunderstanding often result. **3.** Scorpio doesn't want anyone knowing their finances, family, or personal life—only they can share that information. They don't want to have their information misunderstood or mistranslated by anyone. And Gemini thinks the more you talk the better things are. Scorpio has no patience with this or with Gemini's flightiness and seeming superficiality in general. Scorpio will hold Gemini to what they say, with no room for changing direction midstream. **4.** In this relationship, Scorpio will likely drop Gemini—it's just not worth their time and effort. Scorpio wants consistency and loyalty, and they want to see that what Gemini does reflects what Gemini says. Gemini/Scorpio is an okay pairing as siblings or friends (not very close friends, though). This is not a match made in the stars, however. These two aren't the best marriage or domestic partners, and might not work well as business partners, either—there's not enough trust between them. See also *Gemini, Scorpio.* ☯ ☼

Gemini/Taurus   1. Air and earth combine in the Gemini and Taurus pairing. Gemini and Taurus are neighbors in the zodiac, and they make good friends and neighbors in life. **2.** Gemini and Taurus respect each other; Gemini can talk and talk, and Taurus will sit back and listen. ✦ **1.** Taurus's steadfast nature can help Gemini take an idea and make it reality. In this pairing, Gemini is the visionary, and Taurus gets everything down on paper. Taurus is practical and grounded, balancing Gemini's flitting energy. **2.** Gemini/Taurus is a good combination for a parent/child, teacher/student, co-worker, and business partner relationship. And it's pretty ideal for a marriage or domestic partnership, as well. There won't be a lot of sizzle for this pairing, but they will find everyday satisfaction together. See also *Gemini, Taurus.* 🌓 ☼

Gemini/Virgo   1. These two air and earth signs are both ruled by Mercury, and this is the basis of Gemini/Virgo compatibility: these signs really like talking together. **2.** Virgo is the quieter of the two signs, charming and soft spoken. Gemini likes to seek the advantage, taking the lead and scoping out the scene.

✦ **1.** Virgo doesn't want their personal life in the headlines, and Gemini's talkativeness sometimes may seem disrespectful to Virgo, who may also feel that Gemini doesn't listen to them. (This may be true.) **2.** Virgo likes a sense of order in life—this can be an order of their own making that's not always easily visible to others—and this is not natural to Gemini. Virgo likes to take their time, processing things. They express even their creative side in a methodical way. Virgo also wants to improve upon their work, and will rework or reconfigure things to make them better. While Virgo does this, Gemini will have moved on to ten other projects, perhaps moving back and forth between them, and maybe not completing any of them. This can be a big conflict in cohabitation—these two need some time apart to get along well. **3.** Gemini and Virgo communicate well and have enthusiasm for each other, but Gemini's energy can be tiring for Virgo, who really needs a more grounded life partner. These two often don't share mutual respect for each other's way of processing—Gemini doesn't get why Virgo is upset or offended, and Virgo feels Gemini doesn't respect their needs or feelings. Virgo also feels rushed by Gemini. This combination makes good friends and co-workers, and is fine for most partnerships. In marriage/domestic partnership, or in cohabitation, difficulty arises for the Gemini/Virgo pair. See also *Gemini, Virgo.* ☯ ☼

gems **1.** Each sign of the zodiac is associated with a gem or gems. **2.** The gems associated with the Sun signs are: Aquarius: amethyst; Aries: diamond; Cancer: pearl; Capricorn: garnet; Gemini: agate; Leo: ruby; Libra: opal; Pisces: aquamarine; Sagittarius: turquoise; Scorpio: topaz; Taurus: emerald; and Virgo: sapphire. ✴ In addition to your Sun sign, you should consider your rising sign and the sign that rules each house of your birth chart when deciding what gem is appropriate to wear for any particular event or occasion. See also *colors.* **BC** ☯ ⌂ ☼

G

geocentric **1.** Earth-centered. **2.** Astronomer Nicolaus Copernicus believed that the Sun was the center of this universe; before Copernicus, the common belief was that the Earth was the center of the universe. **3.** Traditional astrology continues to operate on this geocentric system, while astronomy focuses on the heliocentric universe. See also *astrology; astronomy; Copernicus, Nicolaus; Earth, planet; heliocentric; Sun.* ◯

gibbous Moon **1.** The fourth of eight lunar phases. Each phase represents the changing relationship between the Moon and the Sun. Each phase is 45 degrees. **2.** The fourth of four waxing phases as the Moon leaves the Sun where it is invisible and approaches greatest visibility or fullness. **3.** The Moon has progressed 135 degrees from alignment with the Sun. A 135-degree angle is a sesquiquadrate. ✴ If you were born during the gibbous Moon phase, you seek self-improvement. Gibbous Moon people constantly analyze themselves for what needs refining. Think of how the Moon is preparing to become full when the Sun's spotlight reveals the greatest breadth of its surface. In the same way, you are preparing yourself for that time when you will be most revealed and visible. See also *Moon phases, sesquiquadrate.*

glyph **1.** A symbol used to represent something or to provide meaning. Glyphs can be part of a writing system or can take the place of that system. **2.** In astrology, each Sun sign and planet is associated with a symbol that relates to it or conveys some meaning about it—some have more than one glyph. There are also glyphs for the asteroids, nodes, and planetary aspects. ✲ **1.** When you look at your birth chart or your aspect grid, you will see symbols—there's not room on the chart for all of the Sun signs, planets, and aspects to be spelled out—it looks cluttered enough using symbols. In astrology, glyphs act as a sort of shorthand, so that every interaction can be recorded in the chart. **2.** Glyphs are like hieroglyphics—these symbols have symbolic meanings. The symbols used in astrology evolved over time, but many were first recorded in the middle ages. The symbol for the Sun, for example, is a simple circle with a dot at its center. This symbol looks like the Sun, but also represents the archetypal combination of the spiritual and physical worlds. See also *aspect grid, planets, Sun sign.* △ **BC** ○ ☼

Glyphs at a Glance

Signs	
Aries	♈
Taurus	♉
Gemini	♊
Cancer	♋
Leo	♌
Virgo	♍
Libra	♎
Scorpio	♏
Sagittarius	♐
Capricorn	♑
Aquarius	♒
Pisces	♓

Planets and Nodes

Sun	☉
Moon	☽
Mercury	☿
Venus	♀
Mars	♂
Jupiter	♃
Saturn	♄
Uranus	♅
Neptune	♆
Pluto	♇
North Node	☊
South Node	☋
Part of Fortune	⊗

Planetoid

| Chiron | ⚷ |

Asteroids

Ceres	⚳
Juno	⚵
Pallas Athene	⚴
Vesta	⚶

G

continues

continued

Major Aspects Between Planets	
Conjunction	♂
Sextile	✳
Square	◻
Trine	△
Quincunx	⊼
Opposition	☍

goddesses/gods   **1.** Roman gods and goddesses associated with the planets in Earth's solar system. Each planet (and many of the asteroids) is named for one of these, and the planets were assigned as planetary rulers of the signs of the zodiac. **2.** The astrological Sun signs are named for constellations, which represent ancient gods and goddesses and their myths. **3.** In older books and resources on astrology, the planets were given different god- or goddess-like energy. The planets were associated with the strengths and characteristics of the gods and goddesses for whom they were named.

Today, when astrologers examine the opportunities and challenges at work in an individual's birth chart, they think of the planets as psychological personalities. See also *Aries, Gemini, Jupiter, Leo, Libra, Mars, Mercury, Pisces, planets, Sagittarius, Scorpio, Sun sign, Taurus, Venus, Virgo.* ◯ ☼

grand cross   **1.** Also called a grand square. This is a rare major aspect created by two pairs of planets. These four planets form squares to each other, creating a cross shape in the birth chart. **2.** The four planets create four squares and two oppositions. **3.** In the birth chart, a grand cross relates to struggle. It is sometimes called a karmic cross because the individual feels constantly pushed and pulled to meet the needs of each of the four planets in the cross. There is no rest for the person with a grand cross until all four missions are completed. If other planets have positive aspects to the planets that create the grand cross, the effects of the grand cross will be softened and the struggle may be a more internal one. **4.** All of the signs in a grand cross are in the same modality: cardinal, fixed, or mutable. Each sign corresponds to a different element, so that all four elements are part of a grand cross. A cardinal cross has four planets in cardinal houses that all want to hurry and make things happen in different areas of life. It's difficult to make much progress when you are pushing yourself in four very different directions. The individual with a fixed cross feels stuck because he can't bring all of his skills, talents, and interests into a single focus or desire. A mutable cross challenges the individual to stand up for his own needs, purposes, and goals. She tends to get caught up in pleasing others and constantly adapts to others' needs.

G

✦ **1.** If you have a grand cross in your birth chart, you are carrying four challenges in your life. The challenges can be seen as karmic debts you are repaying or correcting in this life. You need to finish up these responsibilities, and will likely feel pulled to do so. The four areas of challenge are determined by the four planets and their locations in your chart. The grand cross is a difficult aspect that encompasses a lot of your life. You will definitely be motivated to work hard on these four areas of your life, often to the exclusion of other areas. Those around you may see you as very focused—sometimes to the detriment of anything (or anyone) else in your life, or with disregard for your own well-being. **2.** This aspect is a challenge, and it can mean struggle or obstacles in the areas of the grand cross, but it also means you will experience growth into a more spiritual, enlightened individual. Most people with this aspect in their birth charts are highly motivated. See also *aspects between planets.* △ **BC** 🏠 ○

grand sextile   See *hexagon.*

grand square   See *grand cross.*

grand trine   **1.** A beneficial major aspect between three planets. **2.** Three planets in an equilateral triangle formed because each planet is approximately 120 degrees apart from the other two planets. This aspect is seen as a bit of protection or luck in the birth chart. ✦ **1.** If you have a grand trine in your birth chart, good for you! You came into this life with karmic fortune and are destined to get out of trouble easily, enjoy general good fortune, and pass through life relatively unscathed. If you also have oppositions and squares, the grand trine will ensure that no matter how sticky life gets, you always manage to land on your feet. A grand trine means that much of your old karmic debt was paid off in earlier lives. In this life, you may still encounter difficulties or face struggles, but you will pass through these periods quickly and will bounce back from them quickly. You may reach stability quickly after a crisis. You may keep body, mind, and soul together easier. The hand of God is protecting you as you walk through life, and this is a blessing you earned through hard work in past lives. **2.** What about the areas of the trine? The grand trine affects a lot of your birth chart. It brings ease, opportunity, and protection to the areas of your life represented by the houses in which the planets of the grand trine are located. It also brings ease to the houses bearing cusp signs ruled by those planets. Serendipity follows the planets involved in your grand trine as they progress through your chart throughout your life. (This process can be seen in your solar arc chart.) See also *aspects between planets, solar arc chart.* △ **BC** 🏠 ◯

Greenwich Mean Time (GMT)   **1.** An international standard time based on locations at 0 degrees longitude (the Greenwich meridian or prime meridian), originally calculated at the Royal Observatory in Greenwich, London. Today this time is also called Universal Time (UT). **2.** GMT is five hours later than Eastern Standard Time in the United States. **3.** Astrological birth charts use Greenwich Mean Time to calculate birth time, because GMT is used in an ephemeris. An ephemeris lists planetary locations for every day at noon and midnight GMT. Today computer programs access information from an ephemeris after first translating birth time based on location into GMT. See also *birth place, birth time, ephemeris.* **BC**

harmonic convergence   See *hexagon*.

harmonious   See *beneficial*.

health/medical astrology   In the birth chart, the sixth house and the planets and aspects found there can be interpreted regarding health and vitality. ✦ **1.** What kind of health information can you get from your birth chart? You can't tell if you're going to have a specific condition such as diabetes or cancer, for example, but a health struggle might be indicated. You will also find direction for maintaining your health—maybe you need a certain kind of diet, or you really need exercise. Birth chart information is useful for determining how to benefit well-being, but it can't replace the advice and treatment of licensed medical professionals and specialists. Your birth chart can reveal valuable clues that will aid in a better understanding of your general health and point you toward the right doctor or practitioner to help you get better and stay well. **2.** If you're ill or you're scheduled for a procedure or surgery, you might want to consult an astrologer who specializes in health issues. The astrologer may be able to pinpoint advantageous times for good outcomes, or give insights into how the situation may progress. You might want to know if you will make it through the illness, or maybe you need help deciding on a course of treatment. **3.** You may be more strongly affiliated with your rising sign, in which case the body correspondences for that sign would seem more pertinent for you. You should also consider the sign opposite your sign in the zodiac, too, because opposites are seen to influence health—this is called polarity. See also *barren signs, fertile signs, fertility, sixth house*. △ **BC** ☯

heavens   In astrology, the term for the skies as viewed from the Earth. Look here for the planetary alignments and constellations. See also *celestial equator, celestial sphere, goddesses/gods.* **BC**

heliocentric   **1.** Sun-centered. **2.** It is now known that the planets of this universe are in orbit around the Sun; prior to the studies of Nicolaus Copernicus, the Earth was thought to be the center of the universe. (The term for this is geocentric.) **3.** Traditional astrology continues to operate on a geocentric system, while astronomy focuses on the heliocentric universe. See also *astrology; astronomy; Copernicus, Nicolaus; Earth, planet, geocentric, Sun.* ◯

hemisphere   **1.** Literally, half of a sphere. Used to describe the divisions of the Earth at the equator into the northern and southern hemispheres, as well as into eastern and western hemispheres by meridians at 0 degrees and 180 degrees. **2.** In a birth chart, the circle is divided into halves by the horizon, and the houses above the horizon (houses seven through twelve) create the northern hemisphere, the houses below the horizon (one through six) make up the southern hemisphere. **3.** Western astrology is based on the skies as seen from the northern hemisphere. **4.** Celestial hemispheres are created by an imaginary line coming out from the equator into the sky.

✦ **1.** The upper hemisphere is associated with the Sun, father, daytime, objective conscious awareness, career, and how we are impacted by the world. If you have most of your planets above the horizon, you need to spend time outside, meeting people, making your mark on the world, and learning about yourself through your interactions with society. Fame may figure into your future. **2.** The lower hemisphere is associated with the Moon, mother, nighttime, subjective, unconscious processing, home, and how we are impacted genetically, historically, and emotionally. If you have most of your planets below the horizon, you need cozy downtime at home to process your feelings, family interactions, and insights before going to bed. Home and family are a big focus of your life. **3.** The left hemisphere or eastern hemisphere is associated with sunrise and the start of new activity. If you have most of your planets on the left side, you are inclined toward boldness, risk, leading by example, and doing everything yourself. Independence is a big part of your identity. **4.** The right hemisphere or western hemisphere is associated with response to others and situations. If you have most of your planets on the right side, you tend to take care of others, heal, generate fun and celebration, seek connection, and create in response to limitation. Justice is very important to you. See also *horizon, sidereal zodiac.* **BC**

Herschel   In Britain, the planet Uranus is called Herschel after Sir Friedrich Wilhelm Herschel, the German astronomer and composer who discovered the planet in 1781. See also *Uranus.* ◯

hexagon   **1.** A grand sextile. **2.** A configuration of six planets that are each spaced 60 degrees apart. **3.** The grand sextile is also known as the Star of David configuration and is comprised of two grand trines and two oppositions. **4.** A rare configuration that operates as a vortex when all of the participating planets are consciously expressed by the native. **5.** When transiting planets create two opposing Stars of David, the world experiences a grand sextile. Because its nature includes two oppositions, sometimes a grand sextile includes an eclipse. When it does, it is called a harmonic convergence. **6.** A hexagon configuration includes two of the four elements. **7.** There is tremendous ease associated with a hexagon, as it is comprised of six helpful sextiles. A hexagon or grand sextile tends to unleash a lot of positive energy and resources that magnify and attract more positive energy and want to be used to create opportunities, express talent, and be productive.

✶ **1.** If you see a six-pointed star in the aspect lines in the center of your chart, you probably have a grand sextile. It's important to consider how each planet is most healthfully expressed by you and how all six planets can unify to serve you. **2.** As planets progress within your chart and interact with transiting planets, there may be times when your natal planets, progressed planets, and transiting planets form a grand sextile. See also *angle, aspects between planets, elements, progressions, transiting planets.* △◯

Hindu astrology   **1.** Indian method of astrological interpretation that uses the sidereal approach to dating regarding the precession of the equinoxes. **2.** Also known as Vedic or Jyotish astrology. See also *sidereal zodiac.* **BC**

home signs   **1.** One of the essential dignities of the planets. **2.** When a planet is in the sign it rules, the planet is said to be in its home sign. The home sign pertains to the actual sign and not the house associated with the sign. When in its home sign, a planet has good energy flow. For example, when Saturn is in its home sign of rulership, which is Capricorn, its energy has a natural flow and is balanced and comfortable. **3.** Home sign is used to describe a planet's energy. The planet resonates in its home sign; the planet's energy will not be blocked and there will be no struggle to access the planetary energy. A planet can express itself very easily in the sign it rules, but it can express itself most easily in the sign that exalts it, which is different than the home sign. Only the original seven planets have signs of exaltation. **4.** The opposite of home for a planet is detriment. The energy of a planet's detriment—its opposite sign (Cancer for Saturn)—creates weaker planetary energy. The sign opposite the home sign is where the planet does not feel at home. The opposite sign expresses opposite energies, which means a planet in a sign of detriment has no outlet for expressing its natural character. **5.** It helps to remember the essential dignities as two pairs. The first pair is home and detriment and the second pair is exaltation and fall. **6.** The home sign is also called the rulership sign.

✧**1.** How do you feel when you're at home? You can hang out and relax—you're comfortable. This describes a planet's energy when it's at home. **2.** If you're a Leo, you were born when the Sun was in the sign of Leo, its home sign. You are very comfortable being dynamic, commanding, flamboyant, and the center of attention. Is your Moon in Cancer? If so, you feel right at home crying over old photos and making guests feel as welcome as family. Mercury is at home in Gemini and Virgo. If this is Mercury's placement in your chart, it feels natural for you to quickly assimilate, analyze, and disseminate new information. See also detriment; energy; exalted; fall; planets; planetary ruler. **BC** ○ ☿

homeopathy astrology   **1.** Homeopathy and astrology are both holistic and seek to bring an individual into balance and greater consciousness. Both make interpretations presenting physical, mental, emotional, and spiritual evidence. The homeopath assesses the individual's genetic constitution and the astrologer assesses the individual's planetary constitution. **2.** Homeopathy astrology is a new branch of energetic medicine. The practitioner has in-depth training as a homeopath as well as knowledge of medical astrology. See also *flower essences, health/medical astrology.* ☯ **Z**

horary astrology   In this branch of astrology, the client poses a specific question, called a query, and is therefore referred to as the querent. The astrologer casts a chart for the moment of the question using the astrologer's own present location for the chart's location (not the querent's location or birth place) and the exact time of the query for the chart time. The term horary refers to the hour. The resulting chart reflects the "birth" of the question into the astrologer's conscious awareness. ✦ Horary astrology is amazingly accurate, and is perfect for questions where you need to know the outcome, such as whether you should pursue a lawsuit, or where in the house you left your grandmother's diamond brooch. It doesn't just work for yes or no questions, either—the answer to your query can be very nuanced and detailed, relating information on all of your options in a particular situation, the history of the situation, and the likely outcome. It's essentially a birth chart for the question. See also *birth chart, querent.* **BC**

horizon   **1.** Where the Earth and sky meet in the line of vision. **2.** The beginning of the first house (the imaginary line between the twelfth and first houses) is the horizon in the birth chart. The eastern horizon is where you see the rising sign. **3.** The line running east to west on a birth chart, dividing the chart into halves. The horizon line on a birth chart is what's rising in the east. The rising sign appears here in the sky. ✦ Look out at the Earth—you'll see an imaginary line separating the Earth and the sky. If you're looking at the ocean or across a flat expanse of land, the horizon line is more obvious. When you look at the horizon, it's what you see in the sky. See also *above the Earth, ascendant, below the Earth, hemisphere.* **BC** 🏠

horoscope   **1.** A scope or map of the heavens. **2.** Also a daily astrological forecast, or an astrologer's translation of the planets and their effects on a Sun sign on any given day. Horoscopes are predictions based on general information for a Sun sign (and sometimes also using the transiting Moon). A daily horoscope provides a basic interpretation of the planets and how they are affecting the Sun signs. **3.** Astrologers call a chart they have produced, and its interpretation,

H

a horoscope. The birth chart is like a map; it's a mathematical chart of the planets. ✧ Your birth chart is your very specific personal horoscope based on your birth information and the positions of the Sun, Moon, and planets on the date and in the place of your birth. See also *birth chart, forecast, intuition.* **BC**

house **1.** An astrological chart (birth, progressed, or solar return) is divided into twelve sections, or houses. The 360-degree circle is divided into twelve equal parts of 30 degrees each. **2.** Each house represents an area or theme in life, and planets in the houses color the house and indicate what will be important in that house, or what action will take place in that area of life. **3.** The house can be described as the stage or the setting of the action, which is produced by the planets.

✧ **1.** On a birth chart, the houses are numbered one through twelve, and they appear in counterclockwise order around the circle of the birth chart. The first house is situated below the eastern horizon, which is the left half of the center horizon line (looking down at the Earth from the North Pole, facing south, the east is to your left); the sixth house is located below the western horizon, which is the right half of the center horizon line. Thus, the first six houses are below the center horizon line. Houses seven through twelve are above the center horizon line. The cusp of the first house forms the dividing line between the first and twelfth houses. **2.** More planets in a particular house in your birth chart indicate that you have more work to do in that area of your life. What kind of work depends on the planets and their location and relationship to other planets nearby. **3.** Having no planets in a house in your birth chart means that you have mastered that house's energy and are working on other energies in this lifetime. See also *above the Earth, below the Earth, birth chart, horizon, karma, planets, progressed birth chart, solar return.* **BC**

I

impeded **1.** A planet is impeded when it is poorly aspected or when it is aspected by malefics. **2.** When the Moon conjoins, squares or opposes the Sun, Mars, or Saturn. **3.** Many people have a planet that conjoins, squares, or opposes Mars, Saturn, Uranus, Neptune, or Pluto. ✧ What should you do if you do have an impeded planet? It's important to identify impeded planets in your chart. Most likely, your impeded planet started attracting judgment, ridicule, or resistance when you were a child. It helps to think of your planets as personalities that live within you. Imagine that your impeded planet is getting hassled by the planets that negatively aspect it. The impeded planet needs your help. Its only way of getting your attention is to cause you to be attracted to people who are likely to hassle you in the same way. Eventually, the outer pain you experience through these relationships will cause you to turn within to heal the part of you that is repressed or dysfunctional. You can accelerate the process by contemplating how your impeded planet's pure energy was judged when you attempted to express it. As you reclaim your right to express that characteristic, your impeded planet gains strength and the respect of the malefic planet that aspects it. See also *aspects between planets, malefic.* △◯

Imum coeli See *nadir (Imum Coeli).*

inclination **1.** The angle at which a planet in its orbit crosses the ecliptic. **2.** The movement of a planet toward a position that is not its birth position. **3.** The greater a planet's inclination, the more it challenges reality as commonly accepted on Earth. Think of another planet's orbit as a disc in the solar system that bisects the Earth's orbital disc. If the two orbits are on the same plane, there is little interference. Perhaps they parallel each other or skim each other. If the other planet's disc is on a very different plane than the Earth's, it's as though its orbit slices through our ecliptic. The other planet's orbit is jarring to Earth's. Pluto, the planet that many astrologers consider to be the most impactful upon Earth, has the largest inclination, over 17 degrees. ✷ Do you have any planets that exactly aspect Pluto? Look for planets that are at the same degree number that your Pluto is at. Pluto moves so slowly that it's best to work with an exact degree orb. Because Pluto has such a large inclination, any time transiting Pluto, Mars or any of transiting planets that are the same planets that you have at the same degree as Pluto arrive at the specific degree, dramatic shifts occur. See also *angles between the planets, declination, ecliptic, planets.* **BC** ◯

incompatibility   **1.** The opposite of compatibility. In astrology, incompatibility describes things that do not go together well. **2.** When two elements or signs are not functional or create stress and challenges for each other instead of understanding and peace, they are said to be incompatible. **3.** Any two opposite astrological components that create friction and misunderstanding. ✷ **1.** Some of the Sun sign pairings are more compatible than others. To explore the nuances of Sun sign pairings for specific individuals in a relationship, it is advantageous to look at both birth charts for deeper meanings and insights into whether the partners are compatible or incompatible. **2.** Elemental energies can also be more or less compatible in pairings. **3.** Any time you feel inharmonious energy with someone, this may be a sign of your basic incompatibility. **4.** Incompatibility can depend on lots of things—your Sun sign might not seem the best fit with your best friend's, but you could have other planetary alignments between your birth charts that counterbalance this apparent incompatibility. See also *air, element; compatibility; earth, element; energy; fire, element; relationship astrology; water, element.* ☯ ☼

inconjunct   See *quincunx.*

indirect   **1.** Also called indirect energy. The motion of a planet, when retrograde, creates this energy. **2.** Retrograde planets appear to be moving backward (this is only how they appear from the Earth as they orbit the Sun), and are described as having less direct energy. The planet may not be acting at its fullest potential, or may be expressing itself with a more subconscious, yin energy. ✦ **1.** Do you have any retrograde planets in your birth chart? If you do, this doesn't mean the planet isn't acting in your chart, but the retrograde nature of the action is different from the direct energy of a planet in its normal orbit. You may not have easy access to the areas influenced by a retrograde planet; you may have to work harder toward goals in these areas or experience delays. You may feel an internal struggle or a lack of confidence in your abilities. **2.** Yin, or feminine, energy is indirect energy. The yin signs are Taurus, Cancer, Virgo, Scorpio, Capricorn, and Pisces. See also *direct, energy, planets, retrograde, yang, yin.* **BC** ◯ ℞

indirect energy   See *indirect.*

ingress   **1.** The movement of a planet or other body into a sign or quadrant. This applies to both progressed and transiting planets. Progressed planets move forward as they complete their orbits. For instance, every time Venus orbits the Sun, it moves forward a degree in the native's solar-progressed chart. Solar-arc directed planets move forward a degree every time the Earth orbits the Sun, so all the planets move together preserving the relationships of the birth chart. Transiting planets move through a chart in real time. Ingress is not just about a planet's movement, though; it is about a planet's move into the next sign or next quadrant. Keep in mind that signs typically overlap houses and that quadrants define the houses between axis points. The first quadrant is the houses between the ascendant and the nadir, so the first, second, and third houses. The second quadrant includes the houses between the nadir and the descendant: fourth, fifth, and sixth houses. The third quadrant includes the seventh, eighth, and ninth houses found between the descendant and the midheaven. The fourth quadrant is comprised of the tenth, eleventh, and twelfth houses between the midheaven and the ascendant. **2.** A planet's ingress into different signs and quadrants alters its influence. When a planet ingresses into a new quadrant, there is a distinctive shift in the area of the chart ruled by that planet.

✦ **1.** If the ingress is into the first quadrant, the house ruled by that planet becomes a focal point for you to discover more about yourself. **2.** An ingress into the second quadrant stimulates your desires to create happier relationships in your personal life. **3.** When a planet enters the third quadrant, you get help understanding how people who are different from you also serve as mirrors for the parts of yourself that need more integration. It's an opportunity to increase your acceptance and understanding of others so that you can have more harmony and balance in your life. **4.** The fourth quadrant offers opportunities to find one's place in the world every time a planet crosses the midheaven. See also *midheaven (Medium Coeli), planets, quadrant, Sun signs.* **BC** ◯ ☼

initiating signs   1. Also called the cardinal signs. These are the Sun signs that begin each of the seasons. **2.** The initiating signs are Aries (spring), Cancer (summer), Libra (fall), and Capricorn (winter). **3.** The initiating signs are signs of beginnings. Two of the signs (Aries and Libra) are yang energies; spring and fall create the conditions for the fullness of summer and winter. Two of the signs, Cancer and Capricorn, are yin energies; summer and winter express completeness and the fulfillment of potential, whether outward (summer) or inward (winter). ✷ If you were born under one of the initiating signs or have more than two planets in initiating signs, you are someone who likes to start things. You generate a lot of energy for new enterprises and really like to get things done. You access a lot of energy through setting the conditions for completion. You experience greater success when you look ahead to every aspect of the process of a project. Focusing on what's enjoyable in every phase of a project allows you to relax and enjoy the process more, which in turn helps you to finish what you start. It also helps to remember that failure can be an important part of success. Getting comfortable with failure will help you let yourself explore things that don't come easily to you. The confidence and tenacity to make new starts after failures is a hallmark of the initiating signs; these signs love beginning—that which quickens, fascinates. See also *Aries, Cancer, Capricorn, cardinal, Libra.* ☼

intercepted planet   See *interception.*

intercepted sign   See *interception.*

interception   1. Occurs when two opposing signs within a birth chart are each too large to be accommodated by one house each. These signs squeeze the other signs into the remaining houses so that another pair of signs is sandwiched within their respective houses. **2.** The house system determines the house size. An equal house system assigns the same degree of a successive sign to each successive cusp of each house within the birth chart. **3.** When a sign of the zodiac is confined within a house of a chart, it is described as an intercepted sign. The sign does not express itself as easily as the other signs. This can reflect hidden attributes or skills. People with intercepted signs may not realize these talents or be aware of them until they learn to access that sign through the sign that's on the cusp of the house containing the intercepted sign. **4.** When a sign is intercepted, its opposite sign is intercepted as well. **5.** Charts with intercepted signs are not uncommon and are more likely to occur when the native is born at a more extreme northern or southern latitude or near the equator.

� **1.** What if your Sun sign is intercepted? You'll have to master the qualities of the sign that rules the cusp of the house that your Sun is in. For instance, if you're a Gemini and the house that your Sun in Gemini is in is intercepted, you would have to learn how to express your identity, creativity, and purpose in Taurean ways before you can find your identity as a Gemini. **2.** What does it mean for a planet to be located in an intercepted sign? That planet is called an intercepted planet. Planets in intercepted signs might have their influence hidden or held back until that planet has orbited the Sun enough times to move it out of interception. The planet will again have a direct influence once the sign is no longer intercepted. (This is reflected by a solar progressed chart; planets are moved a degree for every orbit they make around the Sun, and the Sun is moved a degree each year.) See also *house, planets, solar progressed chart, Sun sign.* 🏠⭕☼

interpreting   Using the astrological language of planets, signs, modalities, elements, and houses to relate information. Astrologers are skilled at understanding the meanings of each part of a birth chart, as well as their interactions or combined meanings. Astrologers often use advanced charts containing transits and progressions to ascertain information regarding particular dates, to give further insight into the evolution of the soul and its life path (in this and other incarnations), and to make more sophisticated observations. See also *Akashic Record, astrologer/ist, astrology, birth chart, computer programs.* **BC**

intuition   **1.** Insight, or instinctive knowledge. **2.** Most astrologers rely in some fashion on intuition to assist them in interpreting birth charts. This sixth sense can lead them to see connections and meanings in the chart that would not be obvious to everyone. This is why astrologers seem to know instantly so much about a person by looking at a birth chart, even though no personal information may have been revealed to the astrologer before the reading. Part of this is experience, of course, but it's also an inexplicable awareness. See also *astrologer/ist, interpreting, intuitive arts, solar progressed chart.* **BC**

intuitive arts   **1.** Areas of metaphysics that use intuitive awareness, including astrology, palmistry, tarot, numerology, and psychic intuition. **2.** Practitioners of the intuitive arts use the birth chart, core numbers, a deck of tarot cards, and/or the palm of the hand to reveal and translate symbols or signs into practical information. See also *astrology, intuition, tarot and astrology.* **BC**

inversion   **1.** When an angle that is an aspect is deducted from 180 degrees, the remaining angle is the inversion of the first angle. (Each angle is an inversion of the other.) **2.** The inversion of a trine is a sextile because 180 minus 120 (trine) is 60 (sextile). See also *angle, aspects between the planets, sextile, trine.* △

Aspects that form inversions:

- Semi-Sextile and Quincunx: 30 degrees and 150 degrees
- Semi-Square and Sesquiquadrate: 45 degrees and 135 degrees
- Sextile and Trine: 60 degrees and 120 degrees
- Trine and Sextile: 120 degrees and 60 degrees
- Sesquiquadrate and Semi-Square: 135 degrees and 45 degrees
- Quincunx and Semi-Sextile: 150 degrees and 30 degrees

January 21 to February 19   Birth dates for the Sun sign Aquarius. The position of the Sun during these dates correlates with an astrological Sun sign. Those born between January 21 and February 19 have Aquarius as their Sun sign. See also *Aquarius.* ☼

July 23 to August 22   Birth dates for the Sun sign Leo. The position of the Sun during these dates correlates with an astrological Sun sign. Those born between July 23 and August 22 have Leo as their Sun sign. See also *Leo.* ☼

June 22 to July 23   Birth dates for the Sun sign Cancer. The position of the Sun during these dates correlates with an astrological Sun sign. Those born between June 22 and July 23 have Cancer as their Sun sign. See also *Cancer.* ☼

Juno   **1.** The asteroid Juno was discovered in 1804 by German astronomer Karl Harding. Juno is named for the Roman goddess of marriage and childbirth. **2.** Juno's orbit is highly erratic. The glyph for her astrological symbol is ⚴. **3.** Juno was the most elevated Roman goddess, daughter of Saturn, wife (and sister) of Jupiter, and mother of Mars. Her Greek equivalent is Hera. Jupiter is the king of the universe, which makes Juno the queen. Juno is the goddess of marriage and childbirth, and because the month of June is named for her, it has long been believed that June is the best time for marriage—even today, most weddings are performed in June. On the first of March, Roman women held a festival called Matronalia to honor Juno. **4.** In the same way that Lilith, Adam's first wife, refused to submit to Adam, Juno also insisted that Jupiter treat her as an equal. Both goddesses have endured a lot of bad press for being women's libbers. Juno is known for her strong

temperament, and temper; Juno proved herself a formidable matri-
arch, fiercely protective of (and watchful over) her family ... and her
husband, too.

✦ **1.** Juno relates to marriage and childbirth as well as partnerships. (She is similar to Venus in effect, except that Venus rules what
attracts and excites you about your partner, and Juno is about getting
along on an everyday basis.) She corresponds to the signs of Libra
(marriage) and Scorpio (childbirth). Computer astrology programs
generally include Juno when casting basic birth charts, and most
astrologers will consider Juno when doing astrological readings.
2. Where is Juno—in what house and sign does she appear in your
birth chart? Juno's house placement in your birth chart is where to
look for indications of where you are likely to meet someone with
whom you may have a long-term, committed relationship. The sign
Juno is in tells you how you meet your romantic partner and how to
make your relationship happy. See also *asteroids, planets.* ◯

In what sign do you have Juno in your birth chart?

- **Juno in Aries** needs a relationship that respects each partner's independence.

- **Juno in Taurus** wants financial stability in place before getting married. (The wedding will be a stylish affair!)

- **Juno in Gemini** looks for an excellent conversationalist who enjoys a good road trip.

- **Juno in Cancer** does best in marriage when family comes first and any ex-spouse comes last. Similar food preferences are also important.

- **Juno in Leo** invites a lot of drama and fun into a committed relationship.

- **Juno in Virgo** admires workaholism and needs a partner who is meticulous.

- **Juno in Libra** relaxes when it is clear that the well-being of the relationship is priority number one.

- **Juno in Scorpio** searches for the one and only soul mate. Once they find each other, there could be a lot of passionate hair pulling and back scratching.

- **Juno in Sagittarius** tends to marry a foreigner with a similar life philosophy.

- **Juno in Capricorn** enjoys a famous spouse or at least a confident authority figure.
- **Juno in Aquarius** needs the marriage to include an active social life. Even better if the spouse recycles.
- **Juno in Pisces** wants a lifelong dance partner who shares similar musings.

In what house do you have Juno in your birth chart?

Juno ⚵	Keywords
First house Juno	A romantic partnership full of exuberance and passion that is sometimes competitive.
Second house Juno	A sensuous, down-to-earth, committed relationship that functions better with lots of money.
Third house Juno	A committed yet flirtatious relationship both logical and full of frolic.
Fourth house Juno	A life partnership founded in history together and love of family, but also a need to feel safe and secure.
Fifth house Juno	The committed romantic duo who makes heads turn, has fun, and is sometimes accused of being drama queens.
Sixth house Juno	A practical marriage based on shared values and duties.
Seventh house Juno	Life partners who are super social, refined, and codependent.
Eighth house Juno	Extremely passionate and committed pair who thrives on power and envy.
Ninth house Juno	A royal marriage full of adventure and opinions.

J

continues

continued

Juno ⚹	Keywords
Tenth house Juno	Social climbing, successful, committed couple that inspires others to vote them into office.
Eleventh house Juno	Smart liberals who take forever to commit and who find happiness in an unconventional relationship.
Twelfth house Juno	The committed couple that seeks escape from the pain of the world in fantasy and spirituality.

Juno transits   See *asteroid transits.*

Jupiter   1. Planet known since prehistoric times as a wandering star, named for the Roman king of the gods. In Greek mythology, Jupiter's equivalent is Zeus. **2.** Jupiter is the fifth planet from the Sun, and the largest planet in our solar system. It is the fourth brightest object in the sky, after the Sun, Moon, and Venus. Jupiter travels around the Sun in a slightly elliptical orbit and rotates faster than any other planet. It takes Jupiter about 12 years to complete its orbit around the Sun. **3.** In Roman mythology, Jupiter ruled over laws and social order. He is the son of Saturn (his brothers are Neptune and Pluto), husband (and brother) of Juno, and father of Mars and Mercury. **4.** Along with Uranus and Neptune, Jupiter is known as a social planet because of the expansive natures of these planets. Jupiter relates to luck, good fortune, optimism, and protection from above. **5.** Jupiter ℞ represents the shadow side of Jupiter's direct energies.

✦ **1.** Jupiter's placement in your birth chart can tell you where to look for success and opportunity in life. Jupiter's orbit takes about twelve years, which is the length of this planet's cycle of influence in your life. In other words, every twelve years, a new cycle of expansion under Jupiter will begin. When Jupiter moves into your Sun sign, it is a welcoming time. **2.** Where is Jupiter in your birth chart? In what house and sign does it appear? Wherever its placement, Jupiter always signifies issues relating to abundance; the particular house and sign will give clues to Jupiter's deeper meaning.

3. Your personal philosophy, sense of humor, and how you relate to religion are also related by Jupiter's placement in your birth chart.
4. Jupiter can also indicate overindulgence—there can be too much of a good thing, and your good fortune in certain areas can lead to excess. Jupiter is sometimes connected to weight gain and dieting.
5. In a daily astrological calendar, days and times when Jupiter is in a positive aspect to the Sun, such as conjunct, trine, or sextile, are often good times for meeting new people, scheduling classes, making phone calls, or simply having fun. Days when Jupiter is in more challenging aspect to the Sun, such as square or opposition, can be times to watch overextending yourself, laughing too loud (or long), or doing too much; you may be overprepared for your meeting … and in all the wrong ways, or study the wrong things too hard and miss out on acing the test. See also *Jupiter in the houses, Jupiter in the signs, Jupiter retrograde.* ◯

Jupiter finger   In palmistry, the pointer finger and the base of that finger of each hand relates to a person's Sun sign. The Jupiter finger relates to leadership, self-esteem, authority, ambition, status, and the limelight. See also *Jupiter.* ◯

Jupiter in the houses   **1.** Jupiter is benefic and provides an optimistic and enthusiastic attitude toward the areas of life relating to each of the houses. **2.** Jupiter's chart placement shows areas of growth, opportunity, and expansion. ✦ **1.** Jupiter is good fortune and good luck, no matter where it is placed in your birth chart.
2. Jupiter also has to do with faith—you will believe in your ability or success in the areas of your life influenced by Jupiter. You'll have good luck and opportunity in these areas, but that doesn't mean your life will be problem-free. Jupiter has a desire for a constructive and happy outcome, though, and no matter what problem you encounter, if Jupiter has any say, it will all turn out well. **3.** Because Jupiter can also represent overindulgence, too much of a good thing may turn out to be … too much of a good thing.
♃ **in the first house**   Jupiter in the first house is all about the self and the personality. ✦ **1.** Jupiter plays an important role in your attitude. If you have Jupiter in your first house, you're optimistic and enthusiastic, and have great social abilities. Jupiter's luck will come to you through your personality and charisma. **2.** Jupiter's influence on philosophy and faith may mean that you have strong spiritual

or religious convictions, which will also come through in your personality. **3.** In the first house, Jupiter's excessive side may make you self-indulgent and more than a little bit lazy. **4.** With Jupiter ℞ in the first house, you seek to tame your ego and find a higher code to live by.

♃ **in the second house**   Jupiter in the second house relates to material possessions and what is valued—not necessarily the same thing. ✧ **1.** If your Jupiter is in your second house, you are lucky when it comes to money and other resources. You're good with money and never have difficulty finding a job—even in tough economic times. Earning money is easy for you, and you have the potential to make a lot over the course of your life. **2.** Maybe because it's so easy for you to make money, you may not feel the need to hold on to it. You might not be a saver, because you aren't worried about needing a rainy day fund—you know the sun will shine again after a downpour. You have a tendency to give money away, which is great. You can also spend a lot, which can be wasteful, and you have a tendency toward materialism. **3.** Jupiter ℞ in the second house means you've likely found your ability to earn money a consistent barometer of how you are doing in life.

♃ **in the third house**   Jupiter in the third house of communication relates to thought process as well as early childhood relationships and siblings. ✧ **1.** A third house Jupiter makes you lucky through your optimistic attitude. Your relationships and education in early life were fortunate and serve you well. You're a good conversationalist and have good energy. **2.** Jupiter in the third house likes to uplift others, often using the intellect and voice. You like to observe others, and can read other people well. This gives you an edge in the fields of teaching and writing. You make a great comedian, as well. **3.** How does Jupiter's excess affect you with third house placement? You may enjoy your humor and opinions so much you forget to pause and give others a chance to share. You may also have a tendency to sign up for a lot of classes, blog incessantly, collect a hangar full of vehicles, or get hooked on the slot machines in Vegas. **4.** Jupiter ℞ in the third house means you thoroughly enjoy exploring the capabilities of your own mind.

♃ **in the fourth house**   Jupiter in the fourth house relates to family and home. ✧ **1.** If Jupiter is in the fourth house of your birth chart, you are devoted to family, and family is where you have your luck— you are lucky to have your parents and siblings, and you likely had a

happy, secure childhood. You are protected and prosperous through
family members, especially through your mom or through her
side of your family. **2.** This Jupiter placement can indicate positive
inheritance through family members, of money, material goods, or
good traits. **3.** Jupiter in the fourth house can also make you a little
overindulgent of family members, including your own children. Be
careful of this tendency to spoil those you love. Decide to eat healthfully and take daily walks together, as a positive indulgence that may
also add precious years to keeping families celebrating together as
well. **4.** Jupiter ℞ in the fourth house means you eventually find your
bliss by creating a happy home and family.

♃ **in the fifth house**   Jupiter in the fifth house is all about creativity
and self-expression. ✴ **1.** Your fifth house Jupiter brings you great
luck, prosperity, and enthusiasm through artistic self-expression.
Jupiter in this house makes you very creative and talented in all of
the arts: music, visual art, dance, writing, theater. You're also very
good with children, and your optimistic, social nature makes you an
excellent early-education teacher. Your work with children and the
arts is especially beneficial for you. You may come from a large family
or have your own large family or touch the lives of many children
through your work as a teacher, coach, or parent. Your talents are
visible early in life if you have Jupiter in your fifth house. Your family
may have recognized and nurtured your talents in childhood.
2. Jupiter in the fifth house brings with it lots of social ability—
people like you, and you're good at connecting people. **3.** Jupiter's
tendency toward excess may show up as a collection of drama queen
best friends or overindulged children who don't know the meaning
of the word no. **4.** Jupiter ℞ in the fifth house means you guide your
children to find truth in their own hearts.

♃ **in the sixth house**   Jupiter in the sixth house relates to health
and public service as well as place of work. ✴ **1.** Sixth house Jupiter
brings physical stamina, reserves of good health, and the ability to
overcome disease. You bounce back from emotional, physical, or
spiritual trauma and recuperate quickly from illnesses or accidents.
In addition, you're optimistic about overcoming such health-related
setbacks, and this positive outlook aids your recovery. **2.** Jupiter in
your sixth house brings you luck with your place of employment, as
well. You get along well with your co-workers and your employers.
You harmonize with others well in general, and others recognize this

and tend to give you leadership roles. **3.** Jupiter's indulgent side can bring on health issues caused by overindulgence in food, alcohol, or other substances. You might have issues with your weight—remember that moderation is a good principle to live by in all areas of life.
4. Jupiter ℞ in the sixth house means you seek to serve humanity through simple acts of generosity.

♃ **in your seventh house**   When in the seventh house, Jupiter relates to marriage and partnership. ✶ **1.** If Jupiter is positioned in the seventh house of your birth chart, you benefit through marriage or domestic partnerships, business partnerships, and other partnerships. You tend to attract the people you need into your life and luck and good fortune come to you through partnerships. You have lots of love around you because of the people you attract. All forms of committed relationships are easy for you because you don't have a lot of heaviness or karma to deal with in this area of life. Relationships flow for you. You grow and are successful within partnerships, and receive benefit through these partnerships—you might even inherit through these partnerships, as well. We have a one in twelve chance for this love! You might be one of those people who stay married for 50 years or more. **2.** Be careful not to be so open and giving that you trust the wrong people. Be especially careful when meeting new people through electronic media—face-to-face relationships are best; so meet first and then talk forever online. **3.** Jupiter ℞ in the seventh house means you learn about yourself through your committed relationships and partnerships.

♃ **in the eighth house**   Jupiter in the eighth house is about transformation and new beginnings as well as money and joint resources. ✶ **1.** If you have Jupiter in your eighth house, you are lucky and fortunate psychically and spiritually. You are highly intuitive, and may be able to accurately channel information from heaven or the spirit world. **2.** This Jupiter placement also makes you lucky in money matters, including investments and stocks. Jupiter attracts resources that help and benefit you, so you get lots of luck through resources, money, people, and information from spirit. **3.** Jupiter's tendency toward excess could lead you to overspend—money comes easily to you, and you might not appreciate it. However, you may find yourself a compassionate philanthropist and champion of worthy causes, donating time as well as materials. **4.** Jupiter ℞ in the eighth house means you seek to emulate the right use of power.

♃ **in the ninth house   1.** In the ninth house, Jupiter relates to personal philosophy and religion, as well as higher education, foreign travel, and law. **2.** Jupiter is the natural planetary ruler of the ninth house, and is at home there. ✫ **1.** If you have Jupiter in your ninth house, you are lucky through religious, spiritual, and educational endeavors. Go to school and get a higher education—it will truly benefit you with Jupiter in your ninth house. **2.** Jupiter in the ninth house also rules foreign countries and people. You might travel the globe and will be welcomed everywhere you go. Such travel will be beneficial to you—maybe you will meet people who help you in life, or perhaps you will find yourself in business partnership with foreigners. You blend in well in diverse cultures, and are likely to find great resources through foreigners. **3.** Jupiter's excesses show up as epic adventures that make your life seem exceptional while also preventing you from making commitments and facing your fears of a (seemingly) ordinary life. You may also have a tendency to pick up the check … not just for friends, but for the entire restaurant. **4.** Jupiter ℞ in the ninth house means you internalize your experiences of nature and foreign lands.

♃ **in the tenth house**   Jupiter in the tenth house relates to career, authority figures, and public life and reputation. ✫ **1.** Your tenth house is important in shaping your contributions to society and your career. You are lucky through your career. You may even become famous—your career could bring you public success or you could experience some level of notoriety or high-level recognition through your career. Essentially, your work is the luckiest thing in your life. You are very successful, your achievements are wide and broad, and recognition is assured for your career with this Jupiter placement. You will find the right work at the right time, and you are also lucky overcoming obstacles in your career—if you get fired, a better job is waiting for you. You'll do well in the public arena, including politics, and you are a natural leader. **2.** Tenth house Jupiter also makes you fortunate through hierarchy—namely, your father, your boss or other authority figures, or even through your mother—if you lost your father or your mother's a CEO, police officer, soldier, royalty, or high political figure. **3.** Those with an overindulgent Jupiter in the tenth house may be excessively materialistic, pessimistic, or manipulative. Watch a tendency to use status or material things to control or seduce, or punish or reward someone else. Remember

J

that with success comes a moral responsibility to use stature to achieve societal good as well as personal wealth. **4.** Jupiter ℞ in the tenth house means you choose to succeed in ways that are good for you and everyone involved.

♃ in the eleventh house   Jupiter in the eleventh house relates to hopes and goals, as well as groups or social networks. ✷ **1.** Your eleventh house Jupiter brings you opportunity through your social network—clubs, organizations, and peer groups will all help you get where you need to go. These people guide you along your life path, helping you reach any goal you have in life. Jupiter in the eleventh house also means that if you need something (money, education, a ride to work), if you tell your network, someone will provide what you need. It's a simple matter of asking and receiving with this Jupiter placement. In times of need, you are always protected through your peer groups and friends. **2.** Jupiter's excesses in the eleventh house are all about being different just for the sake of nonconformity or rebellion. **3.** Jupiter ℞ in the eleventh house means you love parties where you can ask people about important issues.

♃ in the twelfth house   **1.** The twelfth house Jupiter relates to karmic duty and debt as well as hidden problems. **2.** Jupiter in the twelfth house has a strong influence on unforeseen events.
 ✷ **1.** Jupiter in the twelfth house of your birth chart brings protection from danger and in unforeseen events. If you are in a dangerous profession, such as law enforcement, Jupiter can't keep you out of dangerous situations, but it can help them turn out favorably. (A criminal with this Jupiter placement might be difficult to catch.) **2.** If you have Jupiter in your twelfth house, you're good at uncovering mysteries and have luck in investigative situations. You have great powers of observation. You see what others don't, which serves you well in careers in law enforcement, as well as in medicine, particularly research. **3.** Jupiter is a co-ruler of Pisces, and is at home in the twelfth house. This placement gives you an innate understanding of people; you may be highly intuitive or even psychic. These abilities would make you a good psychologist or psychiatrist, and also serve you well in astrology or other intuitive arts. Your luck and success comes from your sixth sense—your intuition. You access hidden information very easily. **4.** The karmic duty of the twelfth house is to heal old wounds and help others heal their wounds. This may lead you to a career in service to others, as a doctor, therapist, or social

worker, for example. **5.** The overindulgent side of Jupiter expresses through your impracticality or tendency to fantasize in avoidance of everyday tasks. **6.** Jupiter ℞ in the twelfth house gives you the ability to see the meaning of your life as a dream and your dreams as your life.

See also *house, Jupiter, Jupiter in the signs.*

Jupiter in the signs   **1.** Jupiter is the planet of expansion and opportunity. The sign Jupiter falls in will indicate how luck or opportunity arrives, how the native expresses it, or where his enthusiasm is. **2.** Jupiter ℞ in the signs generally signifies the way you find truth in the world by internalizing your experiences.

♃ **in Aquarius**   Aquarius is a visionary sign of communication and independence. ✦ **1.** If you have Jupiter in Aquarius, you believe that everyone should have equal freedom and prosperity; you also believe that everyone can prosper, if we are all willing to work together to make it happen. You are very altruistic and are enthusiastic in helping others in your community. Open-minded Aquarius has lots of friends and finds great opportunity through them. **2.** Jupiter ℞ in Aquarius finds truth in the world by questioning societal mores.

♃ **in Aries**   Aries is a sign of action. ✦ **1.** Jupiter in Aries likes to experiment and try new things. You are lucky because you have an enthusiastic attitude, and no fear of change. You'll find luck through growth, and will experience good fortune through trying new things. You're a confident leader. **2.** Jupiter ℞ in Aries finds truth in the world by finding ways to be courageous.

♃ **in Cancer**   Cancer is a sensitive sign of emotion and security. ✦ **1.** If Jupiter is in Cancer in your birth chart, you are an eternal optimist with a great sense of humor. You will find opportunity and growth through emotional connections, especially with family—either your family of origin or the one you create. If you work with family, you are enthusiastic about it. You have a nurturing and encouraging tendency, and you use this to help connect others. Your greatest gift might come from a family inheritance of money, talents, or abilities. You receive generational or family luck, and family helps you grow and protects you. Home is lucky for you, and developing home life is good for you. You find good fortune and security at home. **2.** Jupiter ℞ in Cancer finds truth in the world by feeling the pain of those who are starving and then working to feed the hungry.

♃ **in Capricorn**   Capricorn is a practical sign devoted to goals.

⭐ **1.** If you have Jupiter in Capricorn, you are good at business and with the material world. You have luck in these areas, and are serious about and interested in material wealth. You find growth and opportunity when you work hard and persevere to attain a goal. You think you have to physically work and create your own good fortune, and that you earn it with sweat equity. You feel a need to show that you deserve the luck that comes your way. You are very business oriented, practical, and realistic, and are likely to be ambitious and successful in your career. **2.** Jupiter ℞ in Capricorn finds truth in the world by envisioning a corporate existence founded in truth.

♃ **in Gemini**   Gemini is a sign of communication and wit.

⭐ **1.** Your Jupiter in Gemini is related to communication skills. You'll find growth and good fortune through your intellect, education, and communication. You have a strong desire for knowledge, and are enthusiastic and adventurous. Try different ways of communicating— one of them is likely to lead to great things. **2.** Jupiter ℞ in Gemini finds truth in the world by sharing insights gained through turning-point experiences.

♃ **in Leo**   Leo is a charismatic sign of confidence and leadership.

⭐ **1.** Your Jupiter in Leo finds growth and opportunity through your dramatic talents and leadership abilities. Your ability to lead and inspire others may lead you into politics or community leadership. You will likely receive recognition for your leadership skills and your ability to get differing groups to talk to each other and relate. You also have good fortune through public speaking, dramatic arts, and your charismatic ability to pull people to you and direct them successfully in a project or a situation. You can get people enthused and help them to develop pride in what they are doing. **2.** Jupiter ℞ in Leo finds truth in the world by living a life devoted to following the heart.

♃ **in Libra**   Libra is a sign of harmony and balance. ⭐ **1.** Your Jupiter in Libra brings you opportunities and growth through partnerships, including business and marriage or domestic partnership. You find your greatest joy in collaborative or collective projects, because you like to work with partners or groups. Cooperation is important to you, and you will have luck and good fortune through cooperative relationships. **2.** Jupiter ℞ in Libra finds truth in the world through learning to be whole and complete by embracing the qualities sought in a partner.

♃ **in Pisces**   Pisces is a compassionate sign of imagination and faith. Jupiter co-rules Pisces, and is at home in this sign. ✦ **1.** Jupiter in Pisces is expressed in emotional depth. You are very compassionate, with an emotional and intuitive understanding of others. You are interested in everyone having equality, but you will sacrifice for the group if necessary. It's important to you that others do well. You're imaginative, creative, and altruistic. In general, you want everyone to live in peace and harmony. **2.** Jupiter ℞ in Pisces finds truth in the world by seeing how all people are connected.

♃ **in Sagittarius**   Sagittarius is a philosophical and independent sign. Jupiter rules Sagittarius, and is at home in this sign. ✦ **1.** Jupiter in Sagittarius makes you outgoing, optimistic, gregarious, and very lucky in general. Things tend to turn out well for you; you rebound well from all situations. You can fall into a mud puddle and come out looking beautiful. You have strong faith in your chosen belief system as well as a very positive outlook, and you will find growth and opportunity through your beliefs and through travel and education. You have a strong spiritual sense and know that there's a higher power helping you get where you need to go. You're good at helping others lift themselves up, and will always help others in times of difficulty. **2.** Jupiter ℞ in Sagittarius finds truth in the world by listening to the stories of foreigners and travelers and imagining living their lives.

♃ **in Scorpio**   Scorpio is an intense sign of transformation. ✦ **1.** If you have Jupiter in Scorpio, you are very intense and resourceful. You may also have strong psychic and intuitive powers, and will find growth and opportunity through them. You're good with others' resources and with money matters in general, and you take them seriously. You are emotionally attached to your world and want to self-improve as well as to help others self-improve. You put emphasis on transformation in your life. If there's a problem, you know you can grow and transcend it. You don't have to be stuck in any situation, and can rise anew like a phoenix from a crisis. **2.** Jupiter ℞ in Scorpio finds truth in the world by connecting to the dark side for the purposes of bringing what's repressed into the light.

♃ **in Taurus**   Taurus is a grounded and dependable earth sign. ✦ **1.** Your Jupiter in Taurus will bring you opportunity and growth through developing income and managing money. You're a good money manager and will grow through money, which comes easily to you. You're also lucky finding work, even when others aren't; a bad economy isn't a problem for you, because you are resourceful and believe things will turn out fine. You're fortunate in the material world, and like beautiful things; you might be an art collector. **2.** Jupiter R in Taurus finds truth in the world by appreciating that which has lasting beauty and value.

♃ in Virgo   Virgo is practical and analytical. ⚝ **1.** Jupiter in Virgo is very public-service oriented. You want to serve your community in some way (maybe as a doctor or teacher) and will find great growth opportunity and good fortune through such service. You will get recognition and be fulfilled through service. You want others to be healed and resolve their problems, and are serious about helping others heal. You are strong and have great perseverance. **2.** Jupiter R in Virgo finds truth in the world through constant analysis of every-day experience for what feels expansive and therefore true compared to what feels deflating, which they judge to be the false path. See also *Jupiter, Jupiter in the houses, signs.* ◯ ☉

Jupiter/Mars   When Jupiter and Mars create an aspect, Jupiter increases Mars's power—Mars is aggressive and persistent. ⚝ Aspects between Jupiter and Mars in your birth chart could start out fine and later change into extreme behavior. This might cause overindulgence, overreaction, or overly aggressive behavior. Jupiter/Mars aspects will bring you great passion and enthusiasm, but an escalation of these will lead to negative behaviors. See also *aspects between planets, Jupiter, Mars.* △ ☯ ◯

Jupiter/Mercury   Jupiter's positive energy and good luck increase Mercury's enthusiasm for communication. ⚝ Mercury's power to understand and communicate is enhanced by Jupiter when these planets are in aspect in your chart. Jupiter gives Mercury enthu-siastic wit and heightens your communication skills, enabling you to inspire others and make them think. You are a gifted writer and speaker, and a great cheerleader, inspiring others to new heights. See also *aspects between planets, Jupiter, Mercury.* △ ☯ ☯ ◯

Jupiter/Moon   The Moon represents emotional needs and connec-tion, and Jupiter in aspect with the Moon has enhanced nurturing qualities. ⚝ Benefic Jupiter/Moon aspects create good parents and caretakers. Your Jupiter/Moon connection lets you help others to be their best. The best aspects between these planets will bring you fertility, productivity, and prosperity. Negatively, Jupiter/Moon aspects can lead you to be overly sensitive or slow to move. You have a strong creative drive, and are generally content and optimistic. You are a great emotional support for your friends and family. See also *aspects between planets, Jupiter, Moon.* △ ☯ ○

Jupiter/Neptune When these two outer planets connect, major cycles and trends result. ✧ Aspects between Jupiter and Neptune in your chart can affect your spiritual beliefs, but these planets also relate to a major cycle in the world, and these aspects are felt across the globe. When Jupiter touches Neptune, it's an indication that you are a truth seeker. You want to reach a higher level of consciousness and evolve into a new way of thinking. Your religious and spiritual thinking has to do with your community. Groups you belong to will evolve over the period of this cycle. See also *aspects between planets, Jupiter, Neptune.* △ ☯ ○

Jupiter/North Node Jupiter is expansion, and the North Node relates to areas that need to be developed or learned. ✧ **1.** The North Node in aspect with Jupiter indicates how easily you are able to align with your soul's greatest path for growth. **2.** Aspects between Jupiter and the North Node in your birth chart indicate that you're learning to move beyond your comfort zone from what you've always done and to explore new philosophies, religions, cultures, and lands. See also *aspects between planets, Jupiter, North Node.* △ ☯ ○

Jupiter/Pluto These two outer planets also represent transformational societal change. Society will change, and because of Jupiter, the outcome will be beneficial. Before the transformation is complete, there may be extreme behavior or negative behavior. ✧ Jupiter and Pluto aspects in your chart are all about positive transformation, but the path to transformation can be arduous. Even when everyone wants the same thing, it may take a crisis to induce change—change is difficult! Pluto creates change—insists upon it—and Jupiter makes sure the change is beneficial. But Pluto will make you look at challenging things in your life that you might prefer to avoid. The planets have a lengthy cycle, and create a long and gradual period of change. See also *aspects between planets, Jupiter, Pluto.* △ ☯ ○

Jupiter retrograde, personal   **1.** Jupiter is retrograde in a natal chart, creating a personal effect in the native's chart. **2.** Jupiter's orbit around the Sun takes 12 years, and it's retrograde for 120 days during that time. Those born during one of those 120-day periods have Jupiter ℞ in the birth chart. **3.** Retrograde planets travel in a clockwise motion around the wheel of the zodiac, rather than in the typical direct motion. Personal retrogrades have varying influence depending on the activity of other planets in the birth chart.

✧ **1.** Jupiter ℞ in your chart expresses itself in a more passive way than Jupiter in direct motion. Instead of running and jumping into the pool, it dips a toe in first. Jupiter is naturally outgoing, generous, adventurous, jubilant, and over the top, but when it's retrograde, those qualities are tempered. Personal Jupiter ℞ makes you turn inward in your search for truth, adventure, and expansion. See also *Jupiter; Jupiter retrograde, transiting; retrograde planets.* ◯ ℞

Look to the astrological sign of your personal Jupiter retrograde for advice on the best course of action:

- ♃ ℞ **in Aries:** People are shocked by how strong you are—they didn't know you worked out. Your humor tends toward self-deprecation until you let your inner warrior stand up for yourself.

- ♃ ℞ **in Taurus:** You have quite the gift for knowing what things are worth or discerning the authentic from a clever reproduction, so you can be less cautious about making those big purchases.

- ♃ ℞ **in Gemini:** You are so funny and have a killer wit, but you hold back until you are sure your audience gets you. Everyone says foolish things, so you might as well put yourself out there.

- ♃ ℞ **in Cancer:** You crave nurturing, but don't want to ask for it, so it feels like no one cares. There is probably support all around you, even if it's not coming from whom you want it from. You'd be happier letting yourself receive love in whatever form it's offered, as long as the source is pure.

- ♃ ℞ **in Leo:** Your friends envy the way you can look at something in a store window and go home and make it. You need to hire someone to promote you, because you won't do it yourself.

- ♃ ℞ **in Virgo:** Everyone thinks you're so laid back … if only they knew that your mind never stops. Take time every day to expand with some deep breathing and accept your idiosyncrasies as part of what makes you interesting.

- ♃ ℞ **in Libra:** You're always thinking about being in a relationship, but you have a hard time getting started. Try enjoying your own company, and you'll naturally attract who you want.

- ♃ ℞ **in Scorpio:** You find the meaning of life by going deeply into your own emotions and fears. You'd make an excellent shaman.

- ♃ ℞ **in Sagittarius:** All kinds of religions and philosophies call to you. You love applying them to your life to see how they hold up.

- ♃ ℞ **in Capricorn:** You're unaware how much positive impact you've had on everyone in your life.

- ♃ ℞ **in Aquarius:** Though you have a huge circle of friends and acquaintances, you prefer having intellectual discussions or hiking favorite trails with just a few people.

- ♃ ℞ **in Pisces:** You have so much artistic and musical talent, yet you're happiest exploring your painting, performing, or dancing potential at home in your living room.

J

Jupiter retrograde, transiting **1.** Jupiter's transiting retrograde lasts 120 days, or about four months. **2.** Finding ways to channel Jupiter's expansive energy can seem difficult during retrograde periods.

✦ **1.** Sometimes the only thing that seems expansive during Jupiter ℞ is the colossal degree to which everything in your life and in the world around you can seem to spiral out of control. Whether direct or retrograde, Jupiter thinks big. A lot of people begin diets when Jupiter goes retrograde. Other people use the corrective potential of retrograde energy to tap into Jupiter luck by buying lottery tickets, but its luck tends to play out on people, horses, and situations that repeat, so it's best to play the same lottery numbers you've played before. Playing the lottery is a relatively protected Jupiter ℞ experience compared to, say, playing poker, where you could just as easily lose it all to Jupiter as win it big and redeem your cash flow. But you get the message: with Jupiter ℞ you need to calculate the upsides and downsides of potential risks with extra care before you take them. A smart risk is one that comes back to you in an improved scenario, such as a house that you missed out on that has relisted during Jupiter ℞. **2.** When Jupiter is retrograde, it's a good time to travel to the place in the world where you feel most relaxed—a place you've been to before, in the same way that Jupiter is traveling backward to a place where it has been before. Retrogrades, in general, are good for returning to matters put on hold, delayed, or ignored. So not only is returning to a favorite foreign destination a wonderful use of Jupiter ℞ energy, but so is returning to a sport, a philosophy, college, or religious practice. It is also ideal for re-examining what you believe and why you believe it, reprinting an already-published book, realigning your posture, or reconnecting with a teacher, guru, father figure, coach, or even your own higher self. Jupiter rules advertising, so a retrograde is an excellent time to reassess your marketing plan. See also *Jupiter; Jupiter retrograde, personal; retrograde planets.* ◯ ℞

If transiting Jupiter retrograde throws a lot of obstacles your way, look to the astrological sign to throw some light on the situation:

- **In Aries:** Go back to the beginning and consider a more generous or expansive approach.
- **In Taurus:** Is there something you're not saying that really needs to be said? Look for undiagnosed thyroid problems as a possible cause of weight gain.
- **In Gemini:** Think about the decisions and choices you made when Jupiter first went retrograde.
- **In Cancer:** Examine supersized feelings and whether they fit with what's happening.
- **In Leo:** Whose heart needs to be bigger?
- **In Virgo:** What do you hold sacred, and why?
- **In Libra:** What's dangerously out of balance?
- **In Scorpio:** Where's the passion?
- **In Sagittarius:** Are you holding back from taking that grand adventure?
- **In Capricorn:** Post your pros and cons flow chart on your blog.
- **In Aquarius:** Take a brisk walk to get ideas circulating.
- **In Pisces:** Look for a big answer in the most unexpected of places in your heart.

Jupiter return   1. Point at which Jupiter returns to the position it held in the native's birth chart. **2.** Jupiter is in each sign for about 1 year, and has a total orbit time of 12 years. It takes 12 years for Jupiter to return to an exact place in its orbit. ✧ **1.** Because Jupiter returns in your chart approximately every 12 years, you'll be 12 when you have your first Jupiter return, 24 for your second, 36 for your third, and so on. **2.** A Jupiter return is about opportunities to grow, learn, develop, and explore. **3.** Our first Jupiter return at age 12 typically ushers in puberty, a mentor or an important teacher, an interest in other cultures, a desire to travel, and issues of popularity, depending upon our natal Jupiter's situation. **4.** Consider what your natal Jupiter needs to feel fully expressed and make plans to better meet those needs for each Jupiter return. For instance, if you were born with Jupiter in Virgo in your fifth house, then you should find ways to travel as part of your work and plan working vacations for ages 24, 36, 48, 60, 72, and even 84. Virgo rules work and the fifth house rules vacations. See also *Jupiter, planetary returns.* **BC** ◯ **Z**

Jupiter/Saturn   Jupiter brings opportunity and good fortune, while Saturn teaches challenges. Jupiter brings expansion to Saturn's structure. ✴ **1.** Together, Jupiter and Saturn create an opportunity for you: if you learn your lessons, you'll get the benefit of Jupiter. If you are willing to do the work you need to do, really working out the challenges Saturn presents in your charts, Jupiter will reward you. Saturn may be karmic debt you have to repay. You can think of it as a tunnel you have to pass through. And Jupiter is the light at the end of the tunnel. Jupiter takes over after you make it through your Saturn challenge, providing karmic reward. Your life will be better, more prosperous, after your Saturn challenge, when Jupiter is involved. **2.** If you think of your life as a garden, Jupiter would fertilize like crazy to grow the biggest, most sprawling plants possible and Saturn would show up and prune everything back to create orderly paths. Both are needed, but their goals are very different. See also *aspects between planets, Jupiter, Saturn.* △ ☯ ◯

Jupiter/South Node   Jupiter is expansion and opportunity, and the South Node indicates areas of familiarity and comfort. The North Node in aspect to Jupiter indicates a need to explore religion or philosophy more deeply in search of truth, freedom, and happiness. ✴ Aspects between Jupiter and the South Node in your birth chart show a tendency to want to know about everything, but on a superficial level. See also *aspects between planets, Jupiter, South Node.* △ ☯ ◯

Jupiter/Sun   The Sun and Jupiter generally create very beneficial aspects. These two planets interact to mark a fortunate time in life, even if the aspect between them is square. ✴ The Sun is a positive planet, representing your soul or spirit. Jupiter is an outer planet, bringing you good fortune, opportunity, security, protection, and good karma. You'll have blessings and general good luck with Jupiter/Sun aspects. The best aspects between the Sun and Jupiter create a very positive connection, leading to a good home life with a solid marriage and family ties. These aspects are helpful for finding the right marriage partner or the right career. Jupiter/Sun aspects indicate that you've earned blessings for this life. See also *aspects between planets, Jupiter, Sun.* △ ☯ ○

Jupiter transits   **1.** Jupiter as it moves or transits through the signs of the zodiac. **2.** Jupiter's orbit around the Sun takes 12 years; it transits all 12 zodiac signs in this period. **3.** Jupiter's transits can be compared to the placement of Jupiter in a birth chart for predictive purposes. A transit shows the position of a planet at a given moment. **4.** Transiting Jupiter is a catalyst as it enters a new sign or a new house, and as it forms aspects with other transiting planets or planets in both birth and progressed charts. As a catalyst for growth and expansion, Jupiter is used by professional astrologers to predict promotions, appearance of mentors and teachers, long-distance trips, a turn for the better, a major shift in philosophy, publication, winning, and outcome of judgments. ✴ Need to know when to buy a new house or car, start college, or plan a sabbatical of travel? Transiting Jupiter can tell you. As transiting Jupiter moves through each house of your chart, it depicts how your life will unfold in that arena. See also *Jupiter, transiting planets, transits.* ○

> **What can Jupiter transits tell you?**
> - Jupiter transiting your **first house** shows a good time to go Bohemian.
> - Jupiter transiting your **second house** indicates positive outcomes at the bank.
> - Jupiter transiting your **third house** is a great time to write advertising copy or meet with a copywriter.
> - Jupiter transiting your **fourth house** is a great time for moving or moving furniture around or moving forward with expansion plans for your home.
> - Jupiter transiting your **fifth house** is an excellent time to see lots of live entertainment.

- Jupiter transiting your **sixth house** accelerates healing and brings wise health practitioners.
- Jupiter transiting your **seventh house** creates a window for marriage proposals.
- Jupiter transiting your **eighth house** promises great sex.
- Jupiter transiting your **ninth house** brings an invaluable mentor.
- Jupiter transiting your **tenth house** means a promotion at work.
- Jupiter transiting your **eleventh house** brings the best parties and fundraisers.
- Jupiter transiting your **twelfth house** makes meditation easy and yields amazing results.

Jupiter/Uranus   Both Jupiter and Uranus are outer planets. Jupiter is beneficial bringing opportunity and growth, while Uranus elicits radical or abrupt change. ✦ **1.** Uranus brings about unexpected change—maybe through a sudden crisis. Aspects between Jupiter and Uranus in your birth chart can result in extremes. You may experience an unexpected happy surprise (such as a sudden but desired pregnancy)—the unexpected part is Uranus, it's made positive by Jupiter. Perhaps what you thought you couldn't have shows up for you. **2.** The other, less positive side to the Uranus/Jupiter interaction might be a sudden accident or other crisis. Uranus creates the accident, and Jupiter causes some good to result from it. You might meet people who are helpful to you or realize the need for some change in your life. Though the action is unexpected and accidental (and out of your control), the outcome will be positive, thanks to Jupiter. See also *aspects between planets, Jupiter, Uranus.* △ ☯ ○

Jupiter/Venus   Venus rules love life, artistic endeavors, affection, art, beauty, and compassion. ✦ When Jupiter and Venus interact, the results are usually very positive. Jupiter brings encouragement and energy to Venus. Many great artists have some Jupiter/Venus aspect. You will likely have an excellent marriage and home life, as well as financial success and creative abilities. You'll experience heaven on earth with this interaction—it's that good! See also *aspects between planets, Jupiter, Venus.* △ ☯ ○

K

karma   1. The Eastern equivalent of the Western concept of fate. Karma rules what must be corrected in this life; dharma rules purpose and destiny. **2.** The twelfth house of the zodiac relates to karma. **3.** Karmic responsibility is the function of Saturn. **4.** The planetary aspects squares and quincunxes reflect areas of a person's life where karma may be owed and correction or adjustment is needed. **5.** In a birth chart, retrograde planets indicate karmic debt.

✦ **1.** What karmic debts do you have, or what do you need to work on in this lifetime to build up karmic rewards and evolve as a person? Look at your twelfth house, your Saturn placement, and any squares and quincunxes in your birth chart. **2.** If the planetary ruler of your twelfth house cusp, the planets in your twelfth house, or Saturn or Neptune has challenging aspects with other planets, this indicates that these other planets need lots of attention. You'll have to work to clear up past mistakes. **3.** You also have lots to work out—likely including some karmic debts—in any full houses in your birth chart. **4.** You don't have to be fearful of karmic debt you see in your birth chart; this energy can be a powerful force for good in your life as you learn and grow and stretch beyond old patterns to make your life better, and also the lives of those around you. Astrologers look for retrograde planets in your birth chart to reveal karmic obligation and opportunity. Retrograde planets will tell you what you need to review or redo in this lifetime—they pull you to learn or relearn a lesson. You're obligated to work in the area of your life represented by the retrograde planet and the house it's in. You owe it to yourself to complete a lesson in the house where a retrograde planet is located. Planets in direct motion indicate a lack of karmic debt, more free will and karmic reward, as well as the freedom for self-expression in that area of life without lots of lessons. See also *destiny, full house, quincunx, retrograde planets, Saturn, square, twelfth house.* △BC 🏠 ◯ ℞

karmic cross   See *grand cross.*

karmic debt   See *karma.*

karmic reward   See *karma.*

kundalini   See *chakras and astrology.*

last quarter Moon   **1.** Phase when the Moon is 90 to 45 degrees behind the Sun in a birth chart, and half of the Moon appears illuminated in the sky. **2.** Of the eight lunar phases, the last quarter Moon is the seventh phase, preceding the balsamic Moon; it marks the beginning of the final quarter of the Moon's cycle. **3.** In its clockwise orbit of the Earth, the Moon is moving toward Venus and the Sun in the last quarter (as opposed to the first quarter, when it moves away from the Sun and toward Mars).

✦ **1.** A last quarter Moon is part of the Moon's trip back to the side of the Earth where the Sun is, and therefore toward the planet Venus. The return part of the Moon's orbit is yin in nature. Under last quarter Moon you are wrapping stuff up that was initiated in the first half of the Moon's cycle from new Moon to full Moon, and how you accomplish this can be seen through the signs the Moon moves through. **2.** Venus, like Libra, rules response. You can think of the first half of the Moon's orbit as akin to the lower half of a natural horoscope that starts with zero degrees Aries. It's as though the Moon has started at the ascendant and reaches full Moon at zero degrees Libra. The rest of the cycle is like the upper half of a natural horoscope. And just as Aries starts the action, Libra starts the reaction, or response. Aries is cardinal and launches into something new. Libra is an air sign and will mark a period that is thoughtful about how to best bring matters into balance. The last quarter Moon is the response to the first quarter Moon; it's the final chance for you to follow through and restore balance prior to a period of rest. **3.** The last quarter has been divided in half so that it is actually an eighth of the orbit, followed by the final conclusive portion of the Moon's cycle, called the balsamic Moon.

So the last quarter Moon can be seen as a time for you to gather all your data from your period of action (the previous Moon phases) as you prepare to go within during the balsamic Moon. **4.** If you have a last quarter Moon in your birth chart, this will indicate areas of your life that require completion, or phases that will be nearing closure. **5.** The last quarter Moon cycle is a time of each month that is good for finishing things up, organizing, and completing projects; you are still in motion with a last quarter Moon, but slowing down now and generally preparing for the time of rest and introspection that begins with the balsamic Moon. See also *balsamic Moon, Moon, Moon phases*. ◯

latitude   **1.** Used to indicate distance north or south of the Earth's equator. **2.** Latitude and longitude (vertical distances on the Earth's surface) are measured in degrees, and are used to map a specific location. The equator is given a latitude of 0 degrees; latitude indicates degrees north or south of the equator. ✧ In astrology, your place of birth is ascertained and denoted on your birth chart by latitude and longitude. This is why knowing your place of birth is important to creating your birth chart. See also *birth chart, celestial equator, longitude*. **BC Z**

laya centers   **1.** The two natural states that exist when gas becomes liquid or vice versa, or when liquid becomes substance or vice versa. **2.** Saturn rules the conversion of solids into liquids into gases and the reverse process as well. **3.** In astrology, the chakras are locations where matter (the human body) is connected to gas (the soul). **4.** In astrology, the original seven planets, those visible to the naked eye, correspond to the seven chakras. See also *chakras and astrology*.

> **Laya centers activate chakra energy and correspond to planetary energy:**
> - First chakra, Saturn: Energy connects to source
> - Second chakra, Jupiter: Expansion of energy
> - Third chakra, Mars: Intention of energy
> - Fourth chakra, Venus: Refinement of energy
> - Fifth chakra, Mercury: Spoken intention
> - Sixth chakra, Moon: Processing of intention
> - Seventh chakra, Sun: Creation

✦ **1.** Leos enjoy each other's energy, and both like to be the center of attention. If they're both willing to share the spotlight, they'll bask in its glow together quite happily. They'll be very popular together and will have a wide circle of admiring friends. **2.** With their strength and stamina, Leos can get a lot done together. They also boost each other's egos, supporting each other's successes and advancements. They have to shine individually and equally, though. Problems occur when one Leo outshines the other or gets so caught up in personal ego and success that one partner is ignored or neglected. Egos will likely clash at some point with this pair, and when they do, it's rough. Leo is stubborn, remember? Neither partner will admit to being wrong or to needing more attention … or to needing anything, really. And neither partner wants to be the one in the background, holding the bags. **3.** Leo/Leo makes good neighbors, friends, business partners, co-workers, etc. as long as both partners are able to shine. Marriage and domestic partnership is a more difficult balance for Leo/Leo, but it could work, if both partners can keep their egos in check. See also *Leo.* ☽ ☼

Leo/Libra   1. This fire and air combination is very compatible—they bring out the best in each other. **2.** Extroverted, positive, outgoing, leader Leo finds balance with generous, adaptable Libra. ✦ **1.** Leo naturally strives for truth and Libra loves justice. Leo accentuates Libra's cardinal nature and together this pair fights the good fight and works to create a better world. **2.** Leo and Libra are both attracted to beauty. Both Leo and Libra are generous, masculine, and in love with love. **3.** Libra is the great equalizer in this pairing, boosting Leo's ego and balancing Leo's extremes. Libra knows how to soothe Leo in times of stress or difficulty. **4.** Leo and Libra make a great pair, especially when mutually involved in art, music, beauty, justice, and society. Libra doesn't mind Leo's need to make decisions—it may even be a relief. A Leo man thinks of himself as a leader and looks for his Libra woman to provide balance to the relationship. A Leo woman can be a spectacular diva who appreciates the tact and diplomacy of her Libra mate. As long as both are able to shine, this duo makes good neighbors, friends, and business partners, and it's also a compatible pairing for a student/teacher, employer/employee, and marriage or domestic partnership relationship. See also *Leo, Libra.* ☽ ☼

L

Leo/Pisces   **1.** In this mix of fire and water, Pisces tends to wash Leo out. **2.** In the best mix, Pisces helps Leo be more compassionate, and Leo energizes Pisces. ✦ **1.** These two get along when they share the same philosophy, religion, belief system, or background. If they are alike in these foundational ways, they will get along well as friends and be supportive of each other. Pisces loves to let Leo shine, and makes an encouraging audience and supporter of Leo. **2.** Pisces' compassionate nature can get in Leo's way: when Leo's fragile ego is bruised, Pisces needs to help. This simply irritates Leo, who can't be seen as weak, and won't accept nurturing, even if nurturing is what's needed. Leo's rejection and anger will leave Pisces with hurt feelings, and Leo won't likely be willing to smooth things over—they are too busy having their ego flattered by another admirer. **3.** Leo and Pisces can be good friends and co-workers, as well as business partners or a student/teacher pairing—when Leo is the teacher! There would have to be lots going on in the individual birth charts of a Leo/Pisces pair to support a long-term union such as marriage or domestic partnership, unless it's nontraditional. Leo and Pisces might need to live in separate spaces. See also *Leo, Pisces.* ☯ ☼

Leo rising   See *Leo ascendant.*

Leo/Sagittarius   **1.** These two fire signs understand each other's egos. **2.** Sagittarius is easygoing, and won't mind Leo's need for center stage—a big plus. ✦ **1.** Sagittarius is high-minded, and likes to travel and pursue idealistic goals. Leo will support Sagittarius's vision and put enthusiasm into it. Sagittarius tends to be social and spontaneous, with a good sense of humor. Sagittarius is very loving, but recognizes Leo's need for freedom without feeling threatened. **2.** Some Leos like to take credit for any accomplishments, and this can cause even laid-back Sagittarius to bristle. Leo needs to remember to acknowledge Sagittarius' talents and contributions with well-deserved compliments. Too much aggression from Leo can also frighten a more sensitive Sagittarius. It helps to think of Leo as a lion and Sagittarius as a horse. Both are powerful, but the horse will run if the lion flexes its claws. Leo can also be very insistent that cats are the pet of choice, denying Sagittarius the menagerie it longs for. **3.** Leo and Sagittarius really make one of the most compatible partnerships in the zodiac. They are great as neighbors, friends, and business partners, as well as a supportive student/teacher, employer/

employee, or parent/child relationship—especially when Sagittarius is the mentor, business manager, or parent and Leo is the student, budding talent, or child. They also make good marriage or domestic partners. See also *Leo, Sagittarius.* ☯ ☼

Leo/Scorpio   1. This fire sign and water sign combine to make firewater—highly combustible, and a little crazy-making. **2.** There's a lot of intensity when Leo and Scorpio come together. ✶ **1.** Leo and Scorpio both want control over their own lives and each plan to do big things. Each might admire the other's drive, independence, and passion for life, but up close, this relationship is challenging. **2.** If there's not a lot of generosity between Leo and Scorpio, the relationship can devolve into a fight over who's the boss. Neither will be willing to compromise. There's no give and take between these two, so a minor altercation could lead to a major rift. **3.** Leo and Scorpio can work as friends, neighbors, or co-workers. Put them under one roof, though, and all bets are off. It's very hard to mix them together, and with too much togetherness, they'll make each other crazy. Marriage or domestic partnerships between Leo and Scorpio are iffy, but a comparison of birth charts could lead to a compatible pairing. See also *Leo, Scorpio.* ☯ ☼

Leo/Taurus   1. Leo and Taurus combine fire and earth. **2.** When meshed, Leo and Taurus can help each other build up resources. ✶ **1.** Taurus is practical, realistic, loving, down to earth, and devoted. Leo is loyal, responsible, devoted, and steadfast. Both love art and music, and appreciate and desire beauty and richness in their lives and at home. Sounds like they have a lot in common, right? They do. In some ways, they're too much alike. **2.** Leo and Taurus can both be very stubborn and determined (both are fixed signs), so if they have a disagreement, there may be no room for compromise or reconciliation. If these two are at odds, even over something that seems unimportant, it can become a lifelong struggle. If they value the same things, they'll get along better. **3.** This pair makes good friends, neighbors, and co-workers. If they work too closely—in business or other relationships—they may face an unbroachable division. As for marriage or domestic partnership, it's not the best mix. Some Taureans will mesh better with Leo, though, so it's best to look at the compatibility of the individual birth charts before writing this pair off. See also *Leo, Taurus.* ☯ ☼

L

Leo/Virgo 1. The Leo/Virgo fire and earth combination are neighbors in the zodiac. **2.** Leo and Virgo see eye to eye, and there's no conflict this pairing won't be willing to work on and resolve. ✦ **1.** These two do well together working side by side on a common goal. Leo dreams up the big ideas and Virgo organizes the resources, staff, and details to make the dreams a reality. Virgo, terrific with details but also very smart, can get bored when things get too monotonous. Leo, however, is rarely boring. Virgo has a wry sense of humor and loves to sit back and enjoy the show that is Leo's life. Leo can create a lot of drama and needs Virgo's calm, cool ways to smooth over any feathers that Leo has ruffled in others. **2.** Problems can arise if Virgo is stingy with gifts, affection, and admiration or if Leo embarrasses Virgo in public (remember that Leo pride!). Unlike amorous Leo, Virgo is not usually keen on PDAs and may pull away from the unwanted attention, which, of course, Leo revels in. **3.** The Leo/Virgo parent-child relationship works best when Leo is the child; otherwise more mature Virgo (even as a child) has to parent the Leo parent. The Virgo parent should be light-handed with the rules: Leo can't abide by Virgo's narrow standards of perfection around grades, sports, and social behavior. **4.** Leo and Virgo can make good friends, neighbors, co-workers, business partners, and are compatible in a teacher/student, parent/child, employer/employee relationship, as well as marriage or domestic partnership, if each works to understand what the other needs. See also *Leo, Virgo*. ☯ ☼

Libra 1. The seventh sign of the zodiac. **2.** Those born between September 22 and October 23 have Libra as their Sun sign. Libra is a masculine, or yang, cardinal air sign. The ruling planet for Libra is Venus, named for the Roman goddess of love, beauty, and fertility. Venus is all about harmony, balance, and beauty, all of which are integral to Libra. **3.** The glyph for Libra is the scales ♎, which is also Libra's symbol. **4.** Libra is the natural ruler of the seventh house of partnerships and negotiations. Cooperation is a keyword for understanding Libra. **5.** Other associations for Libra are the colors pastel blue and lavender and the gemstone opal.

✦ **1.** The body parts associated with Libra are the skin, veins, kidneys, and lower back. You may have lovely skin, but it's likely sensitive, too. When you're frustrated, angry, or stressed out, it will show up on your face through redness, dryness, or breakouts. What should you do about this? Well, if you can't eliminate stress, try to find an outlet for it. Physical exercise might work, or you could try journaling. Try not to keep your feelings bottled up—or they'll come bursting out. Stay hydrated (good for your kidneys, as well as your skin). And watch out for lower back strain. When planning your diet and exercise routine, just think *balance*. Nothing should be off-limits, but you'll feel it when your body has too much or too little of something. **2.** Is Libra your Sun sign? Libra is a charming diplomat. You are a generous, adaptable, good listener with a strong sense of justice and fairness. Libra is balanced, cordial, and hospitable, and has a kind demeanor and a positive public image. You're a social animal, and you want everyone to get along. Libra likes to negotiate, and really listens. If you're a Libra, you want to understand others, and really get where they're coming from. And you're not just intellectual: Libra is ruled by Venus and so makes you very heart-centered. It's essential that you connect and cooperate with others and that you help others connect and cooperate. Libra is interested in synergies in all that they do. **3.** Libra likes to share. Part of your cooperative nature is that you don't really want to work alone, and you also don't want to celebrate success alone. You want to share what is created, and you also like a consensus. You enjoy working as part of a team, working together to reach a fair and balanced conclusion or position. **4.** As a cardinal air sign, Libra is all about leadership through intellect, as exhibited by fairness, strategy, tact, diplomacy, and the creation of a strong team on which each plays to his or her strength. **5.** What subjects and careers might appeal to Libra? You're a great listener, and would make a good counselor, mediator, or teacher. You also have good leadership skills, but you usually prefer being a *partner*. Your love of beauty may take you to a career in design or the arts. As an air sign, you have an ease with words that makes you well-suited to writing and speaking. Your charm will work to your advantage in sales and diplomacy. **6.** *Watch out for:* your desire to be fair might make you indecisive. You could make an endless list of reasons why one person or another should have that last piece of cake. (Fairness is always important!) Harmony is so essential to you that you might stifle your own feelings to keep the peace. (You may have to work hard to say no.) You are also at risk of losing sight of who you are: you adapt yourself to fit in with

L

different people and groups. As a result, no one (including you) might know the real you. **7. *I'm not a Libra, but my best friend is:*** your Libra best friend is a generous charmer. Libra's also a great listener who is willing to put in the effort to keep your partnership harmonious. Because fairness is important to Libra, your Libra friend can help resolve conflicts you have with others. Be careful not to take your Libra friend's generosity for granted. Libra will be willing to work very hard to win your approval, but will also seek justice and balance in every relationship or situation. See also *Libra ascendant, Libra descendant.* ☼

Libra/Aquarius   See *Aquarius/Libra.*

Libra/Aries   See *Aries/Libra.*

Libra ascendant   Also called Libra rising. The rising sign is Libra, so Libra is the sign on the cusp of the first house in the birth chart and the sign on the eastern horizon at the moment of birth. ✦ **1.** Libra rising presents a Libra image to the world. To others, you appear like Libra. **2.** Libra ascendant has to master Libra qualities in this lifetime. These include learning to cooperate, freedom from discrimination, and working to maintain balance in your life. You need to see that there is balance in life, and learn to recognize the consequences of imbalance in your own life. Libra rising also needs to learn how to adapt and achieve balance without losing their sense of self in the process. Adaptation is a desire for Libra rising, as is fairness, justice, integrity, and cordiality. Strive for balance in yourself and in your relationships with others. **3.** You tend to be very attractive and charismatic. You also have positive energy, and people like you. You're a romantic. Partnerships are your forte and you are usually thinking about your partner, even when you're alone. Marriage seems like a natural state to you, and you may wonder why it is so e'   —until you learn to look for someone more similar to yourself. ...ers see you as partner-oriented, but may also see you as dependent and overly accommodating until they know you better. You have a graceful gait and seem to float across the room. You are at your best in social situations, and are often responsible for setting trends in your social circle. See also *ascendant, Libra, Libra descendant.* **BC** ☼

Libra/Cancer   See *Cancer/Libra.*

Libra/Capricorn   See *Capricorn/Libra.*

Libra descendant   1. The descending sign is Libra; Libra is the sign on the cusp of the seventh house in the birth chart. **2.** The seventh house is the house of partnerships and marriage or significant others, as well as the third sibling, second child, roommate, strangers, and difficult people.

✦ **1.** When your descending sign is Libra, you relate to others in all partnerships (romantic, business, or other) through Libra. You might be any of the twelve Sun signs, but you act like Libra in partnerships when you have this descendant. If you take a look at how Libra behaves with others in partnership, you'll see how you will experience collaboration and sharing. You tend to be protective of your partner and concerned that duties and money be fairly distributed. You think about your partner, but prefer to take care of tasks at hand rather than calling your partner throughout the day. You may be a little aloof and prefer to maintain control of your relationships through your talents of persuasion, tact, and charm. **2.** As a Libra descendent, you are here to work on cooperation and commitment, and will need to find a significant relationship or partnership that grounds you and forces you to work on these issues. You're fair and honorable, and you will behave this way in partnerships. Relationships will be much easier for you if you give up your pride about being independent and admit to needing someone. Part of the joy of loving others is enhancing their life and taking care of them. Your fierce independence can be a challenge for your partner, who struggles to show you love and find new ways to care for you. You'll be happier if you share your deepest feelings and explain what you need and enjoy. **3.** Your descendant also indicates what you will look for, need, or attract in partners. Libra descendant needs someone fair, honest, and just. You'll attract people who make you focus on cooperation and one-on-one commitment. Your Libra descending makes you want freedom, but those you connect with will want you to learn cooperation, and not to have everything your way. Stand up for yourself, but try to let go of your need to be right all the time. People are seldom admired and loved because they are always right.

L

You compromise easily, but you may be testing your partner's sense of fairness as well as their concern for your needs. **4.** Your descendant also rules your relationship with your third sibling and second child. These individuals appreciate your loyalty, integrity, and take-charge personality, but they really appreciate your undivided attention and compassion. See also *Libra, Libra ascendant, descendant.* **BC** ☼

Libra/Gemini   See *Gemini/Libra.*

Libra/Leo   See *Leo/Libra.*

Libra/Libra   **1.** These two air signs are a friendly and cooperative pair. **2.** Together, Libras will talk about important ideas and work on substantial projects. Same sign pairings reveal karmic duty, and this pair may well be exploring the boundaries of integrity in partnerships, and the joy of synergy with each other … creating more together than could be imagined separately.

✦ **1.** Libras believe in fairness, honesty, and integrity. They are attracted to each other and share an appreciation for beautiful things. Libra is an air sign, and generally two air signs get along well, but lack an emotional connection. Venus's presence as Libra's planetary ruler brings depth to Libra's emotional nature. **2.** The Libra need for harmony may cause problems in this partnership. It is possible to be *too* flexible, and a Libra/Libra pairing demonstrates this. When each would prefer to defer to the other rather than express an opinion that could cause a disagreement, well, they're stuck. They'll avoid disagreements at any cost, and are willing to avoid their feelings if they fear the repercussions of expressing them. This can lead either partner (or both) to mislead the other about their true feelings or desires. Not the best foundation for any partnership. If they can find the space and security to be honest, they will learn that they can work through disagreements, and become more balanced and harmonious in their partnership—their goal all along! **3.** Two Libras make good friends, neighbors, co-workers, and business partners, and are an especially good parent/child combination. If this duo has other planets in fire signs, there will be enough passion to make this double Libra combination a good bet for love and marriage or domestic partnership, as well. See also *Libra.* ☯ ☼

Libra/Pisces   1. Air and water: fizzy or flat? Libra and Pisces have the potential to fizz to a froth of ideas and creative energy or fall flat from inertia or indifference. **2.** Libra and Pisces are both gentle signs. Libra gets Pisces's humanitarianism, and Pisces gets Libra's desire for peace and equality. ✦ **1.** Of the water signs, Pisces is Libra's best match. These two can work well together artistically and creatively, with projects in art, music, publishing, or design. **2.** Libra and Pisces need to share the same beliefs and have similar emotional attachments to be truly compatible. Also, if both signs are very passive, there won't be enough energy and aggression to get anything done. **3.** Libra and Pisces make can make great friends, neighbors, and co-workers. Libra may have too many rules for Pisces to want to jump in as a business partner, though. Libra needs rules to keep everything fair, but Pisces sees the rules as suffocating to the creative spirit of the partnership. (Like the fish that represent the sign, Pisces likes to swim without boundaries.) If both partners in a marriage or domestic partnership are artists (or artist/teacher), they'll do well together for the long term. See also *Libra, Pisces.* ☯ ☼

Libra rising   See *Libra ascendant.*

Libra/Sagittarius   1. Air and fire: Libra feeds the Sagittarius fire. **2.** These two are good for each other. Libra provides balance and structure for Sagittarius's bold enterprising will and desire for new experiences. ✦ **1.** Libra balances Sagittarius's fire and independence. Sagittarius is an idealistic visionary, and Libra agrees with and supports Sagittarius in their altruism and high-minded goals. These two generally make a complementary pair. They have a mutual understanding, and get along well intellectually. **2.** Libra tends to be submissive to Sagittarius, and they both are inclined toward procrastination through indecision. Sometimes things just don't get done—this can mean taking out the garbage, paying the bills, completing a class assignment, or keeping a scheduled appointment. Things might fall apart around them, unless one half of this pair is willing to take responsibility. Sagittarius also loves a little risk in life; Libra does not. This is one of those differences that might not show up until after the honeymoon. If life commitment is a possibility, both signs need to know how to deal with this issue or Sagittarius will feel trapped and Libra will be resentful about having to say no to Sagittarius's plans all the time. **3.** Libra and Sagittarius generally make very supportive friends and family members. They are good co-workers and neighbors. As long as procrastination is not a problem, they work well as business partners. They'll need to take care of any issues around Sagittarius's risk-taking for marriage or domestic partnership to work. See also *Libra, Sagittarius.* ☯ ☼

Libra/Scorpio   1. Earth and water combine in these neighboring signs. **2.** This pair of Libra and Scorpio will likely have to weather some ups and downs. Scorpio's intensity can be intimidating to analytical Libra. ✦ **1.** Libra can adapt to Scorpio's intensity, passion, and drive—which is no small feat. **2.** Libra gets hurt feelings because of their need for fairness and honesty; Scorpio could act unfairly in times of emotional intensity causing Libra to feel manipulated in a way that is uncomfortable for them. (Libra is not so accustomed to emotional manipulations or situations where decisions are grounded on feelings and instincts.) Libra will try to help Scorpio maintain a balance—this might not be Scorpio's desire, however. Scorpio's need for a strong emotional connection might fall flat with Libra. **3.** Libra and Scorpio are neighboring signs that make good neighbors and friends. This is a favorable pairing for an employer/ employee, teacher/student, or co-worker relationship. It's not generally the best for marriage or domestic partnership, but, given complementary planetary relationships, it could certainly work. See also *Libra, Scorpio.* ☯ ☼

Libra/Taurus   1. Air and earth signs combine in this pair; Libra is impulsive and intellectual, and Taurus is decidedly grounded, a solid engineering personality. **2.** Libra and Taurus both have Venus as their planetary ruler. ✦ **1.** Their Venus connection means that both Libra and Taurus appreciate and enjoy art, beauty, and travel. Libra energizes Taurus and helps get them moving, while Taurus gives Libra's perspective a firm foundation. **2.** There will be difficulty in this partnership if Taurus gets stuck (in the past or in a past routine). Taurus likes familiar territory, even if it's not the best for them; for Libra, balance and harmony is most important, and they will adapt to achieve it. Taurus is a fixed sign, with an inflexible desire for order, control, security, and routine or discipline. (Once the foundation is set, Taurus will build according to the plan and will be uncomfortable making changes to the blueprint.) Libra is happiest with harmony, but is more spontaneous and flexible than

Taurus. Taurus's need for routine is frustrating for Libra. **3.** Libra/
Taurus is a great combination for a parent/child, employer/employee,
or teacher/student relationship. Libra and Taurus also make good
friends, neighbors, and business partners. Because of the differences
between them, cohabitating might take some hard work, making this
a more challenging marriage or domestic partnership. See also *Libra,
Taurus.* ☯ ☼

Libra/Virgo   1. Air and earth: there's generally a lot of distance
between these two. **2.** Libra and Virgo like to take care of each
other, and both appreciate the sacred beauty of rituals and patterns
in their lives. ✶ **1.** Virgo has a strong sense of order and fairness,
which resonates with Libra. Mercury, which is Venus's neighbor in
the sky, rules Virgo, making Virgo an earth sign that's just quick
enough to keep up with Libra. Virgo is a mutable earth sign, which
means Virgo is flexible, and willing to adapt to make a relationship
work. **2.** These two provide each other with objectivity, and counsel
each other well. Libra and Virgo make a good team on work or
school projects, and for the long-term, both signs like to talk out,
debate, and resolve any problems or issues between them. Libra,
the social butterfly, needs to get out and meet new people. Virgo,
the hermit, usually hates social networking (but paradoxically loves
connections to people). Each sees the other as overly concerned
about what others think, and not being aware of how they project
their own issues on others. Virgo doesn't appreciate Libra's tact and
diplomacy; instead, Virgo hears Libra's words as manipulative. Libra
thinks Virgo's humility is a guise to appear more perfect.**3.** Libra
and Virgo make good friends and neighbors, and are also compatible
business partners, and form a solid parent/child relationship. These
signs don't often join together in marriage or domestic partnership
because their needs are so different. See also *Libra, Virgo.* ☯ ☼

Lilith   One of the newly discovered asteroids that rule goddess
energy and attributes. Lilith rules nighttime, as that is when a
woman tends to contemplate her dilemmas and make her most
difficult decisions. Lilith was Adam's first wife prior to Eve. Lilith
refused to be defined by the role of wife, choosing independence
over tradition and approval by society. ✶ Where is Lilith in your
chart? As you interpret her expression through the sign you find
her in and in what area of your life according to the house she is in,

L

you discover how you can deal with your own resentment, rage, and repression so that you can be a whole person who engages in the kind of relationships that are most suitable and true to your own spirit. This quest for freedom of expression applies equally for both genders: Lilith represents breaking free from stereotypical roles (choosing happiness over the anger and frustration of our shadow selves). See also *asteroids, black Moon.*

longitude   1. Used to indicate distance east or west of the Earth's meridian. **2.** Longitude and latitude (horizontal distances north and south of the equator) are measured in degrees, and are used to map a specific location. The prime meridian in Greenwich, England, is given a longitude of 0 degrees; longitude, then, indicates degrees east or west of the prime meridian. **3.** In astrology, birth location is ascertained by longitude and latitude. This is why it is important to know the place of birth in casting an astrological birth chart. See also *birth chart, celestial equator, latitude.* **BC**

love   1. In astrology, love relationships of all kinds are found in the fifth house of the birth chart. This includes first crushes and love experienced as a child, love for one's children, love for a best friend, and budding love without commitment. Many astrologers take this one step further and designate the fifth house for love relationships, including sexual relationships, where both partners live in separate domiciles without any kind of legal bond, such as marriage, business partnership, or co-ownership of property (without sharing children). Once romantic partners live together, conceive a baby, or marry, the relationship shifts from a fifth-house relationship to a seventh-house relationship. This explains why so many relationships fall apart once the couple marries: they might have harmonious fifth houses and problematic seventh houses. **2.** Marriage and domestic partnership— romantic love—is found in the seventh house. **3.** Eros, the god of innocent love, erotic love, and creativity, was one of the primordial gods born at the same time that Gaia (Earth) was born. He is often depicted as a beautiful young man or as a youth riding a lion. He is associated with the Sun, the Sun sign Leo, and the fifth house. **4.** Venus is the Roman goddess of love; the planet Venus represents how humans receive love through its placement in an astrological birth chart.

✴ Venus rules what we attract and what we are attracted to. This planet represents love, joy, happiness, inner contentment, and beauty. Venus is feminine, the Earth in its fullest of bloom. By looking for Venus in your chart, you'll see where you are encouraged or challenged in love, and which relationships are likely to grow beyond hook-ups to become committed partnerships. See also *fifth house, seventh house, Venus, Venus in the signs.* 🏠 ◯

lower hemisphere   See *hemisphere.*

luminaries   **1.** In astrology, a name used for the Sun and the Moon, which are now usually called planets. **2.** The Sun and Moon are two power points of the astrological birth chart, representing ego and will through the Sun (yang) and the emotional and nurturing sides of the self through the Moon (yin). Some astrologers see the Sun as the higher self and the Moon as the lower self. **3.** The luminaries illuminate the birth chart, or shed light on it, for the astrologer. Other planets connect to the Sun and Moon with aspects; these aspects show what's going on in the chart. In this way, the Sun and Moon light up or highlight areas of importance or significance for the individual whose chart is cast. **4.** The luminaries never go retrograde, and their action in the birth chart is always direct. ✴ Look to the Sun and the Moon in your chart for clues about what lights your way. See also *Moon, Sun.* △ **BC** ◯

lunar cycle   **1.** The 28½-day cycle of the Moon as it orbits the Earth. **2.** In one month the Moon cycles through each of its eight phases. The four major phases are new Moon, first quarter Moon, full Moon, and last quarter Moon. **3.** During the lunar cycle, the Moon transits through all twelve signs of the zodiac. **4.** The new Moon indicates a time for beginnings, while the culmination of the cycle represents fruition or completion. **5.** In astrology, the Moon rules the subconscious mind. Each phase of the Moon's orbit provides a clue as to how best to work with the subconscious. ✴ What part of the lunar cycle were you born in? The Moon's placement in your birth chart will tell you how your subconscious mind works. See also *Moon, Moon phases.* ◯

L

lunar return   **1.** Point at which the Moon returns to the position it held in the native's birth chart. **2.** The Moon's transit through the signs takes 27.3 days; every 27.3 days, the Moon returns to an exact place in its orbit. ✦ **1.** The Moon returns in your chart about every 27 days. **2.** Astrological software makes quick work of calculating each month's lunar return chart to the exact second. The lunar return itself starts a new cycle as depicted by its sign and house. **3.** It's always good to get good sleep the night before and the night of your lunar return as that is when the Moon likes to do its best processing of all your unconscious material. **4.** In looking at your lunar return chart, focus on the relationship between the ruler of the ascendant and the Sun to your Moon for the best insights as to what the month has in store for you. See also *Moon, planetary returns.* **BC** ◯

major aspects **1.** The most influential angles, or aspects, between planets in a birth chart. The birth chart is a circle (360 degrees); major aspects create the most influential relationships between planets in the birth chart. **2.** The five major aspects are conjunction ☌ (planets in the same degree or within 10 degrees), opposition ☍ (planets opposite each other, 180 degrees apart), sextile ⚹ (planets 60 degrees apart), square ☐ (planets 90 degrees apart), and trine △ (planets 120 degrees apart). ✸ **1.** It's likely that you have some major aspects between planets in your birth chart. These aspects indicate the way planets relate to each other and exert influence in your life; the planets in aspect may interact in ways that are beneficial (conjunction, sextile, trine) or challenging (square, opposition). **2.** Major aspects between planets in your chart will have a strong, unavoidable effect on your behavior and personality. When you know which planets are stressed or in harmony, you can choose the best ways to channel their energies. **3.** No matter the aspect, the possibility for positive growth is always present and available to you; look to aspects as clues to right action and avoid getting caught up in whether an aspect seems easy or hard, beneficial or challenging—*every* aspect in your birth chart presents a good opportunity, if used well. See also *angle, aspect grid, aspects between planets, birth chart, conjunction, glyphs, opposition, sextile, square, trine.* △ **BC** ○

malefic **1.** Challenging or difficult. **2.** Certain aspects are considered malefic in a birth chart. Major aspects that are challenging include opposition (180 degrees) and square (90 degrees). **3.** Minor aspects that are malefic include semi-square (45 degrees), sesqui-square (135 degrees), and quincunx (150 degrees). **4.** In astrology, certain planets are considered more challenging than others. Saturn is known as the greater malefic; Mars as the lesser malefic. Uranus can also have malefic effects. **5.** Malefic planets create challenges and obstacles in the birth chart, which are really just opportunities in disguise.

✦ **1.** What if you have malefic aspects or planets in your birth chart? *Malefic* is a scary word—it originates from the Latin word *maleficus*, meaning evil-doing, or wicked. Whoa! Don't worry— malefics aren't really working evil in your birth chart. They are likely creating some challenges for you, though. The purpose of a malefic aspect or planet is to create opportunities for you to grow and change—and sometimes you'll feel growing pains along the way! **2.** If you have malefic planets in their home signs or in their exalted signs, it is a lot easier for you to find ways to more positively express and experience their qualities. **3.** If you have malefics in their signs of detriment or fall, you might spend years wondering when your life will get easier—that is, until you learn all of the lessons of that planet. It's helpful to think of that planet as a person and figure out what this planet may want from you through the study of your birth chart. **4.** If you don't have any malefic aspects or planets in your charts, you're living on easy street, right? Wrong! As you know, everything in your birth chart works together to make you, *you*. Whether you'll face challenges isn't just dependent on malefic aspects and planets, but instead depends on all of the interactions in your birth chart. And even if you were born when all of the planets were in harmony, transiting planets can still make challenging aspects at various times throughout your life. Remember, you have free will, and only you can determine how heavenly energies will manifest in your life. See also *aspects between planets, beneficial, detriment, exalted, fall, home signs, Mars, opposition, Saturn, square, transiting planets, Uranus.* △ ☯ ○

March 21 to April 20   Birth dates for the Sun sign Aries. The position of the Sun during these dates correlates with an astrological Sun sign. Those born between March 21 and April 20 have Aries as their Sun sign. See also *Aries.* ☼

Mars   1. Planet known as the red planet because of its appearance; named for the Roman God of war. **2.** Mars is the fourth planet from the Sun. Its orbit around the Sun takes 687 days. **3.** Mars is the natural ruler of Aries (the Greek name for Mars is Ares) and the co-ruler of Scorpio, as well as the planetary ruler of the first house and co-ruler of the eighth house (with Pluto). **4.** In Roman mythology, Mars is the son of Jupiter and Juno, lover of Venus. A powerful god, Mars is second only to Jupiter. **5.** Mars is a personal or inner planet, associated with action, energy, and desire. The astrological symbol for Mars is ♂. **6.** Mars ℞ internalizes Mars's direct, aggressive energy. Mars in retrograde can lead to introspection and healing, when there is courage to examine and repair sources of conflict and anger. Mars ℞ can present a situation of "worse until it gets better" because it deals with intractable positions, and deeply held beliefs—the kinds of issues that can lead to war.

✦ **1.** Mars is a planet of *action*. The location of Mars in your birth chart can indicate physicality and aggression. What makes you angry, and how's your temper? Are you a go-getter or a wallflower? Mars in your birth chart will tell you about these areas of yourself, and its placement can mean the difference between a lover and a fighter. Your Mars can make you brash and bold, courageous and passionate. It will tell you where you are self-motivated, and can help you figure out what you want to do in life. **2.** Where is Mars in your birth chart? Mars is always about action, but the house and sign will tell you more about what your Mars means to *you*. Whatever your Mars placement, this area of your life will be one where you make things happen. **3.** Mars also relates to desire—and the kind of lover you are. Physical attraction—we're not necessarily talking love—is ruled by Mars. Mars can lend charisma and infectious energy, but can also signal stubbornness and a taste for conflict. Mars can be headstrong and zealous, for better or worse. **4.** In a daily astrological calendar, days and times when Mars is in a positive aspect to the Sun (such as conjunct, trine, or sextile) are usually good times for starting a new creative project or series of healing sessions. These periods are especially portentous for creative or healing ventures that involve sharp instruments, such as sculpting or acupuncture. An astrologer will look for these Mars times when a client needs to select a date for tattooing or piercing, or any kind of cosmetic surgery. Days when Mars is in a more challenging aspect to the Sun (such as opposition or square) can be times when extra caution is wise around surgery, expressing negative feelings with children, playing sports, pursuing a relationship with an unavailable or commitment-phobic person,

M

going on auditions, performing, making investments, and impulsive gambling. See also *Mars in the houses, Mars in the signs, Mars retrograde.* △ ◯ ℞

Mars in the houses   1. Mars brings action and energy to the areas of life relating to each of the houses. Things will happen where Mars is present. **2.** Mars's chart placement shows areas of action, aggression, and desire. ✦ **1.** Mars is action—the house Mars appears in will tell you about how you act in those areas of your life. **2.** Mars also has to do with passion and desire, and the house where Mars lives in your chart reflects the arenas in your life that hold the most attraction for you. Mars is all about what you do … as well as what you *want* to do.

♂ **in the first house   1.** Mars in the first house is all about the self and the personality. **2.** Mars is the natural planetary ruler of the first house, and is at home there. ✦ **1.** Mars is completely at home in the first house—if you have Mars in your first house, you're confident and self-motivated. You have a lot of energy and drive, and you may act impulsively. You are also good at motivating others. You're outgoing and charismatic, but may also appear to be overenthusiastic or overly aggressive. **2.** You are confident sexually and your charisma and intensity makes you a popular lover. **3.** Mars ℞ in the first house can make it difficult for you to know when you need to stand up for yourself or how to present yourself to others.

♂ **in the second house**   Mars in the second house is all about what you value, including what you own. ✦ **1.** Mars in your second house makes you more assertive about money and your security needs. You don't appear to be aggressive, but are more patient, and have consistent, reliable energy. **2.** With this Mars placement, you will be motivated around your security needs. You don't waste resources—time, energy, money, or anything else you value. You are willing to work hard for what you value, and put your considerable energy into meeting your needs. **3.** Mars ℞ in the second house makes it difficult for you to receive compliments, gifts, and money.

♂ **in the third house**   In the third house, Mars relates to communication and intellect. ✦ **1.** Your third house Mars makes you intellectually aggressive, and it might also make you a good public speaker. You certainly communicate well—and with passion. You're persuasive, but sometimes you speak before you think. **2.** Mars in the second house can indicate challenges in your early childhood relationships. **3.** Mars ℞ in the third house means it may take you a while to learn new things.

♂ **in the fourth house**   Mars in the fourth house will explain areas of family and home. ✦ **1.** If you have Mars in your fourth house, you are protective about your family and home. Your family and friends are very important to you, and you are assertively dedicated to them. You may actually be *overly* protective of your home and domestic life. **2.** Mars ℞ in the fourth house can indicate that you and your needs didn't receive adequate attention at home when you were growing up.

♂ **in the fifth house**   In the fifth house, Mars relates to creativity and self-expression. ✦ **1.** Your fifth house Mars makes you aggressive toward social and creative situations. You can create something quickly, and you're very riveting—even magnetic; all eyes will be on you as you do your creative work. **2.** You may be pushy when it comes to romantic involvements. Be careful not to overwhelm a potential lover, or to let yourself become jealous for no reason. **3.** You tend to be protective of children in general, and Mars's aggression can make you overly protective and restrictive of your own children. **4.** Mars ℞ in the fifth house means you attract drama and find yourself in one karmic affair after another.

♂ **in the sixth house**   In the sixth house, Mars relates to health and service, as well as work environment. ✦ **1.** Mars in your sixth house can make you aggressive about your health. You want to protect your health, and you like to be fit. You might become preoccupied with your health and fanatical about exercise and diet—too much exercise isn't a good thing. It can be difficult for you to find a balance between action and rest. **2.** Your place of work is important to you—you may change your work environment frequently, even within the same career. You are driven to succeed. You need a lot of stimulus and are prone to minor altercations in the office. Rein in your passion! **3.** Mars ℞ in the sixth house means that you identify health and work priorities through a process of trial and error.

♂ **in the seventh house**   Mars in the seventh house relates to partnerships of all kinds. ✦ **1.** Your seventh house Mars makes sure you will attract strong partners—in business or marriage and domestic relationships. You likely have a charismatic, self-aware partner (or partners!), and can help them shine. You bring great enthusiasm to your social connections with people and you are good

M

at networking. Problems arise when your competitive side gets in the way. You might want to shine, too. Choose a partner who's not a *constant* challenge, and who wants to share the spotlight—not hog it ... or steal it. **2.** You are generally very charismatic and are good at dealing with the public, but you can also be impatient and restless. **3.** Mars ℞ in the seventh house will lead you to be frustrated by your passive-aggressive tendencies.

♂ **in the eighth house   1.** When in the eighth house, Mars relates to money as well as personal transformation. **2.** Mars co-rules the eighth house (with Pluto) and is comfortable here. ✦ **1.** Mars in your eighth house makes you passionate and persistent. It may also bring you challenges with money matters. You have a strong work ethic and can manage resources well, but your desire to manage your own money can be disastrous if you don't really know what you're doing, and also refuse to admit this. Keeping your savings in the mattress isn't always a safe investment. **2.** You have a strong connection to metaphysics and spiritualism, and are likely very intuitive and observant. **3.** Mars ℞ in the eighth house means you have a secret set of rules by which you expect others to abide.

♂ **in the ninth house   **Mars in the ninth house is related to philosophy and beliefs, education, travel, and law. ✦ **1.** Your ninth house Mars brings you a focus on learning about the world independently. You like to do things your own way, and often learn by doing. Sometimes this means learning the hard way! You're enthusiastic about travel. **2.** You may be a self-made philosopher. Be careful that Mars's natural aggression doesn't lead you to intolerance of other views. **3.** Mars ℞ in the ninth house makes you yearn for travel and higher education, but you find yourself frustrated about how to make that happen for yourself—until you identify the first steps you need to take.

♂ **in the tenth house   **In the tenth house, Mars relates to career, public life, and authority figures. ✦ **1.** Mars in your tenth house makes you a strong worker—your career is very important to you, and you are driven to succeed. You work toward a goal without flagging, and want to get ahead on your own merit. Beware of co-workers who could become jealous of your ambition and success. **2.** You might make your own best boss—you don't like taking orders. **3.** Mars ℞ in the tenth house tempts you to blame outside conditions for your lack of success and fame, but only until you learn tools for manifestation of your hopes and dreams.

♂ **in the eleventh house**   When in the eleventh house, Mars relates to peer groups as well as hopes and goals. ✦ **1.** In your eleventh house, Mars will attract ambitious friends. You might not be particularly aggressive or assertive, but you have friends and peers who are ambitious for you, and push you along to succeed. You have people around you to motivate you and to help you get where you want to go. **2.** Others see you as strong and strong-willed. **3.** Mars ℞ in the eleventh house means you have a lot of powerful friends, but you may not feel comfortable asking them to open doors for you.

♂ **in the twelfth house**   Mars in the twelfth house relates to karmic debt and duty, and hidden areas of life. ✦ **1.** Mars in your twelfth house makes you subdued—you tend to internalize your feelings, and don't show your innermost feelings to others. You don't need a crowd to cheer you on—you're an independent self-starter, and you like to work behind the scenes. Your assertive, aggressive behavior isn't seen by others, but they may *feel* it. Your assertiveness may show up as excitement. You're good at keeping secrets (especially your own), and are passionate about helping others. **2.** You temper your emotions, and this may lead you to hold back when you need to express yourself. You may keep yourself in check too well, and harbor resentments about unexpressed feelings. **3.** Mars ℞ in the twelfth house gives you an interesting ability to make yourself invisible. You hesitate to rely on your intensely psychic nature.

See also *house, Mars, Mars in the signs, retrograde planets.* 🏠 ○

Mars in the signs   1. Mars is the planet of aggression and desire. The sign Mars is in will indicate how a person expresses aggression, or where desire is. Drive, passion, courage, and the ability to accomplish a goal are represented by Mars. **2.** Mars ℞ in the signs generally signifies what energy a person attracts, because a healthier expression of this energy may have been repressed; finding and learning to use the needed energy is paramount here.

♂ **in Aquarius**   Aquarius is an idealistic sign of invention and communication. ✦ **1.** Your Mars in Aquarius brings energy to new ideas. You may like inventing or experimenting in all areas of your life. You'll dissect situations to see how they work, and you may come up with original solutions to problems. You're a communicator, constantly verbalizing your thoughts and energy. You might also be impatient if you're frustrated. When things aren't going the way you want, you can behave erratically. **2.** Mars ♇ in Aquarius attracts eccentrics.

♂ **in Aries**   **1.** Aries is the sign of action. **2.** Mars is at home in Aries. ✹ **1.** Mars in Aries makes you energetic and self-assured. You want to get out there and get things done. You may appear pushy, but you just have irrepressible energy. You aren't afraid to venture out and go in pursuit of a goal. You also tell others how you see things, and don't hold anything back. **2.** Mars ♇ in Aries attracts selfish people, usually male.

♂ **in Cancer**   Cancer is an emotional, nurturing sign. ✹ **1.** Your Mars in Cancer makes you aggressive emotionally. Your feelings are hurt easily, and you tend to hold those hurts inside. You might be volatile or subdued—you're unpredictable, and this can work in your favor, because people don't know what to expect from you. You're intensely protective of family and loved ones, as well as those who appear weak—even if you don't agree with them. You might actually be *overprotective*. You're always on the side of the underdog. When your emotions are triggered, you come out fighting. **2.** Mars ♇ in Cancer attracts clingy or smothering people, usually female.

♂ **in Capricorn**   Capricorn is responsible and self-contained. ✹ **1.** With Mars in Capricorn you're the business person of the zodiac—you can really take care of business with your authoritative and staid nature. You like to keep things on an even keel, and to be in control of your environment. You're very disciplined and structured. Your enthusiasm comes in areas of work and business. You're dutiful and like long-term projects. It takes a lot to make you really angry, and you tend to work your emotions out on your own. **2.** Mars ♇ in Capricorn is attracted to miserly bosses and employers.

♂ **in Gemini**   Gemini is a quick-witted communicator. ✹ **1.** With Mars in Gemini, you are very sharp, intellectually, and are a quick-thinking, fast-acting person. Your intelligence is unparalleled, and you're a great *mental* fighter. You act quickly once you decide to do something—sometimes you don't think it through, though, and act impulsively. You might not be around to see how it turns out, though, so this doesn't bother you. You don't want anything to last too long—you don't have the attention span for it. You get energized when things move quickly. You appear restless or flighty, and get bored easily. **2.** Mars ♇ in Gemini attracts gossipy neighbors at home, at school, or even at work.

♂ **in Leo**   Leo is a shining star—a bright, energetic leader.
✦ **1.** Mars in Leo has big feelings, is generous, talkative, and
enthusiastic. You are good at encouraging others' talents, and your
physical appearance is important to you—you are very attention-
getting in public (people are drawn to your style and signature look)
and confident. You have the ability to stand strong in optimism even
on the brink of disaster. **2.** Mars ℞ in Leo attracts arrogant lovers.

♂ **in Libra**   Libra loves balance and harmony. ✦ **1.** When you
have Mars in Libra you are charming, persuasive, and sensual. You
need to cooperate with others in partnership, and get frustrated
without a productive and balanced relationship of some kind. You
like to study and read, and are always searching for higher balance.
You also have a strong sense of justice, and will work to right wrongs.
2. Mars ℞ in Libra attracts commitment-phobic partners, prompting
this Mars to look for a better balance with less drama; words need to
be backed up with action.

♂ **in Pisces**   Pisces is a compassionate dreamer. ✦ **1.** This placement for Mars in Pisces creates a subtle energy. You don't appear
to be aggressive, but are very intuitive and sensitive to aggressive
behavior in others. You are imaginative and creative, and tend to
put your passion into creative pursuits. You are also inspirational
to others, and are naturally self-sacrificing. You tend to turn your
anger inward, and may self-indulge to make yourself feel better.
Internalizing your emotions can lead potentially to negative health
consequences, so Mars in Pisces needs an emotional outlet—try
something creative! **2.** Mars ℞ in Pisces attracts procrastinators; set
timelines for goals and avoid action without resolution or result. You
want something to show for your creative pursuits and not just a
bunch of unfinished business.

♂ **in Sagittarius**   Sagittarius is the sign of the enthusiastic explorer.
✦ **1.** With your Mars in Sagittarius you are the great adventurer
of the zodiac. You'll be skydiving at age 80! You're courageous and
love to explore new things—cultures, religions, activities. You enjoy
pushing your own boundaries and taking risks. You really love travel,
and may live in a foreign country at some point in your life. You have
a strong, philosophical approach to living, and sometimes you push
these views on others. **2.** Mars ℞ in Sagittarius attracts gamblers and
risk-takers.

M

♂ **in Scorpio   1.** Scorpio is an intense, transformational sign. **2.** Mars is at home in Scorpio. ✵ **1.** In Scorpio, the power of Mars expresses through independence, self-reliance, and self-discipline. You are determined and have powerful desires. You are very focused, and emotionally intense. Your passion drives you, and when you are consumed about something, you will not be deterred. You are often private about what your goals are, and you pride yourself on your self-control. **2.** Mars ℞ in Scorpio attracts hidden sexual energy in ways you may not be prepared to handle. Study martial arts, yoga, and meditation for clues to taming passion and channeling it in productive directions.

♂ **in Taurus**   Taurus, the earthiest of earth signs, is steady and dependable. ✵ **1.** With Mars in Taurus, you are steadfast and determined. You will doggedly pursue a goal once you've decided to—you simply cannot be pushed aside, and the words "give up" are not in your vocabulary. You're methodical and persistent; it's a matter of will, rather than physicality—you aren't a physically aggressive person, but you have a very strong will, and others should get with the program or get out of your way. You also don't forget things— you can hold a grudge. **2.** Mars ℞ in Taurus attracts material girls and boys.

♂ **in Virgo**   Practical Virgo loves order. ✵ **1.** Mars in Virgo man- ifests as *controlled* passion. You work hard to achieve your personal ambitions, and are willing to sacrifice to complete a project—to your very demanding and precise standards. You're a perfectionist with a tendency toward workaholism. You have very high expectations for yourself, and for others. You are detail-oriented and systematic, and have no patience for your own shortcomings. You don't generally show your anger, which is usually directed at yourself. **2.** Mars ℞ in Virgo attracts nitpickers; watch out for a love for people who love detail for its own sake, and remember that sometimes you have to get out of the forest to see the trees.
See also *Mars, signs.* ◯ ☼

Mars/Jupiter   See *Jupiter/Mars.*

Mars/Mercury   Mars brings power and drive to Mercury's natural intellectual abilities. ✵ Mars and Mercury aspect in your birth chart to make you highly intellectual and quick-witted. You talk fast and you think even faster. You love a heated debate—some call it arguing. You're very curious and love to learn. You're a good and persuasive public speaker, and also have great writing skills. It's difficult for you to slow your mind down and relax—you're always thinking. See also *aspects between planets, Mars, Mercury.* △ ☯ ◯

Mars/Moon   Mars brings its considerable energy to the emotional Moon in this combination. ✦ If you have Mars in aspect to the Moon, you can likely feel that Mars energy. You are passionate and energetic. Mars gives you a tendency to be over-excitable and over-emotional. Sometimes it's difficult for you to see past your feelings. You need to stop and take a deep breath. Look for an outlet for your energy and emotions—try some physical activity. See also *aspects between planets, Mars, Moon.* △ ☯ ◯

Mars/Neptune   Neptune's religion and spirituality get a jump start from Mars. ✦ If Mars and Neptune interact in your chart, you may be driven toward the spiritual or religious. You might be an inspirational leader or minister. You'll be fervent in your beliefs. You may be quite charming and creative. You also have an original outlook—you don't see the world as others do. See also *aspects between planets, Mars, Neptune.* △ ☯ ◯

Mars/North Node   Mars is active energy, and the North Node relates to areas that need to be developed or learned. The North Node in aspect with Mars indicates that the power and action of Mars has to be learned. The North Node looks to the future and reveals what you stand to gain (in a karmic sense, too) by mastering Mars energy. ✦ Aspects between Mars and the North Node in your birth chart indicate that you're learning to be assertive and direct. You have to challenge yourself to stand up and be demonstrative and aggressive. See also *aspects between planets, Mars, North Node.* △ ☯ ◯

Mars/Pluto   Mars brings drive and energy to the larger world when these planets are aspected. ✦ Mars and Pluto in your birth chart can help you motivate the public. Mars will push Pluto along to insist on wide-ranging change. As long as the change is positive, this can be a good thing. Be sure of your motivation. See also *aspects between planets, Mars, Pluto.* △ ☯ ◯

M

Mars retrograde, personal   1. Mars is retrograde in the birth chart, creating a personal effect in the birth chart of the native. **2.** Mars is retrograde for 80 days during its 687-day orbit around the Sun. Those born during these 80 days have Mars ℞ in the birth chart. **3.** Personal retrogrades have varying influence depending on the activity of other planets in the birth chart. ✧ **1.** If you have Mars ℞ in your birth chart, you will internalize Mars's action and drive. You'll need to rethink how you do things to find a more effective course of action. **2.** You may also internalize Mars's aggression, turning your anger and frustration inward. Be aware of this and try to find outlets for your anger that help you find productive resolutions and bring you closer to people you love. See also *Mars; Mars retrograde, transiting; retrograde, personal.* ◯ ℞

> **Look to the astrological sign of your personal Mars retrograde for advice on the best course of action:**
>
> - ♂℞ **in Aries:** Graciously accept your role as leader.
> - ♂℞ **in Taurus:** Persevere, persevere, and still persevere.
> - ♂℞ **in Gemini:** Your sense of humor helps you find your way into or out of anything.
> - ♂℞ **in Cancer:** Trust your intuition when making decisions.
> - ♂℞ **in Leo:** It's most satisfying when you get it done while having fun.
> - ♂℞ **in Virgo:** Consider the pluses and minuses before you start.
> - ♂℞ **in Libra:** You'll get more done if you enlist the aid of a partner.
> - ♂℞ **in Scorpio:** Take something in its raw form and transform it into something powerful.
> - ♂℞ **in Sagittarius:** Document the steps you take as you explore how you do something so you can teach it to others later.
> - ♂℞ **in Capricorn:** Delegate the stuff you don't want to do and put energy into what you judge to be important.
> - ♂℞ **in Aquarius:** Do, make, lead, and reform in your own unique and innovative style.
> - ♂℞ **in Pisces:** Meditate to know what it is that you really want and make your dreams come true by envisioning them.

Mars retrograde, transiting   1. Mars's transiting retrograde lasts 80 days; that's about 2½ months. **2.** Transiting retrogrades are the daily retrograde action of the planets that affect everyone on Earth.

3. Finding ways to channel Mars's bold energy can seem difficult during retrograde periods.

✧ **1.** A lot of people are afraid that when Mars goes retrograde it is time to haul out the boxing gloves, because all human interaction will be contentious. Not necessarily. Mars ℞ can turn out to be nothing more than a 100-pound weakling, or a toothless bully. Of course retrograde Mars can also be a fire-breathing dragon. The challenge and potential of using Mars ℞ energy lies in your ability to size up your opponent and situation fairly and honestly. Someone who practices Tai Chi knows how to use their own life force energy as well as their opponent's life force energy to redirect an attack, gain leverage, or protect against vulnerabilities. Knowing how to use Mars ℞ effectively will give you the same advantages. You'll be able to make bold moves, but from sure footing. You'll take the calm measure of your opponent (or partner) and move from a position of strength. **2.** When Mars is retrograde you need to stay mindful of anger, whether it is your own or someone else's. Look for ways to express anger in a positive context; that is, one that is solution-oriented and doesn't place (or take) blame. Use force only when needed, and only in an appropriate amount. Better yet, look for the nonviolent way, and counter your anger with patience toward your anger and its source. Mars ℞ can be a terrific teacher of compassion and tolerance for a willing student. See also *Mars; Mars retrograde, personal; retrograde, transiting.* ◯ ℞

M

If transiting Mars retrograde throws a lot of punches your way, look to the astrological sign to throw some light on the situation:

- **In Aries:** Find the right flow of Aries push and Mars pull.
- **In Taurus:** Sometimes being strong means being flexible.
- **In Gemini:** Study hard and ace the lightning round.
- **In Cancer:** Feelings matter.
- **In Leo:** Courage matters.
- **In Virgo:** Read the fine print to avoid misunderstandings.
- **In Libra:** Find both sides of the story.
- **In Scorpio:** Look through the disguise to see clearly and empower yourself.
- **In Sagittarius:** Being careful doesn't mean being timid.
- **In Capricorn:** Anger can be cool and calculating, too.

- **In Aquarius:** Keep the ideas coming.
- **In Pisces:** To cry or not to cry, that is the question!

Mars return   1. Point at which Mars returns to the position it held in the native's birth chart. **2.** Mars is in each sign for about 57.25 days, and has a total orbit time of 687 days. Therefore, it would take 687 days for Mars to return to an exact place in its orbit. ✱ **1.** Mars returns in your chart every 687 days—that's a little less than 2 years. **2.** If your Mars is not in Taurus, Cancer, or Libra and positively aspected, its return can bring some pretty nice benefits. Typically, a positive Mars brings energy, positive attention, new love, more sex appeal, and improved health. **3.** If your Mars is in its detriment or fall or is negatively aspected, its return can signal a time to curb impulses and stay grounded. **4.** A Mars return brings in a new man. When positive, that's a love affair, investor, best friend, leader, or welcomed rabble-rouser. When negative, that man can be a source of accidents or regrets. See also *Mars, planetary returns.* ◯

**Mars/Saturn   **Mars brings drive to Saturn's orderly nature. Mars provides the youth, zeal, and strength to Saturn's systematic authority. ✱ Saturn and Mars combine to bring long-lasting independence; Saturn sees Mars as a young punk and Mars sees Saturn as the establishment. Aspects between Mars and Saturn in your birth chart make you disciplined, responsible, and possibly an authority figure. You aren't diplomatic, and tend to be overtly aggressive and demanding. You expect others to be as disciplined as you are. The energy of these planets can be constructive—it would work well in the military, for example—and will help you get a lot done. But you may lose relationships along the way, and may feel anger and frustration when the world doesn't live up to your expectations. Exerting discipline is good, but do try not to be an overbearing taskmaster; you want to be loved for your efforts to make the world a better place, not loathed for pushing people over the brink. See also *aspects between planets, Mars, Saturn.* △ ◑ ◯

**Mars/South Node   **Mars is action and aggression, and the South Node indicates areas of familiarity and comfort. The South Node indicates comfort and experience with Mars's active energy. The South Node deals with issues from the past (including karmic ones), and with Mars can reveal that you understand how you experience anger and have mastered this emotion. ✵ Aspects between Mars and the South Node in your birth chart indicate that you're comfortable with assertion and aggression, or at least it's what you are familiar with. You're likely demonstrative, and may be dramatic. You're aware of your power and you use it well! See also *aspects between planets, Mars, South Node.* △ ☯ ○

Mars/Sun   Mars brings energy and drive to the outer self or ego, represented by the Sun. ✵ Aspects between these planets, Mars and the Sun, in your birth chart make you white hot, blinding beautiful and self-challenging. You have a lot of drive and ambition and you are very assertive in pursuit of your goals. You're an enthusiastic self-starter, you're very competitive, and you don't take no for an answer. People may have to squint when they look at you … your aura is so bright. Just keep moving, and others will follow your lead. See also *aspects between planets, Mars, Sun.* △ ☯ ○

Mars transits   **1.** Mars as it moves or transits through the signs of the zodiac. **2.** Mars's orbit around the Sun takes 687 days; Mars transits all twelve zodiac signs in that time. **3.** Mars transits can be compared by astrologers to the placement of Mars in a birth chart for predictive purposes. A transit shows the position of a planet at a given moment. **4.** Transiting Mars is a catalyst as it enters a new sign or a new house, and as it forms aspects with other transiting planets or planets in both birth and progressed charts. As a catalyst for self-assertion, generating an image, and producing the energy for start-ups, Mars is used by professional astrologers to predict important times to be seen, compete, stand up for one's self, and begin an activity. ✵ Need to know when to take action? Transiting Mars can tell you. As transiting Mars moves through each house of your chart, it activates the energy to get you going in that area of your life so that you attract what you need and come up with the ideas and make the decisions to produce results. What can transiting Mars help get you started with? See also *Mars, progressed birth chart, transiting planets, transits.* **BC** 🏠 ○

M

What can Mars transits tell you?

- Mars transiting your **first house** tells you when you are most visible to others and likely to be chosen.
- Mars transiting your **second house** is the perfect time to go shopping or spend the day at the spa.
- Considering a career in journalism? Investigate the leads when Mars enters your **third house**.
- Does the furniture in your home need rearranging? Wait for Mars to enter your **fourth house**.
- Wondering when a new love relationship will come your way? When does Mars enter your **fifth house**?
- When should you change jobs? When Mars enters your **sixth house**.
- Mars moving through your **seventh house** is an excellent time to start litigation.
- Mars transiting through your **eighth house** is ideal for research that boasts results.
- Travel, workshops, and teaching want to happen when Mars moves through your **ninth house**.
- Start your new business when Mars moves into your **tenth house**.
- Best time to throw a party? When Mars enters your **eleventh house**.
- It's easier to face reality and enter therapy when Mars transits your **twelfth house**.

Mars/Uranus   Mars is the match that lights the fuse of unpredictable Uranus—they are explosive together. ✳ These planets, Mars and Uranus, can be volatile together. If they are well-aspected in your chart, you look to the future and may be pioneering and inventive. To others, you might seem to be a crazy genius! You march to your own beat, and think that's the only way to travel. If the aspects between these planets aren't so positive, this interaction can cause unpredictable behavior. See also *aspects between planets, Mars, Uranus.*

Mars/Venus   Mars brings energy to Venus's love of beauty … and love. ✳ Aspects between Mars and Venus in your birth chart make you affectionate and sensual. You are charismatic and have a strong personality. Your energy is very attractive to others. You are very passionate and have a love of beauty and the physical world. You may be motivated to create art or to accumulate art or other material

goods. Mars combined with Venus can give you a strong sex drive.
See also *aspects between planets, Mars, Venus.* △ ☯ ○

masculine principle   **1.** Masculine energy is called yang. This
energy is active and direct. Yang moves, it gives, and lends energy
to its receiver. Traditionally associated with men, this energy can
represent the vital power inherent in taking action, regardless of
human gender. **2.** Masculine energy is focused outward. Air and fire
signs have masculine energy. **3.** The masculine Sun signs are Aries,
Gemini, Leo, Libra, Sagittarius, and Aquarius. �֍ Masculine (yang)
energy is considered more aggressive than feminine (yin) energy.
It's also more active: how you react to things can be influenced by
yang energy, making you more forceful, aggressive, and extroverted.
If your Sun sign is masculine, you may be out to change the world
(for the better, of course!). You have great ideas, an enterprising
spirit, and the intelligence to make things happen. See also *air sign,
Aquarius, Aries, energy, feminine principle, fire sign, Gemini, Leo, Libra,
Sagittarius, yang, yin.* ☯ ☉

May 21 to June 22   Birth dates for the Sun sign Gemini. The
position of the Sun during these dates correlates with an astrological
Sun sign. Those born between May 21 and June 22 have Gemini as
their Sun sign. See also *Gemini.* ☉

mean node   See *Nodes (North, South).*

medical astrology   See *health/medical astrology.*

Medium Coeli   See *midheaven (Medium Coeli).*

Mercury   **1.** Planet named for the very speedy messenger to the
Roman gods. **2.** Mercury is the planet closest to the Sun, and the
second-smallest planet in our solar system. Mercury travels around
the Sun in an eccentric orbit that takes 88 days—the fastest orbit of
any planet in the solar system. **3.** Mercury is the natural ruler of the
Sun signs Gemini and Virgo as well as the third and twelfth houses.
4. In Roman mythology, Mercury was a messenger made extremely
fast by the wings on his feet. He was the son of Jupiter and brother
of Mars. **5.** Mercury is a personal or inner planet, associated with
intellect, communication, and mental action. The astrological symbol
for Mercury is ☿. **6.** Mercury ℞ is a time for rethinking, recasting,
and redoing.

✧ **1.** Mercury's placement in your birth chart can tell you how you think and communicate. Mercury's orbit is so fast that its influence on your chart is as mercurial as the planet itself ... ever shape-shifting and changing direction. This planet's quick orbit promises ample opportunities for change and self-expression. **2.** Where is Mercury in your birth chart? The house and sign in which Mercury appears will tell you more about Mercury's meaning in your life. Wherever you see Mercury, expect some kind of manifestation of the way you make yourself understood, through language and action. **3.** Your thought processes and favored methods of communication (speaking, texting) are revealed through Mercury. **4.** In a daily astrological calendar, days and times when Mercury is in a positive aspect to the Sun (conjunct, trine, or sextile) are usually good times for writing love letters or any creative writing, going on auditions, helping children with school projects, meeting up with your lover, or attending a class about healing, performing, travel, sports, speculation, or one of your hobbies. An astrologer looks for these positive aspects when a client wants to know when they are most likely to hear back from that new guy or girl, when to schedule an audition, launch a webpage, start a relaxing road trip, or have a meeting with creative types. Days when Mercury is in a more challenging aspect to the Sun (opposition or square) are not the happiest for communications or get-togethers with friends, healers, children, investors, fellow sports enthusiasts, or your second sibling. And because Mercury rules medical personnel and the Sun rules the heart, the days with Mercury in a challenging aspect to the Sun are not the best days for seeing a cardiologist—but if you are experiencing heart-rhythm or other heart problems, don't put off seeing a doctor. See also *Mercury in the houses, Mercury in the signs, retrograde planets.* △ ○ ℞

Mercury finger   In palmistry, the little (pinkie) finger and the base of that finger on each hand relate to Mercury. The Mercury finger reveals mental acuity and communication issues. ✧ Hold up your hand and take a look at your little finger. Is it long or short, thin or fat? How long is this finger, compared to your ring finger (the Apollo finger)? A long Mercury finger indicates a quick wit and good communication skills. If your Mercury finger bends away from your Apollo finger, you are likely independent and may have some issues with trust. See also *Apollo finger, Mercury.* ☯ Z

Mercury in the houses   **1.** Mercury represents the mind and intellect, and relates to the native's ability to reason and the thought process, as well as communication. **2.** Mercury's chart placement will indicate areas of life influenced by Mercury's mercurial quicksilver energy. ✦ **1.** Mercury is communication and thinking—the house Mercury appears in will tell you about how you think and communicate in those areas of your life. **2.** Mercury is always a signal that some quick analysis is going on, something needs to be evaluated and information will be shared. Mercury's presence might signal the desire to transform the house through upgrading technology—from a GPS pet collar to solar panels to an e-book reader. **3.** Mercury's perambulations may be so swift they cause a tangle of ideas or even migraines; slow down and think and rethink each strand through.

☿ **in the first house**   Mercury in the first house is all about the self and the personality. ✦ **1.** Mercury in the first house makes you think about yourself a lot. You aren't necessarily egotistical; but you think a lot, and are introspective. You like to analyze yourself. **2.** You communicate well with the public, and have good public speaking skills. You're also friendly and affable. It's important to you that you look and sound good when you are speaking in public, again, not because you're egotistical—you analyze your performance to make sure it works well for you and for your listener. **3.** Mercury ℞ in the first house means you learn differently from other people and you are sometimes challenged in your ability to say what you mean because you have so many thoughts circling round in your head. You also get sidetracked in making decisions until you filter out the distractions. Others might see you as shy, but really it just takes you a while to formulate your opinions.

☿ **in the second house**   Mercury in the second house is all about what you value, including what you own. ✦ **1.** Mercury in your second house means you think a lot about your values. You then make plans based on those values, and you follow through to make your plans a reality. You have the ability to visualize something and then make it material. You are stimulated by thinking about what makes a good investment and what you hold dear—this can include money, stocks and bonds, people, and time. You sometimes overthink and worry about realizing your dreams. **2.** Mercury ℞ in the second house means you get fixed on certain ideas about money that can actually stop you from moving forward with the opportunities that are in front of you.

M

☿ **in the third house**   Mercury is the natural ruler of the third house of communication. ✳ **1.** Your third house Mercury makes you an excellent communicator and public speaker. You might be a comedian, and are very good with languages. You might be a translator or interpreter, and you have excellent verbal skills. You love books and study, and improving your mind is likely a favorite hobby. You likely enjoy travel as a way of expanding your mind—and keeping you interested. **2.** Mercury in the third house lends itself to communicating about early childhood. **3.** Mercury ℞ in the third house gives you a tendency to talk in circles while you are pulling your more important points together inside your head.

☿ **in the fourth house**   Mercury in the fourth house will explain areas of family and home. ✳ **1.** If you have Mercury in your fourth house, you enjoy talking about home and family, and you create extended family with your friends and neighbors. Your home might be the congregating place for extended family gatherings. **2.** You are interested in your family history, and genealogy may be an interest you pursue and share with others. **3.** Mercury ℞ in the fourth house makes it difficult for you to separate your ideas from your feelings. It helps to put your feelings down on paper.

☿ **in the fifth house**   In the fifth house, Mercury relates to creativity and self-expression. ✳ **1.** Your fifth house Mercury helps you communicate and express your thoughts through creative endeavors. You're an excellent writer/blogger, visual artist, dancer, or actor. You'd also do well in media, such as journalism. You're quick-witted and clever, and others have a difficult time keeping up with you. **2.** Fifth house Mercury also communicates well with children, and vice versa. You can communicate on a child's level, and this would make you a good elementary education teacher. **3.** Mercury ℞ in the fifth house compensates for a lack of confidence by speaking in a superior tone.

☿ **in the sixth house**   **1.** In the sixth house, Mercury relates to work environment, as well as health and service. **2.** Mercury is at home in the sixth house. ✳ **1.** Mercury in your sixth house makes you preoccupied with work. Communicating and succeeding at work is important to you, and you use your communication skills to develop good relationships with co-workers. You're great at research—you want to know everything, and are very detail oriented. You might be a group spokesperson at work. **2.** Your health is important to you and can be another preoccupation or worry for you.

3. Mercury ℞ in the sixth house can generate obsessive worry. If you can see yourself objectively in this cycle, your brain will realize something bigger than it is still in charge. This will help you relax right away.

☿ **in the seventh house**   Mercury in the seventh house relates to partnerships of all kinds. ✳ **1.** Your seventh house Mercury means that you need a partner. You like to talk with someone—all the time! You'd run a business well with a partner or work on a project with someone well. You communicate best with a partner who's your intellectual equal. When you find someone who is intellectually compatible with you, you stick with them. They can understand and challenge you. **2.** You make a good debater, lawyer, or arbitrator. You don't enjoy working in isolation. **3.** Mercury ℞ in the seventh house likes to ask everyone else what they think before committing to an opinion or decision.

☿ **in the eighth house**   In the eighth house, Mercury relates to money as well as personal change and transformation. ✳ **1.** If you have Mercury in your eighth house, you accomplish change in your life through communication. You excel at research and investigation of all kinds—the more complicated, the more you enjoy it. You like to go beneath the surface and find information no one else knows, and then share it. **2.** You enjoy behind the scenes work; public speaking isn't usually your thing. **3.** Mercury ℞ in the eighth house has you searching so deeply for meaning that the obvious may escape your notice.

☿ **in the ninth house**   Mercury in the ninth house is related to philosophy and beliefs, education, travel, and law. ✳ **1.** Your ninth house Mercury makes you a great orator—you can give a speech like no one else. You can use this ability well as a teacher, a politician, or a pastor. You love school and might be a student during your entire life. You're an adventurous learner, and you want to share what you learn with others. You'd like to be able to help others with what you know. **2.** You love to travel, and it stimulates your mind. **3.** Mercury ℞ in the ninth house may cause you to hear things in exaggerated terms, provoking some pretty foolish responses from you.

☿ **in the tenth house**   In the tenth house, Mercury relates to career, public life, and authority figures. ✳ **1.** Mercury in your tenth house makes you focused on career, which is where you put your communication skills to good use. You are a good speaker and have great communication abilities. Lots of politicians and speech writers have this placement; you give a good speech, and often have a desire to educate others or share your ideals through language. **2.** You tend to travel for work. **3.** Mercury ℞ in the tenth house knows a better way to run things, but finds it difficult to assume the necessary authority to convey this message to others.

☿ in the eleventh house   When in the eleventh house, Mercury relates to peer groups as well as hopes and goals. �֍ **1.** In your eleventh house, Mercury creates a need to share your ideas—talking an idea out is part of your thought process. You have an intellectual need to share ideas and information with a group. You want everyone in your community to share in what you know, and you like to be able to go to them for information, as well. **2.** You like to have others' opinions, but you don't necessarily take their advice. **3.** Mercury ℞ in the eleventh house gives you fantastic ideas for inventions, but you tend to think everybody gets these kinds of ideas, so they never make it to the patent or trademark attorney.

☿ in the twelfth house   Mercury in the twelfth house relates to karmic debt and duty, and hidden areas of life. ✖ **1.** If you have Mercury in your twelfth house you won't tell people what you're thinking all of the time. You are a great observer, and you can assess and analyze a person or a problem quickly and easily. **2.** You tend to be contemplative and introspective; you aren't a great talker, and are concise when you speak. It takes you a long time to decide what you think and whether to share it (and with whom to share it). You are likely intuitive and may have psychic abilities. You would make a good counselor, spiritual advisor, or investigator. **3.** Mercury ℞ in the twelfth house causes you to speak in a way that confuses others. See also *Mercury, Mercury in the signs, retrograde planets.* 🏠 ◯

Mercury in the signs   **1.** Mercury is the planet of intellect and communication. The sign Mercury is in will indicate how the native thinks and communicates. Mercury reveals the connections we make and how we relate to each other through language and technology. **2.** Mercury ℞ in the signs generally signifies a conflict in the processing of internal cues with incoming information, so that the individual needs an additional moment or two to sort out thoughts before speaking. The sign Mercury ℞ is in gives an indication of what a conflict is about. Keep in mind that a planetary retrograde draws in fated or karmic circumstances. Retrogrades offer some of the best learning opportunities.

☿ **in Aquarius**   Aquarius is an innovative sign of communication and new ideas. ✴ **1.** If you have Mercury in Aquarius, you might be a bit eccentric—some of your ideas are "out there," or at least other people with less bold vision might think so …. You need your friends and family to bounce ideas around with—you like to share your thoughts. You like to relate your ideas and you really need others' feedback. You're a creative thinker—a visionary—and you like to cooperate with others. You are also a good listener. You really pay attention. **2.** Mercury ℞ in Aquarius makes it difficult for you to stay connected to the here and now.

☿ **in Aries**   Aries is the active go-getter of the zodiac. ✴ **1.** Mercury in Aries has an active, forward-pushing mind. You communicate—a lot. You're outgoing and extroverted, and are a very direct speaker. You say what you think, and don't hold back. You work out your thoughts while speaking, and your ideas may not come through clearly, even to you. But the end result can be a grand scheme for bold implementation. **2.** Mercury ℞ in Aries challenges your focus by leaving your thoughts incomplete; you don't have the will to think the idea through enough to manifest an action plan that will work.

☿ **in Cancer**   Nurturing Cancer is all about family. ✴ **1.** Mercury in Cancer processes thought through emotions. Before you speak, you feel things out—you're very attuned to others' feelings, and will be careful of them. You speak compassionately and have an excellent memory—you remember names, conversations, and events from long ago. You speak from your past experiences, which reach others. You have a tendency toward nostalgia. Anything you say has some basis in the past or in emotion. **2.** Mercury ℞ in Cancer means you have a tendency to cling to what you were taught.

☿ **in Capricorn**   Steady Capricorn is responsible and self-controlled. ✴ **1.** If your Mercury is in Capricorn, you're a serious, deep thinker. You are very good at obtaining practical information. You're pragmatic and will take your time with things, but once you've obtained information, you remember it. You hold others to what they've said—you often remember it better than they do. You have good executive abilities, and are a straightforward, direct thinker and speaker. You are able to see the bottom line and how to improve it. You're also a great problem solver, and think constructively.

2. Mercury ℞ in Capricorn can get you so stuck in rational thought that you forget to include *feelings* in your decisions.

☿ **in Gemini   1.** Airy Gemini is an intellectual communicator. **2.** Mercury rules Gemini. ✹ **1.** Mercury in Gemini is a great communicator—your mind works fast, and you communicate fast, too. You are very intelligent and witty, and are always ahead of the curve. No one wants to debate with you—it's impossible to win. Because you don't slow yourself down to consider what you're saying and to whom, you are sometimes tactless. You get easily bored, and are ready to flit on to the next topic of conversation before anyone around you has had a chance to grasp what you just said. You might have to interrupt others with your insightful comments, which can become annoying. **2.** Mercury ℞ in Gemini can make you seriously scattered.

☿ **in Leo**   Leo is the proud leader of the zodiac. ✹ **1.** Mercury in Leo is the grand communicator. You're an entertainer, and make a great television personality or satellite radio DJ. You speak dramatically and can uplift others. You like to read up on a topic before talking about it, and are very good at putting your own spin on things to make it entertaining. You like to embellish. **2.** Mercury ℞ in Leo makes it difficult for you to be wrong. It may help to contemplate how we rarely love others for being right all the time.

☿ **in Libra**   Libra insists on balance and harmony. ✹ **1.** Mercury in Libra is the balanced mind. You want to be fair, and will weigh things carefully before you decide what you think. Sometimes this makes you indecisive—you look at both sides of any situation, again and again. This frustrates you as well as those around you. You are idealistic, and want to make your decisions based on fair and balanced judgment. You need an intellectual equal. You're often an excellent speaker, editor, debater, and diplomat. **2.** Mercury ℞ in Libra means you have to double-check that you heard others correctly and that they understood what you said.

☿ **in Pisces**   Dreamy Pisces is compassionate and intuitive. ✹ **1.** Mercury in Pisces makes you a very compassionate, understanding thinker—your thoughts are often focused on others. You are often in a service profession, helping others in some way. You are a kind, gentle thinker and speaker. You will observe how your voice affects others and change your tone or voice modulation accordingly. You're also imaginative, and do well in the arts. You're an excellent, empathic listener. **2.** Mercury ℞ in Pisces has you wondering which thoughts are your own and which thoughts you are picking up psychically.

☿ **in Sagittarius**   Sagittarius is a sign of enthusiasm and independence. ✦ **1.** If you have Mercury in Sagittarius, you're bright, easygoing, and outgoing. You want everyone to get along and are great at networking. You don't like a silent room, and will talk just to get things going—sometimes this means creating an argument, which you enjoy much more than silence. You don't want to be put in a position of holding your tongue; you need to share your thoughts and ideas to get feedback. **2.** Mercury ℞ in Sagittarius means you often remember *afterward* that a little tact goes a long way; sometimes you just flat out like to start trouble with a few choice words and see what happens.

☿ **in Scorpio**   Intense Scorpio has a powerful, emotional energy. ✦ **1.** Mercury in Scorpio has a very intense mind. You have excellent observational skills and a probing mind, and can assess a person or situation quickly and accurately. Your memory is excellent and you know how to get information out of people—you really like to discover or uncover information. You'll do lots of investigating before you speak, and you'll analyze what you learn in an emotional way. You see beneath the surface of things and may hold back information to protect your privacy or someone else's. You have trouble hiding your passion when you love an idea; you are a devoted managing editor. **2.** Mercury ℞ in Scorpio means you tend to communicate through sarcasm; emotion may cloud your thinking.

☿ **in Taurus**   Earthy Taurus is slow and steady. ✦ **1.** Mercury in Taurus makes you want to think before you speak. You like to take your time and consider what you're going to say before you say it, blog it, or act on it. You take your time to process your thoughts, but when you do express yourself, you're eloquent, and your thoughts are well presented and easily understood. Once you've figured out what you think about something, that's it—it's very difficult to change your mind. You're likely an excellent writer. **2.** Mercury ℞ in Taurus means you may speak in a way that sounds narcissistic.

☿ **in Virgo**   **1.** Virgo is all order and practicality. **2.** Mercury is at home in Virgo. ✦ **1.** Mercury in Virgo is an analyzer. You want to know how things work or why they don't. You'll probe all angles of a situation, and you won't give up until you've exhausted all areas of exploration. You're a direct, no-nonsense speaker, which sometimes can be hurtful to others. You don't intend to create hurt feelings, of course—you're just too focused on your own thoughts to see past them. You articulate well, and can be a good public speaker. Accuracy is very important to you. You recognize sacred patterns in words and language. **2.** Mercury ℞ in Virgo means you may struggle with obsessive-compulsive tendencies. See also *Mercury, signs*. ○ ☿

Mercury/Jupiter   See *Jupiter/Mercury*.

Mercury/Mars   See *Mars/Mercury*.

Mercury/Moon   Mercury is the planet of communication; both of these planets are known as personal planets. ✴ If your Mercury and Moon are in aspect, this means that you communicate through your emotions, and you also communicate your emotions well. You express your emotional self through your intellectual self—no matter what you talk about, your emotional self is involved. What you say is who you are. Everything you write, or do from a communication standpoint, speaks from the heart. See also *aspects between planets, Mercury, Moon*. △ ☯ ○

Mercury/Neptune   Mercury is about communication, and Neptune is a spiritual planet. Together they make a spiritual communicator. ✴ When Mercury and Neptune connect in your birth chart, it indicates that you communicate with others in a spiritual or religious way. You communicate in an imaginative way—you might hear music others can't hear, and you communicate with a higher level of consciousness. You might use poetry to express what you feel. You think along spiritual and religious lines and communicate on this level, as well. See also *aspects between planets, Mercury, Neptune*. △ ☯ ○

Mercury/North Node   Mercury is communication, and the North Node is unfamiliar territory—these combine to indicate areas of learning and growth around communication. Karmic destiny provides opportunities to master Mercury's energy. ✴ When Mercury is influenced by the North Node, it indicates that you're very intelligent, but you may not feel comfortable saying what's on your mind. Talking and using your intellectual capacity is important for you. You have to conquer your shyness to learn this lesson. See also *aspects between planets, Mercury, North Node*. △ ☯ ○

Mercury/Pluto   Pluto has a very long orbit time, and its influence is generational. Mercury interacts with Pluto to create a wide-ranging influence. ☀ Communicating with the masses is key to aspects between Mercury and Pluto. Think mass media. If you have these two planets in aspect in your birth chart, you might be drawn to television, radio, or the web for communication purposes. Think about keeping a blog! You are able to express ideas that resonate for individuals personally, but when added up, you've influenced a lot of people on a large scale. If you create a product, everyone will think it has been made just for them, and everyone will have to have it! See also *aspects between planets, Mercury, Pluto.* △ ☯ ○

Mercury retrograde, personal   1. Mercury is retrograde in the birth chart, creating a personal effect in the birth chart of the native. **2.** Mercury's orbit around the Sun takes 88 days, and it's retrograde for 24 days three times each year. Those born during one of those 24-day periods have Mercury ℞ in the natal chart. **3.** Personal retrogrades have varying influence depending on the activity of other planets in the birth chart.

☀ **1.** If you have Mercury ℞ in your birth chart, you are an original thinker who might be misunderstood. You also might not communicate in the same way or in the same time frame as others, leading to some miscommunication. **2.** If you have a personal Mercury ℞ in your birth chart, you may find that periods of transiting Mercury ℞ are very comfortable for you. Because what's in the sky resonates with and enhances what's in your natal chart, you can get a lot done. You are *on* during transiting Mercury ℞—things align for you, and you get productive and decisive. Unlike everyone else, you don't have to slow down or back up your data. For you transiting Mercury ℞ is three weeks, three times each year when you can plan on getting things done! If this is you, break out your calendar, and schedule some really productive activities for yourself during transiting Mercury ℞. See also *Mercury; Mercury retrograde, transiting; retrograde, personal.* ○ ℞

M

Need some tips for handling your personal Mercury retrograde? Check the sign:

- ☿ ℞ **in Aries:** Slow down and get centered.
- ☿ ℞ **in Taurus:** Connect to what's going on through *all* of your senses.
- ☿ ℞ **in Gemini:** Start your day by identifying your top priorities.
- ☿ ℞ **in Cancer:** Be less concerned with how to say something and more focused on why you want to say it.
- ☿ ℞ **in Leo:** Imagine speaking through lips on your heart.
- ☿ ℞ **in Virgo:** Take a moment and contemplate everything that is right in your life.
- ☿ ℞ **in Libra:** Remind yourself that you are whole and complete right now just as you are.
- ☿ ℞ **in Scorpio:** Ask yourself: *What is the outcome that I want to achieve?*
- ☿ ℞ **in Sagittarius:** There is always more to learn. Take a break from learning and have fun applying what you know so far.
- ☿ ℞ **in Capricorn:** Ask yourself: *How would I express myself if I were fearless?*
- ☿ ℞ **in Aquarius:** Reassure yourself by telling yourself: *The best part of me is the weird part of me.*
- ☿ ℞ **in Pisces:** Make a daily declaration: *I choose to only be influenced by truth.*

Mercury retrograde, transiting **1.** Mercury's transiting retrograde lasts 24 days and happens three times every year. **2.** Finding ways to channel Mercury's quick energy can seem difficult during retrograde periods. Many people find transiting Mercury retrograde to be an optimal time to finish projects, to think about a new way of doing something, or to look for flaws that need fixing. **3.** Transiting Mercury ℞ brings about a three-week period of review and reflection. Mercury is all about how people think and communicate; when it's retrograde, it's time to *rethink*. During Mercury ℞, look at areas of concern and review old thinking patterns to see what's been working well and what hasn't. Rather than engaging in direct communication (Mercury ℞ can cause miscommunication, communication slow-downs, or electronic snafus), look inward. Mercury's influence makes this a great time to shift an attitude or make a change of mind. Once Mercury is direct again, act on this new way of thinking.

✦ **1.** Most astrologers accept that transiting Mercury retrograde signals breakdowns in communication, and many will counsel you not to sign contracts or make formal agreements during these times (certainly not without reading the fine print or getting the assistance of a professional to help you). This can be a time when nothing seems to happen fast and everything seems to take forever. In fact, Mercury ℞ can be the right time for the ultimate do-over and can be very supportive of efforts to rethink, redo, rework, revise, or revisit. Think about *how you think.* **2.** Current astrology theory holds that the energy of Mercury ℞ is less about snafus, missed appointments, or busted hard drives, and more about creating opportunities to make improvements. Did you drop your cell phone in a toilet …? Time for an upgrade! Lost your luggage at the airport? Time for some vacation shopping! When Mercury is in retrograde, you've got a constant prompt to do better, to find the flaw and introduce a new way. It is also a great time to catch up on something or to complete something that's been hanging around unfinished. Take care of all of the work in progress! **3.** Some experts say that any cars, electronics, or equipment purchased while Mercury is retrograde will prove disappointing or will break down a lot; maybe … but maybe not. This retrograde energy allows you to decide whether your technology is working for you and what you want to do with it. See also *Mercury; Mercury retrograde, personal; retrograde, transiting.* ◯ ℞

M

If transiting Mercury retrograde grinds your fast-paced world to a halt, look to the astrological sign to throw some light on the situation:

- **In Aries:** Push harder, and then stand back.
- **In Taurus:** Wear protective gear.
- **In Gemini:** Twice the inspiration yields exponential gain.
- **In Cancer:** Always keep an extra at home or in your car.
- **In Leo:** Keep the message big; increase your font size.
- **In Virgo:** Get those symptoms checked out this time … your body wants your attention.
- **In Libra:** When something breaks, it's not fair. Let go of the past and start fresh.
- **In Scorpio:** Who's got time for secrets and shadows? Don't be misled.
- **In Sagittarius:** Tenacity means never being afraid to start over.

- **In Capricorn:** Reboot the system and see what happens.
- **In Aquarius:** Keep your feet on the ground and your nose in a book.
- **In Pisces:** Swim against the tide, or go with the flow, or both at the same time … it's whatever works!

Mercury return   1. Point at which Mercury returns to the position it held in the native's birth chart. **2.** Mercury is in each sign for a little more than 7 days, and has a total orbit time of 88 days. Therefore, every 88 days Mercury returns to an exact place in its orbit. ✴ **1.** Because Mercury returns in your chart every 88 days, you'll have a Mercury return about four times every year. **2.** Mercury returns bring vital information that you want or need, as well as new ideas, greater focus, and meetings with important people. See also *Mercury, planetary returns.* ◯

**Mercury/Saturn   **Saturn is all about responsibility and discipline. These planets combine to create a serious communicator. Saturn and Mercury create success through attention to detail and clear communications. ✴ These two planets create a serious, thoughtful influence. Mercury and Saturn might create a teacher or minister— someone speaking seriously about an important topic. You take action on a problem with this aspect, and you need to help others understand the importance of your beliefs and actions. Mercury's innate mutable nature understands Saturn's rules. See also *aspects between planets, Mercury, Saturn.* △ ☯ ◯

Mercury/South Node   1. The comfort zone of the South Node in combination with Mercury indicates that areas of communication are already well known. **2.** Past karma supports knowledge of self-expression that will help growth in other areas of the birth chart. ✴ **1.** Mercury in aspect to your South Node says that you're intelligent, and you have amazing communication skills. You're very articulate—you can talk to anyone about anything … and you do! See also *aspects between planets, Mercury, South Node.* △ ☯ ◯

**Mercury/Sun   **The Sun relates to the outer self and the ego. Mercury is the closest planet to the Sun, and when Mercury and the Sun interact, Mercury is like the Sun's personal messenger. ✴ Mercury combines with the Sun to make you speak about your ego. You'll communicate the Sun's values: you'll translate what the Sun has to say for everyone to understand, and you will be able to tell others what the Sun (*your* Sun) *really* wants. See also *aspects between planets, Mercury, Sun.* △ ☯ ◯

Mercury transits   **1.** Mercury as it moves or transits through the signs of the zodiac. **2.** Mercury's orbit around the Sun takes 88 days; Mercury transits all twelve zodiac signs in that time. **3.** Mercury transits can be compared to the placement of Mercury in a natal chart for predictive purposes. A transit shows the position of a planet at a given moment. **4.** Transiting Mercury is a catalyst as it enters a new sign or a new house, and forms aspects with other transiting planets or planets in both birth and progressed charts. As a catalyst for expression and movement, Mercury is used by professional astrologers to predict important announcements, messages, conversations, meetings, ideas, arrivals, and departures. ✭ Need to know the best time to send an important message, set up a meeting or class, or get work done on your car? Transiting Mercury can tell you. As Mercury transits through each house of your chart, it helps you to get moving and express yourself. Where do you need Mercury's help? See also *Mercury, progressed birth chart, transiting planets, transits.* BC 🏠 ◯

M

What can Mercury transits tell you?

- Mercury transiting your **first house** tells you when to enter a writing competition.
- Mercury moving through your **second house** is a great time to buy something decorative or therapeutic for your hands or arms.
- Mercury transiting your **third house** is when you'll get a straight answer from your mechanic or engineer.
- Get out the photos and put a scrapbook together when Mercury moves through your **fourth house**.
- Mercury transiting your **fifth house** is the best time to have fun with your siblings or neighbors.
- Need a check-up? Go when Mercury is moving through your **sixth house**.
- Want to settle a pending lawsuit? Initiate your offer when Mercury enters your **seventh house**.
- If you need to take care of matters regarding a will, investments, taxes, or life insurance, do it when Mercury is in your **eighth house**. This is also the time to see a medium about talking to someone who has passed on to spirit.

- Mercury transiting your **ninth house** is the best time to contact a publisher about getting your book published or to submit your dissertation or thesis. It's also great for a walking tour in a foreign destination.
- Mercury transiting your **tenth house** is a great time to ask your boss for additional responsibility or to send out a memo outlining the accomplishments of those under you. This is also a good time to see your dermatologist, dentist, or chiropractor.
- Planning your wedding or a special event? Make the important decisions while Mercury moves through your **eleventh house**. This is also when you'll get your best ideas for inventions.
- Mercury transiting through your **twelfth house** tends to bring prophetic dreams and messages from the depths of your psyche.

Mercury/Uranus   The transpersonal planet Uranus is a planet of unexpected change. When Mercury interacts with Uranus, the big change is prefaced by logical thought and planning. ✦ When these planets interact in your birth chart, Mercury will communicate a desire for knowledge and information before Uranus begins a big change. These planets can work together or they can be at odds— Uranus just wants the change, while Mercury wants practical, logical change. See also *aspects between planets, Mercury, Uranus*. △ ☯ ◯

Mercury/Venus   Generous, kind, and affectionate Venus relates to Mercury to combine heart and mind. ✦ Venus and Mercury influence each other to help you think of compassion, engagement, and a desire for peaceful resolution of conflict. Meaningful communication is important to you, as is communicating in a kind and compassionate way. Part of communicating for you is listening, and your desire is to have everyone satisfied and at peace, even when they disagree. See also *aspects between planets, Mercury, Venus*. △ ☯ ◯

meridian   See *longitude*.

midheaven (Medium Coeli)   **1.** Highest point on the astrological birth chart, indicating the highest point of the Sun on the date of birth. **2.** The midheaven is on the cusp of the tenth house of career and career calling, public life, and reputation, and authority figures. **3.** Opposite the midheaven is the lowest point on the birth chart, the *nadir*. ✦ **1.** Your midheaven is the high noon of your chart. It appears at the top of the chart, on the cusp of the tenth house. **2.** You can find your midheaven by looking for the line with an arrow pointing upward in the top half of your birth chart. It's always on the cusp of the tenth house. Check to see what sign your midheaven is in for clues to how you can best decide your contribution to humanity. **3.** The tenth house cusp relates to career, but it's bigger than career. It's your career calling, your public reputation, your vocation. Look at your midheaven to find out how and where you are meant to contribute to the world. See also *nadir (Imum Coeli)*.

midpoint   1. The midpoint is the degree between two planets. It's not a planet itself, but rather the halfway point. Usually it forms aspects with the two planets it divides. For instance, it could semi-square each planet on either side of it. **2.** Many astrologers use the midpoint to help the planets it divides. If two planets are squaring each other, advising the native how to express the midpoint may soften a situation. It can also be helpful to focus on the Sabian symbol for the midpoint. See also *aspects between planets, planets, Sabian symbols*.

minor aspects   1. Specific angles, or aspects, between planets in a birth chart. The birth chart is a circle (360 degrees); minor aspects create influential relationships between planets in the birth chart. (Major aspects are considered more influential.) **2.** The four minor aspects are quincunx ⚻ (planets 150 degrees apart), semi-square ∠ (planets 45 degrees apart), sesquiquadrate ⬚ (planets 135 degrees apart), and semi-sextile ⚺ (planets 30 degrees apart). ⚹ **1.** The minor aspects aren't as easy to spot as the major ones, and they also aren't considered as influential. Minor aspects bring the opportunity for growth to your life, and it's up to you to use your free will to take advantage of the opportunity. Minor aspects are not as stable as major aspects and this off-kilter energy adds a sense of jump start and catalyst to the planetary relationships they inform. Like the tarot's Minor Arcana cards, astrology's minor aspects often highlight decisions you can make that will redefine your path or situation. **2.** If you created your birth chart on a computer, the aspects (major and minor) can be seen on the chart or in an accompanying aspect grid—you just have to recognize the aspect glyphs. See also *angle, aspect grid, aspects between planets, birth chart, glyphs, major aspects, quincunx, semi-square, semi-sextile, sesquiquadrate*. △ BC ○

modality   See *quality*.

money   **1.** Certain areas of the astrological birth chart relate to money and finances. **2.** The second house relates to earning capacity and possessions, and the eighth house provides insight into shared resources as well as karmic duty around money. **3.** The planets Venus and Mars (planetary rulers of the second and eighth houses) are also indicative of money-related matters in the birth chart.

✦ **1.** Having money issues, or wonder what you need to do to earn big bucks? Any money lessons or abilities you have will be represented in your second and eighth houses. Have a lot going on in those houses? You might have some work to do on money issues. **2.** If these two houses are empty in your birth chart, this shows that you've already worked through lots of lessons related to these houses. You may be versatile, and have no trouble finding work and making money. If you still want to know about your ability to make money, look for Venus's location in your chart as this will tell you the areas where you're especially skilled and have great earning potential. Venus's presence indicates a vocation rather than simply a career—money you earn in areas related to your Venus will also bring you a sense of self-worth. You'll likely be drawn to these areas, and can make money there, even if you think it an unlikely prospect—trust the stars! **3.** Venus and Mars and their aspects will indicate how money is likely to come into your life. If they are in harmony, they work together like a happy marriage and bring you work that you love that also makes you lots of money. When Mars feels good about Venus, other people want to give you money. When Venus feels good about Mars, you love the people who pay you. If Mars and Venus have a challenging relationship, such as a square, you tend to feel you shouldn't be paid very much for what you do or others are skeptical of your value and want to pay you less than you deserve. It can be helpful to bring a little Pluto energy in—Pluto is the modern ruler of Scorpio and other people's money. If you have tension between Venus and Mars, think of your money as being sourced by the universe and not by specific people, situations, employers, governments, or economies. This will lighten the planetary relationship as well as your attitude toward your own worth and those who pay you. See also *business astrology, eighth house, Mars, Pluto, second house, Venus.* 🏠 ◯

Moon **1.** Heavenly body orbiting the Earth in a 27.3-day cycle. **2.** The Moon's North Node and South Node are important in astrology as the points where the Moon crosses the ecliptic, causing solar eclipses. **3.** The Moon is the natural ruler of the Sun sign Cancer as well as the fourth house. **4.** The Moon is a luminary that relates to emotions and emotional connections. **5.** The Moon correlates to the yin or feminine principle. The Moon is also associated with mothering, nurturing, and the subconscious mind. The astrological symbol for the Moon is ☽. **6.** The Moon and the Sun (the luminaries) never go retrograde; the Moon's energy is always direct.

✧ **1.** The Moon is your emotional life and your inner self. It also represents your nurturing side. Want to understand your mother better? Look at your Moon placement—and your mom's too—for clues to this maternal relationship. If you are a woman, want to understand your own mothering style better? Look at your children's Moon placements in relation to your own. **2.** Where is the Moon in your birth chart? Look at the house and sign your Moon is in to learn more about how you express yourself emotionally. **3.** Your intuition and your intuitive nature are represented by the Moon. **4.** If your birth date or birth time is not completely accurate, your birth chart may not show your correct Moon sign. This is because the Moon moves fast—it goes through each sign in about two and a half days. Try to get the exact place of your birth and a to-the-minute birth time, if you can. **5.** In a daily astrological calendar, you can follow the Moon's transit through each of the signs and get a heads up as to the primary emotion encompassing the globe for the day. You can also see when the Sun and Moon are at odds with each other—when the Moon is in the opposite sign from the Sun's sign. See also *luminaries, Moon in the houses, Moon in the signs, Moon retrograde, North Node, South Node, yin.* △ ○ ℞

Moon in the houses **1.** The Moon brings dedication to the areas of life relating to each of the houses. **2.** The Moon's chart placement shows areas of emotional connection and bonding. **3.** The Moon is always direct, never retrograde. ✧ **1.** The Moon is emotion—the house the Moon appears in will tell you about how you *feel* in those areas of your life. **2.** The Moon also has to do with intuition and nurturing. What is revealed in the pale glow of moonlight illuminates the subconscious and the dreamscapes of your psyche.

☽ **in the first house**   The Moon in the first house creates an emotional connection to the outward self. ✵ **1.** First house Moon means you're dedicated to yourself, you have an emotional connection to your outward appearance, and you're passionate about how you express yourself to the outside world. **2.** There's an emotional connection for this Moon to your rising sign (the sign on the cusp of your first house). **3.** When you're in public, you'll show your emotions—what you see is what you get. Your outward appearance and how you relate to the world is emotional. You relate to the outer world emotionally.

☽ **in the second house**   A second house Moon relates as an emotional need for security. ✵ **1.** With second house Moon you're dedicated to security needs, including earning money. You might have an emotional attachment to material goods and the material world. **2.** The Moon is a personal planet, and you feel better when you can make your own money. You're connected to what you value, and you have an emotional attachment to feeling safe and secure. **3.** Your self-worth increases as your sense of safety increases. Conversely, you get nervous if you feel your needs have not been met.

☽ **in the third house**   Emotions are attached to thoughts when the Moon is in the third house of communication. ✵ **1.** Your thoughts and ideas have a strong emotional influence on you with a third house Moon. You are moved by how you speak and relate to others, as well as a desire to communicate and remain attached to siblings. **2.** You have a need to connect to people verbally, and your arts of persuasion have strong emotive power. **3.** You feel with your mind.

☽ **in the fourth house**   A strong emotional connection and bond to family comes with a fourth house Moon. ✵ **1.** You might react strongly to what family members expect or ask of you with fourth house Moon. You are likely dedicated to family, and don't like to disappoint them. **2.** You have a strong belief in loyalty to whomever you consider to be your family, your primary social network. **3.** You may have a special connection to mothering and motherhood.

☽ **in the fifth house**   A fifth house Moon creates an emotional connection to children and passion for creative self-expression. ✵ **1.** You're an entertainer with fifth house Moon. Your emotional connection may be through children—your own or others, or your own attachment to childhood pursuits. **2.** You may be childlike and very creative yourself, or you may be passionate about children's causes. **3.** Romance, performance, and fun are your pursuits.

☽ **in the sixth house**   The Moon in the sixth house brings an emotional resonance through career and service to others. ✦ **1.** You are dedicated to your health, to your daily routine, and to public service. **2.** You are passionate about your well-being, and you have an emotional attachment to co-workers and your place of work. You might become a workaholic. **3.** You feel emotionally satisfied by helping others.

☽ **in the seventh house**   A seventh house Moon brings dedication to partnership and cooperation. ✦ **1.** You really need and want a partner—business, marriage, or domestic partnership. You're dedicated to these partnerships, and develop strong emotional attachments to your partners. **2.** You really want others to cooperate well together, and you'd likely make a good counselor, mediator, or lawyer.

☽ **in the eighth house**   An emotional release around money and shared resources is expressed through the Moon in the eighth house. ✦ **1.** You are dedicated to transformation and rebirth with an eighth house Moon. **2.** You're emotionally connected to money and resources—you'd like to help others attain financial success. **3.** With this Moon you are very intuitive, and possibly even psychic. You're dedicated to the unknown, and love the mysteries of life, beyond the material world. You're bonded to the mysteries of life, and are always asking why—finding out secrets may be your passion.

☽ **in the ninth house**   Religion or belief system, higher education, and foreign travel are the areas of emotional dedication associated with a ninth house Moon. ✦ **1.** You're dedicated to religious or spiritual work with a ninth house Moon. **2.** You likely enjoy learning and may have advanced degrees. You want to know everything, and may try to understand why others think and behave as they do—here and in other cultures. You're emotionally attached to seeking higher wisdom, and you need to develop religious, spiritual, or educational desires. **3.** Your passion is likely study and education, and travel also likely invigorates your passion.

☽ **in the tenth house**   The Moon in the tenth house brings a sense of dedication to career and public life. ✦ **1.** You are dedicated and passionate about your career. Your colleagues are very important to you, and you are connected to and bonded to your career calling—you have an important place in the world through your career contribution. **2.** You might be a leader, dedicated to public service

M

with a Moon in the tenth house. You feel that you have a calling, and your calling brings you emotional fulfillment.

☽ in the eleventh house A strong dedication to social networks and personal hopes come with an eleventh house Moon. ✶ **1.** You're dedicated to friends with eleventh house Moon, and you need to bond with and socialize with your network; it's where you're emotionally attached. **2.** Clubs, organizations, and social networks bring you emotional fulfillment—it may not be your family. You have many friends and followers and you love the intimacy of the instant message.

☽ in the twelfth house A twelfth house Moon is connected to karmic duty and debt, as well as psychic abilities. ✶ **1.** You're sensitive to others with this twelfth house Moon and have an emotional need to connect to your inner intuition. **2.** You may be somewhat insecure emotionally, and you tend to hold back with those you don't know. You don't like to expose yourself emotionally. You're a great observer of others, and are very compassionate. **3.** You might also be overly sensitive. Your great compassion and observational skills make you a wonderful and caring counselor, psychiatrist, pastor, or psychic counselor. **4.** You love to work behind the scenes and tend to be an introvert. You might become sacrificial, if you aren't careful.

See also *luminaries, Moon, Moon in the signs, Moon retrograde.* 🏠 ○

Is your Moon above or below the horizon? People with their Moon above the horizon, in houses seven through twelve, really get recharged in foreign cultures and through travel. Those with the Moon below the horizon, in houses one through six, tend to be homebodies. The first six houses are more personal and domestic—foreign travel makes those with the Moon in these houses long for home or at least appreciate home. And houses six through twelve are more inquisitive—those with their Moon in these houses look outside themselves more and are energized and enriched by experiences outside the domestic sphere.

Moon in the signs **1.** The Moon is the planet of nurturing and emotion. The sign the Moon is in will indicate how the native feels and expresses emotion. **2.** As a luminary, the Moon is always direct, never retrograde.

☽ in Aquarius Aquarius is a sign of freedom and innovation. ✶ If you have the Moon in Aquarius, you are intellectual, and have an emotional need to communicate. If you can find someone on your level to talk with, you're happy. You can accidentally hurt others with your abruptness or impulsivity. You're creative and independent. You love your family and can be a humanitarian, but you don't always do well one on one. Too much emotion is uncomfortable for you, and you may run from it.

☽ **in Aries**   Aries is a sign of action and beginnings. ✴ If you have the Moon in Aries, you're outgoing, and you emote easily and instantaneously. You need to be free and independent. You don't want too many emotional bonds—that feels confining. You trigger people's emotions, but don't always handle the response well.

☽ **in Cancer**   Cancer is a sign of emotion and family. The Moon is at home in Cancer. ✴ If you have the Moon in Cancer, home, family, and security are all important to you. Anyone you have an emotional attachment to is like a family member to you. You are devoted to those you love. You are sensitive and emotional and you feel everything deeply. You can be moody, and tend to hide your hurts away. You're also intuitive and imaginative.

☽ **in Capricorn**   Capricorn is a sign of practicality and discipline. ✴ If you have the Moon in Capricorn, your emotions are deep. You are hardworking and can seem serious and unfeeling, but you just don't express your emotions verbally. You like to stay busy and are success oriented. You also enjoy nature and the great outdoors— you are calmed by outdoor pursuits. Your mother may thrive on your outer world achievements so much you feel compelled to draw a line as to what you have earned on your own and what is due to her support and encouragement.

☽ **in Gemini**   Gemini is a sign of intellect and communication. ✴ If you have the Moon in Gemini, your mind is connected to your emotions, and you talk out your emotions. You're very self-expressive, and you have an emotional need to express your feelings. You're quick to share your feelings with others—once you've thought them through.

☽ **in Leo**   Leo is a sign of leadership and heart. ✴ If you have the Moon in Leo, you're demonstrative and strong-willed. You are a bit dramatic, as well as generous and kind. You are good at drama and performing, and can inspire others easily. You need to lead and are good at it. Loyalty is important to you—you need to feel appreciated.

☽ **in Libra**   Libra is a sign of balance and justice. ✴ If you have the Moon in Libra, you need a partner. You have an emotional need

M

to find compatible partners in life. You don't like doing things alone, and feel enriched by working with others cooperatively or bringing others together. You're a good negotiator.

☽ **in Pisces**   Pisces is a sign of intuition and compassion. ✳ If you have the Moon in Pisces, you are highly emotional and intuitive. You are likely psychic, and you read others well. You feel compassion for others and seek a soul mate. You're idealistic, though, and you may not attract what you think you want. The people you attract usually have some karmic connection to you—this can be challenging, but you're devoted and you need to help others transform. You're fine living on your own, and you're great with children and animals.

☽ **in Sagittarius**   Sagittarius is a sign of adventure and philosophy. ✳ If you have the Moon in Sagittarius, you're optimistic and genuinely concerned for others. You enjoy attention, and can be a risk-taker in love. You get bored when things are too steady, and you may go looking for adventure. You see well in the moonlight and are not intimidated by strong emotions and deep feelings; but you are more likely to be seduced by a new experience than a new person.

☽ **in Scorpio**   Scorpio is a sign of intensity and magnetism. ✳ If you have the Moon in Scorpio, you are intensely passionate and sensual. Privacy is very important to you. You are sometimes judgmental, and are easily induced to drop people who hurt you—they may not know what they did, because you'll keep it to yourself. You likely love a good mystery, and enjoy digging for answers. You may be highly intuitive or insightful, and likely have psychic abilities—though you may not tell anyone else about this.

☽ **in Taurus**   Taurus is a sign of calm dedication. ✳ If you have the Moon in Taurus, feeling snug and safe is important to you. You're affectionate and romantic, and very loyal when committed. You're emotionally balanced and stable. Others can count on you for emotional support. You are the kind of person who will find out what makes other people feel comfortable, especially family, and then supply it if you can.

☽ **in Virgo**   Virgo is a sign of order and control. ✳ If you have the Moon in Virgo, you are organized and methodical. You tend to analyze your own feelings. You might be disappointed in others—it's difficult to meet your expectations. You love to complete tasks—in the best possible way. You approach whatever you're concentrating on doing with methodical zeal, and you love order, even in your emotions. See also *Moon, signs.* ◯ ☼

Moon/Jupiter   See *Jupiter/Moon.*

Moon/Mars   See *Mars/Moon.*

Moon/Mercury   See *Mercury/Moon.*

Moon/Neptune   Neptune relates to the spirit and imagination. When Neptune interacts with the Moon, dedication to imagination is the result. �֍ **1.** No matter the aspect, a Moon/Neptune connection enhances your imagination. The Moon draws you to imagination and creativity, and when combined with Neptune, you'll be drawn to the arts—drama, art, fantasy, and psychic awareness. You might become an actor, dancer, singer, or religious or spiritual leader. You do well in drama or writing, because you really enjoy becoming another person in your mind for a while. You slip into your imaginative world easily and fully—your surrender to this side of yourself is almost trancelike. **2.** You might be able to channel information and guidance from the other side. You will also have a desire for spiritual development and religious awareness, and you will be profoundly devoted to your calling. You may be altruistic and spiritual. See also *aspects between planets, Moon, Neptune.* △ ☯ ◯

Moon/North Node   The Moon is emotion, and the North Node is what has to be learned. The North Node can indicate the karmic destiny of this, and future lives. ✖ When the Moon and the North Node interact, this indicates that you have to learn to be open with your emotions—not something you're comfortable with at all! You're learning to be aware of your emotions as well as how to connect emotionally with others. You're likely very intuitive, but you have to learn to trust your intuition. See also *aspects between planets, Moon, North Node.* △ ☯ ◯

Moon phases   **1.** The Moon's orbit around the Earth takes 27.3 days. In this time, the Moon passes through the twelve signs of the zodiac. **2.** The Moon has four major phases, which can be further broken down into eight total phases. Moon phases are a result of how the Moon reflects light from the Sun. Sun and Moon aspects create the four major Moon phases: new Moon, waxing Moon, full Moon, and waning Moon. **3.** The eight Moon phases are: new Moon, crescent Moon, first quarter Moon (waxing Moon), gibbous Moon, full Moon, disseminating Moon, last quarter Moon (waning Moon), and balsamic Moon. **4.** The Moon phases are important to the practice of the Wiccan faith, in which the ceremony to draw down the Moon is a powerful affirmation of Goddess energy. Many cultures and spiritual practices throughout history and around the globe incorporate the Moon phases into ritual and belief. ☆ Do you know what Moon phase you were born in? Find out and then look up that phase to see what meaning your birth date's moonlight has for you. See also *balsamic Moon, crescent Moon, disseminating Moon, first quarter Moon, full Moon, gibbous Moon, last quarter Moon, Moon, new Moon.* **BC ◯ Z**

What phase of the Moon were you born in?
- **New Moon:** 0 to 45 degrees ahead of the Sun.
- **Crescent Moon:** 45 to 90 degrees ahead of the Sun.
- **First quarter Moon:** 90 to 135 degrees ahead of the Sun.
- **Gibbous Moon:** 135 to 180 degrees ahead of the Sun.
- **Full Moon:** 180 to 135 degrees behind the Sun.
- **Disseminating Moon:** 135 to 90 degrees behind the Sun.
- **Last quarter Moon:** 90 to 45 degrees behind the Sun.
- **Balsamic Moon:** 45 to 0 degrees behind the Sun.

Moon/Pluto   The luminary Moon interacts with the outer planet Pluto to create dedication to transformation. ☆ The Moon interacts with Pluto in a powerful way. If you have an aspect between the Moon and Pluto, you are likely connected to a higher consciousness—you may be ultra-sensitive to what's happening around you, in your community, and the world. You feel the emotions of the world around you, and you feel the energy of a crowd. You see the big picture and are attuned to a higher plane. A strong connection here means you are able to help others transform and attain a higher level of consciousness. You have the potential to impact the world—recognize this and be aware of how your actions influence others. Secrets—good or bad!—may be revealed when these two planets are in aspect. See also *aspects between planets, Moon, Pluto.* △ ☯ ◯

Moon retrograde   As luminaries, the Moon and the Sun are always direct, never retrograde. See also *luminaries, Moon, Moon phases, Sun.*
○ ℞

Moon/Saturn   The Moon brings devotion to Saturn's responsibility and discipline. ✦ Your Moon/Saturn aspects will show a realistic, practical approach. You have the opportunity to complete tasks and are likely dutiful and responsible. You have a desire for order and practicality. Getting the job done is very important to you—your physical comforts can fall by the wayside if necessary to complete the task at hand. You'll be learning about devotion and responsibility. Discipline is like freedom for you. Saturn will control your emotions, and the Moon will provide you with self-discipline. See also *aspects between planets, Moon, Saturn.* △ ☯ ○

Moon sign   **1.** The astrological sign the Moon was transiting through at the time of birth is the Moon sign. **2.** The Moon stays in each sign for about two and a half days, as it appears in the sky from the Earth, moving through each of the Sun signs in its 28½-day orbit.

✦ **1.** What's your Moon sign? The zodiac sign the Moon was in when you were born tells you about your emotions and how you express them. How you nurture others is expressed in your Moon sign, as well. **2.** Your Moon sign indicates how you *emotionally* project the characteristic energies of your Sun sign. **3.** Astrology is full of yin and yang, such as with feminine and masculine signs. The Moon is the yin or feminine luminary that plays out the other side of the yang or masculine Sun. In the same way that your Sun sign tells you about your yang side, the Moon—and your Moon sign—helps you understand your yin side. **4.** While the Sun is about your more developed or higher self, the Moon holds answers about your more primal origins: the nature of your soul *before* you started your journey in this lifetime. As your soul chose to have a particular experience in this life, it stored all the memories of who you have been before this lifetime in your unconscious mind (which is ruled by your Moon). The more you understand your Moon sign, the more you understand your unconscious behaviors. A professional astrologer can give you a lot of detail about your past life experiences by reading your Moon's sign, placement, and aspects. **5.** The Moon

M

is about your relationship to your mother and to Mother Earth. It is also about your most immediate survival needs. Your Moon sign tells you what you need to survive and how you feel when your needs are unfulfilled. **6.** The Moon rules instinct; your Moon sign indicates your instinctual prowess—or dysfunction. **7.** The Moon rules your intuitive nature, or what you can feel at a visceral level. Your Moon sign tells you how your intuition operates. **8.** In a man's chart, the Moon sign indicates how he relates to his emotions, his internal feminine, and to women in general. A man tends to live out his Sun sign more naturally and will grow to include his Moon sign. If he works to embrace his Moon sign more consciously, he releases emotional resistance and baggage and is able to more fully enjoy life. In other words, he evolves more easily. **9.** In a woman's chart, the Moon sign indicates her comfort with her own body's cycles, nurturing others, and the various phases of motherhood from expectant/ new mother to grandmother. A woman typically feels most herself as her Moon sign and makes a conscious effort to become the best example of her Sun sign. See also *Moon, Moon in the signs, Sun sign, yang, yin.* **BC** ☽ ○ ☼

Moon/South Node   The Moon is the inner self and emotion; the South Node is the comfort zone. This combination indicates familiarity with the emotional self. The karmic connotation of the South Node means this Moon sheds light on past lives with emotional clarity. ✳ If your Moon and South Node are in aspect, you are likely someone whose emotions are easily triggered—you might cry at weddings, at movies, in everyday conversation! You bond easily with others. You feel deeply and are wide open, making yourself vulnerable. You're compassionate and empathetic—maybe too much. You might be oversensitive to others' emotions, or just plain oversensitive. You feel what you feel, and what everyone else feels, too. You're also highly intuitive. See also *aspects between planets, Moon, South Node.* △ ☽ ○

Moon/Sun   The Moon is all about emotions, and the Sun is about the outer self. Together, the two luminaries create harmony between the inner and outer self. ✳ The Moon connects to the Sun and creates a feeling of harmony—your inner life is aligned with your outer life, and your emotional self is in harmony with your ego. You're likely vital and energetic, determined, and emotionally supportive of others. The bond between these two planets in your birth chart brings out your intuition and instinct. Sun/Moon connections are emotional, and you are opened up to that emotional energy with such a connection. See also *aspects between planets, Moon, Sun.* △ ☯ ○

Moon transits **1.** The Moon's motion or transit through the signs of the zodiac. **2.** The Moon's orbit around the Earth takes 27.3 days; the Moon transits all twelve zodiac signs in that time. **3.** The Moon's transits can be compared to the placement of the Moon in a birth chart for predictive purposes. Because the Moon moves pretty quickly, most astrologers do not spend a lot of time predicting what will happen with each shift of the Moon from sign-to-sign, but the position of the transiting Moon can be very important for choosing a date that is safe and comfortable for events ruled by the Moon or allotted to the house with a Cancer cusp in your chart. For instance, you would want a harmonious placement of the Moon for an open house, a real estate transaction, conception, baby shower, moving into a new home, finding the right home for your mother, hiring a nanny, a family reunion, or even the right date for a fishing trip.

✦ **1.** Need to know what date to schedule your visit to your allergist or midwife? You can choose a date by comparing what sign your Moon was in when you were born with what signs the Moon will be in throughout the month. Start by finding the Moon in your birth chart. Once you know your Moon sign, you can check to see when the transiting Moon is in a sign that is harmonious with your Moon sign. If the Moon is in a sign that is two or four signs away from your Moon sign, then matters of the Moon go easily. For instance, if you were born with your Moon in Aries, look for when the Moon is in Gemini (two signs away counterclockwise), Aquarius (two signs away clockwise), Leo (four signs away counterclockwise), or Sagittarius (four signs away clockwise). **2.** You can also find dates that may be problematic for Moon activities. If the Moon is in a sign that is three, five, or seven signs away from your Moon sign, you may want to choose another, more harmonious date. See also *Moon, transiting planets, transits.* **BC** ○ ☼

Moon/Uranus The outer planet Uranus combines combustible effect with the luminary Moon to stir up emotional action or change. ✦ If you have the Moon in aspect to Uranus in your birth chart, be prepared for the unexpected! This pairing will result in unusual, bizarre, and sometimes impulsive action, as well as strong emotion and great emotional tension. You may have very passionate energy and heightened psychic abilities. You might also be drawn to clandestine relationships. The pattern these planets create may be disruptive. You likely have great ambitions, and rapidly fluctuating moods. You'll never have a dull moment with the planetary interaction of the Moon and Uranus! See also *aspects between planets, Moon, Uranus.*

Moon/Venus   Venus is all about love, and the Moon is emotion— what a great combination! ✴ The Moon and Venus can create a life of happiness and balance. You are likely charitable and friendly. You have a positive outlook and a love of beauty and art. Romantic love and home life are important to you. You're sensitive to affection, and have a strong desire to socialize and connect with others. Even challenging aspects between the Moon and Venus will lead you to affection and compatible connections with others. Loving, kind relationships are your forte. You enjoy a big extended family dinner! See also *aspects between planets, Moon, Venus.*

morning sky, planets in   **1.** Physically, the planets appear in the morning sky based on their rotations. **2.** In astrology, the planets in the morning sky are those in the eleventh and twelfth houses. Planets in these houses appear above the ascendant in the birth chart, and change monthly. **3.** The planets in the morning sky each day are those that rule the astrological sign for that date. ✴ **1.** The early rising morning sky planets focus on new beginnings, and opening doors to allow new things in. You can check the planets in the morning sky each day, for clues about what's in store that day. **2.** If you have a lot of planets in the morning sky—in the eleventh or twelfth houses of your birth chart, you are ahead of your time and have a unique concept and vision of the future. You are detached, but compassionate, which allows you to love unconditionally. You have faith in the new generation and can see how technology and spirituality will one day dovetail. Your enlightened view is an inspiration to others and you probably share your visions through your work, be that a cause, fine art, music, photography, journalism, a documentary, poetry, break-through television, the web, or the pursuit of a cure to a devastating disease. See also *eleventh house; evening sky, planets in; planets; twelfth house.*

mothers and mothering   See *Moon*.

mundane astrology   **1.** Branch of astrology dealing with world events. **2.** The word *mundane* means "world"; this branch of astrology focuses on politics and world affairs. **3.** Mundane astrology uses all of the houses and planets to create a birth chart for an event such as a presidential inauguration. A mundane astrological chart is used to forecast events and outcomes. See also *astrology, birth chart, house, planets*. **BC Z**

mutable cross   See *grand cross*.

mutable (quality)   **1.** One of the three qualities used to classify the astrological signs (the others are cardinal and fixed) that influence behavior. **2.** Mutable signs are Gemini, Virgo, Sagittarius, and Pisces, representing each of the four elements: air, earth, fire, and water. **3.** The mutable signs are the final sign in each season, the time when the seasons shift. Mutable signs represent change. They are the most adaptable in the zodiac.

✦ **1.** If you're a mutable sign, you're likely easygoing. You get along with pretty much everyone, and you really want others to get along, too. You might wear many hats—you're very flexible, and can move from one task to another—or a few others—easily. You're the poster child for multitasking. Be careful that your multitasking doesn't become a lack of focus. You may come across as scattered, but you really can carry on a conversation with three people (on three different topics) at once. **2.** You may have lots of planets in mutable signs in your birth chart, and if this is the case, you might be flexible, with a tendency to go with the flow in life. You aren't rigid, but can change direction at the drop of a hat. Do you have a lot of planets in Gemini? You are like a chameleon. You can quickly read another person's character and adapt yours so that you express yourself in a way that makes the other person very comfortable and relaxed. The problem is that the other person assumes that you're the same as they are and they never bother to ask you questions about yourself. Loads of planets in Virgo? Whatever is needed, you shift gears and get it done. Mary Poppins probably had lots of planets in Virgo because she could tidy, cure, inspire, counsel, and summon up magic with a snap of her fingers, yet always knew when it was time to go. Do you have many planets in Sagittarius? You

M

could be a laid-back perpetual student who travels the world. It doesn't bother you one iota that when you learn something new and profound, you might have to surrender up your current philosophy. You just love learning and often update your beliefs about what constitutes truth, justice, and reality. More than a few Pisces planets? You are more than flexible: you are boundless, like the ocean. You are psychic, sympathetic, empathetic, and sincerely forgiving because you totally get that all people are connected like the cells of one big body. You read and transmit thoughts as easily—and unthinkingly—as you breathe. **3.** Of the four mutable signs, Gemini is the *most* changeable and Virgo is the most stable. See also *cardinal (quality), fixed, Gemini, Pisces, Sagittarius, Virgo.* ◯ ☼

mutual reception   **1.** Occurs when two planets are each in the sign that the other is exalted in. For example, Mercury is exalted in Virgo and Jupiter is exalted in Cancer. If Jupiter is in Virgo and Mercury is in Cancer in the same chart, these two planets are said to be in *mutual reception.* **2.** Some astrologers consider two planets in mutual reception when each is in the sign or house ruled by the other. So if Venus is in Leo and the Sun is in Libra, then Venus and the Sun are in mutual reception. Or if Venus is in the fifth house and the Sun is in the second or seventh house, then Venus and the Sun would also be in mutual reception. See also *exalted, house, planets, ruler.* 🏠 ◯

mythology   See *goddesses/gods.*

nadir (Imum Coeli, or IC) **1.** The beginning of the fourth house, or the line between the third and fourth houses in the birth chart. **2.** The nadir is also called the *north point.* **3.** Opposite the nadir in the birth chart is the *midheaven.* **4.** The nadir represents the resolution of life, as well as life foundations. How will things conclude? This is the question answered by the nadir.

✦ **1.** Your nadir is the midnight or the lowest point of your chart. It's on the bottom half of your birth chart, on the cusp of the fourth house, which relates to home and family. **2.** You can find your nadir by looking for the arrow pointing downward from the center of your birth chart. This line is the nadir. The top half of this line (an arrow pointing upward) is your midheaven. **3.** In the birth chart, the sign on your nadir will tell how you conclude this life. **4.** There's a generational effect to the nadir: the fourth house includes ancestors, so the nadir relates to your contribution to your family of origin. The nadir can give you information on how you entered this life, how you utilized your talents and gifts while here, and how you'll exit this life. Ask yourself: What mark will you leave on your family of origin? Did you take care of your elders? How many cell phones will you go through in your lifetime, talking to the people in your life? **5.** Your nadir can also give you clues about how a pregnancy will conclude, so you'll know what to expect when labor arrives. **6.** The nadir also helps you understand what you need to feel secure and comfortable in your body and in your family. See also *birth chart, fourth house, midheaven* (Medium Coeli). **BC** 🏠

natal astrology The use of astrology to create and interpret birth charts. See *birth chart.* **BC Z**

natal chart   See *birth chart.*

native   Another name for the owner of a birth or natal chart.
✦ You are the native of your own birth chart. See also *birth chart.*
BC ☯ Z

natural chart   An equal house chart, in which each house is exactly
30 degrees, that has 0 degree, zero minute Aries on the ascendant,
the cusp of the first house. See also *ascendant, birth chart, first house.*
BC 🏠

natural house ruler   **1.** The planetary ruler associated with each
of the twelve houses of the zodiac in a natural chart. **2.** Each of the
twelve houses of the zodiac correlates with a zodiac sign, and each
zodiac sign has a natural planetary ruler. ✦ The natural ruler of
each house is important because of the influence the planet has in
that house. Remember that if you have no planets in a particular
house, the house ruler is where you look for planetary influence
there. See also *birth chart, house, planets, zodiac.* BC 🏠 ○ ☼ Z

House	Planetary Ruler (Zodiac Sign)
First	Mars (Aries)
Second	Venus (Taurus)
Third	Mercury (Gemini)
Fourth	Moon (Cancer)
Fifth	Sun (Leo)
Sixth	Mercury (Virgo)
Seventh	Venus (Libra)
Eighth	Mars, Pluto (Scorpio)
Ninth	Jupiter (Sagittarius)
Tenth	Saturn (Capricorn)
Eleventh	Uranus, Saturn (Aquarius)
Twelfth	Neptune, Jupiter (Pisces)

negative sign   **1.** Another name for the indirect or feminine energy ascribed to the planets and zodiac signs in astrology. The terms *negative sign* and *positive sign* are used more in the sense of alternating current, and not at all in the sense of bad and good. **2.** The negative, or yin, signs are the earth and water signs: Taurus, Cancer, Virgo, Scorpio, Capricorn, and Pisces. See also *feminine principle, positive sign*, yin. ☯○☼

Neptune   **1.** The planet discovered in 1846 and named for the Roman god of the sea. **2.** Neptune is the eighth planet from the Sun. Its orbit takes 165 years, and it spends about 14 years in each zodiac sign. Because its orbit is so lengthy, Neptune has a generational influence: everyone born during each 14 year period when Neptune is in a particular sign will have Neptune in that sign in the birth chart. **3.** Neptune is the natural ruler of Pisces, and the planetary ruler of the twelfth house. **4.** According to Roman myth, Neptune is the son of Saturn, and brother to Jupiter and Pluto. The Greek equivalent of Neptune is Poseidon. **5.** Neptune is one of the outer planets, also called the transpersonal planets, and is associated with dreams and inspiration. The astrological glyph for Neptune is ♆. **6.** Neptune ℞ heightens sensitivities and minimizes boundaries. If other planets have difficult aspect to a retrograde Neptune, escape from reality becomes strongly desired and fantasy may begin to replace reality. Night and day can also get all turned around as sleep patterns may be polarized. If other planets positively aspect a retrograde Neptune, psychic abilities are heightened, as is imagination, passion for music, compassion, and a sense that all people are universally connected.

✦ **1.** Neptune is the planet of dreams, spirituality, and the unknown. In what sign is Neptune in your birth chart? This can give you clues about what inspires you and how you relate to the world spiritually—and psychically. Neptune will help you figure out your spiritual needs. **2.** Which house does Neptune occupy in your birth chart? Neptune is about inspiration and dreams, but the house and sign your Neptune is in will tell you more about what Neptune means in *your* life. **3.** Neptune also relates to psychic awareness, and is the natural ruler of the twelfth house of karma and the unconscious. **4.** The dark side of Neptune can be an overworked imagination, leading to fantastic visions, fanaticism, or infatuations with various belief systems. **5.** Neptune relates to your spiritual life, which could include organized religion, but it doesn't have to. Your expression of the spiritual could also include meditation, nature hikes, and astrology, to name a few. It just depends on your personal spiritual needs, which your Neptune placement can help you discover. Both organized religion and spiritualism have shadow sides or extremes. For organized religion, it's fanaticism, and for spiritualism, it's channeling. **6.** In a daily astrological calendar, days and times when Neptune is in a positive aspect to the Sun (such as conjunct, trine, or sextile) are usually good times for fun in, on, or at the water, as well as dancing, forgiveness, playing music, painting, and healing in a hospital. Days when Neptune is in a more challenging aspect to the Sun (such as opposition or square) can be times when confusion, denial, or narcissism appears. Worry can creep in, so it's best to focus on the beauty of nature and those you love. Charitable work helps alleviate suffering or sorrow. See also *Neptune in the houses, Neptune in the signs, retrograde planets.* △ ◯ ℞

Neptune in the houses   1. As Neptune goes through the houses, it represents spiritual growth and devotion to a calling. **2.** Neptune placement in the birth chart reveals the source of devotion.
✷ **1.** Neptune is the part of you that goes to church, meditates, and prays. You can learn about how you express yourself spiritually by looking at the house your Neptune lives in. **2.** You'll be most spiritually inclined and devoted to a higher calling wherever Neptune lands in your chart—the house is very important to Neptune's influence in your life.

Ψ in the first house   Neptune in the first house self-identifies with religion or spirituality. ✷ **1.** If Neptune is in your first house you are inclined to be religious or spiritual. You want peace and tranquility, and you need a spiritual calling. You're devoted or may spend your life looking for philosophical direction or looking for a Higher Power. You're creative and focused on your religious and spiritual ideals, and that's how you appear to others. You also desire spiritual/creative qualities in others. **2.** You may be extreme in your beliefs, or you may express extreme behavior through escapism—your own fantasies and delusions may be the basis for self-delusion. **3.** Neptune ℞ in the first house compensates for internal confusion and worry through aggression.

Ψ **in the second house**   In the second house, Neptune relates to money and the material or physical world. ✦ **1.** Here second house Neptune might take a spiritual approach to money matters. You're likely altruistic and generous with your physical possessions. You may also be creative with money. Spiritual values are important to you, as are your religious ideals. **2.** Neptune ℞ in the second house brings nightmares about being homeless. Once you understand that Neptune ℞ magnifies things out of proportion, its energy can be used to visualize and manifest mountains of money.

Ψ **in the third house**   Neptune in the third house relates to communication and self-expression. ✦ **1.** If you have Neptune in your third house, your imagination flows well, and your creative self-expression is good. You may excel at acting or writing. Religious or spiritual values are important to you in communication, and you likely communicate in a religious or spiritual way. **2.** Religion or spirituality also might have been highlighted in your childhood. Perhaps you were conditioned to certain beliefs, and if so, you would likely stick with those beliefs into adulthood. **3.** Neptune ℞ in the third house can make learning a challenge unless information is conveyed through hands-on experience.

Ψ **in the fourth house**   Neptune in the fourth house is about family and home. ✦ **1.** This Neptune placement makes family, as well as how you were raised and taught about spiritual and religious philosophy, important to you throughout your life. **2.** You want to help others be compassionate and giving, and you are willing to sacrifice for or devote yourself to your home and family of origin. You feel devoted to where you came from, without question. **3.** Neptune ℞ in the fourth house can show up as a food addiction or extreme insecurity, which can be rectified by identifying what the soul *truly* desires. Your emotions provide all the clues: if what you want doesn't give you a cozy or pleasant floating feeling, it's probably a substitute for what your soul wants—something you don't dare to hope for.

Ψ **in the fifth house**   In the fifth house, Neptune relates to birth and rebirth, as well as children and creative expression. ✦ **1.** Neptune in your fifth house makes you musical, creative, and/or artistic. Careers in the fine arts, design, or entertainment—artist, writer, architect, actor—all appeal to you. **2.** You work well with children and understand the childhood imagination. You are devoted to children, creativity, and self-expression. You might also have a childlike aura. **3.** Neptune ℞ in the fifth house feels ashamed for needing attention and should be encouraged to start by giving their inner child more attention.

Ψ **in the sixth house**　In the sixth house, Neptune relates to health and work environment. ✴ **1.** Sixth house Neptune makes you devoted to work and to your employer/ees and co-workers. You want to make a contribution to your workplace. You're inclined to take on a lot of responsibility in your work, and when you find your calling in work, you will be consistently devoted to it. **2.** You need to stay grounded and realistic about your health. Don't mislead yourself about your health or rationalize overindulgence. The self-deceptive side of Neptune can lead you into denial about your health and well-being, and you have to resist this. **3.** Neptune ℞ in the sixth house tends to generate hypochondria until health is understood to be an interactive relationship between the body, mind, and spirit.

Ψ **in the seventh house**　A seventh house Neptune relates to partnership. ✴ **1.** Your seventh house Neptune makes you idealistic: you want the highest and the best. You want a spiritual partner, and would prefer someone with a spiritual calling. That's what you seek in partnerships—someone who equals you in philosophy or spiritual beliefs. You also want devotion; once you make a connection to a partner, you will be devoted to that partner or to the path you enter with that partner. **2.** Be careful not to delude yourself about your partner. Don't think of him or her as your savior. You tend to see the highest in your partner, and while this is generally a good thing, it may be an illusion. Some partners will try to live up to how you see them, though. **3.** Neptune ℞ in the seventh house hides their outrage about a partner's insensitivity. Instead of sharing your feelings, you strive to be a perfect mate who continually sacrifices for the good of the relationship.

Ψ **in the eighth house**　Rebirth, transformation, and shared resources are the domain of an eighth house Neptune. ✴ **1.** Neptune in the eighth house might mean that you're clairvoyant—you definitely pick up on things others don't understand. You've got psychic gifts, and may touch the other side, and be able to communicate with or somehow connect to the spirit world. You're also very intuitive. The grandeur of the spirit world attracts you—makes sure that illusion doesn't cloud your psychic judgment. **2.** You may be good at collecting resources or, if you follow your self-deceptive side, you might be a gambler. **3.** Neptune ℞ in the eighth house indicates karma around possessiveness or jealousy. The retrograde causes you to imagine these familiar souls as still jealous and plotting revenge or betrayal. Past life regression can be very helpful in releasing the stuck trauma so that you can forgive those you're in power play with.

♆ **in the ninth house**   In the ninth house, Neptune relates to philosophy and religion, as well as travel and higher education. ✴ **1.** With a ninth house Neptune, you're really connected to your spiritual beliefs and religion, which could be metaphysical, spiritual, or traditionally or otherwise religious. Your belief system might supersede everything else in your life; they come first for you. **2.** You're an idealist, devoted to being peaceful and kind. You might attract a following as a spiritual leader, and would make a good minister, guru, or nurse. Don't be led astray by self-delusion, and be sure that it's *your* belief system you're following, not someone else's! **3.** Neptune ℞ in the ninth house makes you see your survival as dependent upon deceiving others—until you feel the presence and protection of an all-powerful being or energy.

♆ **in the tenth house**   In the tenth house Neptune relates to career and career calling, public service, and authority figures. ✴ **1.** If you have Neptune in your tenth house, your career is your devotion, and your desire to contribute to society is your calling. You are devoted to getting out into the world to make spiritual or religious connections with others. You might do this through music or art. Your career is your life calling, and you will utilize your spiritual, religious, and creative ideas in a career. You have the power to get others to see humanity, and you have a spiritual and creative sense of your work in the public. **2.** Neptune ℞ in the tenth house struggles with oversensitivity to perceived abandonment and rejection. It helps to make a list of the *facts*.

♆ **in the eleventh house**   In the eleventh house, Neptune relates to friendship and wishes. ✴ **1.** You have a strong connection to and need devotion from your friends, co-workers, social groups, and peers. You need to feel a sense of belonging outside of family. In fact, your network can become your extended family. You're devoted to friends, and they may relate to your goals and wishes. Sometimes, the only way for you to reach your personal goals is through your social groups. You may need others to help you with your calling. **2.** You might be a follower, rather than a leader, and this can be dangerous, depending on the people you choose to include among your friends and in your social network. **3.** Neptune ℞ in the eleventh house may over-identify with the underdog and become lost in a cause—or become a rebel without a cause. Any spiritual philosophy that helps put suffering into perspective is a huge assist in integrating into society.

Ψ **in the twelfth house   1.** In the twelfth house, Neptune is all about the subconscious and karmic duty. **2.** Neptune is at home in the twelfth house. ✧ **1.** If you have Neptune in your twelfth house, you may have hidden talents or abilities. You likely have a strong devotion to your belief system, whatever it is. You're also devoted to karma and karmic debt. You're willing to sacrifice yourself, and will be quiet about what you believe in order to get along. You might be metaphysically spiritual and private about your beliefs, but you will live your beliefs, you just might not talk about them all the time. **2.** You understand persecution and discrimination, and fight on behalf of those who haven't been treated fairly. Your strong sense of empathy leads you to help others through difficult times or trauma. **3.** Neptune ℞ in the twelfth house often sees life on Earth as something to be endured until set free by death and reunited with friends and angelic realms in spirit. It helps to contemplate Earth as a rare opportunity to apply spiritual practices.

See also *house, Neptune, Neptune in the signs, retrograde planets.*

Neptune in the signs   1. Neptune is the planet of religion and spirituality as well as inspiration. The sign Neptune is in will indicate how the native expresses spirituality or spiritual needs. **2.** Neptune stays in each sign for up to 14 years—everyone born during that 14-year period has Neptune in that sign. That's why it's called a generational planet. **3.** Neptune ℞ in the signs generally signifies how the individual is overly sensitive and seeks escape from everyday reality.

Ψ **in Aquarius   **Aquarius is an original, communicative sign. ✧ **1.** If you have Neptune in Aquarius, you're innovative, maybe even eccentric. You don't like groupthink or group mentality, and find the rules of organized religion stifling. Freedom and independence is important to you. You might take an interest in the mystical or spiritual instead of more traditional religion. You have humanitarian desires. **2.** Neptune ℞ in Aquarius is overly sensitive to the moods of friends and seeks escape through television or the Internet.

Ψ **in Aries** Aries is an active entrepreneurial sign. ✦ **1.** Neptune is devotion and creativity, as well as religious and spiritual ideals. With Neptune in Aries, you are innovative in your approach to spiritualism and religion. You are open to all religions and want to experiment with religion and philosophy. You might question traditional religion, but you do this because you want to understand. You'll test many theories of religion. You also test the word *devotion*. You believe it's fine for everyone to have their own religion. **2.** Neptune ℞ in Aries is overly sensitive to comparison and seeks escape by clearing the decks and starting over.

Ψ **in Cancer** Cancer is intuitive and emotional. ✦ **1.** If your Neptune is in Cancer, you are very devoted to family. Your religious or spiritual beliefs are connected to family and community. You likely go to church or temple every week, or follow some other ritual that appeals to you. You're emotionally attached to your beliefs. If you have a family belief system, you'll follow it because it makes you feel emotionally connected to your family. You'll stick with a belief system even if it's not really your belief, if it works for your family. **2.** You're likely psychic, and may have a powerful prayer life or meditation routine. You have intuitive feelings about God, and may be convinced that there is a spiritual world (which may include God and heaven, but it also may not). You believe that if you pray and nurture your religious beliefs, a Higher Power will protect you. Your faith is unshakable. **3.** Neptune ℞ in Cancer is hyper-vigilant about possible danger and stays home to escape dealing with the world.

Ψ **in Capricorn** Capricorn is practical and responsible. ✦ **1.** In Capricorn, Neptune is reserved and logical. If you have Neptune in this sign, you are likely critical of religion, even your chosen one. You might be conservative, because you like order, structure, and authority. For these reasons, organized religion appeals to you. **2.** Neptune ℞ in Capricorn is overly sensitive about being told what to do and escapes reality through depression.

Ψ **in Gemini** Gemini is innovative and intellectual. ✦ **1.** If you have Neptune in Gemini, you're an innovative thinker, and you like to think about and analyze religion and your own religious beliefs. New concepts are interesting to you. You might believe in something or you might not, but either way, you're sure to weigh it all out before you decide. You can be devoted, but you want to follow logic toward religion, and make an intelligent choice. You like to ask questions as part of your research: Why do you believe this? How did you get to this belief? You like to philosophize and study theology to make sense of God and the spiritual. You may spend your life seeking proof, because you need logic to bring you to God. **2.** You're also creative, perhaps musical. You have a creative imagination and are good at coming up with new approaches to things. **3.** Neptune ℞ in Gemini is compulsive about needing to know what to do and seeks escape through classes and workshops.

♆ in Leo Leo is a charismatic leader with a dramatic flair. ✧ **1.** If your Neptune is in Leo, everything is dramatic and theatrical to you. Think about healing with the laying on of hands, for example. That kind of religious spectacle, a very dramatic spiritual or religious experience, is the essence of Neptune in Leo. You can be a charismatic religious leader. You might also be moved by a charismatic leader. **2.** Your dramatic flair makes you excel in the arts, including music, dance, and dramatic and fine arts. You're generous, you like excitement, and you're devoted to family and to your public. You like to make others feel great about themselves through religion, art, and creative use of the imagination. **3.** Neptune ℞ in Leo is overly sensitive about their need for luxury and seeks out affairs for escape from everything ordinary.

♆ in Libra Libra longs for beauty and harmony. ✧ **1.** If you have Neptune in Libra, you want balance and harmony in religion. You seek the ideal in religion, and may look at things through rose-colored glasses. In difficult times, you can be seen as unrealistic. You'll be the one holding up the peace sign at a rally for the troops. You see God as benevolent. You follow the golden rule, and think it's important to treat others as you want to be treated—fairly and with respect. You can't stand persecution based on religious beliefs. You love beauty and want peace and love to reign. That's how you seek religion: through peace and universal love. **2.** Neptune ℞ in Libra is overly sensitive about being single and seeks escape through romance novels.

♆ in Pisces **1.** Pisces is the intuitive dreamer of the zodiac. **2.** Neptune is the natural ruler of Pisces. ✧ **1.** You very much want to help others. You love everyone and everything—animals, plants—and you try to see God in all living things. You tend to have humanitarian impulses and can be selfless in service to others. You're not judgmental, and are more likely spiritual than religious. You have an emotional and intuitive connection to your beliefs. **2.** Neptune in Pisces is very intuitive and creative. **3.** Neptune ℞ in Pisces is overly sensitive to others' moods and may seek escape through drugs, music, alcohol, and movies.

Ψ **in Sagittarius**   Sagittarius is the zodiac's philosopher. ✧ **1.** Neptune in Sagittarius is a philosopher. You like to explore and study religion or theology. You don't need to adhere to one set of beliefs, and are happy to learn about as many as you can. You're intuitive and idealistic. **2.** Be wary of fanaticism. **3.** Neptune ℞ in Sagittarius is overly sensitive about religion and seeks escape through other people's problems.

Ψ **in Scorpio**   Powerful and intense—that's Scorpio. ✧ **1.** If you have Neptune in Scorpio, you are firmly devoted to your chosen belief system. Your faith is unwavering, and your beliefs are the foundation for the rest of your life. **2.** Scorpio's intensity can lead to passionate and possibly extreme beliefs. Neptune in Scorpio might embrace nontraditional ideas of religion, including the paranormal. Mind-altering activities also might be equated with the spiritual. **3.** Neptune ℞ in Scorpio hears blame whenever problems are discussed and seeks escape through seduction.

Ψ **in Taurus**   Taurus is the gentle, dependable zodiac sign. ✧ **1.** With Neptune in Taurus, you take a pragmatic approach to spiritualism and religion. You likely participate in a traditional religion, and you follow the rules! You listen to what others say and will follow the religious leadership of your chosen faith. You're devout, don't question, and don't want to experiment. You feel a sense of responsibility toward your church. You also want to participate and be part of the group—your church group. **2.** Neptune ℞ in Taurus is overly sensitive about deserving things and seeks escape through shopping.

Ψ **in Virgo**   Virgo can be described as analytical and orderly. ✧ **1.** Neptune in Virgo is the analyzing sign combined with the clairvoyant. You embrace the philosophical/theological side of religion and as with everything, you are particular about religion. In Virgo, Neptune wants structure in religion, but also questions the structure. You can't stand hypocrisy. You participate in and believe in religion, but you also question and criticize it. **2.** An iconoclast, you might reject the traditional religion of your culture for a different religion. You could also be at risk for an addictive devotion to drugs or another harmful substance. Generally, though, you pay a lot of attention to your health and appearance. **3.** Neptune ℞ in Virgo is overly sensitive toward criticism and seeks escape through purification.

See also *Neptune, signs.* ◯ ☼

Neptune/Jupiter   See *Jupiter/Neptune.*

Neptune/Mars   See *Mars/Neptune.*

Neptune/Mercury   See *Mercury/Neptune.*

Neptune/Moon   See *Moon/Neptune.*

Neptune/North Node   Neptune brings devotion to the North Node's need to learn. There is a karmic destiny to evolve spiritually. ✷ Aspects between Neptune and the North Node in your birth chart can help you to see the whole picture, and figure out what brings about your greatest spiritual growth. More challenging aspects can cloud your ability to see your spiritual potential. See also *aspects between planets, Neptune, North Node.* △ ☯ ◯

Neptune/Pluto   Neptune's spirituality combines with Pluto's transformational capacity. ✷ Aspects between these planets, Neptune and Pluto, in your birth chart can help you to gracefully release what you've outgrown. Hard aspects might lead you to stay in destructive situations or relationships for too long—you have a difficult time moving on. See also *aspects between planets, Neptune, Pluto.* △ ☯ ◯

Neptune retrograde, personal   **1.** Neptune is retrograde in the birth chart, creating a personal effect in the birth chart of the native. **2.** Neptune's orbit around the Sun takes about 165 years, and it's retrograde for 158 days in each twelve-month period. Those born during one of those periods have Neptune ℞ in the birth chart. **3.** Personal retrogrades have varying influence depending on the activity of other planets in the birth chart. ✷ If you have Neptune ℞ in your birth chart, you struggle to see yourself as you really are. You may avoid therapy or counseling because you fear that you'll be confronted with a person you don't like—*you*—but really, you would discover your humanity and magnificence. You might benefit tremendously from watching movies in which the protagonist finds self-forgiveness, self-acceptance, and inner peace. See also *Neptune; Neptune retrograde, transiting; retrograde, personal.* ◯ ℞

Need some tips for handling your personal Neptune retrograde? Check the sign:

- ♆℞ **in Aries:** Strive to do only what you *really* want to do.
- ♆℞ **in Taurus:** Reassure yourself that you are worthy just in being who you are.
- ♆℞ **in Gemini:** Let people know when you are at a loss for words.
- ♆℞ **in Cancer:** Make a family out of the people who care about you.
- ♆℞ **in Leo:** Discover your creative spark through a child's craft project.
- ♆℞ **in Virgo:** Imagine how you would feel if you loved yourself just as you are.
- ♆℞ **in Libra:** Make your time alone special.
- ♆℞ **in Scorpio:** Become more of what you want to attract.
- ♆℞ **in Sagittarius:** Make a list of what you know in your heart to be true.
- ♆℞ **in Capricorn:** Think about all of the things you wanted to do and then did.
- ♆℞ **in Aquarius:** Not fitting in gives you a lot of freedom to just be yourself.
- ♆℞ **in Pisces:** Let art and music nurture your soul.

N

Neptune retrograde, transiting **1.** Neptune's transiting retrograde lasts 160 days, which is a bit more than five months. **2.** Transiting retrogrades are the daily retrograde action of the planets that affect everyone on Earth. **3.** Finding ways to channel Neptune's intuitive energy can seem difficult during retrograde periods. ✳ **1.** People who are Neptune-challenged may feel overwhelmed by life's vicissitudes and not up to the task of navigating stormy emotions or volatile situations. Transiting Neptune ℞ can make it hard to know what the best thing to do is, or how to sort things out. But Neptune in retrograde also presents a valuable chance to explore whatever is under the surface and to allow it to emerge into the light of day. Neptune ℞ is a great time to start a dream diary, to test the boundaries of infinity and beyond, or to risk confusion in search of clarity.

2. Now, remember that it sometimes feels out of control to be out of your comfort zone and Neptune ℞ may take you into uncharted waters whether you like it or not. But like Columbus, you may just find a New World on the other side of that ocean, full of strange and unimagined wonderments as reward for your bravery of spirit. Don't be afraid to explore! See also *Neptune; Neptune retrograde, personal; retrograde, transiting.* ◯ ℞

If transiting Neptune retrograde sends a tsunami your way, look to the astrological sign to throw some light on the situation:

- **In Aries:** Shutting down emotionally doesn't make it easier to push.
- **In Taurus:** Practice the fine art of losing.
- **In Gemini:** Don't breathe through your nose underwater, metaphorically speaking; stay calm and think things through.
- **In Cancer:** Look for the right color.
- **In Leo:** Finger paint; do art therapy.
- **In Virgo:** Allow what is sacred to speak without rules or reasons.
- **In Libra:** Offer harmony for turmoil.
- **In Scorpio:** Study tarot's Moon card.
- **In Sagittarius:** Boldly go where no one has been before.
- **In Capricorn:** Your dreams need an infrastructure … ask yourself *why* you want what you do.
- **In Aquarius:** Go for a spontaneous hike with a little barefoot time to get yourself grounded again.
- **In Pisces:** This is a fantastic time to ask yourself what you can do to really, truly forgive and accept yourself.

Neptune return   1. Point at which Neptune returns to the position it held in the native's birth chart. **2.** Neptune is in each sign for about 14 years, and has a total orbit time of 165 years. Therefore, it would take 165 years for Neptune to return to an exact place in its orbit. ✳ Neptune's lengthy orbit makes it very unlikely that Neptune will return to its position in your birth chart during your lifetime—at least not in today's world! If you want to be around for your Neptune return, you'll have to consider being cryogenically frozen (though there is no proof that such an undertaking will extend human life). See also *Neptune, planetary return.* ◯

Neptune/Saturn Saturn brings a love of order to Neptune's spiritual/religious nature and discipline to Neptune's ideals.
✳ Aspects between these planets, Neptune and Saturn, in your birth chart can bring about the necessary discipline to help you turn your dreams into reality. The planets combine to establish a system to inspire humankind. Learn to listen to your soul before following the guidance of authority. If the aspect between Neptune and Saturn is challenging, this can manifest as depression, gloom, and phobias. See also *aspects between planets, Neptune, Saturn.* △ ☯ ○

Neptune/South Node Neptune is religion and spirituality, and the South Node indicates areas of familiarity and comfort, including the karma of past lives. The South Node indicates comfort and experience with religion or the spiritual world and karma going forward.
✳ Aspects between Neptune and the South Node in your birth chart show that you came into this lifetime with beliefs that create a comfortable foundation for you as you explore new ways of looking at life, your family's religion, other religions, and spiritual concepts. Difficult aspects between Neptune and your South Node might cause you to cling to your beliefs, religion, and spirituality—or lack of spirituality—that has been defined for you. See also *aspects between planets, Neptune, South Node.* △ ☯ ○

Neptune/Sun Neptune brings devotion to the Sun's ego.
✳ Aspects between Neptune and the Sun in your birth chart can allow you to draw from the many talents and wisdom you acquired in past lifetimes. More challenging aspects between Neptune and your Sun may cause you to rely too much upon others or what is already known to you. See also *aspects between planets, Neptune, Uranus.* △ ☯ ○

Neptune transits 1. Neptune as it moves or transits through the signs of the zodiac. 2. Neptune's orbit around the Sun takes 165 years; Neptune transits all twelve zodiac signs in that time. 3. Neptune transits can be compared to the placement of Neptune in a birth chart for predictive purposes. A transit shows the position of a planet at a given moment. 4. Transiting Neptune is a catalyst as it enters a new sign or a new house, and forms aspects with other transiting planets or planets in both birth and progressed charts. As a generational planet, Neptune brings about big, long-lasting changes.

✦ **1.** Transiting Neptune can help you review your life, resolve issues, and move on to a new period of growth. As Neptune transits through the houses of your birth chart, it makes you question—everything. **2.** As transiting Neptune makes positive aspects to other key planets, you are able to see who you are and how what you do fits into the bigger picture of your family, your field of work, your community, and the world. You are able to align with your deepest longings and dreams. Your psychic abilities increase, as do your compassion and feelings of unity with others. Latent artistic and musical abilities also make themselves known. **3.** When transiting Neptune creates challenging aspects to other planets, you may feel confused, overwhelmed, plagued by ghosts or multiple personalities, or lost. Addictions can be activated by your perception that the world is full of sorrow that you must escape. See also *Neptune, progressed birth chart, transiting planets, transits.* **BC** 🏠 ◯

What can Neptune transits tell you?

- Neptune transiting your **first house** reassures you that the whole is not complete without your unique, individual contribution.
- Neptune moving through your **second house** moves you to make money by following your dreams and ideals.
- Neptune transiting your **third house** helps you to express your feelings and fantasies.
- Neptune traveling through your **fourth house** heightens your intuitive powers and reunites family members.
- Neptune transiting your **fifth house** inspires your creativity and love of life.
- Neptune moving through your **sixth house** beckons your exploration of the body-mind connection.
- When Neptune enters your **seventh house**, it brings you face to face with your shadow self as it projects upon strangers, frenemies, your partner, roommate, third sibling, paternal grandfather, or maternal grandmother.
- Neptune in your **eighth house** unifies your being with your lover's for nights of ecstasy.
- Neptune transiting your **ninth house** is the best time to get your screenplay sold, go on an island vacation, or take up horseback riding at the beach.

- Neptune transiting your **tenth house** dissolves the fears that have blocked your success.
- Neptune moving through your **eleventh house** tends to wreak havoc with computers, your website, and friendships. It's best to focus on the outcomes you want.
- Neptune transiting through your **twelfth house** brings you the peace of knowing that progress occurs whether you feel it or not.

Neptune/Uranus   Uranus brings a love of order to Neptune's spiritual/religious nature. �֍ Aspects between Neptune and Uranus in your birth chart help you make the best use of your emotions as a gauge of what's right for you. Challenging aspects between Neptune and Uranus can create denial or delusion around people and situations when what you need is to be alert to what's really going on. See also *aspects between planets, Neptune, Uranus.* △ ☯ ○

Neptune/Venus   Venus brings a love of beauty to Neptune's devotion. �֍ The most beneficial aspects between Neptune and Venus generate an ideal harmony for romance, music, and artistic pursuits. If you have a challenging aspect between Neptune and Venus, you might be overly sensitive to other people's moods, habits, and smells. See also *aspects between planets, Neptune, Venus.* △ ☯ ○

N

new Moon   **1.** Phase when the Moon is 0 to 45 degrees in front of the Sun in the birth chart. Because the unilluminated (by the Sun) side of the Moon is facing Earth, the Moon appears dark in the sky and may not be visible at all. **2.** Of the eight lunar phases, the new Moon is the first phase, and follows the last quarter Moon by about one week. ✖ If you were born during a new Moon, you have a lot of energy, vitality, and physical strength. You look and feel young your whole life. You're naturally assertive, you thrive on competition, and you may anger easily. You like getting things done—the sooner, the better. Others find you to be open, passionate, bold, and impetuous. You like start-ups and beginnings and may need to monitor your desire for change just for the sake of doing something different. See also *Moon phases.* ○

ninth house   **1.** In astrology, the ninth house relates to philosophy, religion, and higher education. **2.** The ninth house also represents foreign travel and politics. **3.** This is also the house to check for answers about the fourth sibling, brothers- and sisters-in-law, and issues with the hips, thighs, and butt! ✳ **1.** What's your personal belief system? Do you have a philosophy of life? The ninth house relates to your spiritual, religious, and moral beliefs, as well as organized religion: how you look at a Higher Power and your practice of your faith, and what role religion plays in your secular life. **2.** The ninth house is also where to look for information on out-of-country travel, as well as your attitude and interactions with foreign people and cultures. This is the house of law, so you'll find how you deal with court and legal systems in your own country here. Higher education is in this house, as well. Are you going to college? Applying? Look at your ninth house for help with these decisions. **3.** The ninth house is naturally associated with Sagittarius, and is ruled by Jupiter. **4.** What does it mean if you have lots of planets—or very few—in this house? Lots of planets indicate that the areas relating to this house—social areas such as higher education and travel—will be very important to you in this lifetime. If you don't have a lot of planets in your ninth house, you may not need to focus on these areas of your life this time around. Having difficulties in your life with areas covered by the ninth house? Look not only in the ninth house but also in its opposite, the third house. See also *house, Jupiter, Sagittarius.*

🏠 ○ ☼

nodal   Of, or pertaining to, the North and South Nodes. See also *North Node, South Node.* **BC Z**

noon birth chart   **1.** Noon, or midday, is used to create a birth chart when the birth time of the native is unknown. **2.** Astrologers use noon because it produces the best odds for accuracy, because the native's actual birth time is not more than twelve hours off (either earlier or later than noon). See also *birth chart.* **BC** ☯

North Node   **1.** Also called the Dragon's head in Vedic astrology. The ascending node of the Moon's orbit. **2.** The point in the Moon's orbit when it is moving from south to north and it crosses the ecliptic. **3.** Because it's not a planet, the North Node doesn't have a planetary ruler, and it's not associated with a particular house. **4.** As the North Node and the South Node are exactly 180 degrees apart, most astrologers set their astrological program preferences to display only the North Node. Once you have memorized all the signs and their polarities, it's easy enough to determine the position of the South Node in your mind. **5.** The North Node can illuminate karmic issues and opportunities for this life, and going forward. The astrological glyph for the North Node is ☊.

✳ **1.** The North Node's location in your birth chart will tell you what you have to learn in this life. It's sometimes called the Point of Destiny, because it's where you *have* to go. Its placement will be unfamiliar territory, and you'll have to go outside your comfort zone to work on your North Node issues, because you are growing in new areas when you go toward your North Node. You may have to overcome fears to do this work, but it's worth it. Growth in your North Node area will also lead to karmic rewards. **2.** What house placement does the North Node have in your birth chart? That's what you have to learn. **3.** You might not be comfortable working out your North Node issues until you're in your late 20s or early 30s, after your Saturn return. **4.** In a daily astrological calendar, positive aspects between the Sun and the North Node (such as conjunct, trine, or sextile) generate a sense of joyful anticipation for the challenges each day brings. Magical meetings happen and people say yes to your ideas. Difficult aspects between the Sun and the North Node (such as opposition or square) are frustrating. Sometimes it feels like you can't get a break around your creative projects or with your children. It's important to focus attention on what is working creatively or what is going well with your child. When you put your focus there, the North Node will work with your subconscious mind to bring you more and more of these kinds of experiences. See also *Nodes (North, South), North Node in the houses, North Node in the signs, Saturn return, South Node.* △ ◯ ℞

North Node in the houses **1.** The North Node represents the lessons you have to learn (including karmic lessons and opportunities), and your areas of potential growth. **2.** The North Node's placement in the birth chart indicates the areas of life influenced by the North Node's energy. **3.** Because the North and South nodes are always opposite each other in the birth chart, the North Node placement indicates the South Node placement: North Node in the third house means that the South Node is in the ninth house. ✳ The North Node relates to your future, and is what you still have to learn. The house the North Node is in will tell you where you have to go—and grow—in the future. You'll feel called, or pulled, to work in these areas of your life.

☊ **in the first house**   The North Node in the first house is all about the self and the personality. ✷ **1.** In the first house, the North Node indicates a need to learn about the self and self-identity. **2.** Your first house North Node leads you to learn about yourself. You'll have to conquer your fears and insecurities with this placement. You're here to learn to be independent and self-reliant.

☊ **in the second house**   The North Node in the second house relates to money and the material world. ✷ How do you value yourself? This North Node placement challenges you to take care of yourself financially. You'll develop a new sense of self-worth and will work with money in new ways, or will have a new approach to money. You'll have to conquer your fears about money, and when you do, your financial situation will improve.

☊ **in the third house**   In the third house, the North Node relates to communication and expression, as well as early childhood. ✷ You'll learn new ways to deal with issues and obstacles from your childhood, and you will overcome these obstacles through your North Node work. You are gifted with communication, but you have to discover your communication skills.

☊ **in the fourth house**   The North Node in the fourth house is all about home and family. ✷ You'll be led to build your home life—and maybe even build your own home—with the North Node in your fourth house. Family will be an area of growth for you, and home is important to your growth and development. You might go back to your family of origin, or you might work to create a new kind of home life.

☊ **in the fifth house**   The North Node in the fifth house is all about creative self-expression. ✷ You have hidden talents in the arts, and your lessons will lead you to realize these talents. It's also beneficial to you to work with children in some way—you have some lessons to learn from them, and you might need to work on behalf of children.

☊ **in the sixth house**   The North Node in the sixth house relates to health, work environment, and public service. ✷ **1.** This North Node placement leads you to an understanding of your own physical health. You will be able to read your health well, and you might be

drawn to new healing technologies or philosophies, either for yourself or for others. **2.** You will likely be fortunate with employment,
but you might need to think outside the box when you need to find
work.

☊ in the seventh house   The North Node in the seventh house
is all about cooperation and partnership. ✦ With this North Node
placement, you are committed to and want to cooperate with significant others in your life. Marriage, business, and domestic partners
will be important to your growth; going it alone is not in your best
interest. For you, great lessons can be learned through fully accepting partnership.

☊ in the eighth house   The North Node in the eighth house
relates to joint resources and money, as well as psychic intuition.
✦ **1.** Your eighth house North Node will pull you to develop your
psychic awareness and to discover your ability to reach out to others
in time of need. You need to develop your intuition, and learn to
trust your gut feelings and insights—they will prove very accurate.
Part of what you have to learn with this North Node placement is
to accept and trust what you feel. This may not seem sensible to you,
but with practice, you'll grow to accept your intuitive powers. **2.** You
also have power in areas of investment, but you might be shy about
testing your power. Don't be afraid—trust yourself.

☊ in the ninth house   The North Node in the ninth house is
about religion and spirituality, as well as travel and higher education.
✦ This North Node placement calls you to seek new adventures.
You push your own envelope, making yourself get out there and gain
new experiences in education, foreign travel, dealing with people
from other countries, or religious beliefs. You may question your old
beliefs or decide to try something new. You have an open mind, and
you benefit greatly from such questioning and exploration.

☊ in the tenth house   In the tenth house, the North Node relates
to career and authority figures. ✦ You may feel pulled to learn to
become an authority figure—a supervisor of some kind—with the
North Node in your tenth house. You won't be used to wielding
authority, but you need to learn how to do it. You might be surprised
to learn that you can stand strong as a leader—leading others is not
your comfort zone. But learn to lead well, and you will find great
personal gratification.

N

☋ **in the eleventh house**   In the eleventh house, the North Node relates to your social network and peer groups, as well as your hopes and wishes. ✳ You will find that your friends and peer groups will be able to help you with your goals and wishes. You have to learn to *let them*. You'll have to accept your role as part of the group, and become a team player. You'll learn that teamwork can work very well—and that going it alone takes too long and is far less fun! Learning that it's okay to ask for help when you need it is difficult for you, but you'll also realize that assisting others on their path is very rewarding.

☋ **in the twelfth house**   A twelfth house North Node relates to karmic debt as well as the shadow self or hidden areas of the self, dreams, and intuition. ✳ Your twelfth house North Node will insist that you learn to cultivate your dreams, which may require you to shine a little light on those hidden parts of yourself—needless fear, or shame, for example—that may be holding you back. This inner, hidden self is just as real to you as the world outside yourself, and it's difficult for you to believe your feelings aren't necessarily based in reality, because they are so deeply rooted in your subconscious. The North Node in the twelfth house calls you to let go and trust your-self and the world around you. See also *Nodes (North, South), North Node in the signs.* 🏠 ◯

North Node in the signs   **1.** The North Node relates to what has yet to be learned. The sign in which the North Node resides in the birth chart will indicate areas of growth for the native. **2.** Because the North Node and South Node are opposite each other in the birth chart, North Node in Aries is in the same place as South Node in Libra. Together these opposites create a yin/yang balance in the fabric of the universe between the past and the future.

☋ **in Aquarius**   Aquarius is a sign of intelligence and independence. ✳ The North Node in Aquarius gets you motivated toward altru-ism, compassion, intellectual studies, and a desire to know every-thing. You know that the future is more important than the past, and you live life that way.

☋ **in Aries**   Aries likes to start things, so the North Node has extra energy for exploration now. ✳ In Aries, the North Node gives you a pioneering spirit, need for adventure, love of the unknown, and a desire to create. You see the future as a world with no boundaries.

☊ **in Cancer** Cancer is intuitive and emotional. ✧ Your North Node placement in Cancer makes you devote energy to creating a home and family, as well as a desire to learn about nurturing—children, a garden, your community, or your global family. You believe everyone is interconnected, and your catchphrase might be, We are all in this together!

☊ **in Capricorn** Capricorn is responsible and ambitious. ✧ The North Node in Capricorn motivates you toward leadership roles in your career or your calling. You may have untapped leadership or executive abilities that you can apply in business, medicine, or religion. You can lead with authority and discipline.

☊ **in Gemini** Gemini is intelligent and witty. ✧ If your North Node is in Gemini, you love to study and want to learn everything there is to learn. You may have hidden intellectual abilities and communication skills—you'll be surprised at how articulate you can be. Take the initiative: educate yourself and all doors will open.

☊ **in Leo** Leo is a generous leader. ✧ With the North Node in Leo, you want to share your knowledge with others. You're generous and understand the needs of those around you—help others gain this understanding. Create a plan for the future that includes everyone, because we need not go through life alone! You not only want to get there yourself, you have the strength and desire to get everyone else there (whether loved ones, or even more generally just people in society) with you.

☊ **in Libra** Libra seeks harmony and beauty. ✧ The North Node in Libra wants cooperation. You'll learn that partnership, marriage, and the idea of partnering up is not as scary as it seems to you at first. You'll also learn that cooperating with others gets things done faster—and it can be more fun than working alone. Develop a commitment to partnership and cooperation, and enhance your life.

☊ **in Pisces** Pisces is intuitive and compassionate. ✧ The North Node in Pisces motivates you to move past your fears and apprehensions about life. You realize you can be both a dreamer and a doer. When you do, your creative, compassionate side will emerge as an asset and you'll have a deep understanding of the human condition, along with a newfound ability to affect change.

☊ **in Sagittarius** Sagittarius wants to understand the world. ✧ The North Node in Sagittarius gives you an interest in philosophy and religion and the desire to study the cultures of the world.

You seek a higher truth, and the future is yours when you shoot for the stars—don't worry where your arrow lands! So start drawing new maps and the rest of us will learn and follow.

☊ **in Scorpio**   Scorpio is powerful and transformational. ✸ With your North Node in Scorpio, you have great power of persuasion. Your intuition and ability to read human behavior is powerful, and you can use it well as a healer, medical advisor, or investigator. Try to bring out the power of transformation and rebirth in yourself as well as others. Remember that your passion is a wonderful part of you—rather than tame or control it, learn to use your strong passions to teach and heal yourself and others.

☊ **in Taurus**   Taurus is gentle and reliable. ✸ A Taurus North Node makes you well suited to work in the financial or material world. But you'll have to ask yourself what you value. Your ability to learn about the financial/material world is great, and you're learning to balance the material with the spiritual—key to success and happiness.

☊ **in Virgo**   Analytical Virgo loves routine. ✸ The North Node in Virgo motivates you in areas of health and well-being. Health, work, and daily routines are a necessity to you. Your future is sound when you work in service to others and to yourself. Balancing these will benefit you and make you feel accomplished! For you, a contemplative life must be combined with action; so you'd do well as a teacher or cleric (nun or monk). See also *Nodes (North, South), signs*.

○ ☼

North Node/Jupiter   See *Jupiter/North Node*.

North Node/Mars   See *Mars/North Node*.

North Node/Mercury   See *Mercury/North Node*.

North Node/Moon   See *Moon/North Node*.

North Node/Neptune   See *Neptune/North Node*.

North Node/Pluto   Pluto brings transformation to the North Node's calling to learn. ✸ The North Node and Pluto aspect in your birth chart means you have the ability to transform yourself. You'll be positively influenced or motivated by the masses—the community around you, for example. You might learn lessons through or be transformed by work with your community. See also *aspects between planets, North Node, Pluto.* △ ☯ ○

North Node, retrograde   See *Nodes (North, South).*

North Node return   **1.** The North Node of the Moon returns to the position it held in the native's birth chart. **2.** North Node returns happen every 18½ years or so. ✦ **1.** The North Node will return to where it was when you were born just about every 18½ years. So you'll have a nodal return when you are 18, 37, 55, 74, 93, and so on. **2.** The North Node is also known as the Point of Destiny, and you will feel destiny kick in during the years of your North Node return. This might be most apparent when you look back at the turning points of your life. See also *North Node, planetary return.* ○

North Node/Saturn   Saturn is the self-disciplined teacher and the North Node brings a calling to learn. Saturn brings a serious note to the aim of erasing karma and fulfilling the soul's purpose on Earth. ✦ When the North Node and Saturn interact in your birth chart, you need to develop self-discipline, focus, and structure in your life. If you do this, you'll have success. Self-discipline can lead you to a new—and better—future. You have a duty to be responsible in some area of your life (family, community, health), and once you assume this duty and follow through with it, you'll gain karmic rewards. If you ignore Saturn's influence, this planet may begin to express itself more as taskmaster than helper; allow the North Node to temper this effect through curiosity and devotion. Aspects between Saturn and the North Node quickly correct you when you stray from your soul's path. See also *aspects between planets, North Node, Saturn.* △ ☯ ○

N

North Node/South Node   See *Nodes (North, South).*

North Node/Sun   The Sun brings ego and energy to the North Node's calling to learn. ✦ If you have the Sun and the North Node in aspect in your birth chart, you are charismatic, and may have talents you aren't aware of. You'll need to motivate yourself to uncover these talents, especially as you're likely skeptical about their existence. Follow your instincts, and don't take the safe route—your best success and karmic rewards will take work. See also *aspects between planets, North Node, Sun.* △ ☯ ○

North Node transits   **1.** The North Node as it moves or transits through the signs of the zodiac. **2.** North Node transits can be compared to the placement of the North Node in a natal chart for predictive purposes. A transit shows the position of a planet at a given moment. **3.** Transiting North Node is a catalyst as it enters a new sign or a new house, and forms aspects with other transiting planets or planets in both birth and progressed charts. �֍ Transiting North Node can help you discover hidden gifts and abilities in areas where you usually have resistance and fear. See also *North Node, progressed birth chart, transiting planets, transits.* **BC** 🏠 ◯

What can North Node transits tell you?

- The North Node transiting your **first house** brings the opportunity to step up and ask for what you want.
- The North Node moving through your **second house** offers you insights about resistance you may have around receiving or being rich.
- The North Node transiting your **third house** challenges you to share your ideas and opinions despite fears of judgment, criticism, or humiliation.
- The North Node moving through your **fourth house** encourages you to put roots down and start a family.
- The North Node transiting your **fifth house** helps you take a chance and do what you've always wanted to, especially creative ventures, travel, and performing.
- The North Node moving through your **sixth house** elicits feelings of reverence for a well-lived, simple life, down-to-earth people, and everyday acts of kindness.
- When the North Node enters your **seventh house**, you strive to understand yourself through your committed relationships.
- The North Node in your **eighth house** offers gain by putting a powerful team together.
- The North Node transiting your **ninth house** is the right time for religious or spiritual studies at a university.
- The North Node transiting your **tenth house** helps you achieve success and fame when you build your career and reputation in alignment with your higher self.
- The North Node moving through your **eleventh house** wants you to wake up and recognize how you've sold out or failed to take a stand for what you believe.
- The North Node transiting through your **twelfth house** is your opportunity to let down your hair, take down your walls, and learn to go with the flow.

North Node/Uranus   Uranus brings sudden change to the North Node's calling to learn. ✦ Uranus and the North Node will connect to produce a rebellious side in you. You may need to break your old patterns, and find a new way of thinking or doing things. You could have a revelation and be radicalized to do or be something very different. The change may be dramatic and quite difficult, but it will likely be liberating. Once you take the new path, there's no turning back. See also *aspects between planets, North Node, Uranus.* △ ☯ ○

North Node/Venus   Venus brings a need for love and harmony to the North Node's calling to learn. ✦ The North Node and Venus connect in your birth chart to make you learn about your need for love in your life. You might find love in unexpected places or when you aren't looking for it. You might be a free-spirited artist who finds love with an investment banker (or vice versa). You have to learn to accept the seeming disparity, and through this experience, you'll release your expectations and will be more open to love in a universal, tolerant way. See also *aspects between planets, North Node, Venus.* △ ☯ ○

north point   See *nadir (Imum Coeli).*

northern hemisphere   See *northern signs.*

northern signs   **1.** Also called *commanding signs.* Aries, Taurus, Gemini, Cancer, Leo, and Virgo are the northern signs. **2.** The northern signs are the signs that correspond to the first six houses found in the lower hemisphere of the chart. Just as the nadir or cusp of the fourth house rules the northern-most point in the chart, the lower half of the chart is ruled by the north. See also *Aries, Cancer, Gemini, hemisphere, Leo, nadir (Imum Coeli), Taurus, Virgo.* 🏠 ☼

November 22 to December 22   Birth dates for the Sun sign Sagittarius. The position of the Sun during these dates correlates with an astrological Sun sign. Those born between November 22 and December 22 have a Sagittarius Sun sign. See also *Sagittarius.* ☼

October 23 to November 22   Birth dates for the Sun sign Scorpio.
The position of the Sun during these dates correlates with an astrological Sun sign. Those born between October 23 and November 22
have Scorpio as their Sun sign. See also *Scorpio.* ☼

old soul   **1.** One whose soul has had either thousands of earthly
incarnations or at least a sufficient number of earthly incarnations to
resolve any remaining karmic issues in this or the next lifetime, with
the possibility to do so without generating new karmic debts. **2.** An
old soul birth chart has half or more than half of its planets close in
degree—they will all be placed near 20 degrees in whatever house
they occupy, for example. **3.** A birth chart will be defined as an old
soul chart when its planetary ruler, the planet that rules the sign on
the ascendant, along with the Sun or Moon, and Saturn or Neptune
are at the same exact degree. For instance, if the chart's ascendant is
3 degrees Aries rising, and Mars, the Moon, and Neptune are all at 3
degrees, the chart is an old soul chart. **4.** When the Sun conjoins Saturn or Neptune within a 5 degree orb, the chart is an old soul chart.
For example, if the Sun is at 11 degrees Taurus and Saturn is located
somewhere between 6 and 17 degrees Taurus, the chart is an old soul
chart. (And the rule follows that the tighter the orb, the older the
soul.) **5.** When the Sun or Moon conjoins Saturn, Uranus, Neptune,
or Pluto at the exact same degree and exact same minute, the chart
is an old soul chart. An example would be when the Moon is at 14
degrees, 5 minutes Aquarius, and Neptune is at 14 degrees, 5 minutes
Aquarius. **6.** Many astrologers contend that an old soul's chart is
intense or challenging—that a young soul would never choose to take
on such a chart. An intense chart may have any of the aforementioned,

or it may have a lot of retrograde planets, Saturn or Pluto in the twelfth house, or any of the outer planets conjunct the Sun or the Moon within 7 degrees. See also *aspects between planets, birth chart, Chiron, karma, North Node, young soul.* BC 🌓 🏠 ◯ Z

opposition **1.** This is one of the five major aspects, or angles, between planets in astrology. **2.** The glyph for an opposition is ☍. On a birth chart, planets are in opposition when they create a 180-degree angle, or are opposite each other in the birth chart. Planets are also considered in opposition when they are within 10 degrees of this 180-degree angle. **3.** Oppositions are generally seen as creating a challenging relationship between planets.

✦ **1.** An opposition isn't necessarily a negative thing—really, it's an opportunity for growth and change. The key to managing an opposition is to remember to give *both* planets expression in your life rather than favor the one that's easier for you to deal with. **2.** Charts with opposing stelliums (three or more planets bunched together within 10 degrees) usually manifest as a double life unless other planets connect the opposing energies through trines and sextiles. See also *aspect grid, aspects between planets, stellium.* △ 🌓 ◯

outer planets **1.** In astronomy, the five outermost planets in this solar system: Jupiter, Saturn, Uranus, Neptune, and Pluto. **2.** In astrology, the three transpersonal planets: Uranus, Neptune, and Pluto. ✦ What do the outer planets mean in your birth chart? Check the sign and house each planet is in. The sign that Uranus is in shows you where you're most conscious and the house tells you in what area. It's also where you exhibit genius. Neptune's sign and house are clues about your areas of denial and confusion. Neptune also indicates your best tools for psychic awareness. Pluto's sign and house show your prior incarnations. The sign that Pluto is in helps you know the best way to transform, renew, and revitalize yourself. See also *Neptune, orbit, personal planets, Pluto, transpersonal planets, Uranus.* ◯

Pallas **1.** Also called *Pallas Athene*. An asteroid discovered in 1802 by Heinrich Olbers. Pallas is named for Athena, the Greek goddess of wisdom and war who emerged full-bodied and armor-clad from the head of her father, the king of the gods, Zeus. Her Roman counterpart is Minerva. **2.** The glyph for Pallas's astrological symbol is ⚴. **3.** Pallas was a strong, independent female figure; she did not take a husband or lover, nor did she have children. Though a warrior, she is peace-loving, and bestowed the olive branch to the Greeks.

✦ **1.** In astrology, Pallas's wisdom can translate to psychic abilities, as well as power as a healer. In the birth chart, Pallas can be seen as a female version of Chiron, the wounded healer, in that Pallas also equates power to the mind and spirit and believes one should rule the body and emotions. This asteroid is a link to your higher self, guiding you toward the truth of our earthly plane of existence. In your birth chart, Pallas's job is to wake you up and make you aware of what you already know. Pallas corresponds to the signs of Leo, Libra, and Aquarius. Computer astrology programs generally include Pallas when casting basic birth charts, and most astrologers include this asteroid in their astrological readings. **2.** In what house and sign does Pallas appear in your birth chart? Pallas's house placement is where you already have wisdom: the house indicates the areas of life where you can take care of yourself, and don't need help or guidance. The sign Pallas is in tells you how you express your intelligence and your ability to discern patterns and cycles. See also *asteroids, planets*. ◯

In what sign do you have Pallas in your birth chart?

- **Pallas in Aries** makes you keenly aware of your path and what helps or hinders it.
- **Pallas in Taurus** is where intelligence and beauty come together vocally, artistically, and with heightened self-esteem.
- **Pallas in Gemini** gives you incredible insights into human nature that you can write about or teach.
- **Pallas in Cancer** gives you a sharp mind and memory that quickly identifies behavior patterns in yourself, in others, and in history.
- **Pallas in Leo** is the performer who brings added depth, wisdom, and healing to a dance, song, or role.
- **Pallas in Virgo** is highly functional, super-smart, and always right about everything.
- **Pallas in Libra** gives you the upper hand in your relationships and you tend to temper that advantage with respect and grace.
- **Pallas in Scorpio** may cause you to intellectualize or *conduct* sex rather than abandon yourself to passion. Pallas in Scorpio makes for a very wise shaman.
- **Pallas in Sagittarius** gives you heightened awareness of your higher self. You are able to teach, inspire, and heal others through that spiritual understanding and wisdom.
- **Pallas in Capricorn** gives you a tremendous career advantage, as all the bigwigs admire your brains and ability and seek you out for your wisdom.
- **Pallas in Aquarius** shows up as high IQ, innovative group leader, and public speaker for human rights.
- **Pallas in Pisces** makes you not only super-psychic, but gives you a good head for business and an ability to heal through music.

In what house do you have Pallas in your birth chart?

Pallas ⚷	Keywords
First house Pallas	No-nonsense: you know what you want and no one gets in your way.
Second house Pallas	Very self-confident, excellent taste, smart with money.
Third house Pallas	Eloquent, confident driver, and a little too good at card games.

Pallas ⚴	Keywords
Fourth house Pallas	It's only a home once the books are on the shelves. Incredible memory.
Fifth house Pallas	Relates to children as whole people; very talented with crafts and practical arts.
Sixth house Pallas	Heals through imagery, knowledge, and purity of intention. Animal communicator.
Seventh house Pallas	Brilliant mediator, litigator, and fighter for justice.
Eighth house Pallas	Amazing detective; unafraid of death; shrewd investor.
Ninth house Pallas	Natural teacher; sharp, philosophical wit; disciplined athlete.
Tenth house Pallas	Rises quickly up the ranks of success; speaks and carries self with authority.
Eleventh house Pallas	Prodigy; original thinker; superb networker. Inspires community planning and evolution.
Twelfth house Pallas	Visionary, medical intuitive, musical genius.

Pallas Athene See *Pallas.*

Part of Fortune **1.** Also called *fortuna.* Arabic astrology works with calculated points in space known as parts. **2.** The Part of Fortune indicates natural talents and inherent abilities that lead to good fortune or success on a world scale. The astrological glyph for Part of Fortune is ⊗.

✧ **1.** If you were born before noon, your Part of Fortune is calculated by adding your ascendant to your Moon and deducting your Sun. **2.** If you were born after noon, your Part of Fortune is calculated by adding your ascendant to your Sun and deducting your Moon. **3.** The sign that your Part of Fortune is in indicates how your talents and abilities are expressed. In Aries, it's a talent for leadership. In Taurus, it's a talent for recognizing value. In Gemini, it's a talent for communication. In Cancer, it's a talent for caretaking. In Leo, it's a talent for showmanship. In Virgo, it's a talent for analyzing. In Libra, it's a talent for diplomacy. In Scorpio, it's a talent for transformation. In Sagittarius, it's a talent for listening. In Capricorn, it's a talent for management. In Aquarius, it's a talent for networking. In Pisces, it's a talent for seeing the bigger picture. **4.** The house that your Part of Fortune is in indicates the area of life in which you will manifest success, health, and abundance. In the first house, it's image. In the second house, it's income. In the third house, it's school. In the fourth house, it's real estate. In the fifth house, it's the stage or playing field. In the sixth house, it's the health field. In the seventh house, it's partnership. In the eighth house, it's insurance. In the ninth house, it's foreign lands. In the tenth house, it's government or self-employment. In the eleventh house, it's community. In the twelfth house, it's oil, the sea, or institutions. **5.** Planets that conjoin the Part of Fortune or the ruler of the sign that the Part of Fortune is in and any aspect formed between the two signifies the extent of the power and impact of the Part of Fortune. Fortunately, even challenging aspects are beneficial, just less potent. See also *aspects between planets, Moon, Sun.* △ 🏠 ○

partile   **1.** When two planets are in exact aspect. **2.** Planets are considered in aspect within 10 degrees of a particular aspect, so planets forming a 65-degree angle are considered sextile; the exact angle for sextile is 60 degrees. Planets creating an exact sextile, or 60 degree angle, are partile. **3.** Planets that share the same degree number naturally form aspects to each other, even if the aspect is a conjunction. For instance, if your Mercury is at 18 degrees Cancer and your Jupiter is at 18 degrees Virgo, those planets have a partile aspect. ✴ **1.** If you have partile aspects in your chart, what does this mean? Partile or exact aspects are much stronger than aspects formed between planets with different degrees. Each partile aspect's degree number is vibrationally charged in the chart. Every time a transiting planet reaches that degree number, every other natal or progressed planet is catapulted into activity. **2.** Many astrologers believe that the presence of partile aspects in the birth chart is an indication of an old soul. See also *angles between planets, old soul, progressed birth chart.* △

passive planets **1.** The luminaries: the Sun and the Moon. **2.** The luminaries are considered passive because their energies are completely filtered through the signs they are located in and the planets that form strong aspects to them. Passive, however, does not mean the influence of the luminaries is not potent … just filtered. See also *luminaries, Moon, Sun.* ○

personal planets **1.** In astrology, the three personal planets are Mercury, Venus, and Mars. These are sometimes called the inner planets, because they are the three planets closest to the Sun (excluding the Sun). **2.** The orbits of these planets are relatively short, making their influence more personal than generational, as they move fairly quickly through the signs of the zodiac. Mercury's orbit takes 88 days (about 7 days in each sign); Venus takes about 225 days to orbit the Sun (19 days in each sign); and Mars has an orbit of 687 days (57 days in each sign). **3.** Western astrology views the inner planets as rulers of an individual's inner and personal reality. **4.** The inner planets rule the first quadrant of the horoscope: Mars rules the first house, Venus rules the second house, and Mercury rules the third house.

✧ **1.** What do the personal planets mean in your birth chart? Collectively, your personal planets tell you what experiences you draw to yourself that help you to know your path, what you want, your value, and how to interact with other people. **2.** The personal planets relate your most personal experiences—those that create your beliefs. They also indicate what you focus on in your personal life, which creates your personal reality. **3.** What sign and house are your personal planets in? The sign that Mercury is in depicts the nature of what you focus upon and the house it's in indicates where your personal experiences take place. Venus's sign indicates how you develop your self-esteem and its house tells you what area of your life activates its development. The sign and house of your Mars indicates how and where you'll have personal experiences that help you to know what you want and how to identify your life's path. See also *Mars, Mercury, outer planets, Venus.* ○

Pisces **1.** The twelfth sign of the zodiac. **2.** Those born between February 19 and March 21 have Pisces as their Sun sign. Also called the fishes, Pisces is a yin, or feminine, mutable water sign. Pisces has two ruling planets: Neptune, the Roman god of the sea (the Greek equivalent is Poseidon), and Jupiter, the Roman king of the gods (Zeus in Greek mythology). Neptune is the planet of spiritual energy and dreams, while Jupiter is all about expansion and opportunity. **3.** The glyph for Pisces is ♓, which resembles two linked fish, and the symbol is the two fishes, linked together but swimming in opposite directions. **4.** Pisces is the natural ruler of the twelfth house of karma, psychic intuition, hidden or unconscious self, and dreams. **5.** Other associations for Pisces are the ocean's colors, turquoise and pale green, and the aquamarine.

✦ **1.** The body part associated with Pisces is the feet. Pisces also rules the lymph system. If you're a Pisces, you likely have well-shaped, handsome feet. Treat them well: wear supportive shoes—the right size!—and give yourself the luxury of a regular foot massage or pedicure. Try not to be on your feet all day, and also give your feet a breather and go barefoot! **2.** If your Sun sign is Pisces, you are compassionate, intuitive, and very sensitive. You're so sensitive and intuitive that you can be overwhelmed with all of the feelings swirling around you, and you might be tempted to escape reality with some addictive behavior. You don't like to leave things unfinished: bills, relationships, you name it, Pisces needs closure. **3.** Pisces is very good at sizing people up. You have an intuitive understanding of the world, and if you trust your intuition, it will take you far—your hunches are rarely wrong. You're also very spiritual, and have a strong connection to your spiritual life. **4.** As a mutable water sign, Pisces is flexible and fluid—sometimes too fluid. You feel everything around you, and you might have a hard time distinguishing between your feelings and someone else's. You need to create and be vigilant about your personal boundaries to have peace. **5.** In school, Pisces needs the bigger picture of the subject being taught. You learn best in a gentle environment and do really well with classical music that harmonizes the two spheres of your brain. If the teacher or topic feels intimidating, Pisces tends to escape into fantasy or a self-induced trance that *appears* interested. You can also make yourself invisible so as not to be questioned. Because you feel such compassion for others, you really want to help, and can apply this in careers in the health field, particularly as a therapist. You're very creative and have a vivid imagination, which will serve you well in most artistic careers. **6.** *Watch out for:* You're so compassionate that others can take advantage of you. Your sensitivity is a strong point, but it also makes you vulnerable to great pain and sadness. If you don't feed your own emotional and spiritual needs, you may feel pulled toward addictive behavior and overindulgence. You can be your own worst enemy, especially if you don't learn to work with your intuitive nature. Like those fishes, you may be trying to swim in two directions at once. **7.** *I'm not a Pisces, but my best friend is:* Your Pisces best friend is sensitive and compassionate. This friend is always there for you when you need a shoulder to lean on—and is a great listener, too. To be a good friend to Pisces, take care of your Pisces friend—pamper and appreciate this delicately strong person. Be there to lend support when your Pisces friend is feeling blue. See also *Pisces ascendant, Pisces descendant, signs.* ☼

Pisces/Aquarius   See *Aquarius/Pisces.*

Pisces/Aries   See *Aries/Pisces.*

Pisces ascendant   Also called Pisces rising. The rising sign is Pisces, so Pisces is the sign on the cusp of the first house in the birth chart and the sign on the eastern horizon at the moment of birth. ✧ **1.** If your rising sign is Pisces, you present yourself to the world as a Pisces, and that's how the world sees you. **2.** Pisces rising is sensitive, caring, and creative. You appear very flexible and somewhat shy or introverted. You're devoted to what you hold dear, and express your compassion through humanitarian endeavors. You'll sacrifice yourself to help others. Pisces rising likes to see the best in others—and sometimes you have to invent it. You tend to see life through rose-colored glasses, and this can make you vulnerable. You're helpful, and like to appear generous and kind. **3.** Pisces rising can also be moody and irrational or impractical. You're very sensitive and might throw yourself into causes as a way of losing yourself and avoiding your feelings. You also get personally involved in your causes, and suffer because of this. **4.** You're attracted to spiritual and creative endeavors, and may live through your imagination. Holistic practices such as yoga and meditation appeal to you, and can be beneficial. See also *ascendant, Pisces, Pisces descendant.* **BC** ☼

Pisces/Cancer   See *Cancer/Pisces.*

Pisces/Capricorn   See *Capricorn/Pisces.*

Pisces descendant   **1.** The descending sign is Pisces; Pisces is the sign on the cusp of the seventh house in the birth chart. **2.** The seventh house is the house of partnerships and marriage or significant others. ✦ **1.** If you have Pisces on the cusp of your seventh house, you relate to others in partnership like compassionate Pisces. **2.** A Pisces descendant has Virgo rising. You will attract Pisces qualities, such as sensitivity, compassion, and kindness in partners of all kinds: a business partnership, roommate, spouse or life partner, stranger, or even enemy. You will also attract partners who appear somewhat shy, reserved, sensitive, intuitive, and very spiritual and creative. You want a partner who's the romantic ideal—you're looking for a knight in shining armor, and you might project these qualities onto your romantic partner. You want a partner who is devoted to you. You might be holding out for someone who doesn't exist, because it will be difficult for anyone to live up to your fantasy. **3.** Your descending sign also expresses your alter ego, or the aspects of yourself that you repressed when you were seven or eight years old. It also describes your maternal grandmother, paternal grandfather, third sibling, and second child. See also *descendant, Pisces, Pisces ascendant.* **BC** ☼

Pisces/Gemini   See *Gemini/Pisces.*

Pisces/Leo   See *Leo/Pisces.*

Pisces/Libra   See *Libra/Pisces.*

Pisces/Pisces   **1.** This water and water combination flows. **2.** Pisces and Pisces get along swimmingly. Same-sign pairings often reveal a shared karmic destiny; for Pisces, this may be an opportunity to explore the depths of compassion but can also run the risk of becoming disengaged from society and caught up only in their own dreams. ✦ **1.** Pisces and Pisces understand each other. If they share spiritual beliefs and values, they are a great pairing. Both are compassionate and caring, with a strong humanitarian ethic. They will support each other and each can understand how deeply the other feels. **2.** Without someone to ground them, these two might live in a world of imagination and spirit—with no one to pay the bills or get them to work on time! Together, they might find it too easy to avoid the real world. **3.** Pisces and Pisces are compatible in friendship, in business and work relationships, and in marriage or domestic partnerships. See also *Pisces.* ☯ ☼

Pisces rising   See *Pisces ascendant.*

Pisces/Sagittarius   When these water and fire signs combine, fiery Sagittarius might feel their enthusiasm dampened, while Pisces may feel that Sagittarius is too thrill-seeking to be trustworthy with their hearts. ✳ **1.** Pisces and Sagittarius are both mutable signs, making them flexible. They both love travel and humanitarian work, and are very generous. Religion and spiritual development are also important to both of these signs. **2.** Pisces can be needy, and this doesn't sit well with independent Sagittarius, who might feel smothered or oppressed by Pisces. Pisces, on the other hand, might feel that Sagittarius is aloof and uncaring when Pisces needs them most. **3.** Pisces and Sagittarius can be compatible in friendship and in business and work relationships. This pair might face difficulties in marriage or domestic partnerships, mainly because of their differing emotional needs. See also *Pisces, Sagittarius.* ☯ ☼

Pisces/Scorpio   **1.** This water and water combination is very fluid. **2.** Pisces and Scorpio are emotionally intense. ✳ **1.** Pisces and Scorpio are both intense, and they attract each other. Pisces is flexible, and Scorpio is fixed—if Scorpio is the leader in the relationship, they will get along very well. Both are devoted and loyal. Pisces likes alone time, and gives Scorpio much-needed privacy. **2.** Pisces and Scorpio are compatible in friendship, business relationships, and in marriage or domestic partnership. See also *Pisces, Scorpio.* ☯ ☼

Pisces/Taurus   **1.** This water and earth combination go together like … water and earth: Pisces and Taurus can grow a beautiful garden together. **2.** Pisces and Taurus make a harmonious pair. ✳ **1.** Pisces is the nurturer, and Taurus is earthy dependability. They both value security, home, and family. These two can make a beautiful, stable home together. They nurture each other and are very patient and devoted to each other. **2.** Among the signs of the zodiac, Pisces might be most compatible with Taurus. This pairing works well in friendship, in business and work relationships, as teacher/student or employer/employee, and in marriage or domestic partnerships. See also *Pisces, Taurus.* ☯ ☼

P

Pisces/Virgo   1. This water and earth combination creates balance. **2.** Pisces and Virgo bring out the best in each other. ✸ **1.** Pisces and Virgo are opposite each other in the zodiac, and they have many opposite qualities, but they attract and balance each other. Pisces needs the analytical, organized, workaholic energy of Virgo. Virgo will work very hard to accomplish their goals, including the goals they have in their relationship with Pisces. Virgo will really listen to Pisces' needs, and will work to meet them. Pisces nurtures Virgo and cheers Virgo on. **2.** Pisces and Virgo are a very compatible pairing in friendship, in business and work relationships, and in marriage or domestic partnerships. See also *Pisces, Virgo.* ☯ ☼

planetary angles   See *angles between planets.*

planetary cycles   1. A planet's transit through the zodiac from 0 degrees Aries to 30 degrees Pisces. **2.** A planetary cycle depicts everything happening on Earth that relates to that planet. See also *planet, zodiac.* ◯ **Z**

planetary metals   1. Originally, the seven metals associated in alchemy with each of the first seven planets discovered (including the luminaries, and excluding the Earth). **2.** The metals and their associated planets are as follow: gold/Sun, silver/Moon, copper/Venus, iron/Mars, tin/Jupiter, mercury/Mercury, and lead/Saturn. **3.** The outer planets, Uranus, Neptune, and Pluto, which are modern-day discoveries, each have two metals associated with them. Uranus is associated with radium and zinc, Neptune with lithium and cobalt, and Pluto with tungsten and bismuth. See also *planets.* ◯

planetary order   In astrology, planets can be listed in ephemeris order, which is different from the order of the planets according to their distance from the Sun in our solar system. See also *astronomical order of the planets, ephemeris order of the planets.* ◯ **Z**

planetary physiques   Astrophysiognomy is the study of traits that pertain to the astrological correlation of planets, signs, elements, and qualities to physical characteristics in human beings. See also *chakras and astrology, health/medical astrology, planets.* ☯ ◯ ☼ **Z**

planetary return   **1.** When a planet returns to the exact position it held in the birth chart. **2.** The returns of the planets Jupiter, Saturn, and Uranus are most influential, though for Uranus, it is the halfway point that is marked. **3.** The returns of these planets create long-term or permanent change within a lifetime. A Jupiter return occurs every 12 years; Saturn every 30 years; for Uranus the halfway return point is every 42 years. ✦ **1.** Planetary returns can mark big changes. Look at a planetary return as an opportunity to revisit the energy of a planet in a particular position in your birth chart. **2.** Each planetary return marks the beginning of a new cycle in your life. **3.** A Jupiter return indicates exploration of new philosophies and foreign lands. **4.** A Saturn return signals the falling away of old ways that are no longer of use and the election of a new code, abandonment or commencement of a marriage, often a dramatic change of employers or career, and a passage into adulthood, parent-hood, or retirement. **5.** A Uranus half-return occurs at age 42 and is typically associated with a midlife crisis and perimenopause and its equivalent in men. The midlife crisis seems like a disaster, which is very Uranian. Looking back, you'll see that Uranus's mid-return was a blessing in disguise that pushed you to abandon behaviors borne of guilt or to reject oppressive situations and people. Uranus always wants you to wake up and get yourself unstuck, no matter what it takes—short of death. See also *Jupiter return, planets, Saturn return, transiting planets, Uranus return.* **BC ◯ Z**

planetary ruler   **1.** The planet associated with each of the twelve signs of the zodiac. **2.** The planetary ruler of a house is the planet that rules the sign on the cusp of the house. **3.** The planetary ruler of a birth chart or a solar return chart is the planet that rules the sign on the ascendant. See also *cusp, natural house ruler, solar return chart.* ⌂ ◯ ☼ **Z**

planetary transits   See *transiting planets.*

planetoid   **1.** A smaller planet-like entity. **2.** This term is often used interchangeably with the word *asteroid* to describe bodies in orbit around the Sun that are larger than meteoroids but smaller than a planet. **3.** Sometimes used only to describe the larger asteroids, such as Ceres and Chiron, and sometimes used interchangeably with

P

dwarf planet, which is the astronomical classification of Pluto, as of 2006. Eris is another dwarf planet. See also *asteroids, Ceres, Chiron, Eris, planets, Pluto.* ◯

planets   **1.** Heavenly bodies of a certain mass and shape in orbit around the Sun. **2.** Astrology utilizes ten planets in a birth chart, including the luminaries, the Sun and Moon. Each planet is the ruler of a house and sign of the zodiac. **3.** The planets have energy, which interacts with other energy in the birth chart. **4.** Each planet is named for a god or goddess from Roman mythology, and shares some qualities of that deity, and each is associated with one of the four elements, as each sign is associated with one of the elements. ✴ In your birth chart, the houses tell you *where* in your life action takes place, but the planets *create* the action. Each planet has its own orbital energy, and additional energy and influence is created when the planets interact by creating angles to one another in your birth chart. See also *angles between planets, elements, house.* △◯

planting   See *gardening.*

Pluto   **1.** Planet discovered in 1930 and named for the Roman god of the underworld. **2.** In 2006, Pluto was also reclassified as a dwarf planet for the purposes of astronomy; it is still considered a planet in astrology. **3.** Pluto is the ninth planet from the Sun. Its eccentric orbit takes 248 years, and it spends 12 to 21 years in each sign. **4.** Pluto is the natural ruler of Scorpio and the planetary ruler of the eighth house of the zodiac. **5.** Pluto's Greek counterpart is Hades. Pluto was also the god of wealth. **6.** Pluto is one of the outer or transpersonal planets, associated with external energy, others' resources, and transformation or regeneration. The astrological glyph for Pluto is ♀. **7.** Pluto ℞ internalizes Pluto's transformative power.

✴ **1.** Pluto is a planet that effects your transformation. Pluto key-words: Others' resources, sex, birth, death, destruction of everything not built upon truth, creation, regeneration, healing, renewal, power struggles, upheaval, surgery, and investigation. **2.** Where is Pluto in your birth chart? Pluto is always about change, but the house and sign will tell you more about the kind of change. The house position of Pluto is key to understanding which area of life will enact the most dramatic transformation. It's often the area that you grasp for with the most longing, but where it seems difficult or even impossible to attain your ideal vision. Your birth chart might point to a lifelong meditation on some issue, and no planet dogs us like Pluto does. Its potent medicine helps you burn away what is not necessary, through your own initiated changes, as well as changes caused by external sources. Pluto's transformation can be very challenging, but remember that we often have to undergo an agonizing letting-go process and build faith in life itself, for miracles to occur. **3.** In a daily astrological calendar, when transiting Pluto makes positive aspects to your natal or progressed planets, you feel motivated to release burdens, negative thinking, and ignorance and seek out people and situations in the world that empower you and restore your vitality and passion for life. See also *Pluto in the houses, Pluto in the signs, retrograde planets, transpersonal planets.* ○

Pluto in the houses **1.** Pluto brings transformative energy to the areas of life relating to each of the houses. **2.** Pluto's chart placement shows areas of transformation and regeneration. ✧ **1.** Pluto brings dramatic change or upheaval—the house Pluto appears in will tell you about how Pluto will transform those areas of your life, and how you might struggle through this change to reach the power on the other side. **2.** Pluto also relates to community, and often the change in your life will involve breaking from or transcending societal expectations.

♇ in the first house Pluto in the first house relates to the self and the personality. ✧ **1.** With this Pluto placement, you have to learn how to transform old ideas, philosophies, and attitudes in order to attain independence and reach your personal power. You want to stand out on your own, and you'll have to re-create yourself to make this happen. Once you do, you can help others transform. **2.** Pluto ℞ in the first house wants you to reconsider whether your ego and pride are in the way of your advancement on your life path.

♇ in the second house Pluto in the second house relates to money and values. ✧ **1.** Second house Pluto means that your values will likely transform—how you handle money will also change in your lifetime. You'll learn that you have earning capacity, but it can be a difficult transformation—you might have to learn new values around the money you earn, also. You want to be self-sufficient, but you'll have to figure out what you really value to get there. Is it money, or what money can buy, or the change it can create? Work through your money issues, and you'll come out fine. **2.** Pluto ℞ in the second house wants you to look inward, not outward, for all the evidence you need that you are lovable and deserving.

♀ **in the third house**   In the third house, Pluto relates to siblings and family. ✳ **1.** Third house Pluto makes you very curious about how people think, and why they come to their decisions. You will likely need to transform away from your family or origins or from the beliefs you were raised with. **2.** Siblings might be catalysts for change in your life. **3.** Pluto ℞ in the third house wants you to revise your thoughts so that they are more empowering.

♀ **in the fourth house**   Pluto in the fourth house relates to family. ✳ **1.** Fourth house Pluto means that your family of origin is the place of your personal transformation. You might need to free yourself from issues with your family—you'll have to accept them before you can change them. You could leave family behind at some point in your transformation—you'll move across the country, or settle in a city, if you were raised on a farm. **2.** Pluto ℞ in the fourth house wants you to listen to your emotions and follow what makes you feel good.

♀ **in the fifth house**   Pluto in the fifth house means change relating to children, creativity, and romance. ✳ **1.** Pluto in your fifth house? Experiences with children and love (physical and romantic) can create a change in your consciousness and your experience of life. You might also need to let go of old ideas of romantic love expectations about children to move into your power. You might want to try a new path—marriage and traditional family, or traditional marriage, might not be for you. **2.** You're also very creative, and will need to figure out how to use your creativity to transform yourself and others. **3.** Pluto ℞ in the fifth house wants you to let go of being a victim and take responsibility for making decisions that create a happy life.

♀ **in the sixth house**   Pluto in the sixth house relates to work and public service. ✳ **1.** If Pluto is in your sixth house, you'll need to transform through work and service to the public. You are likely very work oriented, and you might serve the public through your work. You might not fit into the standard work world—you might start your own business. You might have lessons to learn about the value of service over work—you might have to let go of your tendency toward workaholism. **2.** Pluto ℞ in the sixth house wants you to connect with your body's consciousness on a deeper level.

♀ **in the seventh house** Seventh house Pluto creates transformation through partnerships. ✳ **1.** With a seventh house Pluto, you're working on transforming your attitude toward partnerships of all kinds. You have to learn to participate in relationships without giving up yourself or needing to be in full control. This balance can be difficult for you, but it's important to a successful relationship. **2.** Pluto ℞ in the seventh house wants you to take back ownership of the side of yourself that you were taught to judge and abandon—it's actually your passion.

♀ **in the eighth house** **1.** Eighth house Pluto relates to transformation and regeneration. **2.** Pluto is the natural planetary ruler of the eighth house, and is at home there. ✳ **1.** If you have Pluto in your eighth house, you can come into your power by utilizing your charisma and energy in the world. You likely face some roadblocks on the way there, though. You can break through your limitations, but you have to work through your bad habits and negative thought processes to transcend them—they won't just go away. The first step is realizing that you need to transform. **2.** Pluto ℞ in the eighth house wants you to come to terms with your secrets and find ways to share them.

♀ **in the ninth house** Pluto in the ninth house relates to religion and philosophy as well as travel and education. ✳ **1.** With a ninth house Pluto, you likely have a strong belief system, and might try to convert others to your beliefs—you might also experience a transformation in your own religious beliefs. **2.** Travel and higher education can move you to transformation and regeneration; the process of expanding your mind through education or travel in different cultures can create dramatic changes in you. **3.** Pluto ℞ in the ninth house wants you to listen to your Higher Self and follow its advice no matter who it upsets.

♀ **in the tenth house** Pluto in the tenth house creates change through career, public reputation, and authority figures. ✳ **1.** If you have Pluto in your tenth house, you are learning how to establish your identity and authority in this lifetime. Career is very important to you, and you might be put into a position of authority in your career, and in the public. You will likely change your community, yourself, or your co-workers through your leadership. **2.** Pluto ℞ in the tenth house wants you to take responsibility for getting your personal and public needs met.

P

♀ **in the eleventh house**   Pluto in the eleventh house relates to peer groups and goals. ✴ **1.** Pluto in your eleventh house? Your friends are very important to you—they're like family. You will transform yourself and others through your social network. Your wishes and goals are likely outside the mainstream, and your diverse social network reflects this. You can bring this varied group together, and motivate them into awareness and change. **2.** Pluto ℞ in the eleventh house wants you to detach from the demons in your mind by thinking about what makes you feel light and free.

♀ **in the twelfth house**   Twelfth house Pluto relates to psychic ability and karma. ✴ **1.** With Pluto in your twelfth house, you have the potential for transcendence, and are constantly seeking a higher plane. You'll need to learn to trust—and manage—your intuitive powers in order to get where you want to go. You also might have to let go of yourself to transform. You need to merge your power and spirit in the world—but don't sacrifice yourself for every perceived higher good. **2.** Pluto ℞ in the twelfth house wants you to moan, cry, and grieve losses you experienced earlier in your life or in past lifetimes.

See also *Pluto, Pluto in the signs, retrograde planets.* 🏠 ◯

Pluto in the signs   **1.** Pluto is the planet of transformation and regeneration. Pluto's sign will indicate how the native is likely to transform. **2.** Pluto is a generational planet, remaining in each sign for twelve to twenty-one years. **3.** Pluto ℞ in the signs demands that you find ways to connect more deeply with your soul. ✴ The sign your Pluto is in gives you a clue as to how to make a deeper connection to your inner or higher self.

♀ **in Aquarius**   **1.** Pluto is the sign of transformation, and Aquarius is an innovative individualist. Pluto in Aquarius is transformation through invention and original thought. **2.** Pluto will enter Aquarius in 2024. ✴ **1.** Pluto in Aquarius ends networking as we know it and ensures a quantum leap for electronics, automation, and robotics. **2.** Pluto ℞ in Aquarius brings people together through cutting-edge technology, science, disaster, and brotherhood.

♀ **in Aries**   **1.** Pluto is the sign of transformation, and Aries is all about action. Pluto in Aries is transformation through right action. **2.** Pluto was in Aries from 1822 to 1852. (It returns to Aries in 2068.) ✴ **1.** This was a period of great innovation as well as war.

The generation born during this period shared a pioneering spirit that was unwavering even in the face of war or death. Risk-taking was a path to transformation. **2.** Pluto ℞ in Aries revisits causation, and what's needed to lead, free of ego.

♀ **in Cancer   1.** Pluto in Cancer is transformation through family and instinct. **2.** Pluto was in Cancer from 1914 to 1938. (It returns to Cancer in 2158.) ✷ **1.** This generation was focused on the homeland, on family and on building security within the family, community, and country. Ownership of property was essential for the purposes of feeding, nurturing, and developing family and nation. Those born during this period shared a desire to own their own land or home and to have a personal stake in creating a solid footing for family. **2.** Pluto ℞ in Cancer stirs up the subconscious mind so that current and ancestral family dysfunction is felt, acknowledged, and transformed.

♀ **in Capricorn   1.** Pluto in Capricorn creates transformation through ambition and structure. **2.** Pluto is in Capricorn from 2008 until 2021. ✷ **1.** The collective focus of this generation will be on the world economy. The worlds of business and finance will be the focus of transformation. The collective desire of this group is to get back to basics, reassessing their financial and economic needs. They will rethink how we handle resources, including money, land, and the environment, and they will work to preserve and conserve precious resources. They will ask how we can change the world's financial systems and still maintain future security. **2.** Pluto ℞ in Capricorn tests systems and corporate structures for validity and ethical use of resources.

♀ **in Gemini   1.** Pluto in Gemini means transformation through communication, transportation, and primary education. **2.** Pluto was in Gemini from 1884 to 1914. (It returns to Gemini in 2132.) ✷ **1.** Communication was essential to this generation, which forged new paths of information and education with the telephone, newspapers, journals, and global travel. **2.** Pluto ℞ in Gemini questions why information is processed in a particular way, and creates lateral applications.

♀ **in Leo   1.** Pluto in Leo creates change through children, entertainment, and courageous leadership. **2.** Pluto was in Leo from 1938 to 1957. (It returns to Leo in 2183.) ✷ **1.** If you're part of the Pluto in Leo generation, you may support strong leadership to protect the

P

homeland, its values, and security. This generation shares a desire to protect and maintain the gains made when Pluto was in Cancer. The leaders of this generation developed via war and civil unrest, after tests of power and domination. This generation found that charisma created leaders. If you have Pluto in Leo, you grew up believing that you had the power to be and do anything. Entertainment is a big part of your life and your children's lives. Your generation enjoys death-defying sports. **2.** Pluto ℞ in Leo demands an alignment with the truth that can only be found in the heart.

♀ **in Libra   1.** Pluto in Libra transforms to create justice and harmony. **2.** Pluto was in Libra from 1971 to 1983. (It returns to Libra in 2217.) ✴ **1.** Were you born into this generation? If so, your focus is on enacting legal and civil rights into law. Libra demands fairness and justice and will negotiate the differences between groups. This generation is attentive to global diplomacy, international relations, civil rights, international trade, and wants to transform old laws to serve the present society and a need for equal rights and justice under the law. **2.** If you have Pluto in Libra, you personally transform through partnerships and marriage. Pluto ℞ in Libra wants integration with the alter ego.

♀ **in Pisces   1.** Pluto in Pisces transforms through spiritual transcendence. **2.** Pluto will enter Pisces in 2044. ✴ **1.** Hospitals, sanitariums, prisons, and institutions in general transform through Pluto's transit of Pisces. Music, dance, photography, and film will be Pluto's vehicles for transformation of the collective unconscious by revealing what has been cloaked in mystery or confusion. Psychology will undergo a major upheaval as Pluto moves through Pisces. The upcoming generation with Pluto in Pisces will find new resources in outer space. **2.** Pluto ℞ in Pisces urges deep introspection into the soul.

♀ **in Sagittarius   1.** Pluto in Sagittarius transforms through higher education, law, and religion. **2.** Pluto was in Sagittarius from 1995 to 2008. (It returns to Sagittarius in 2241.) ✴ **1.** The collective focus of this generation is in the transformation of all social systems, including higher education, athletics, religion, and law. They will experience a reawakening of religion and fighting for religious rights or beliefs. This generation's collective consciousness will free themselves of dogma by realizing that their old beliefs are no longer productive. They will debate the fundamentals of and differences between religion and science and this will result in innovative discoveries. Pluto seeks integration and Sagittarius rules foreign lands. This transit pushed for invasion of foreign lands in pursuit of resources. This later generates greater awareness and acceptance of different cultures and peoples. **2.** Pluto ℞ in Sagittarius awakens the inner voice of truth as a transformative, religious experience.

♇ **in Scorpio   1.** Pluto is at home in Scorpio, a sign of power and intensity. **2.** Pluto in Scorpio transforms through public money and resources. **3.** Pluto was in Scorpio from 1983 to 1995. (It returns to Scorpio in 2229.) ✸ **1.** If you were born when Pluto was in Scorpio, your generational focus is on resources and making fortunes, working with money, and investing in the global market. Money and making it fast was the key in this time and for this generation, especially through joint resources, lending, and insurance. This generation experienced phenomenal success with goods and services, but they had to deal with issues of health, and with the need to develop a universal approach to disease as well as care of the environment. **2.** This generation is in a position to resolve or generate karma. Pluto ℞ in Scorpio seeks reassurance that life is eternal and death no more than a release from the physical dimension.

♇ **in Taurus   1.** Pluto in Taurus transforms through values and the material world. **2.** Pluto was in Taurus from 1852 to 1883. (It returns to Taurus in 2098.) ✸ **1.** This generation found power in security and possessions and a shared desire for ownership. Owning property, banks, art, copper, wheat fields, and precious gems fulfilled their need for security and desire for financial power and control. The action of this collective consciousness was to control others via wealth and ownership of property (as well as enslavement). **2.** Pluto ℞ in Taurus urges fulfillment through artistic or musical acquisitions.

♇ **in Virgo   1.** Pluto in Virgo transforms through analyzing and problem solving. **2.** Pluto was in Virgo from 1957 to 1972. (It returns to Virgo in 2203.) ✸ **1.** If you're part of this generation, your focus is on solving problems and creating efficiency in pet care, health care, and employee benefits through intelligent research, detailed analysis, and highly skilled teams. This generation is studying and perfecting better ways to create and sustain health, in pursuit of universal care. This generation has a strong desire for education, employment, and implementation of new discoveries in science and technology. **2.** Pluto ℞ in Virgo seeks internalized transformation of the physical body.

See also *Pluto, signs.* ◯ ☼

P

Pluto/Jupiter   See *Jupiter/Pluto.*

Pluto/Mars   See *Mars/Pluto.*

Pluto/Mercury   See *Mercury/Pluto.*

Pluto/Moon   See *Moon/Pluto.*

Pluto/Neptune   See *Neptune/Pluto.*

Pluto/North Node   See *North Node/Pluto.*

Pluto retrograde, personal   **1.** Pluto is retrograde in the birth chart, creating a more personally transformative effect in the life of the native. **2.** Pluto's orbit around the Sun takes 248 years, and it's retrograde for 160 days each year. Those born during one of these periods have Pluto ℞ in the natal chart. **3.** Personal retrogrades have varying influence depending on the activity of other planets in the birth chart. ✵ If you have Pluto ℞ in your birth chart (and with Pluto in retrograde for 160 days each year, that's a lot of people with a retrograde Pluto in their birth charts), you will attract intense people or situations according to the sign and house placement that cause you to seek a deeper understanding of yourself and meaning of your life's purpose. See also *Pluto; Pluto retrograde, transiting; retrograde, personal.* ◯ ℞

Need some tips for handling your personal Pluto retrograde? Check the sign:

- ♀℞ **in Aries:** When you feel excited about an idea, stick with it.
- ♀℞ **in Taurus:** Focus on the money you have to create more space to receive.
- ♀℞ **in Gemini:** Think of your mind as linked to a universal cloud computer.
- ♀℞ **in Cancer:** Focus on the love and caring already in your life.
- ♀℞ **in Leo:** Seek out opportunities to perform for others.
- ♀℞ **in Virgo:** Pay attention to your hunches.
- ♀℞ **in Libra:** Pick an activity that you prefer to do alone.
- ♀℞ **in Scorpio:** Death is a long way off for you and the transition will be easy.

- ♀ ℞ **in Sagittarius:** The part of you that knows the difference between a thought born of worry and a thought born of hope is always present and ready to guide you when you stop racing around. Breathe deeply, and feel yourself in your body.
- ♀ ℞ **in Capricorn:** Decide to be your own ultimate authority.
- ♀ ℞ **in Aquarius:** Consider the benefits of being an outsider.
- ♀ ℞ **in Pisces:** Look for the silver lining in your life situations.

Pluto retrograde, transiting   1. Pluto's transiting retrograde lasts 160 days; that's a little more than five months. **2.** Finding ways to channel Pluto's transforming energy can seem difficult during retrograde periods. ✳ **1.** Retrograde Pluto has two speeds: slow, and slower. It's like the effect physicists relate about traveling at the speed of light: everything and everyone around you seems to be standing still … but you're on the threshold of the transforming change that can only occur at top speed. **2.** Pluto ℞ is a shape-shifter. To use retrograde Pluto wisely, you need to be willing to experience change down to a molecular level; you need to be willing to challenge the status quo; you need to be willing to reinvent your world … and then reinvent it again. Holding on to notions about self, about the past or the future, is dangerous now. With Pluto, you live completely in the moment, and are ready to brush aside the current reality at a moment's notice to make room for a new understanding. Much like a monk brushes away an intricate sand mandala at its moment of completion, Pluto ℞ teaches nonattachment to particular outcomes as well as a bold curiosity. See also *Pluto; Pluto retrograde, personal; retrograde, transiting.* ◯ ℞

P

If transiting Pluto retrograde challenges your expectations, look to the astrological sign to throw some light on the situation:

- **In Aries:** Resist your impulse to insist on doing it your way and form a team.
- **In Taurus:** If you wouldn't buy it all over again, get rid of it.
- **In Gemini:** Being versatile is great preparation.
- **In Cancer:** Holding hands can make change less frightening.
- **In Leo:** Be creative about creating something new.
- **In Virgo:** Look for blessings.
- **In Libra:** Look for justice.

- **In Scorpio:** Be soulful, sensual.
- **In Sagittarius:** Be enterprising.
- **In Capricorn:** Be specific.
- **In Aquarius:** Be smart.
- **In Pisces:** Everything old is new again.

Pluto return   Pluto's return occurs every 248 years, well beyond the human life span. Frenchwoman Jeanne Calment is the oldest human being whose age can be documented accurately. Born in Arles, she lived to age 122, nearly halfway through her Pluto return. As medical technology advances and more people reach the halfway point of the Pluto return, doubtless mystical revelations will prove transforming to all humanity, holding valuable clues to the secrets of enjoying long life. See also *planetary return, Pluto.* ◯

Pluto/Saturn   Pluto is transformation, and Saturn is self-discipline. Pluto brings a need to transform Saturn's stable reality. ✸ When these two planets, Pluto and Saturn, positively connect in your birth chart, you possess a natural executive ability for maximizing resources and making a profit. A more challenging aspect encourages suspicion around corporations, government leaders, police, and authority figures. The fear is Saturn's skepticism about the future and the excitement is Pluto's anticipation about the evolutionary process of life. Pluto empowers and Saturn manifests … reality. When you feel afraid of death, abandonment, or loss, remember that you have the power to create your future through the choices you make every day. See also *aspects between planets, Pluto, Saturn.* △ ☯ ◯

Pluto/South Node   Pluto is transformation, and the South Node is the comfort zone. ✸ When Pluto and the South Node connect positively in your birth chart, you are more easily able to release what you've outgrown. A more challenging aspect can make you feel that you are never in the right place at the right time until you align with the destiny described by your North Node. See also *aspects between planets, Pluto, South Node.* △ ☯ ◯

Pluto/Sun Pluto is transformation, and the Sun is self and the external world. ✦ When Pluto positively connects in your birth chart to the Sun (one of the luminaries), others will look to you for leadership. A challenging connection may cause you to bully others into serving you. Check your intentions. See also *aspects between planets, Pluto, Sun.* △ ☯ ○

Pluto transits **1.** Pluto as it moves or transits through the signs of the zodiac. **2.** Pluto's orbit around the Sun takes 248 years; Pluto transits all twelve zodiac signs in that time. **3.** A portion of Pluto's orbit is within the orbit of Neptune. This means that there are periods of time—close to twenty years—when Pluto and Neptune swap positions as the outermost planet. **4.** Pluto transits can be compared to the placement of Pluto in a natal chart for predictive purposes. A transit shows the position of a planet at a given moment. **5.** Transiting Pluto is a catalyst as it enters a new sign or a new house, and forms aspects with other transiting planets or planets in both birth and progressed charts. As a generational planet, Pluto brings about big, long-lasting changes.

✦ **1.** Transiting Pluto gives you the courage to end unhealthy situations or the appetite to delve into the dark side. As transiting Pluto makes positive aspects to other key planets, you are able to attract the people and raw resources you need to empower your life. If you are in alignment with your passion, you magnetically attract investors. **2.** When transiting Pluto makes difficult aspect to other planets, you may feel drawn to individuals who betray you, seek to use you sexually, or demean you in some way. You may also feel obsessed about death—your own or others'—and you may find yourself caught in a web of self-destruction because of your focus on dark and negative energies. See also *Pluto, progressed birth chart, transiting planets, transits.* BC 🏠 ○

What can Pluto transits tell you?

- Pluto transiting your **first house** is a good time for plastic surgery, branding your persona, image makeover, and divorce to get your freedom and independence back.
- Pluto transiting your **second house** requires radical measures to avoid bankruptcy. Focus on paying off one bill at a time. It's a good time to sell jewelry and art.

- Want to transform your car? Find out when Pluto enters your **third house**. Pluto likes red, black, and sexy with plenty of power.

- Pluto in the **fourth house** makes it easier to let go of the past, bad habits, and nagging family members.

- If you want the kind of lover who turns heads, commands a room, and sweeps you off your feet, just hang in there until Pluto finds its way into your **fifth house**. Be forewarned: you might get a married lover.

- Your job may end when Pluto enters your **sixth house**. Pluto wants you to do a little research and find a new position where you will have more power and money.

- Pluto moving through your **seventh house** usually means marriage or divorce. Avoid a divorce by looking for what needs healing and transforming before Pluto arrives.

- Pluto transiting through your **eighth house** is the best time to make big money through joint ventures.

- Pluto attracts publishing and travel opportunities when it moves through your **ninth house**. It's also a good time to get your degree.

- Your employer could go under when Pluto moves into your **tenth house**. After some initial loss of stability, you'll get your sea legs and find greater success in a new career.

- Friendships end or transform when Pluto enters your **eleventh house**. Pluto will be happiest getting involved in some kind of social reform during this time.

- Pluto transiting your **twelfth house** is pretty intense. Buried trauma from this life and prior lives loosens and floats to the surface to be transformed and released. Jungian dream analysis, past life regression, or auto-hypnosis can help.

Pluto/Venus   Pluto is transformation, and Venus is beauty, harmony, and love. ✦ **1.** When Pluto and Venus positively connect in your birth chart, you accept the fleeting nature of physical life and appreciate the beauty of nature—and humanity—all the more. When Pluto and Venus are harshly aspected, you tend to cling to your money, assets, and loved ones to prevent loss and delay any encounter with death. **2.** Pluto and Venus hold a natural polarity in that they are natural rulers of opposing signs in a natural chart. Venus rules Taurus, the sign of attachment and beauty made flesh. Pluto rules Scorpio, the sign of detachment and loss of integrity of flesh. Both are involved with money. Venus rules the private use of money and Pluto rules the public sphere of money, as well as joint ventures. When both planets are consciously expressed either in a natal chart or during times of progressions and transits, money functions at its best. See also *aspects between planets, Pluto, Venus.* △ ☯ ○

Point of Destiny See *North Node.*

Point of Loss See *South Node.*

polarity **1.** A relationship of mutual opposition. **2.** The Earth is polar (the North Pole, the South Pole), and exists with a magnetic polarity. **3.** Astrology is full of polarities because it reflects the state of physical existence on Earth. **4.** Concepts and ideas can also be polarities: hate and violence are polarized by unconditional love and kindness. Yin and yang are astrology's two energies and their polar energies combined will unite in perfect balance and harmony. See also *Earth, planets, yang, yin.* ☯ ○ **Z**

> **Travel around the zodiac, and you'll find these sets of polarities:**
> - **Aries** is independent; **Libra** is partnership.
> - **Taurus** is attachment; **Scorpio** is detachment.
> - **Gemini** is speaking; **Sagittarius** is listening.
> - **Cancer** is intuition; **Capricorn** is logic.
> - **Leo** is personal love; **Aquarius** is love of humanity.
> - **Virgo** is detail; **Pisces** is the big picture.

P

positive sign **1.** Another name for the direct or masculine energy ascribed to the planets and zodiac signs in astrology. **2.** The positive, or yang, signs are the air and fire signs: Aries, Gemini, Leo, Libra, Sagittarius, and Aquarius. Positive is used here more in the sense of electricity's alternating current (positive and negative), than in the sense that positive is good, while negative is bad. See also *masculine principle, negative sign, yang.* ☯ ☼

prediction See *forecast.*

progressed birth chart **1.** An astrological birth chart that is fast-forwarded from birth to now or to any significant date from the time you were born and off into the future. **2.** How is this done? Well, most astrologers will look at how many degrees or minutes a planet moves in one day, and that will become the movement for one year in a progressed chart. For a lunar progression, the Moon is moved forward 1 degree for every 28-day cycle since birth. **3.** Another type of progressed chart is the solar arc chart. In this case, the Sun is moved a degree for every year since birth and all the other planets maintain the same ratio to the sun (solar arc) as found in the birth chart.

✦ **1.** Your birth chart represents a moment in time—the moment of your birth. It can be used to guide you throughout your life, but the planets keep moving in their orbits around the Sun and through the zodiac. A progressed birth chart can help you figure out how you have changed or will change over time. **2.** If you want more understanding about an event from your past or an upcoming event, your astrologer will most likely cast your solar progressed chart, your solar arc chart, and the transits for the date of query and compare those with your birth chart. The planet that rules the nature of the event, the chart ruler, and Mars and Pluto will all be checked in the transits chart to see what they were triggering internally and externally in your natal and progressed charts. These four charts are viewed in a quad-wheel. As the term suggests, this is a chart that places your natal chart wheel in the center, surrounded by your solar progressed planets in a second wheel, surrounded by your solar arc planets in a third wheel, and finally surrounded by the transiting planets in the fourth, the outermost, wheel. See also *birth chart, planets, solar arc chart, solar progressed chart, transits.* **BC** ☯ ◯ **Z**

progressed planet   1. A planet as it has moved from the time a birth chart was created. **2.** As the planets progress, they can create aspects, or angles, with the planets in the natal chart. And because a planet's daily motion is used as one year's motion in a progressed chart, these aspects usually last for years. ✦ **1.** Progressed planets can tell you about how you will grow and change over time. **2.** As the planets progress, they can also change the house and sign they're in. Because every degree of the 30 degrees that comprise a sign holds a different expression of the sign, you grow and acquire wisdom as your planets progress through the various signs. See also *birth chart, progressed birth chart.* **BC**

progressions   1. Imagined or predicted movement of the planets in their orbits, used to create a progressed birth chart for an individual, corporation, or a Davison relationship chart. **2.** Planets do not actually progress out in the solar system. The progression of planets is a system of moving a planet forward. **3.** One of the two most popular systems is called secondary progressions: each day of movement after your birth date represents a year in the progressed chart. **4.** The second most popular system of progressions is solar arc directed: the Sun is progressed in the same way as the solar progression, but the rest of the planets are not progressed according to their own rate of travel. Instead, they are moved forward the same distance as the Sun. This is the solar arc: the distance the Sun has moved from where it was when you were born. A solar arc chart looks just like your birth chart in that all of the planets are the same distance from each other, but they have been moved forward, counterclockwise, about the same number of degrees as you are old. **5.** Transits show the actual location of planets where they are in the solar system in relationship to the Earth. **6.** Progressions are not usually triggers in themselves unless they change signs, directions, or houses. Progressed planets are poised, waiting for a transiting planet to activate them. See also *Davison relationship chart, progressed birth chart, progressed planet, solar arc chart, solar progression.* **BC ☯ ◯ Z**

P

quadrant **1.** A section of the zodiac when it is divided into four parts along the horizon and meridian. **2.** Each quadrant contains three of the twelve houses of the birth chart.  Do you have lots of planets in one quadrant of your birth chart? If so, you find more happiness and satisfaction in this life by identifying any resistance you have to the challenges of that quadrant and expanding to embrace the qualities of its three houses. See also *birth chart, house.* **BC**

Do you have lots of planets in one quadrant of your birth chart?

Birth Chart Quadrant	Houses	Keywords
First	First, second, and third	Spring, internal, discovery of self; path, values, and expression
Second	Fourth, fifth, and sixth	Summer, internal, growth through family relationships, love relationships, and work
Third	Seventh, eighth, and ninth	Fall, external, expansion through integration via committed partnership, shared resources, and foreign exploration
Fourth	Tenth, eleventh, and twelfth	Winter, external, active contribution to business, community, and humanity

quadrate   **1.** Another name for the aspect between planets known as the square. **2.** A 90-degree angle between planets. **3.** Considered challenging or malefic. See also *aspects between planets, square.* △○Z

quadruplicity   **1.** A group of four zodiac signs of each of the three qualities. **2.** The three qualities are cardinal, fixed, and mutable. **3.** The cardinal quadruplicity includes Aries, Cancer, Libra, and Capricorn. **4.** The fixed quadruplicity includes Taurus, Leo, Scorpio, and Aquarius. **5.** The mutable quadruplicity includes Gemini, Virgo, Sagittarius, and Pisces. See also *cardinal (quality), fixed, mutable, quality.* ☯☼

quad-wheel   See *progressed birth chart.*

quality   **1.** Used to describe the characteristic energy of the astrological signs. The three qualities are cardinal, fixed, and mutable. **2.** The cardinal signs are Aries, Cancer, Libra, and Capricorn. These signs are the active initiators of the zodiac. They are also the first sign of each season. **3.** The fixed signs are Taurus, Leo, Scorpio, and Aquarius. These signs are persistent and consistent. They are the second sign of each of the four seasons, and represent the immobile center. **4.** The mutable signs are Gemini, Virgo, Sagittarius, and Pisces. These signs are flexible and changeable. They mark the end of each of the four seasons, just before the season shifts. ✴ How is the quality of your Sun sign important? It's one more piece of the puzzle of your birth chart. The quality indicates how the sign is alive, animated, and in motion. See also *cardinal (quality), fixed, mutable.* ☯☼

Quality	Signs	Keywords
Cardinal	Aries, Cancer, Libra, and Capricorn	Birth, initiating, and energy that pulls away or pushes outward
Fixed	Taurus, Leo, Scorpio, and Aquarius	Physical life, stabilizing, and energy that draws toward or pulls inward
Mutable	Gemini, Virgo, Sagittarius, and Pisces	Transition, release, and energy that spirals

quartile Another name for the aspect between planets known as the square. See also *square*. △ ○ **Z**

querent **1.** One who queries, or ask questions. **2.** The name for someone asking questions (of an astrologer, tarot card reader, or intuitive, for example). ✦ When you visit or speak to an astrologer or intuitive and ask questions about your life path—general or specific questions—you are the *querent*. See also *astrologer/ist, intuitive arts*. ☯ **Z**

quincunx **1.** Also called *inconjunct*. One of the minor aspects between planets in astrology. **2.** The glyph for quincunx is ⚻. On a birth chart, planets are in quincunx when they create a 150-degree angle in the birth chart. Planets are also considered in quincunx when they are within 10 degrees of this 150-degree angle. **3.** Quincunxes are generally seen as creating a challenging relationship between planets that requires adjustments from both planets. **4.** The planets do not relate to each other very easily because they are in different signs, different elements, and different modalities.

✦ **1.** Check your birth chart for the quincunx symbol: ⚻. If you find one, figure out which planets form the quincunx. This will help you understand how to give each planet what it needs so that they can harmonize. **2.** In which houses of your birth chart are the planets creating the quincunx located? This will give you clues about the areas of your life that are likely to be most affected by the planetary interaction. **3.** Now check the signs the planets in quincunx appear in. This will indicate how to give expression to each of the planets so that neither is favored over the other. **4.** A quincunx doesn't have to be seen as negative, though it can cause you a fair amount of frustration, until you find a way to make each of the included planets more conscious in your life. The planets in quincunx have no common ground, nothing they share. To get these planets to work together, you need to unite disparate energies; if you can pull it off, you'll have a genius result beyond anything you could have thought possible. (So don't give up on this quincunx aspect without giving it your best.) See also *aspect grid, aspects between planets*. △ ☯ ○

Q

quintile   **1.** One of the minor aspects between planets in astrology. **2.** The glyph for quintile is Q. On a birth chart, planets are in quintile when they create a 72-degree angle in the birth chart. Planets are also considered in quintile when they are within 10 degrees of this 72-degree angle. **3.** Quintiles are generally seen as creating a positive or beneficial relationship between planets. **4.** Quintiles are not typically included in a reading, perhaps because there are so many different interpretations as to what they represent. **5.** The number 72 is often equated with material gain through perseverance. **6.** A quintile is one fifth of a circle and quintiles are often associated with Mercury in Taurus, which rules the number five. Mercury in Taurus can be expressed as a magical gift that turns an ordinary substance into gold, much like alchemy that transmutes lead into gold.

�֍ **1.** Check your birth chart for the quintile symbol if you have a printout of a chart that includes the minor aspects: Q. If not, you can eyeball your chart to see whether you have a pair of planets that appear to be separated by one fifth of a circle, and then you can do the math and see whether they are. If you have one of these, look at the planets that are creating the quintile for clues about which planets give you a talent for turning ordinary work or products into wealth. **2.** In which houses of your birth chart are the planets creating the quintile located? This will tell you about the areas of your life that are most likely to produce wealth. **3.** Now check the signs the planets in quintile appear in. This will indicate your magical talents for making money. **4.** A quintile is an aspect that indicates a special talent or gift for creating wealth. See also *aspect grid, aspects between planets.* △ ☯ ○

radical chart See *birth chart.*

reaping lifetime **1.** When most of the planets are in the western half of the birth chart, in houses four through nine. **2.** A reaping lifetime is one in which the native gains the rewards of work done in previous lifetimes. **3.** When most planets are in the eastern half of the native's birth chart, in houses ten through three, the native is said to be in a sowing lifetime. ✸ Does your chart show that this is a reaping lifetime for you? If so, this should be a good life for you—you have already worked off most of your karmic debts in previous lives, and in this lifetime, you get to enjoy your karmic rewards. You can maximize this good fortune by working to resolve conflicts with others by owning your part in disputes and disharmony. Do this by developing positive expression of the planets that are in difficult aspect in the eastern half of your chart, in houses ten through four. See also *birth chart, sowing lifetime.* **BC ☯ Z**

reception **1.** When one planet is in the sign in which an aspected planet is exalted or is the ruler. The ruling or exalted planet receives the second planet and extends a beneficial relationship. **2.** The aspect can be a conjunction, sextile, square, trine, or opposition. An example would be the Sun squaring Mercury in Leo, the sign the Sun rules. ✸ Do you have a planet in reception in your birth chart? Make a note and find out when a transiting planet aspects that planet as it will trigger an event. See also *aspects between planets, conjunction, exalted, house, mutual reception, natural house ruler, opposition, sextile, square, trine.* △ 🏠 ◯ ☼

rectification **1.** Using major life events to ascertain a birth time for a native whose birth time is unknown. **2.** Life events used to rectify a birth chart include those that pertain to the angle houses (the first, fourth, seventh, and tenth houses). An astrologer needs a minimum of fifteen life events to rectify a chart. **3.** Rectification is most accurate with precise dates and times of life events. If the event time is unknown, noon is used. If the event date is not known, the 15th of the month is used. If the month is not known, July 1st is used for the month. **4.** There are some excellent computer programs for chart rectification. Using these, the astrologer enters the client's birth date and place and any bracket of possible birth time if known.

✧ How does an astrologer rectify your birth chart? If you know you were born just before dinnertime and your family always ate at 6 P.M., the astrologer could enter 5:00 to 6:30 P.M. for the time range. Then the astrologer enters the fifteen or more life events you've provided, and the program weighs the events according to pertinence and accuracy and then calculates the most probable times in order of probability. The astrologer can then test those times through looking at progressions and transits. See also *birth chart, birth time.* **BC ☯ Z**

> **Here are events that qualify as rectification events in the angular houses:**
> - **First house events:** Times of recognition and becoming independent (such as leaving home), a divorce, or being singled out from a group (such as being selected from an audience).
> - **Fourth house events:** Include long-term additions or losses from your home, conception of first child if you are a woman, adoption by stepmother, mother's passing, and purchase of real estate.
> - **Seventh house events:** Dates of legal partnerships in business or marriage, or the date a long-term roommate moved in, and dates of lawsuit filings.
> - **Tenth house events:** Birth of first child if you are a man, adoption by stepfather, passing of father or boss, and hire dates with new employers.

reincarnation **1.** Some astrologers believe that the soul is embodied on Earth many times, and during each lifetime, the soul works to release karmic debt and create karmic rewards. Souls that have lived few lifetimes are young souls; souls with many lifetimes behind them are old souls. **2.** The eighth house, Pluto, and Scorpio rule reincarnation and also depict existence in the hereafter. **3.** Karmic debt is ruled by the tenth and twelfth houses, Saturn and Neptune, Capricorn and Pisces. **4.** The fifth house, the Sun, and Leo provide information about past lives and your soul. The ninth house, Jupiter, and Sagittarius give clues about future lives. See also *karma, old soul, reaping lifetime, sowing lifetime, young soul.* **BC** 🌓 **Z**

relationship astrology   The branch of astrology that studies relationship and compatibility, known as *synastry*. See also *compatibility, composite chart, fifth house, love, seventh house, synastry, Venus.* △ 🌓 🏠 ◯ ☼ **Z**

relocation astrology   **1.** Branch of astrology also known as geographic, locational, or locality astrology. **2.** Relocation charts are maps. There is importance attached to whether the relocation is to the east or west. West of the ascendant is more of a first house influence; east of the ascendant line is more twelfth house experience. West of the midheaven is tenth house energy; east of the midheaven is ninth house influence. West of the descendant is seventh house territory; east of the descendant is sixth house. West of the nadir is fourth house influence; east of the nadir is third house orientation. See also *ascendant, birth chart, descendant, first house, fourth house, midheaven (Medium Coeli), nadir (Imum Coeli), seventh house, tenth house.* △ 🌓 🏠 ◯ ☼ **Z**

retrograde, personal   **1.** The placement of a retrograde planet in the native's birth chart. **2.** Retrograde motion can internalize or stifle the normal direct energy of the planet. The astrological symbol to designate a retrograde planet is ℞, as in Jupiter ℞.

✦ **1.** In your birth chart, a retrograde planet means that you will have resistance, hesitation, or inhibition around giving that planet expression. You may not be drawn to what that planet represents or you might not give it much thought. Instead, your focus is elsewhere and the retrograde planet's manifestation is delayed. **2.** A retrograde planet can also mean that you have internalized the nature of the planet. For instance, if you were born with Mars retrograde you might tend to avoid confrontation, which is an outward expression of Mars, but you might be very independent, which is an inner expression of Mars. **3.** Do you have multiple retrograde planets in your birth chart? You may feel like you are waiting for your life to start. As planets progress, they continue to be retrograde according to how long those planets were retrograde after you were born. Progressed personal planets eventually go direct, and periods of transiting retrograde can heighten these planets' influence. See also *Jupiter retrograde, personal; Mars retrograde, personal; Mercury retrograde, personal; Neptune retrograde, personal; Pluto retrograde, personal; retrograde planets; Saturn retrograde, personal; Uranus retrograde, personal; Venus retrograde, personal.* **BC** ◯ ℞ **Z**

retrograde planets   **1.** The positioning of the planets in their orbits so that, from the Earth, they appear to be moving backward, though they are not. **2.** Retrogrades happen when the Earth passes a planet moving slower than the Earth does, or when a faster-moving planet passes the Earth. The Sun and Moon don't have retrogrades in astrology because the Sun doesn't have its own orbit (the Sun doesn't orbit itself!) and the Moon circles the Earth; the other planets—Mercury and Venus (faster-moving planets), and Mars, Jupiter, Saturn, Uranus, Neptune, and Pluto (slower-moving planets)—all exhibit retrograde behavior. **3.** Retrogrades are designated by the astrological symbol ℞, as in Mercury ℞. **4.** Astrologers say that a planet goes retrograde when it begins its apparent backward movement and goes direct when apparent forward movement resumes. **5.** The planets beyond the Earth that are more distant from the Sun retrograde more frequently: Mars retrogrades for 72 days every 25 months; Jupiter for 121 days every 13 months; Saturn for 138 days every 12 months; Uranus for 151 days every 12 months; and Neptune for 158 days every 12 months. **6.** Planets appear retrograde when they are closer to the Sun in their orbit, and this can create an intensification of energies in the chart. The native may face challenges with the retrograde planet, or may have to work to reveal the planet's energy.

✦ **1.** If you were born with planets in retrograde, you tend to have a much easier time when those same planetary transits are also retrograde. **2.** Retrogrades are generally regarded as negative, but you can turn this energy around by working with it. Approach the retrograde with a question as to what in that area of your life needs rethinking or redoing. This will start an internalization process of that planet's nature within you and help you to identify what you can do to help it be more functional in your life when the retrograde is over and the planet goes direct. See also *retrograde, personal; retrograde, transiting*.

General activity of the retrograde planets:

- **Mercury** ℞: Excellent cycle for returning to abandoned projects, ideas, and writing.

- **Venus** ℞: Replaces desperation for love with awareness of your own lovability.

- **Mars** ℞: Slows down the fast pace and aligns with activities that result in joy.

- **Jupiter** ℞: Wants internal reflection on whether religion or philosophy is one's truth.

- **Saturn** ℞: Reveals how setting impossible standards is not generating more success, satisfaction, or happiness.

- **Uranus** ℞: Is in the moment of social awkwardness and finds acceptance and relief with it.

- **Neptune** ℞: Makes use of super-sensitivity to replace worries with slightly more positive affirmations.

- **Pluto** ℞: Karmic situations reappear to be acknowledged, atoned, forgiven, and released.

retrograde, transiting   1. The motion of the planets in their orbits, as they transit, or move, through each house and sign of the zodiac. **2.** Planetary cycles always include retrograde periods and astrologers refer to these periods as transiting retrogrades. When a planet exhibits transiting retrograde behavior, its influence affects everyone here on Earth. **3.** Each transiting retrograde planet has its own signature energy.

✧ **1.** When you observe the heavens, a retrograde planet appears to be moving backward, but that's just an illusion. **2.** Knowing when transiting retrogrades will be coming up and how long they will last can help you understand how to plan ahead and to use retrograde energies for your best benefit. A good astrological calendar will include the dates when transiting retrogrades begin and end during the year for each planet. **3.** Until recently, most astrologers interpreted transiting retrogrades as times with challenging or negative influences on people. Today's astrologers are more open-minded about transiting retrogrades and view them more as a shift in energy or as a way to correct something, rather than as an indicator of anything inherently bad. How you work with the energy of a transiting retrograde can determine whether these times present you with insurmountable obstacles or with opportunities to grow. Whether you like them or not, retrogrades happen; you can learn to welcome their energy rather than dread it. **4.** The astrological sign in which a transiting planet goes retrograde or goes direct can give you extra clues about how to interpret its energy. For example, if Mars goes retrograde in Gemini, then expect that the power of sharp words might carry anger that can cut both ways, either to build or destroy. Either way, Mars ℞ in Gemini requires that you nurture quick thinking to avoid the confusion that can come in the wake of Mars's blindsiding force (especially if you haven't checked your astrological calendar and are unprepared for its effect). **5.** If you have one or more retrograde planets in your birth chart, the energies of those planets will be amplified or enhanced for you personally during their periods of transiting retrograde. See also *Jupiter retrograde, transiting; Mars retrograde, transiting; Mercury retrograde, transiting; Neptune retrograde, transiting; Pluto retrograde, transiting; retrograde, personal; retrograde planets; Saturn retrograde, transiting; Uranus retrograde, transiting; Venus retrograde, transiting.* ◯ ℞ **Z**

return   See *planetary return.*

rising sign   See *ascendant.*

ruler   **1.** The planet associated with an astrological sign or house. **2.** The planet's energy and associated characteristics will influence the zodiac sign and color the house with which it is associated. See also *natural house ruler.* 🏠 ◯ ☼ **Z**

rulership sign   See *home signs.*

Sabian symbols **1.** System developed in the 1920s by astrologer Marc Edmund Jones and Elsie Wheeler, creating a correlating symbol for each of the 360 degrees in the zodiac. **2.** Using Sabian symbols, every degree on the birth chart has a particular meaning or interpretation. **3.** The Sabian symbols are archetypal images used to add an interpretive layer to the birth chart; many contemporary astrologers use Sabian symbols, and there are astrologers who are Sabian symbol specialists. ✳ Some astrologers assign clients sacred rituals based on the Sabian symbols images. For instance, if you have two planets that trine each other and you see that a related transiting planet will be making an exact grand trine at an upcoming date within a specific time frame, you could look up the Sabian symbols for those three planets and create a ritual that incorporates all three. This would make the three planets in the grand trine configuration very conscious and it would activate the luck they contain. See also *archetype, degrees, zodiac.* **Z**

Sagan, Carl Like Galileo Galilei (the great Italian Renaissance physicist and astronomer) before him, American astronomer and astrophysicist Carl Sagan continued the quest to link the metaphysical nature of human existence to the heavenly bodies of the universe. While astronomy and astrology have become divergent disciplines in our modern world, exploring and understanding the universe and our human place within it is the passion of both. Carl Sagan and colleague Francis Drake created a plaque sent into space on Pioneer 10 and on 11 satellites with images meant to help intelligent extraterrestrial beings plot a course to planet Earth. From ancient to modern times, from Copernicus to Einstein, the quest for understanding moves the human spirit. See also *Copernicus, Nicolaus; universe.* ☯ **Z**

Sagittarius   **1.** The ninth sign of the zodiac. **2.** Those born between November 22 and December 22 have Sagittarius as their Sun sign. Also called the archer, Sagittarius is a yang, or masculine, mutable fire sign. The ruling planet for Sagittarius is Jupiter, named for the Roman king of the gods. Jupiter is the planet of expansion and opportunity. **3.** The glyph for Sagittarius is ♐, which looks like an arrow, and the symbol is the archer. **4.** Sagittarius is the natural ruler of the ninth house, the house of religious beliefs or philosophy, higher education, foreign travel, and law. Sagittarius is an optimistic, outgoing sign. **5.** Other associations for Sagittarius are the color violet-purple and the gemstone turquoise.

✦ **1.** The body parts associated with Sagittarius are the liver, hips, and thighs. If you're a Sagittarius, you tend to put on weight in the hips and thighs. You also have to protect your liver—don't ingest toxins, and consider doing a liver detox once a year. **2.** If your Sun sign is Sagittarius, you are optimistic. Like the arrow that represents Sagittarius, you shoot for the stars. You always look on the bright side, and your enthusiasm in infectious. You're courageous and outspoken, and you do everything in a big way—that's Jupiter in action. You won't be overlooked. **3.** Sagittarius is very good at sharing their optimism and inspiring others. You steer others toward education—it will help them, you know it will, and everyone should be as informed as possible about what's happening in the world. **4.** As a mutable fire sign, Sagittarius is energetic and flexible. You like change and are spontaneous, which is why you travel so well. Mutability creates your natural inclination to expand, which often means incorporating new knowledge, new friends, new adventures, new philosophies, and, always, new admirers. **5.** Sagittarius loves school. Education, particularly higher education, is like home for you. You love learning new things, and enjoy visiting foreign lands to learn about new cultures. You're open-minded. You excel at athletics, cultural integration, law, philosophy, literature, and religion, and all with a whopping dollop of humor. This is why you would be successful in so many professions, such as professor, travel guide, advertising exec, judge, clergy, minister of foreign affairs, publisher, or life coach. **6.** *Watch out for:* Sometimes you're too optimistic—you don't like to think things won't work out, so you ignore the negative, and have a hard time redirecting yourself and others when a scheme goes awry. Forming a plan B is not your forte, and you feel responsible for a failure that affects others. You can also be just as down as you were enthusiastic. You have a tendency toward procrastination—you'll especially put off unpleasant tasks, and you might say yes to too many things. **7.** *I'm not a* Sagittarius, *but my best friend is:* Your Sagittarius best friend makes everyday adventures exciting. This friend is enthusiastic about whatever you do together—generous and independent. Don't be hurt if Sagittarius is out of touch for a while. Sometimes, you just have to give this intrepid explorer space. See also *Jupiter, ninth house, Sagittarius ascendant, Sagittarius descendant.*

Sagittarius/Aquarius   See *Aquarius/Sagittarius.*

Sagittarius/Aries   See *Aries/Sagittarius.*

Sagittarius ascendant   Also called Sagittarius rising. The rising sign is Sagittarius, so Sagittarius is the sign on the cusp of the first house in the birth chart and the sign on the eastern horizon at the moment of birth. **1.** If you're a Sagittarius rising, Sagittarius is how you present yourself to the world—it's how the world sees you. **2.** If your rising sign is Sagittarius, you are outgoing, enthusiastic, and generous, and you have a good sense of humor. You're open-minded and love foreign travel and culture. Be careful not to take on too much—you won't be able to do everything you promise to everyone. **3.** Sagittarius rising is philosophical, and might also be religious or spiritual. This is part of what makes you optimistic about society and about other people. You have faith in a positive outcome; negative outcomes can lead you to overindulge. You take any perceived failure out on yourself, and on your health. When you're feeling positive, you're focused and can accomplish anything. See also *ascendant, Sagittarius, Sagittarius descendant.* **BC**

S

Sagittarius/Cancer   See *Cancer/Sagittarius.*

Sagittarius/Capricorn   See *Capricorn/Sagittarius.*

Sagittarius descendant   **1.** The descending sign is Sagittarius; Sagittarius is the sign on the cusp of the seventh house in the birth chart. **2.** The seventh house is the house of partnerships and marriage or significant others. **1.** Do you have Sagittarius on the cusp of your seventh house? If so, you relate to others in partnership like optimistic, outgoing Sagittarius. **2.** A Sagittarius descendant has Gemini rising. You attract the Sagittarius qualities of optimism and support. Your partner is enthusiastic, but might be restless or get bored easily, and you'll have to work to make sure your partner isn't bored. They might not do well with the routine of relationships. Spontaneity is important. Travel can keep things fresh—it breaks up routine, and you'll both enjoy exploring new cultures. **3.** Your descending sign also reveals your alter ego, or the aspects of yourself you repressed when you were seven or eight years old. It also describes your maternal grandmother, paternal grandfather, third sibling, and second child. And it will tell you what you will attract in a business partnership, roommate, spouse or life partner, stranger, and enemy. See also *descendant, Sagittarius, Sagittarius ascendant.* **BC** ☼

Sagittarius/Gemini   See *Gemini/Sagittarius.*

Sagittarius/Leo   See *Leo/Sagittarius.*

Sagittarius/Libra   See *Libra/Sagittarius.*

Sagittarius/Pisces   See *Pisces/Sagittarius.*

Sagittarius rising   See *Sagittarius ascendant.*

Sagittarius/Sagittarius   **1.** These two fire signs want the same things in life. **2.** Sagittarius is attracted to other fire signs. ✸ **1.** These partners are both ruled by expansive Jupiter. You're both optimistic and enthusiastic, and you can inspire each other, especially if you share the same values and beliefs. This is key to intellectual freedom— Sagittarius is a thinker. **2.** These two make good business partners and friends and are also positive parent/child or boss/employee relationship. In marriage or domestic partnerships, so long as the belief systems are shared, this pairing works well. See also *Sagittarius.* ☯ ☼

Sagittarius/Scorpio   **1.** These two signs create firewater. **2.** Sagittarius and Scorpio are neighbors in the zodiac. ✸ **1.** Sagittarius can bring private Scorpio out of their shell, and Scorpio will make Sagittarius connect on a deeper level. If they have shared beliefs around life philosophy and money, they get along well. For Scorpio, having resources is the deal-breaker. Scorpio is scrupulous about money matters, and especially does not tolerate secrets around money.

These partners really must have similar beliefs on abundance. **2.** These two are good as friends, neighbors, and business partners or co-workers. They can also work in parent/child, teacher/student relationship. Marriage or domestic partnerships work well as long as everything is clear about money. See also *Sagittarius, Scorpio.* ☯ ☼

Sagittarius/Taurus   1. This pair joins fire and earth. **2.** Sagittarius can feel stifled by steady Taurus. ✳ **1.** Sagittarius brings enthusiasm to Taurus, and Taurus steadies Sagittarius. This can work well in some partnerships, but often, these two don't mesh. **2.** Taurus loves routine and security, and Sagittarius is restless, and likes spontaneity. Taurus is fixed, and doesn't want to change—even when Taurus is energized by Sagittarius, they might not move fast enough, and spontaneity is generally outside Taurus's comfort zone. **3.** Taurus and Sagittarius can be great friends, co-workers, and business partners. In the parent/child or boss/employee relationship, as well as for marriage or domestic partnerships, these two want different things in daily life, and—depending on other influences in the birth chart—may not be compatible. See also *Sagittarius, Taurus.* ☯ ☼

Sagittarius/Virgo   1. Fire and earth unite in this pair. **2.** Sagittarius and Virgo are both mutable and adaptable. ✳ **1.** These partners communicate well together. They like to debate. Sagittarius's enthusiasm offsets Virgo's critical tendencies. They might butt heads, but they also have an attraction based on their shared intellectual nature. They help each other along in work or with creative projects. For close relationships, they'll have to be willing to work at it. **2.** These two make good friends and business partners. They work especially well as co-workers, also positive parent/child or boss/employee relationship. The head-butting might get in the way of a happy marriage or domestic partnership, depending on other influences in the birth chart. See also *Sagittarius, Virgo.* ☯ ☼

S

Saturn   1. Planet named for the Roman god of agriculture. **2.** Saturn is the seventh planet from the Sun. Its orbit around the Sun takes 29.5 years; it spends about 2.5 years in each sign of the zodiac. **3.** Saturn is the natural ruler of Capricorn and the planetary ruler of the tenth house of career and reputation. **4.** In Roman mythology, Saturn is the father of Ceres, Jupiter, Pluto, and Neptune. His Greek equivalent is Cronos. Saturn rules the primal father and the public father figure or authority. **5.** Saturn is one of the social planets, and brings discipline and organization. The astrological glyph for Saturn is ♄. **6.** Saturn ℞ learns about boundaries as the victim of a bully or an intimidating parent, or under such binding rules and structures that there's no opportunity to learn to trust their own judgment.

✴ **1.** Saturn is a planet of order. The location of Saturn in your birth chart can indicate where you have self-discipline. It will also tell you where you are dutiful and orderly. **2.** Where is Saturn in your birth chart? Saturn always brings discipline and order, but the house and sign will tell you more about Saturn's activity in your chart. **3.** Saturn's aspects to the Moon in your chart will tell you a lot about how you maintain balance between your emotional needs and your ambitions. If Saturn is the father, the Moon is the mother. The Moon brings emotions into Saturn's stern, logical equations. **4.** Saturn is the letter of the law; it wants order regardless of your situation. In a daily astrological calendar, days when Saturn is in a positive aspect to the Sun are best used for sales presentations, celebrating with parents, lunching with the boss, leading your team to victory, and organizing your entertainment media. When transiting Saturn makes an adverse aspect to the Sun, watch for a tendency to doubt yourself, to accept responsibility that's not yours to own, or to build mountains out of molehills. See also *retrograde planets, Saturn in the houses, Saturn in the signs.* ○

Saturn finger   In palmistry, the middle finger and the base of that finger of each hand relates to the native's Saturn sign. The Saturn finger relates to executive prowess, political ambition, success, fame, money, and most of all, responsibility. ✴ Take a look at your middle finger. Is it average, long, or short? If your Saturn finger is more than three-eighths of an inch longer than your Jupiter pointer finger and your Sun ring finger, it is longer than average and shows that you are a natural-born authority figure. See also *Saturn.* ☯○**z**

Saturn in the houses   **1.** Saturn brings discipline and order to the areas of life relating to each of the houses. **2.** Saturn's chart placement shows where you will be serious and disciplined in your life. ✴ **1.** Saturn is rules and regulations—the house Saturn appears in will tell you about the areas in your life where you exert the most discipline and where you are most regimented. **2.** Sometimes Saturn indicates areas where you feel *too* restricted.

♄ **in the first house**   Saturn in the first house is responsible and self-disciplined. ✲ **1.** If you have Saturn in your first house, you are serious and grounded. You're down to earth and self-disciplined, and make a good teacher and a serious student. **2.** Saturn ℞ in the first house may find you in the role of the fall guy until you treat yourself with more respect.

♄ **in the second house**   Saturn in the second house relates to values. ✲ **1.** You're serious about the application of your values in your life. Saturn in the second house means that you can earn money steadily. You might sometimes feel that money is unattainable, but when you focus on your talents, Saturn will bring financial security into your future. **2.** Saturn ℞ in the second house may have you thinking you can't be trusted with money. Stop that lie by making a list of all the ways you have been responsible with money and possessions.

♄ **in the third house**   Saturn in the third house relates to early childhood experiences, siblings, and communication. ✲ **1.** You probably learned in younger years to be responsible and take on responsibility well with this Saturn placement. You may have had difficulties in early childhood, but you learned how to be responsible and concerned in dealing with them. **2.** Saturn ℞ in the third house inhibits your expression. Think about all the foolish things you hear coming out of other peoples' mouths and that will help you feel better about taking a chance and putting your own opinion out there.

♄ **in the fourth house**   In the fourth house, Saturn relates to family and home. ✲ **1.** If you have this Saturn placement, family matters greatly to you, and your family of origin was extremely important to you in some way. They may have been strict and made you take life seriously. Or maybe you were the responsible one in the family. Either way, you learned about responsibility from how your family members took care of each other. **2.** Saturn ℞ in the fourth house may present itself as obsessive-compulsive behavior rooted in a fear lingering from a past lifetime. You might want to find a good hypnotherapist who can clear the trauma from that past life.

♄ **in the fifth house**   Saturn in the fifth house relates to creative self-expression and relationships with children. ✲ **1.** Romance, children, and creative self-expression are all tied together for you. You take these matters seriously. Children remind you how to be a child yourself. Saturn in the fifth house can bring difficulties with romance, but you just need to realize what you truly need from a

S

relationship. Learn patience and it will pay off for you. **2.** Saturn ℞ in the fifth house makes for a pretty somber and serious childhood. You were made to feel ashamed for enjoying yourself and preferring fun to chores. You can channel some of that discipline into a creative hobby, something fun *and* productive.

♄ in the sixth house　In your sixth house, Saturn relates to health, daily work life, and public service. ✦ **1.** With this Saturn placement, work and public service are very important to you. You are responsible and hardworking in your place of work. Sometimes, Saturn in your sixth house will give you more than you expect: people may give you more responsibility because your work ethic shows that you can handle it. **2.** You need to learn not to overwork yourself and not to worry over work, because it can cause health issues for you. Exhaustion and stress can lead to health problems. **3.** Saturn ℞ in the sixth house makes you feel like you're always paying your dues to move up in your career. If you're going to work this hard, you definitely want to choose a job you enjoy.

♄ in the seventh house　Saturn in the seventh house relates to partnerships, including marriage and domestic partnerships. ✦ **1.** In your seventh house, Saturn teaches lessons about relationships—all relationships: marriage, business, and any form of contractual relationships. It can be difficult for you to find the best match. Saturn brings longevity in relationships, but because commitments are felt deeply, Saturn encourages you to take your time and not jump into a relationship too quickly. Make sure you really want this partner, and ask yourself, Will this relationship limit me or enhance me? **2.** Saturn ℞ in the seventh house has you waiting a while to find your life partner. Just when you think it's never going to happen, Saturn relents and it's your turn to cut the cake.

♄ in the eighth house　In the eighth house, Saturn relates to joint resources, values, and transformation. ✦ **1.** You will feel responsibility to others, and take care of others' legal and money matters. Saturn here can make you a disciplinarian or overcautious about money matters. Learn to take one thing at a time so you don't get overwhelmed with those responsibilities. **2.** It may be difficult for you to access your psychic ability with this placement, but as you get older, you will develop wisdom and intuition. You'll recall life experiences and realize life lessons as you age. **3.** Saturn ℞ in the eighth house makes you overly anxious about dying even though it also indicates that your death happens when you are very, very old.

♄ in the ninth house Saturn in the ninth house relates to philosophy and religion, foreign travel, and law. ✷ **1.** Your Saturn placement gives you the desire to continue to learn and expand your awareness, further your education, and travel the world. You'll have experiences and education that will help you as you grow. Higher education, religion, spiritual work, medicine and science, and politics and government hold an attraction to those with Saturn in the ninth house. Education can be your wealth. **2.** Saturn ℞ in the ninth house makes you worry that you'll never find the time and money to see more of the world. You can work with Saturn ℞, though. Start by picking places you want to go—maybe some less expensive destinations at first—and then research the best time of year to go and where to stay. Figure out a minimal budget and the fewest number of days you'll need for your travels. Saturn will respond to these actions and help manifest the opportunity for you. Bon voyage!

♄ in the tenth house **1.** Saturn in the tenth house relates to career and career calling as well as public service. **2.** Saturn is the natural ruler of the tenth house, and is at home here. ✷ **1.** You are self-reliant and have a disciplined focus toward career and personal power. Contributions to society are also very important to you. You will develop a strong sense of responsibility toward family, community, career, and public service. You are learning leadership and responsibility—not only to your career, but to others who look up to you. You are a leader whether or not you wish to be. You will take on positions of power and leadership and may be expected to lead others to security and prosperity. **2.** Saturn ℞ in the tenth house is probably pushing on you to plaster your work wall with diplomas and certificates as proof of your credibility. Saturn ℞ in the tenth house indicates someone who has worked in the same profession they are most drawn to in this lifetime. So if you could list your experience from all of your past lives, you would relax because you'd know that you are actually the most experienced candidate in your field. It's time to start acting the part.

♄ in the eleventh house Saturn in the eleventh house relates to peer groups and aspirations. ✷ **1.** Your friends and peer groups look to you for guidance and to encourage them through difficulties. You can also count on receiving the same help in return when you are in need. Your friends, social groups, and the clubs and organizations you belong to can help you develop self-discipline and organization. They will keep you focused and help you attain

S

your goals and desires. Look to your friends for help in these arenas, and remember to be patient: all good things will come with time, perseverance, and a little help from your friends! **2.** Saturn ℞ in the eleventh house makes you reluctant to ask for help. You might feel as though you should be smart enough not to ever *need* help. Well, that's no way to collaborate, is it? To work through this, start asking for help as much as possible. With Saturn ℞ in the eleventh house, your friends will be glad to have an opportunity to repay some of the karma they owe you.

♄ in the twelfth house   Saturn in the twelfth house relates to karmic debt and psychic abilities. ✴ **1.** You need to learn not to get carried away by a too serious approach to life. Try not to get depressed over the small things in life. When things are difficult and need resolution, you just have to dig deep—and ask for help when you need it. You have amazing resiliency and can surface from difficulties even stronger than before—and then you can share those experiences to help others. You will teach from personal experience. You're here to learn many lessons, but the rewards will be great. You'll become self-sufficient and self-reliant and will be able to teach those skills to others. **2.** You work well in service professions as an anesthesiologist, interior designer, dance instructor, psychologist, spiritual teacher, holistic practitioner, police officer, and in work related to serious tasks, such as a hospital administrator or prison warden. **3.** Saturn ℞ in the twelfth house can make it difficult for you to see how your life is evolving, which is probably how a caterpillar feels while it is metamorphosing inside the cocoon. Have faith and patience; in time you'll emerge as the butterfly you are destined to be.

See also *retrograde planets, Saturn, Saturn in the signs.* 🏠 ◯

Saturn in the signs   **1.** Saturn is the planet of responsibility and discipline. The sign Saturn is in will indicate how you manifest as Saturn rules time and space. The sign also indicates how you can be shut down by fear. **2.** Saturn R in the signs generally shows how you make life harder than it needs to be, at least until you figure out how to manage your self-doubt or transform it into confidence.

♄ in Aquarius   Aquarius is an idealistic sign of invention and communication. ✴ **1.** Your Saturn in Aquarius creates the desire for freedom and order. Your challenge is to learn how to curb your urge for freedom with the need to learn discipline; for you, discipline is freedom. **2.** The blessing of Saturn in Aquarius is the ability to reinvent the wheel: you will apply innovation, rebelliousness, and revolution toward a constructive outcome. **3.** Saturn ℞ in Aquarius causes you to avoid groups of people even though you feel lonely.

♄ in Aries   Aries likes to get things started, but often sacrifices structure for speed. ✸ **1.** The lesson and challenge for Saturn in Aries is to learn independence and self-reliance. Don't be afraid to push your own envelope. **2.** You have a pioneering spirit and an inventive drive that might lead you to make a breakthrough from old systems into new. You can create a new future, a new world for the community around you. You have the ability to manifest ideas into reality, getting concrete results. Go where no man or woman has gone before and be proud of it! **3.** Saturn ℞ in Aries prefers not to compete rather than come in second. This holds for sports, work, and love.

♄ in Cancer   Cancer loves home and family. ✸ **1.** The lessons and challenges for Saturn in Cancer are learning about responsibility to family and family cooperation. Your childhood experiences and childhood issues will come up as challenges that could hinder your emotional security or create a fear of intimacy. **2.** You can make breakthroughs with your family and community and become compassionate and nurturing toward others. You now understand the universal principle: home is where the heart is. **3.** Saturn ℞ in Cancer makes family feel burdensome until you are comfortable saying no.

♄ in Capricorn   **1.** Capricorn is a serious, ambitious sign. **2.** Saturn is the planetary ruler of Capricorn. ✸ **1.** Your Saturn in Capricorn challenge is to learn how to develop your ambition and your goals toward career. You have to figure out how your work ethic can contribute to or delay your wishes. Perseverance, constructive focus, and discipline are required. Keep the faith and forge ahead with integrity. Your efforts will be rewarded both financially and spiritually. **2.** Saturn in Capricorn can sometimes focus on what you don't have, when what you need to do is slowly build into what you will have—when your work pays off. **3.** Saturn ℞ in Capricorn makes others feel like you are judging them. Reassure them that what they are feeling is your insecurity about your own success.

♄ in Gemini   Gemini is intellectual and communicative. ✸ **1.** Saturn in Gemini challenges you to learn to communicate your thoughts, ideas, and plans. You have a great ability to problem solve, and you need to relate your problem-solving ideas to others.

Knowledge is power, and Saturn in Gemini knows this! You'll discover that debating and talking things out with others can truly resolve problems. You'll encourage others to further their knowledge by researching and learning new information with them. **2.** Saturn ℞ in Gemini makes learning slow in the beginning and fast once you've got the gist of it.

♄ in Leo   Leo brings drama and charisma. ✴ **1.** The challenge of Saturn in Leo is to learn that taking the lead and developing leadership in any way, shape, or form is important for you. More than you know, leadership is what you are supposed to learn and become in this lifetime. You are the boss, whether you want to be or not! You have creative management abilities you can use to move a group forward. **2.** Children and youth will be attracted to you and will need your constructive leadership for their growth. **3.** Saturn ℞ in Leo makes you doubt your creative potential. Just keep at it, and the time will come when you'll be shocked by your talent.

♄ in Libra   Libra loves beauty and harmony. ✴ **1.** Your Saturn in Libra challenges you to learn about partnership, including marriage and domestic partnerships, friendships, and business partnerships. It's not always easy to cooperate or negotiate with others, but for you to have a long-lasting relationship—no matter the type—you'll need to learn that cooperation and adaptation are a necessity. The good news is that you'll experience enduring and enriching connections that will enhance your life. **2.** Saturn ℞ in Libra worries that getting married may derail the energy you need to put toward your career. You just need to find a partner that is very supportive of your ambition.

♄ in Pisces   Pisces is a compassionate, intuitive sign. ✴ **1.** Saturn in Pisces has to learn to sacrifice for the highest good of everyone and to adapt to the needs of others. You'll learn humility and compassion you didn't know you had. You might learn this lesson by observing or partaking in some universal crisis. You will run when duty calls and will learn acceptance. You'll also learn trust: trust in others and trust that a helping hand will be there for you or for your community when you need it. You'll also gain trust in the universe and you'll know that when things aren't going as you'd like, there is a silver lining somewhere. Everything happens for a reason. **2.** Saturn ℞ in Pisces has you afraid to believe in your own psychic abilities. Once you accept they are real and develop them, you'll find that you are so masterful in reading energies that you can do it professionally.

♄ **in Sagittarius**   Sagittarius is a philosophical, free-spirited sign.
✳ **1.** Your Saturn in Sagittarius challenge is to not be focused on your need for independence. You love your freedom and long to be free of any type of restriction. You have to learn moderation and patience and go with the flow in any circumstances. Moderate your impulses and desires. You'll develop a newfound faith that will help you release your fear of being restricted or confined to others' expectations. You have always been free; you just have to realize it!
2. Saturn ℞ in Sagittarius is conflicted between wanting to stay put and see how far you can go with what you have and venturing into something new that would bring you exciting adventures. You'll be happier and even more successful if you go with the adventurous option.

♄ **in Scorpio**   Scorpio brings power and transformation.
✳ **1.** Saturn in Scorpio makes you serious, thoughtful, and very responsible whenever it is required. Try not to go overboard in your ideas of duty and responsibility—you might resent it in the end. Your personal drive and power is far reaching—just make sure to reach out without hanging yourself up. You'll be rewarded with the wisdom of your insights, your intuition, and your healing powers. The intensity of your beliefs and convictions are unwavering.
2. Saturn ℞ in Scorpio makes you come across as pretty serious and intense. You'll feel better if you decide reality is not as real as the news leads you to believe and decide to look for the ways the world is better than it's ever been.

♄ **in Taurus**   Taurus is a gentle, steady sign. ✳ **1.** Saturn in Taurus is challenged in working with resources, financial matters, and security needs. You are great at working toward a goal, but you need to become more flexible in case you have to go to plan B—it can work just as well as your first plan, maybe even better. Use patience to help you develop security, financial stability, and overall stability in the material world. Do everything in moderation. You'll be blessed with an abundance of resources and wealth, but you must remember that there is plenty for everyone! **2.** Saturn ℞ in Taurus has you holding on tightly to your first dollar. You'll have more money if you make room for it, which means you'll have to spend some.

♄ **in Virgo**   Virgo is hardworking and analytical. ✳ **1.** Saturn challenges you to take care of your health and well-being. Pay attention to your surroundings and the physical world. Your body is your temple, so take care of it. Your home is your castle, so repair it before it falls

S

apart. Your community is your village, so participate with them. Do these things and you will live in an environment where everyone seeks to live in harmony and to enjoy the simple things. Your hard work will pay off, not just for you, but for everyone you are responsible for. **2.** Saturn ℞ in Virgo needs structural support, such as a caring chiropractor or osteopath.
See also *Saturn, signs.* ○

Saturn/Jupiter See *Jupiter/Saturn.*

Saturn/Mars See *Mars/Saturn.*

Saturn/Mercury See *Mercury/Saturn.*

Saturn/Moon See *Moon/Saturn.*

Saturn/Neptune See *Neptune/Saturn.*

Saturn/North Node See *North Node/Saturn.*

Saturn/Pluto See *Pluto/Saturn.*

Saturn retrograde, personal **1.** Saturn is retrograde in the birth chart, creating a personal effect in the birth chart of the native. **2.** Saturn is retrograde for 140 days each year. Those born during these 140 days have Saturn ℞ in the natal chart. **3.** Personal retrogrades have varying influence depending on the activity of other planets in the birth chart. ✧ If you have Saturn ℞ in your birth chart, you have fear or karma to work out according to the sign and house Saturn is in. Consider what your fear might be and become aware of how you can be more receptive and less resistant to whatever form it shows up in. See also *retrograde planets; Saturn; Saturn retrograde, transiting.* ○ ℞

Look to the astrological sign of your personal Saturn retrograde for advice on the best course of action:

- **♄℞ in Aries:** Take initiative without worrying about how it affects others.
- **♄℞ in Taurus:** Seek a position that pays what you're worth.
- **♄℞ in Gemini:** Work with smoky quartz crystals, preferably tabby-shaped … they look like a rectangle on one end with the corners clipped off.

- ♄℞ **in Cancer:** Learn enough feng shui to keep your home clear.
- ♄℞ **in Leo:** Schedule fun and creative time.
- ♄℞ **in Virgo:** Develop a health maintenance routine that includes herbs.
- ♄℞ **in Libra:** Find a happily married or partnered couple to be role models for you.
- ♄℞ **in Scorpio:** Sex needs to be a little primal so that you don't get so bored that it becomes a chore.
- ♄℞ **in Sagittarius:** Think a lot about what it will feel like to have abundance.
- ♄℞ **in Capricorn:** Focus only on the very next step to take toward success and the rest of the steps will take care of themselves.
- ♄℞ **in Aquarius:** Entertain friends at home so that you can control the situation.
- ♄℞ **in Pisces:** Learn to play an instrument as a pastime with the understanding that it will take you a while to figure it all out.

Saturn retrograde, transiting Saturn's transiting retrograde lasts 140 days; that's about 4½ months. Finding ways to channel Saturn's self-disciplined energy can seem difficult during retrograde periods. When Saturn appears to be in reverse, it can feel like the universe has sent humanity to stand in a cosmic time-out in the corner because mere mortals can't do anything "right." ✧ With transiting Saturn ℞, you're being taken to task and Saturn will make sure that after you've stood your ground, you'll receive your marching orders and know exactly what targets you are expected to reach … that's right, *expected.* Saturn may feel harsh and even military, but this is all for your own good, or would be, if you let it be. Fight Saturn in retrograde and you may find you're doing battle with your own Jungian shadow side. And, as in therapy, what you learn may surprise you. Saturn in retrograde teaches self-knowledge and self-awareness, and when you believe you are the least capable of figuring anything out, suddenly, you've got it mastered. But don't let Saturn ℞ turn you into a know-nothing know-it-all, either. Be humble and persistent in pursuit of knowledge and Saturn will reward your efforts by bringing you closer and closer to becoming the artisan you are in training to be.

If transiting Saturn retrograde delivers a stream of delays your way, look to the astrological sign to throw some light on the situation:

- **In Aries:** Don't give up when you've only just started.
- **In Taurus:** Accept the rules.
- **In Gemini:** Make your own rules.
- **In Cancer:** Feelings get hurt when you highlight why nothing fits.
- **In Leo:** Explore who is drawing outside the lines.
- **In Virgo:** Jettison rules that don't make sense.
- **In Libra:** You have to *find* your balance to lose it.
- **In Scorpio:** Figure out who is over the top.
- **In Sagittarius:** Easy on the sarcasm.
- **In Capricorn:** You may be trying too hard.
- **In Aquarius:** Look for new ideas in unconventional places.
- **In Pisces:** An oxymoron can express equal truth.

Saturn return   1. Point at which Saturn returns to the position it held in the native's birth chart. **2.** Saturn is in each sign for about 2.5 years, and has a total orbit time of 29.5 years. Therefore, it would take 29.5 years for Saturn to return to an exact place in its orbit. ✦ **1.** Because Saturn returns in your chart nearly every 30 years, you'll be about 30 when you have your first Saturn return. Your next Saturn return hits when you're about 60. **2.** Saturn is a teacher—sometimes the lessons are difficult ones. This is an opportunity to review the previous 30 years to see where you've been and what you've accomplished—or what you need to accomplish. It's an opportunity to reassess and realign yourself, and reconfigure your path, if necessary. It's a second chance at finding your bliss. Your Saturn return bestows adult values and maturity. With your Saturn return, you can accept your karmic responsibilities and feel sufficiently connected and supported by the Earth to enjoy uncomfortable experiences because they cause you to grow spiritually. See also *Saturn, planetary returns.* ◯ **Z**

If Saturn is in harmony with other planets, you'll have a powerful ally. Difficult Saturn aspects create limitation or strain. For example, a Saturn square to Venus can cause you to feel isolated and to experience many obstacles to happy relationships. Saturn is linked to depression because of the cloud of self-doubt it casts. But Saturn also helps you build faith in yourself, because you've got to walk through the "dark night of the soul" to overcome these mysterious built-in pressures, fears, and losses.

Saturn/South Node Saturn brings discipline and order to the South Node's lessons learned. ✧ You're attracted to your old habits and patterns—but you're also a little repelled by them. You have a difficult time breaking your old patterns, and may feel limited by your connection to the past. You want to break away, but you see the benefits of your past experiences. You want to stick to what you know, but over time, your old plan doesn't work well. See also *aspects between planets, Saturn, South Node.* △ ☯ ○

Saturn/Sun The Sun brings energy to Saturn's discipline. ✧ When Saturn and the Sun connect in your birth chart, Saturn wants you to be serious and focused, determined and persevering. If you learn discipline, you'll find it freeing. You have an ability to follow through. You endure and persevere. See also *aspects between planets, Saturn, Sun.* △ ☯ ○

Saturn transits **1.** Saturn as it transits the signs of the zodiac. **2.** Saturn's orbit around the Sun takes about 29.5 years; it transits all twelve zodiac signs in that time, spending about 2.5 years in each sign. **3.** Saturn transits can be compared to the placement of Saturn in a birth chart for predictive purposes. A transit shows the position of a planet at a given moment. **4.** Transiting Saturn activates and awakens other heavenly bodies as it enters a new sign or a new house, and as it forms aspects with other transiting planets or planets in both birth and progressed charts. Saturn is used by professional astrologers to predict when things manifest in the physical; issues with father, boss, and authority figures; the best time for construction, success, bestowal of honor, acknowledgment, or awards; bouts of anxiety or depression; bankruptcy; hardship; opportunities to resolve karma; abandonment; rejection; blood clots; skeletal and dental needs; the onset of pain or suffering; times of stability; and lifelong relationships.

✧ Transiting Saturn makes you pay attention to the house it appears in. It has lessons to teach you in that house. Every house or angle Saturn transits forces you to look at what's important, pay attention to the details, and meet your responsibilities in that area of life. You have to get serious about the areas Saturn visits for each 2.5-year span. You might face crises or become aware of an issue you need to resolve—you have to be responsible about the issues in that house; you simply can't ignore them. Confront these issues, figure out how to resolve them, and ask for help when you need it. You can develop understanding, strength, and wisdom from Saturn's lessons. See also *Saturn, transiting planets, transits.* ○

What can Saturn transits tell you?

- Saturn transiting your **first house** tells you when you will be most visible as an authority in your field.

- Saturn transiting your **second house** can be a time of financial stability or loss, depending on the foundation you've put in place.

- Saturn entering your **third house** can be a time when siblings abandon you.

- When Saturn enters your **fourth house**, it's time to start construction on your home.

- When Saturn enters your **fifth house**, create more daily structure for your children.

- When Saturn enters your **sixth house**, go see the chiropractor and the dentist.

- Saturn moving through your **seventh house** attracts lifelong partners.

- Saturn transiting through your **eighth house** builds a credible reputation in the occult sciences or intuitive arts.

- When Saturn moves through your **ninth house**, travel is best for business or practical purposes.

- When Saturn moves into your **tenth house**, get assertive about taking on more responsibility or starting your own business.

- Saturn transiting your **eleventh house** is the time to build your reputation via television and the Internet.

- When Saturn transits your **twelfth house**, you can get a handle on rooting out addictions even though you might have to contend with mild depression at the same time.

Saturn/Uranus   Saturn and Uranus aspects combine discipline with rebellion. It's a conflicted combination. ✳ **1.** Saturn is structure and discipline: stay the course and victory is yours. Uranus is a rebel welcoming erratic and unusual behavior and prone to tearing down the old to make something new. Recognize this inherent conflict: Saturn wants to limit and define your freedom, and Uranus just wants the freedom—freedom now will give you more to be disciplined with later. You likely remember your history and know that structure is good, but you might also be rebellious. Know that a little rebellion is okay—restrict Uranus too much, and you'll cause a big reaction. **2.** With this combination, be careful of constructive/destructive behavior. Uranus wants to tear down what Saturn builds up, no matter what it is. But change is not always good, and you won't know when you need to change until you follow through. If things don't work out, let Uranus in to mix things up. See also *aspects between planets, Saturn, Uranus.* △ ☯ ○

Saturn/Venus Venus brings a love of beauty to Saturn's discipline. ✳ **1.** Saturn and Venus combine to find beauty in order and harmony in structure. **2.** It might be difficult to find the right romantic partner with this interaction—it's difficult for anyone to meet your expectations. Saturn has lots of requirements, and doesn't like the lack of discipline Venus brings. See also *aspects between planets, Saturn, Venus.* △ ☯ ○

Scorpio **1.** The eighth sign of the zodiac. **2.** Those born between October 23 and November 22 have Scorpio as their Sun sign. Also called the scorpion, Scorpio is a yin, or feminine, fixed water sign. The ruling planets for Scorpio are Pluto, named for the Roman god of the underworld who received all transpired mortal souls who awaited his judgment, and Mars, named for the Roman god of war. Pluto is a planet of transformation and resources. Mars is an active, aggressive planet. **3.** The glyph for Scorpio is ♏, which looks like the scorpion's stinger, and the symbol is the scorpion, a deadly and secretive creature. The scorpion is the ruler of Scorpio's lower nature and the eagle is the ruler of Scorpio's higher nature. **4.** Scorpio is the natural ruler of the eighth house, the house of birth, death, and psychic ability. **5.** Other associations for Scorpio are the colors crimson, black, and deep blue-green and the topaz.

S

✳ **1.** The body parts associated with Scorpio are the reproductive organs. If you're a Scorpio, you need to be careful of urinary tract infections and diseases of the reproductive organs. Female Scorpios should be sure to make it to an annual gynecological appointment. Stay well hydrated by drinking plenty of water—when you're stressed out, you're more likely to get a UTI. **2.** If your Sun sign is Scorpio, you are intense and passionate. Scorpios are transcendent: you'll help in a transition or will encourage change in others. You're often not demonstrative with words or gestures, and don't show much emotion, no matter how deeply you feel. People think you're mysterious, because it's so difficult to know you. **3.** Scorpio is sometimes called the psychic healer. You are deeply moved by others' pain, and you feel everything deeply. You will work with devotion to help in a crisis, and are loyal and committed once you decide to trust someone. Your fear of betrayal can sometimes cause you to bond with someone you can trust even if the person is inept or negative. **4.** As a fixed water sign, Scorpio's emotional nature naturally resists ups and downs. **5.** In school and work, you defy fatigue and rarely admit defeat. In school and work, it's important that you feel really interested or intrigued by what you're doing. You like intensity—even a little danger!—and will get bored with work that doesn't stir you up a little. You're great at money-related careers, including banking, real estate, and investing, and you make a good financial counselor. Your ability to dig beneath the surface of a situation makes you a great researcher, investigator, reporter, detective, police officer, or military leader. You're the most intuitive sign in the zodiac, and could find satisfaction in psychic work. **6.** *Watch out for:* Your intensity means that you have trouble with moderation—you just don't get the point. You can be extreme in your passion: you love something or hate it. You also have a tendency to hold a grudge. Your secretive nature means that even those closest to you don't know how you truly feel—or how deeply you feel—until long after the fact. Say what you feel before it's too late—you won't lose power by opening up to others. **7.** *I'm not a Scorpio, but my best friend is:* Your Scorpio best friend is very private. It may take a long time for them to open up to you—they don't trust easily. Once they do, they are yours for life. Your Scorpio friend will be devoted to you. Don't misunderstand a quiet reserve for a lack of emotion, and remember that if your Scorpio friend is angry, it's likely too late to diffuse the situation: if this Scorpio is upset enough to lose composure, feelings have been building for a while. See also *eighth house, Mars, Pluto, Scorpio ascendant, Scorpio descendant.*

Scorpio/Aquarius   See *Aquarius/Scorpio.*

Scorpio/Aries   See *Aries/Scorpio.*

Scorpio ascendant   Also called Scorpio rising. The rising sign is Scorpio, so Scorpio is the sign on the cusp of the first house in the birth chart and the sign on the eastern horizon at the moment of birth. ✦ **1.** If you're a Scorpio rising, Scorpio is how you present yourself to the world and how the world sees you. **2.** If your rising sign is Scorpio, you are steadfast and emotionally charged. You're passionate about work or family or whatever matters most to you. You're stoic: you don't usually show your feelings and are private. You're in tune with the emotions of those around you—even if you aren't aware of this. You respond well in times of need, focused on getting done what needs to be done. You can be counted on to follow through. **3.** You sometimes attract people who are out of control and feel a need to help them through their situation. **4.** Scorpio rising appears to be very calm, cool, and collected. You might be undergoing all kinds of turbulent emotions, but you don't show it. Others can't tell what you're feeling or thinking, and you're so self-contained that you can be misunderstood or misread as unfeeling or not engaged. See also *ascendant, Scorpio, Scorpio descendant.* **BC** ☼

Scorpio/Cancer   See *Cancer/Scorpio.*

Scorpio/Capricorn   See *Capricorn/Scorpio.*

Scorpio descendant   **1.** The descending sign is Scorpio; Scorpio is the sign on the cusp of the seventh house in the birth chart. **2.** The seventh house is the house of partnerships and marriage or significant others. ✦ **1.** Is Scorpio the sign on the cusp of your seventh house? If so, you relate to others in partnership like intense, secretive Scorpio. **2.** A Scorpio descendant has Taurus rising. You attract those Scorpio qualities of intensity and passion. Your partners might be mysterious and secretive, or even manipulative. You might want peace and harmony—those Taurus qualities—and you will get some of this from your partner, but it's difficult to get to know them. Once they have examined you completely and decide to trust you, they'll open up a little more. This can take years. **3.** Your descending sign reveals your alter ego, or the aspects of yourself you repressed when you were seven or eight years old. It also describes your maternal grandmother, paternal grandfather, third sibling, and second child. And it will tell you what you will attract in a business partnership, roommate, spouse or life partner, stranger, and enemy. See also *descendant, Scorpio, Scorpio ascendant.* **BC** ☼

Scorpio/Gemini   See *Gemini/Scorpio.*

S

Scorpio/Leo   See *Leo/Scorpio.*

Scorpio/Libra   See *Libra/Scorpio.*

Scorpio/Pisces   See *Pisces/Scorpio.*

Scorpio rising   See *Scorpio ascendant.*

Scorpio/Sagittarius   See *Sagittarius/Scorpio.*

Scorpio/Scorpio   1. These two water signs are intense and power-ful. 2. Scorpio is attracted to other water signs, but this combination might be too passionate. With the same-sign pairing of Scorpio and Scorpio this pair might be seeking karmic work: they may soar in the heights of power and passion as the eagle, or they may descend into the scorpion's sudden and stealthy sting. Either way, as a couple they will be exploring and working out the extremes of the Scorpio nature. ✦ 1. Scorpio paired with Scorpio is intense. These two work well together and get a lot done, and they're also loyal, pas-sionate, and sensual. 2. Both of these partners need privacy, and lots of it. Because neither wants to share their feelings too soon, a simple situation can turn into a giant blow-up. They accuse each other of secretiveness, and they're right! If these two have a fight, that may be the end of the relationship, and the beginning of a determined war. 3. These two can make good business partners, co-workers, and friends. It can be difficult for Scorpios to live together day in and day out without misunderstandings, which makes this pairing iffy for marriage or domestic partnership. See also *Scorpio.* ☯ ☼

Scorpio/Taurus   1. This Scorpio water and Taurus earth combina-tion are both fixed. 2. Taurus and Scorpio are opposite signs, and opposites attract. ✦ 1. These partners are both sensual, and both are also fixed. This means they can stand their ground with each other. They are also loyal, once committed. When working together, they get a lot done. 2. These partners can overwhelm each other with passion or overindulgence. Their fixed nature also can make them stubborn and unwilling to bend or compromise to solve a problem. 3. These two have a strong attraction. They work well together in business relationships and as co-workers, and are also compatible for friendship and marriage or domestic partnerships if they can learn balance and be a little flexible. See also *Scorpio, Taurus.* ☯ ☼

Scorpio/Virgo   This Scorpio water and Virgo earth combination create harmony. Virgo's devotion and fascination with sacred patterns works well with Scorpio's determined passion and creative drive. Both also harbor a secretive need for private personal rituals that may be shared together or indulged in as individuals (with mutual respect for alone time). This pair can be meticulous and loyal. ✦ **1.** Virgo wants to make the relationship work, and will be tenacious in getting Scorpio to open up and get committed. Scorpio loves the Virgo tendency to improve everything. These two agree that they will do their best in whatever they do. Virgo is also fine with Scorpio's need for privacy, and can also adapt to Scorpio's intensity and strong will. **2.** These two make great friends, co-workers, or business partners and friends and are also good in a parent/child or boss/employee relationship. This is also a positive pairing for marriage or domestic partnerships. See also *Scorpio, Virgo.* ☯ ☼

second house   **1.** In astrology, the second house is the house of financial capacity and resources, including the ability to earn income (not inherit money). **2.** The second house also indicates what is valued and how the native reacts to the material world, material goods, and the physical world. **3.** Parts of the body associated with the second house are the lower part of the face and neck, specifically ears, mouth, lower jaw, throat, and neck. ✦ **1.** How you do feel about money? Can you make money, or is that a struggle for you? **2.** The second house is also the house of values and the ability to evaluate, especially material values. **3.** Your spouse's first sibling's spouse (your in-law) is also ruled by the second house, as is your father's second sibling, your mother's second sibling's mate, and your lover's father. **4.** The second house also rules whom you attract, what you attract, and who and what you find attractive. **5.** The second house is naturally associated with Taurus, and is ruled by Venus. **6.** The planets you have in your second house will tell you what's important to you. They'll also tell you about your earning capacity, and how you can best—and most easily—earn money … and if you have no planets in your second house, its natural ruler, Venus, or the ruler of the sign on the cusp of your second house, will give you this insight. See also *house, planetary ruler, Taurus, Venus.*

secondary progressions   **1.** Solar progressions. **2.** Chart created using one day to one year; each planet's daily movement is used to represent the progression of that planet for one year. **3.** Secondary

S

progressions are used to predict important developments or culminations. ✦ How can a secondary progression be useful to you? Astrological software can show you your progressed chart in moments. Many programs allow you to animate your progressed chart so that you can see the progressed planets move forward either day-by-day, month-by-month, or year-to-year. Pay attention to when the planets change signs or houses, enter angular houses, and form important aspects to each other. These changes indicate important developments according to the signs and houses. Goals, relationships, and aspirations that you have been working toward tend to come to fruition when their ruling progressed planets form important aspects or enter the related houses. See also *progressed planet, solar progression.* △ ◯ **Z**

secondary ruler   See *subruler.*

semi-sextile   **1.** One of the minor aspects, or angles, between planets in astrology. **2.** The glyph for semi-sextile is ⊻. On a birth chart, semi-sextile planets are those at an angle that is half of a sextile (60 degrees), or 30 degrees apart or within 10 degrees of this 30-degree angle if the semi-sextile involves the Sun or the Moon or within 8 degrees if the semi-sextile is between nonluminary planets. **3.** A semi-sextile creates a relatively weak planetary influence, but does indicate areas of opportunity for the native, especially around replacing negative beliefs with slightly more positive beliefs. ✦ **1.** Do you have a semi-sextile in your birth chart? Look for its symbol: ⊻. The planetary relationship is harmonious, but the planets creating the angle will determine the specific meaning of the semi-sextile. **2.** The houses your semi-sextile planets appear in will tell you where this planetary action takes place in your life. **3.** The signs of the semi-sextiled planets influence how it affects you. **4.** A semi-sextile is like a sextile, but weaker. There is the possibility for opportunity in the areas of the semi-sextile, but they are easy to overlook. You'll have to find the opportunities and then work to take advantage of them. See also *aspect grid, aspects between planets, sextile.* △ ☯ ◯

semi-square   **1.** One of the minor aspects, or angles, between planets in astrology. **2.** The glyph for semi-square is ∠. On a birth chart, planets are said to be semi-square when they are at an angle that is half of a square (90 degrees), which is 45 degrees (or when they are within 10 degrees of this 45 degree angle if the Sun or the Moon are involved or within 8 degrees for nonluminary planets). **3.** To understand a semi-square, think about the square. Semi-squares are challenging, but it is a weaker aspect than a square. ✦ **1.** If you want to find out if you have a semi-square in your birth chart, just look for its symbol: ∠. The meaning of the semi-square is determined by the planets involved, but the relationship between the planets is generally challenging or frustrating. **2.** Check the houses your semi-square planets appear in to find out where this planetary action takes place in your life. **3.** The signs of your semi-square planets influence how it affects you. **4.** A semi-square generates tension that often leads to growth and development, unlike a square, which usually creates frustration and blockages. See also *aspect grid, aspects between planets, square.* △ ☯ ○

September 22 to October 23   Birth dates for the Sun sign Libra. The position of the Sun during these dates correlates with an astrological Sun sign. Those born between September 22 and October 23 have Libra as their Sun sign. See also *Libra.* ☼

sesquiquadrate   **1.** One of the minor aspects, or angles, between planets in astrology. Also called a sesquisquare. **2.** The glyph for sesquiquadrate is ⌑. On a birth chart, planets are said to be sesquiquadrate when they are 135 degrees apart or are within 10 degrees of this 135 degree angle if the Sun or Moon are involved or eight degrees if between two non-luminary planets. **3.** Sesquiquadrates are similar to semi-squares, creating a somewhat challenging planetary interaction. ✦ **1.** You'll know if you have a sesquiquadrate in your birth chart if you see its symbol in your aspect grid: ⌑. The planets creating the sesquiquadrate will determine its specific meaning, but the planetary relationship is challenging. **2.** The houses the sesquiquadrate planets appear in will tell you where this planetary action takes place in your life. **3.** The signs of the sesquiquadrate planets influence how it affects you. **4.** A sesquiquadrate generates friction that helps effect needed changes in your life. See also *aspect grid, aspects between planets, semi-square.* △ ☯ ○

sesquisquare   See *sesquiquadrate.*

S

seventh house   1. In astrology, the seventh house is the house of partnerships of all kinds: marriage, domestic partnerships, business partnerships, work partnerships, and temporary partnerships, such as roommates. **2.** The seventh house rules the alter ego that seeks acknowledgment by projecting itself upon the partner or strangers. **3.** Cooperation and contracts are covered in the seventh house, as are openly identified enemies.

✴ **1.** What personalities or self-identities do you attract? Information on the types of partners you attract is found in your seventh house. **2.** How you cooperate and collaborate with others in partnership, as well as how you negotiate, is also found in the seventh house. **3.** If you sign a contract, that's covered in the seventh house. **4.** Your father's father, your mother's mother, your third sibling, and your second child if you are a man are all ruled by the seventh house. **5.** The seventh house also rules your lower back and kidneys. **6.** The seventh house is naturally associated with Libra, and is ruled by Venus. **7.** The planets you have in your seventh house will help define how you relate in partnerships … and if you have no planets in your seventh house, its natural ruler, Venus, or the ruler of the sign on the cusp of your seventh house, will give you this insight. See also *house, Libra, planetary ruler, Venus.*

> Your seventh house alter ego is also known as the disowned self or shadow. It's the part of you that you don't identify with. It's the same gender and age as you, but possesses all the talents and abilities that you've rejected, either because you were taught to judge such expression or because you lack the confidence to own that side of your nature. The shadow seeks integration with the ego so that you will become whole in self-knowledge and expression. For this reason, the disowned characteristics are projected upon partners and strangers in hopes that you will identify their desirability and recognize it as your own. This is one of the reasons people fall instantly in love with others who possess qualities they do not. It is also why people may grow to despise those same qualities if they are unable to recognize the projection and accept the disowned qualities as their own.

sextile   1. One of the five major aspects, or angles, between planets in astrology. **2.** The glyph for sextile is ✶. On a birth chart, planets are said to be sextile when they are 60 degrees apart or are within 10 degrees of this 60-degree angle. **3.** Sextiles are generally considered to produce a beneficial interaction between planets. ✴ **1.** Do you have a sextile in your birth chart? Look for its symbol: ✳. The planets creating the angle will determine the meaning of the sextile, but the relationship between the planets is harmonious. **2.** The houses the planets in sextile appear in will tell you where this planetary action takes place in your life. **3.** The signs of the sextiled planets influence how it affects you. **4.** A sextile can help you come out of difficulty without trauma, and you can even learn from your struggle and feel good about it afterward. This aspect brings harmony to a situation. A sextile is a beneficial aspect—the sextiled planets bring you opportunities, but you'll have to work to make the most of them. See also *aspect grid, aspects between planets.* △ ☯ ○

shadow self   See *descendant.*

sidereal zodiac   **1.** Also called sidereal astrology. Astrological system based on the position of the constellations. **2.** The 12 constellations named for the signs of the zodiac are the ring through which the Sun seems to pass every year as seen from the earth's orbit. This ring is called the ecliptic. Because of a process called precession of the equinox, the dates for the Sun signs (as viewed in tropical, or Western, astrology) no longer align with the constellations. What this means is that the tropical sign of Aries is now within the constellation of Pisces. Sounds complicated, right? It has to do with the gravitational shift in the Earth's rotational axis. In tropical astrology, the signs are linked to the seasons, based on the vernal equinox; the sidereal system links the signs to the actual position of the stars in the sky. Aries goes from March 20 to April 19 in Western astrology, but in sidereal, or Hindu, astrology, Aries covers the period from April 18 to May 14. See also *astrology, constellation, ecliptic, Hindu astrology.* **Z**

S

signs   **1.** Also called Sun signs. Astrological or zodiac signs. **2.** Each of the twelve houses of the zodiac is associated with a Sun sign. The twelve signs are: Aries (March 21–April 20), Taurus (April 20–May 21), Gemini (May 21–June 22), Cancer (June 22–July 23), Leo (July 23–August 22), Virgo (August 22–September 22), Libra (September 22–October 23), Scorpio (October 23–November 22), Sagittarius (November 22–December 22), Capricorn (December 22–January 21), Aquarius (January 21–February 19), and Pisces (February 19–March 21). See also *house, zodiac.* ☉ **Z**

sixth house   1. In astrology, the sixth house is the house of health and well-being and public service. **2.** Daily work life and environment are also found in the sixth house. **3.** The sixth house rules employees, domestic help, co-workers, and pets. ✶ **1.** How do you take care of your body? Your health and well-being are in the sixth house. **2.** The sixth house is also the house of public service and the role of public service in your life. How do you serve your community? **3.** How you work at work, meaning your daily activities at work, is also found in this house. This isn't the house of career, but rather what you do within your job. What's your workday like? What are your daily concerns at work? This is found in your sixth house. **4.** Your mother's first sibling, your father's first sibling's spouse, and your second child, if you are a woman, are also ruled by the sixth house. **5.** The sixth house also rules your lower abdomen and intestines. **6.** The sixth house is naturally associated with Virgo, and is ruled by Mercury and the asteroid Chiron. **7.** The planets you have in your sixth house will give you clues about your health, your daily work life, and the role of public service in your life. If you have a lot of planets in your sixth house, you might have lots of jobs, pets, and hobbies. When you're older, you might inherit money from friends. If you have no planets in your sixth house, its natural ruler, Mercury, or the ruler of the sign on the cusp of your sixth house, will give you insight about your health, work life, and public service. See also *house, Mercury, planetary ruler, Virgo.* ◯ 🏠 ☼

social planets   1. In astrology, the social planets are Jupiter and Saturn; Uranus is often included. These were the planets visible to the human eye beyond the personal planets that were identified before the invention of the telescope. Modern astrologers tend to include Uranus as well. **2.** Jupiter rules banquets, celebrations, ceremonies, etiquette, hospitality, jubilation, pageants, parades, public functions, and social gatherings. Saturn rules social climbing. **3.** The orbits of these planets are long, making their influence broad, as they move through the signs of the zodiac. Jupiter's orbit takes 12 years (so, about 1 year in each sign); Saturn takes about 29.5 years to orbit the Sun (about 2.5 years in each sign). **4.** In Western astrology, the social planets rule social areas of life, including the ninth house areas of higher education, religion, and foreign travel; tenth house areas of career and reputation; and the social networks of the eleventh house. **5.** Planets in the ninth, tenth, and eleventh houses will express themselves through your interactions with society. See also *eleventh house, Jupiter, ninth house, outer planets, personal planets, Saturn, tenth house.* ☯ ◯

solar arc chart   1. A birth chart that has been rotated forward a degree for every year of the native's age is called a solar arc–directed chart. Every planet is advanced forward a degree so the solar arc chart looks just like the birth chart except everything in the chart has moved forward. **2.** The position of the Sun in the solar-progressed chart and the solar arc chart will be at the same degree in the same sign. **3.** A solar arc chart is paramount in the accurate prediction of events. When the solar arc planets have moved forward enough so that one of them makes an exact aspect to a natal planet, the energies of the two planets are engaged and the stage is set for *action.* When a transiting planet also aspects the solar arc planet and the natal planet, it becomes extremely likely that an event will occur that relates to the natal or solar arc planet.

✴ **1.** Your solar arc chart gives you another perspective of how you have consciously evolved since you were born. The Sun rules your conscious self and all of the planets in a solar arc chart are moved forward according to the Sun's movement, not their own. Your birth chart reveals the map of your life that you started out with and your solar arc chart gives you insight as to how far you have come. **2.** Your birth chart remains your primary chart. Your solar arc chart shows your spiritual development and alignment with your heart. See also *birth chart, solar progression, Sun.* **BC** ☯ ◯ ☼ **Z**

solar progressed chart   An astrological chart that shows how all the planets have moved forward (or backward in cases of retrogrades) since the native's birth. ✴ Your birth chart is still the most important astrological image you have of yourself; think of your birth chart like your astrological DNA. Your solar progressed chart shows your psychological development. See also *birth chart, Sun.* **BC** ☯ ◯ **Z**

solar progression   In a solar progression, each planet is moved a degree forward (counterclockwise, unless retrograde) every time it orbits the Sun. ✴ How can a solar progression work for you? A solar progression depicts your evolution through each of your planets. See also *progressions, solar progressed chart.* **BC** ☯ ◯ **Z**

S

What to expect when your solar progressed (SP) planets form positive aspects to your natal Sun, especially when transiting Mars hits the same degree of either:

- SP Moon to Sun = deep sense of security and confidence
- SP Mercury to Sun = brilliant, creative ideas spring forth
- SP Venus to Sun = happy romance
- SP Mars to Sun = smart decisions and choices generate happiness
- SP Jupiter to Sun = wonderful, fun-filled vacation abroad
- SP Saturn to Sun = heart's desires actually manifest
- SP Chiron to Sun = able to see and heal primary past-life wound
- SP Uranus to Sun = new, true friendship or conception of child
- SP Neptune to Sun = self-forgiveness and acceptance
- SP Pluto to Sun = able to see and end destructive relationships

What to expect when your solar progressed (SP) planets form negative aspects to your natal Sun, especially when transiting Mars hits the same degree of either:

- SP Moon to Sun = no support for following heart's desire
- SP Mercury to Sun = too busy to enjoy life
- SP Venus to Sun = irrevocable differences in love
- SP Mars to Sun = rage or obsession destroys true love
- SP Jupiter to Sun = overindulged or overinflated ego
- SP Saturn to Sun = innocence and joy shut down from negativity
- SP Chiron to Sun = can't allow self to be happy
- SP Uranus to Sun = can't connect to make friends
- SP Neptune to Sun = unable to trust own feelings
- SP Pluto to Sun = self-destruction

solar return   See *solar return chart.*

solar return chart   **1.** An astrological chart calculated for the native's birthday. **2.** A solar return is cast for when the Sun arrives at the same degree and minute as at the native's birth. Adjustments are made for where the native currently lives or for where the native is located when the Sun makes this return to its original degree and minute. **3.** As the chart changes according to location, many astrologers advise their clients about the best place to be to create the best possible chart for their birthday. **4.** The solar return chart is active from the birthday in the year that the chart is created until the birthday of the following year. Because our calendar is based on a 365-day year instead of the actual 365 and one-quarter days it takes the Sun to travel the zodiac, a solar return may not always be the native's exact birthday. Some years it may be the day before or the day after the actual birthday. ✦ Why create a solar return chart? Your solar return chart tells you what to expect for your birthday year. The ruler of the sign on the ascendant is the chart ruler. The chart ruler, along with planets it aspects, tells you the most about what to expect for the year. See also *birth chart, Sun.* **BC** ☯ ◯ **Z**

solar system   **1.** Our solar system is located in the Milky Way galaxy, which is in turn located in the universe. **2.** The Western astrological system is based on the luminaries, planets, and other heavenly bodies in Earth's solar system. See also *universe, Western astrology.* ◯ **Z**

solstice   **1.** Term derived from the Latin words *sol,* meaning Sun, and *systere,* meaning stand motionless. **2.** Times during the Earth's orbit when the Sun is farthest north (summer) or farthest south (winter) of the celestial equator. **3.** The two solstices are the summer solstice (northernmost point), when the Sun is poised motionless over the Tropic of Cancer, and the winter solstice, (southernmost point), when the Sun stands still over the Tropic of Capricorn. **4.** The summer solstice is the longest day of the year, and occurs in June, when the Sun is in Cancer; the winter solstice is the shortest day of the year, and occurs in December, when the Sun is in Capricorn. **5.** During a solstice, the Sun appears to stand still. **6.** The summer solstice is when the Sun is at 0 degree Cancer and the winter solstice is when the Sun is at 0 degree Capricorn. ✦ Where is 0 degree Cancer and 0 degree Capricorn in your birth chart? This natural axis is like two doorways between polarities in your chart. The summer solstice point at 0 degree Cancer is a doorway into your subconscious mind, where you can ask for those desires you wish to manifest during the winter solstice. The winter solstice point at 0 degree Capricorn aligns your innermost desires with the forces of time and space so that your subconscious mind's hidden desires can be birthed into physical reality. See also *Earth, planet, Sun.* ☯ ☼ **Z**

S

South Node   1. Also called the Dragon's tail in Vedic astrology. The descending node of the Moon's orbit. **2.** The point in the Moon's orbit when it is moving from North to South and it crosses the ecliptic. **3.** Because it's not a planet, the South Node doesn't have a planetary ruler, and it's not associated with a particular house. **4.** The North Node and the South Node are exactly 180 degrees apart, so most astrologers set their astrological program preferences to display only the North Node. Once the signs and their polarities are known, it's pretty simple to calculate the position of the South Node. **5.** The South Node is sometimes associated with issues of past karma. The astrological glyph for the South Node is ☋.

✳ **1.** The South Node will tell you about your past. It's what you've come from or what you've already done. The South Node is familiar territory, and represents what you fall back on when you're in a bind. Because it's where you're comfortable, you go here when you're stressed—it works as surely as comfort food to calm your anxiety. It's comfortable and nice to return to from time to time, but it's not where you'll grow spiritually. **2.** In what house is the South Node in your birth chart? That's where you're most comfortable— and perhaps a little stuck. **3.** In a daily astrological calendar, positive aspects between the Sun and the South Node (such as conjunct, trine, or sextile) mean there are also positive aspects between your Sun and your North Node. Those positive aspects help you let go of your attachment to your South Node and to explore the scary and magnificent domain of your North Node. A conjunction between your Sun and your South Node gives you more information about your past lives, acquired abilities, and mastered knowledge. All of that seems great—so why would you want to let go of it? Because you have already mastered it. Why keep repeating the eighth grade when you could move on to high school? While you may have been afraid to go on to middle school or high school, it was just too boring and awkward to stay behind. All the excitement in life comes from letting go of our South Node and embracing the unknown of the sign and house of our North Node. In the case of a conjunction between your Sun and South Node, you will have to let go of child- hood, personal attention, and desires, and commit yourself to more altruistic goals. **4.** Challenging aspects between the Sun and your South Node (such as opposition or square) in a daily astrological calendar can cause you to hang on to your childhood friends, sports, and talents for dear life. Yet, you will actually be happier serving humanity in some way in this lifetime. See also *ecliptic, node, North Node, South Node in the houses, South Node in the signs.* △ ◯ ℞

South Node in the houses   1. The South Node represents areas of familiarity or lessons already learned. **2.** The North Node's house placement in the birth chart indicates the areas of life influenced by the South Node's energy. **3.** Because the South and North Nodes are always opposite each other in the birth chart, the South Node placement indicates the North Node placement: for example, the South Node in the third house means that the North Node is in the ninth house. ✷ The South Node relates to your past, and is what you learned in past lives. The house the South Node is in will tell you where you have been—and what you learned—in the past. In times of distress or discomfort, you'll want to return to these areas of your life, where you feel confident, comfortable, and at ease.

☊ **in the first house**   South Node in the first house is all about the self and the personality. ✷ This South Node placement indicates that habits from your early life are still with you. You have a desire to return to what you remember as your own personal habits or routine. You feel comfortable with your old routine, personality. They may be good habits, but still, you have to try not to fall back on them. It's difficult for you to leave old conditions or health habits to change to a new habit or routine.

☊ **in the second house**   The South Node in the second house relates to values and the material world. ✷ Your second house South Node makes you concerned about money and financial security—you want to do it your way. You can be steadfast in your money habits and your value system. You know how to take care of yourself financially and your earning capacity is good. You may have a difficult time letting go of possessions or material goods you have grown accustomed to. You have accomplished many good lessons about money and possessions, and now it's time to relax and pat yourself on the back!

☊ **in the third house**   In the third house, the South Node relates to communication, self-expression, and early childhood. ✷ Your childhood and childhood memories are very influential, and you hold on to these memories for security. You might develop nostalgia

S

for the past. You find comfort in your memories and you have great recall on the events of your life. You use your memories—usually family memories—as your foundation.

☬ **in the fourth house**   The South Node in the fourth house relates to family and home. ⚹ Family matters are very important to you! You lean on family—or they lean on you—for security: there is a strong bond within your family unit. You have a desire to care for people, but have to make sure you don't go overboard. You can be so overly concerned with the welfare of others that you neglect yourself.

☬ **in the fifth house**   The South Node in the fifth house relates to creative self-expression and relationships with children. ⚹ You need a lot of attention, respect, or recognition from others. Either your own children, or young people in general, can be a focus and concern for you, and you can be a leader for them. You have a strong drive toward creative self-expression and you develop artistic skills with ease. You can utilize many talents from your past to create the attention you desire.

☬ **in the sixth house**   The South Node in the sixth house relates to health and well-being, work environment, and public service. ⚹ You can be a perfectionist when it comes to your health, work environment, and public service. You are very devoted to your work and have developed a strong work ethic. You are very familiar with and work comfortably toward perfecting what you do at work and taking care of your health. Sometimes you're overly focused on these areas of your life—you need to learn to relax.

☬ **in the seventh house**   The South Node in the seventh house relates to cooperation and partnerships of all kinds. ⚹ You enjoy marriage and all forms of partnerships and worked hard on these areas in the past—it's familiar territory for you. You may have a problem being alone or have some insecurity about standing out on your own. You're adaptable and very cooperative in any partnership you enter into. Be careful not to become too dependent on others. Remember that you can go it alone if you have to; you're perfectly capable.

☬ **in the eighth house**   The South Node in the eighth house relates to money, joint resources, and psychic intuition. ⚹ You long for connections to others and have a deep emotional and psychological need to connect. You love the mystery of deep intimacy, and you crave energy and power not only from within, but that which other people can bring into your life. You get a (contact) high from human intimacy. You love passion and have great charismatic energy.

☋ **in the ninth house**   The South Node in the ninth house relates to religion and spirituality, foreign travel, and higher education. ✵ You have strong and clear beliefs and philosophy, and you fall back on these beliefs when the going gets tough. Your spiritual/religious beliefs are unshakable. You are focused on seeking the truth and finding answers. If you need extra education or help of some kind, you will seek it. You aren't afraid to seek wise advice and counsel from authority figures.

☋ **in the tenth house**   In the tenth house, the South Node relates to career, public reputation, and authority figures. ✵ You work hard and are self-motivated to succeed and take on responsibility and leadership. Your strong drive to succeed keeps you on task. Overworking and taking on too much responsibility can cause you physical and emotional depletion. Status is important to you, but you'll be wiser to focus on maintaining your health.

☋ **in the eleventh house**   In the eleventh house, the South Node relates to your social network and peer groups, as well as your hopes and wishes. ✵ Your friends and associates give you a sense of belonging. You may be dependent on these friends and groups, which comfort you. You need to be cautious about your need to fit in or to be accepted. You need to work on participating with others rather than being led by others.

☋ **in the twelfth house**   A twelfth house South Node relates to karmic debt, dreams, and intuition, as well as the shadow self or hidden areas of the self. ✵ You are very practical and realistic and maintain order and discipline in your life. You have a strong spiritual life. Loyalty, devotion, and self-sacrifice come easily to you. You have to learn not to sacrifice so much that you lose yourself in the process. You want to be of service, but don't become subservient. See also *house, Nodes (North, South), South Node in the signs, South Node retrograde.* 🏠 ◯

South Node in the signs   **1.** The South Node indicates areas of comfort and familiarity. In the birth chart, the sign the South Node is in will indicate areas of routine for the native. **2.** Because the North Node and South Node are opposite each other in the birth chart, South Node in Aries is the same as North Node in Libra.

S

℧ **in Aquarius**   Aquarius is a sign of intelligence and rebellion.
✴ The South Node in Aquarius creates comfort and understanding of universality. You know that we're all in this together. You understand others' needs and want to help them—you want to help the community. You are altruistic and compassionate, and have a vision of the future. You know when things or systems are obsolete, and you can easily let go of what's obsolete. Change doesn't bother you—it's the path to the future. You're happy to tear down the old to make way for the new.

℧ **in Aries**   Aries likes to start things. ✴ In Aries, the South Node means that you know yourself well. Life may be all about you—you relate to the world through *I am*. You are independent, self-reliant, and self-confident—these are the areas of life you are comfortable with. Less comfortable for you: your internal self, thoughts, and beliefs.

℧ **in Cancer**   Cancer is intuitive and emotional. ✴ Your South Node says, *I feel*. You are a good caretaker and feel comfortable nurturing others. You can be a strong mother figure. You understand how to give to others and have a knack for giving others what they need. Domestic tranquility and family are very import to you, and you create a harmonious home life with ease and joy.

℧ **in Capricorn**   Capricorn is about structure and responsibility. ✴ The South Node in Capricorn understands life's highs and lows, wealth and poverty, success and failure. With this placement, you are at home with ambition, but you might also have experience being used by others to achieve their own ambitious ends.

℧ **in Gemini**   Gemini is intelligent and witty. ✴ If your South Node is in Gemini, you're right at home with intellectual pursuits. You have a good memory and are very intelligent. Studious discipline is comfortable for you. You communicate well, and have a good sense of humor.

℧ **in Leo**   Leo is dramatic and generous. ✴ With the South Node in Leo, what you know is drama. You're entertaining and generous, and have comfort in leadership positions. You're at home in the spotlight, and have loads of charisma. You're aware of your talents and ego.

℧ **in Libra**   Libra wants justice and harmony. ✴ The South Node in Libra knows how to work with partnerships—you're comfortable in them and really enjoy cooperating with others. You've done different kinds of partnerships before, and they are easy for you. You don't fear commitment, but find love and harmony in partnerships.

☋ **in Pisces**   Pisces is sensitive and intuitive. ✴ The South Node in Pisces creates compassion for the world. You are devoted to healing, nurturing, and changing the lives of others for the better. You're comfortable giving to others, especially emotionally. You understand sacrifice. You understand the depths of despair that your neighbor or friend might experience, and can help them through these difficult times, based on your own experiences.

☋ **in Sagittarius**   Sagittarius is a freedom-loving philosopher. ✴ With your South Node in Sagittarius you're an educator and philosopher. Higher education is a comfort zone for you—you might be a student for life. You have a great memory and learn from your past experiences. You also love foreign travel and are comfortable in foreign cultures. Religion and spirituality are also familiar to you, and you might turn to religion for comfort in times of stress.

☋ **in Scorpio**   Scorpio is intense and transformational. ✴ With your South Node in Scorpio, you are familiar with power and charisma. You can manipulate the world to suit yourself, and you also mask your own true feelings very well—you manage a situation to make it better. You utilize resources well and with ease. You have a strong link to your intuition and identify with the mysteries of life. You're familiar with these areas of life, and access your intuition and psychic abilities easily.

☋ **in Taurus**   Taurus is stable and grounded. ✴ A Taurus South Node feels comfortable with having and owning. You can make money easily and manage it well. The physical world and material possessions are your comfort zones—you have mastered these areas. You have strong convictions.

☋ **in Virgo**   Virgo is an analytical perfectionist. ✴ The South Node in Virgo is right at home with hard work. You're a perfectionist, and are disciplined and orderly—you are very comfortable with self-discipline. You don't do things halfway, but will finish a job and finish it *well*. You are also familiar with service, and it comes easily to you.

See also *signs, South Node*. ○ ☼

S

South Node/Jupiter   See *Jupiter/South Node*.

South Node/Mars   See *Mars/South Node*.

South Node/Mercury   See *Mercury/South Node*.

South Node/Moon   See *Moon/South Node.*

South Node/Neptune   See *Neptune/South Node.*

South Node/North Node   See *Nodes (North, South).*

South Node/Pluto   See *Pluto/South Node.*

South Node retrograde   See *Nodes (North, South).*

South Node return   **1.** The South Node of the Moon returns to the position it held in the native's birth chart. **2.** South Node returns happen every 18.5 years or so. ✦ **1.** The South Node will return to where it was when you were born just about every 18.5 years. So you'll have a nodal return when you are 18, 37, 55, 74, 93, and so on. **2.** The South Node is also known as the Point of Loss. Don't panic! you just need to check in with yourself about what you want to lose or let go of when you have your South Node return. See also *South Node, planetary return.* ◯

South Node/Saturn   See *Saturn/South Node.*

South Node/Sun   The Sun brings energy to the South Node's familiar patterns. ✦ When the Sun and the South Node are in aspect in your birth chart, the South Node brings old routines and patterns to the forefront. You have a lot of recall of your old behaviors, and you fall back on them. You have a very difficult time breaking old patterns, even when they aren't healthy. These patterns and behaviors are very entrenched, and can make you your own worst enemy. You might feel an internal struggle. Of course, if your patterns are positive, you can be very productive in your old patterns, but you'll still have difficulty moving on to something new. See also *aspects between planets, South Node, Sun.* △ ⚉ ◯

South Node transits   **1.** The South Node as it moves or transits through the signs of the zodiac. **2.** South Node transits can be compared to the placement of the South Node in a natal chart for predictive purposes. A South Node transit shows the position of a sensitive point at a given moment. **3.** Transiting South Node acts as a catalyst as it enters a new sign or a new house, and forms aspects with other transiting planets or planets in both birth and progressed charts. ✴ Transiting South Node can help you have confidence about what you have mastered and let go of its pursuit. If you have a habit of enrolling in self-improvement classes, a South Node transit will signal completion of learning in the respective sign and house. When the South Node transit conjoins the planet that rules your boyfriend, it may be time to move on. See also *South Node, transiting planets, transits.* **BC** 🏠 ◯

What can South Node transits tell you?

- The South Node transiting your **first house** shows possible loss of independence through impulsive acts.
- The South Node moving through your **second house** can mean financial loss because you are not letting go of what is not working for you.
- The South Node transiting your **third house** can point to mechanical problems resulting from lack of focus and distraction.
- The South Node moving through your **fourth house** can be a time of insecurity—until you recognize your *own* path in the world that differs from your family's designated path for you.
- The South Node transiting your **fifth house** may cause you to lose out on performing or creative opportunities if you insist on doing it your way.
- The South Node moving through your **sixth house** can be challenging with co-workers as they sense your critical eye.
- When the South Node enters your **seventh house**, a partnership takes a hit unless you find a way to be fresh and energetic about it.
- The South Node in your **eighth house** can mean a loss around joint ventures if you don't exercise more self-control.
- The South Node transiting your **ninth house** is not the best time to travel to foreign lands, but is a good time for a domestic road trip.
- The South Node transiting your **tenth house** can be a demotion in title because you sided with the wrong team instead of going with your gut.
- The South Node moving through your **eleventh house** brings losses around friendships if you have become too dependent on them for support.
- The South Node transiting through your **twelfth house** feels very sad and confusing until you take practical steps to put your life in order.

S

South Node/Uranus The outer planet Uranus brings radical change, and the South Node relates comfort with familiar patterns. ✧ When the South Node and Uranus interact in your birth chart, the results can be *combustive*. What if you're comfortable with change, chaos, and unusual behavior? You might express explosive behavior or experience a radical event in your life. Your free will can't stop Uranus—it's karmic. You can look back at the behavior or the event to determine what caused it, but you can't know when it'll happen again. See also *aspects between planets, South Node, Uranus.* △ ☯ ○

South Node/Venus Venus relates harmony and love, while the South Node relates lessons learned. ✧ When the South Node and Venus interact in your birth chart, you attract old loves to your life and are very attracted to and comfortable with them. You might have unfinished business with this person or experience, and you have difficulty releasing it from your life. Try not to let the relationship or situation control you, and let it go when you've resolved the remaining issues. Remember why the situation or relationship was in the past to begin with—why didn't it work out before? See also *aspects between planets, South Node, Venus.* △ ☯ ○

southern hemisphere See also *hemisphere, southern signs.*

southern signs **1.** The signs of the upper hemisphere of the chart, specifically Libra, Scorpio, Sagittarius, Capricorn, Aquarius, and Pisces. **2.** The astrological signs that occupy the third and fourth quadrants. ✧ **1.** These astrological signs help you learn to be more objective about yourself and about the world. **2.** The southern signs also rule your public life. See also *Aquarius, Capricorn, Libra, northern signs, Pisces, Sagittarius, Scorpio.* ☼

sowing lifetime **1.** When most planets are in the eastern hemisphere of the native's birth chart, in houses ten through three. **2.** A sowing lifetime is one in which the native is planting the seeds for future lives. This is a time for exploring many avenues. **3.** When most planets are in the western hemisphere of the native's birth chart, in houses four through nine, the native is in a reaping lifetime. ✧ **1.** Are you in a sowing lifetime? Get out there and get planting! A sowing lifetime is one in which you're putting lots of energy out there, possibly in many directions. You're working out some issues and trying to deal with some karmic debt. You won't be reaping the rewards of your hard work in this lifetime, though; that has to wait for the reaping lifetime, which is down the road for you. **2.** Even though your long-term soul growth will be realized in a future life, you can still make use of the first house's ability to discern what you want, the second house's ability to know you are deserving, the third house's ability to focus, the tenth house's ability to manifest, the eleventh house's ability to choose worthwhile goals that make life a unique adventure, and the twelfth house's ability to visualize. Do this by choosing a worthwhile goal that you really want and focusing on why you want it (first, third, and eleventh houses). Visualize the end result and feel the joy of having it (second and twelfth houses). Have faith that it will manifest and enjoy the results (tenth and eleventh houses). See also *birth chart, eleventh house, first house, reaping lifetime, second house, tenth house, third house, twelfth house.* **BC** ☯ **Z**

square **1.** One of the five major aspects, or angles, between planets in astrology. **2.** The glyph for a square is □. On a birth chart, planets are squared when they create a 90-degree angle in the birth chart. Planets are also considered squared when they are within 10 degrees of this 90-degree angle. **3.** Squares are very powerful aspects, and are generally seen as creating a challenging or frustrating relationship between planets. **4.** Planets that are positively aspected in a birth chart produce tangible results when one of them is transiting the other. For example, in a birth chart in which the Moon is at 20 degrees Cancer and Mars is at 22 degrees Pisces, the Moon and Mars are in a positive trine to each other. When *transiting* Mars is at 20 degrees Aries, it forms a square to the natal Moon, which generates tension. As the nature of Mars's and the Moon's relationship is harmonious, the tension from the square pushes them to work together constructively through the signs of Aries and Cancer.

☆ **1.** Do you have any squared planets in your birth chart? Check your aspect grid for the square symbol: □. If you find one of these, figure out which planets form the square. The planets will help you understand the meaning of the square. **2.** In which houses of your birth chart are the squared planets located? This will tell you what parts of your life are likely to be most affected by the planetary interaction. You might be uncomfortable or frustrated with the two houses involved in the square, and this will lead you to resolve some

S

issues there. You'll have to figure out what's frustrating or blocking you, and how to deal with it—really deal with it, and not just get angry. Once you understand and resolve the issue, you can move on and will be stronger and more self-disciplined. **3.** Now find out the signs of the squared planets. The signs tell you how to identify what is positive about the square's presence in your life. **4.** A square isn't really negative—it does muck up the energies of the planets creating the square, though. You have to do some extra work to sort things out and get the planetary energies moving again. This will be beneficial in the long run, as it will cause you to grow. **5.** No squares in your chart? You'll still have some challenges in life, and you might miss out on some great growth opportunities. Squares keep you from getting complacent or lazy. See also *aspect grid, aspects between planets, challenging.* △ ☯ ◐ ◯

star-crossed   **1.** Not compatible. **2.** Two astrological signs can be considered star-crossed if they are not compatible. The stars don't align for these signs. **3.** Think about Shakespeare's famously star-crossed lovers, Romeo and Juliet. **4.** Refers to two people whose North Nodes connect, but whose other planets relating to marriage or partnership are not harmonious. See also *compatibility, synastry.* BC ☯ ◯ Z

star time   Sidereal time. See also *sidereal zodiac.* Z

stars   **1.** Gaseous heavenly bodies held together with gravity. **2.** In our solar system, the Sun is a star. **3.** In astrology, which means the study of stars, all heavenly bodies are considered to be stars. See also *heavenly bodies, Sun.* ◯ Z

stationary   **1.** A planet when it appears to be unmoving. **2.** A planet is stationary just before it moves from direct to retrograde or from retrograde to direct. **3.** As with retrograde motion, stationary is an illusion; a planet is always in direct motion. ✦ **1.** How can you tell if you have a stationary planet in your birth chart, and what does it mean if you do? Instead of ℞ for retrograde, you will see an *S* following the minutes of the planet's position equation. **2.** Stationary retrograde, the time just before a planet goes retrograde, is the perfect time to plan how to make the best use of the upcoming retrograde. Stationary direct, the time just before a planet goes direct, is very powerful for setting an intention about how you want the energy gathered during the retrograde to manifest. See also *direct, planets, retrograde.* ◯ ℞

stellium   1. A configuration of three or more planets bunched together in the birth chart within 10 degrees. **2.** Multiple planets in conjunction. The higher the number of planets, the more powerful and impactful the stellium. Three planets are the minimum to form the configuration, but four creates enough impact that it becomes an important dynamic in interpreting the chart. **3.** If all of the planets are in the same sign or in the same house or both, the stellium is more powerful and impactful. **4.** The tighter the orb, the more powerful and impactful the stellium. The fewer the number of degrees between the planets and the fewer degrees that all of the planets encompass overall create greater synergy. ✦ **1.** Do you have a stellium in your birth chart? If so, the planets in the stellium are more powerful because they can borrow energy from each other. Imagine the planets that form the stellium as people brought together to form a task force. Their combined experience, skills, and talents enable them to get the job done in the most effective and efficient manner. **2.** The sign and house in which the stellium is located will be emphasized in your life. See also *aspects between planets, conjunction.* △ **BC** ◯ **Z**

stem planet   See *T-square.*

subruler   1. Secondary ruler of a house or sign in the zodiac. **2.** Several signs in the zodiac have two planetary rulers. They are Scorpio, Aquarius, and Pisces. Sometimes the Sun is seen as a secondary ruler of Aries. **3.** Mercury, Venus, Mars, Jupiter, and Saturn have all served double-duty as rulers of two signs. **4.** As new planets are discovered, they are assigned to the proper signs. Mercury continues to rule both Gemini and Virgo, but a faction of astrologers believes the planetoid Chiron is the true ruler of Virgo. Venus also continues to rule both Taurus and Libra, but the newly discovered planet Eris will eventually assume primary rule of Libra and Venus will become a subruler of Libra. Mars once ruled both Aries and Scorpio, but upon the discovery of Pluto, it became Scorpio's subruler. In addition to Sagittarius, Jupiter ruled the sign of Pisces until the discovery of Neptune. Jupiter is now the subruler of Pisces.

S

Saturn once ruled both Capricorn and Aquarius until the discovery of Uranus. Saturn is now the subruler of Aquarius.

✸ If you are a Scorpio, Aquarius, or Pisces, you can gain more insight into your chart by analyzing the relationship between the ruler and subruler of your sign. For example, when you have Scorpio rising, your chart has two rulers: Pluto and Mars. As transiting Pluto moves so slowly, pay special attention to transiting Mars to predict what is most likely to be activated in your chart. See also *natural house ruler.* 🏠 ◯ Z

succedent house   1. The second, fifth, eighth, and eleventh houses in the birth chart. The succedent houses are those following the angular houses. **2.** Succedent houses correlate to the fixed astrological signs: Taurus, Leo, Scorpio, and Aquarius. **3.** The second house relates to values and material possessions. **4.** The fifth house relates to creative self-expression and relationships with children. **5.** The eighth house relates to transformation. **6.** The eleventh house relates to peer groups and aspirations. ✸ **1.** Planets in your succedent houses in your birth chart tend to be fixed in their effects. **2.** The effect of any planet in a succedent house is to augment, stabilize, and further empower the ruler of the preceding angular house and its planetary residents. You may think of the ruler of an angular house as its boss, and the planets in the succedent house are its wingmen. **3.** Angular houses are the most impactful and powerful abodes. Succedent house residents are the second most powerful. Cadent house residents are only powerful in their ability to adapt so that their respective quadrant gets its needs expressed. See also *angular house, Aquarius, cadent house, eighth house, eleventh house, fifth house, house, Leo, Scorpio, second house, Taurus.* **BC** 🌓 🏠 ◯ ☼

Sun   1. Along with the Moon, one of the luminaries in the birth chart. **2.** The Sun is the center of Earth's solar system; all of the planets orbit this heavenly body. **3.** The Sun is the natural ruler of the Sun sign Leo as well as the fifth house. **4.** The Sun is a luminary that relates to the outer self and action. **5.** The Sun correlates to the yang or masculine principle. **6.** The Sun (and the Moon) never goes retrograde; the Sun's energy is always direct.

✣ **1.** The Sun represents your soul, your ability to love, and your higher self. It's a positive, energizing planet. **2.** What's your Sun sign? Look at the house and sign your Sun is in to learn more about how you express yourself creatively. **3.** The Sun also tells you about the condition of your heart and upper back, your second sibling, your friends' mates, and the types of people you get romantically involved with. **4.** Want to understand your father better? Look at your Sun—and his. **5.** Problems with a lover or your cat? Close your eyes and get a sense where the Sun is in the sky. If it's nighttime, you can imagine where the Sun is, below the Earth. Send the Sun a message inviting it to send some of its energy to where you are in the form of an avatar; this is what your Sun looks like as it lives in your psyche. Its energy is as real as you are. Ask your Sun avatar what area of your life it rules. Then ask the Sun avatar what it can teach you about that and listen up. Then ask what you should do to be in harmony with your lover boy or girl … or your kitty-cat. The astrological symbol for the Sun is ⊙. **6.** In a daily astrological calendar, you can follow the Sun's transit through each of the signs to see when vitality, connection to Spirit, romance, creative projects, and time with children or your father go really well. Look for those months when the Sun is in the same element as it was when you were born. If you were born when the Sun was in Taurus, an earth element, romance unfolds when the transiting Sun is in earth signs: Taurus, Virgo, and Capricorn. See also *elements, luminaries, Sun in the houses, Sun in the signs, yang.* △ ○ ℞

Sun in the houses **1.** The Sun brings energy and enthusiasm to the areas of life relating to each of the houses. **2.** The Sun is the illuminator—it shines a spotlight on the house it rests in. ✣ The Sun represents the self—the house the Sun appears in will tell you about your personality. It will uplift and revitalize the house it appears in.
⊙ **in the first house** **1.** The Sun in the first house is an energetic, outgoing individual. **2.** The Sun is at home in the first house. ✣ If you have the Sun in your first house, you are jovial and vital. You have a positive outlook and are optimistic and focused. Your talents relate to your personality: you're charismatic and have a good public presence and leadership abilities.

S

☉ **in the second house**   In the second house, the Sun shines light on money matters. ✸ The Sun in your second house is all about earning money. You have great earning potential and can meet your security needs. You're positively focused on these areas, and have great energy to achieve your financial goals. You're really good at finding work and making money—it's not difficult for you. Your values are important to you, and you are confident in them. You can attain what you need to in this house.

☉ **in the third house**   The third house Sun is an enthusiastic communicator. ✸ If you have the Sun in your third house, you're a great communicator. You have talent and enthusiasm in writing, speaking, or otherwise communicating, and can reach others with your enthusiasm. You really enjoy and are energetic about education: you love to learn. You may have had enlightening experiences in early childhood. You may have discovered your talents in childhood. If you had difficulties in childhood, you are likely optimistic about the outcome and about your ability to overcome them. You likely get along well with siblings and may be the family negotiator.

☉ **in the fourth house**   The Sun in the fourth house illuminates family. ✸ If you have the Sun in your fourth house, you bring good energy and optimism into your family life. You likely learned a lot from your family of origin—and are able to let go of negative family experiences from childhood. You're gifted at nurturing and caring for family, and you want your home to be a peaceful and harmonious retreat. Your home and family revitalize you.

☉ **in the fifth house**   The Sun in the fifth house is energetic with children and creative self-expression. ✸ **1.** If you have the Sun in your fifth house, you identify with the fun things in life, and are really good with young people. You bring energy to your relationships with children, and they energize you. You're in touch with your inner child and want to bring out childlike qualities in others. **2.** You're gifted at creative self-expression, and excel at all creative arts. You appreciate the beauty and romance of life and want to bring joy to life. **3.** You also have a natural gift for leading and inspiring others.

☉ **in the sixth house**   The Sun in the sixth house highlights daily work life, health, and public service. ✸ **1.** If you have the Sun in your sixth house, you're productive and devoted to work. You're always able to find work and you feel vitalized in the workplace and by your co-workers. Your enthusiasm there is inspiring—you might use this ability in public service work, to inspire others to action. You have a positive attitude about work and the workplace. **2.** You're vital and rebound from illness quickly. You're proactive about your health, and you encourage others to meet health goals, as well. You'll do well in careers in the health field, where you can share your positive message about health and well-being. **3.** You also do well with land—you nurture the land and animals and make a conscientious farmer or veterinarian.

⊙ **in the seventh house**   The Sun in the seventh house is an enthusiastic partner and negotiator. ✦ **1.** The Sun in your seventh house gives you jubilation in marriage. You bring great enthusiasm to your relationships, and partnerships of all kinds revitalize you. You aren't afraid of commitment and feel great about marriage or domestic partnership. You get along well with others and are optimistic about the outcome of any partnership you enter into. **2.** You're a good negotiator or advisor. You listen to others and can mediate disagreements well and fairly.

⊙ **in the eighth house**   The Sun in the eighth house brings enthusiasm to money and joint resources. ✦ **1.** If you have the Sun in your eighth house, you're great with money and can easily accrue resources. You can manipulate resources and grow money. Banking, investments, insurance, land—all kinds of resources come easily to you. You have the personal power to attain and work with resources. You're also a good networker, and this is helpful to your abilities with resources. **2.** You're a healer, as well, and feel connected with your psychic abilities. You like digging into the mysteries of life, and aren't afraid of the unknown.

⊙ **in the ninth house**   The Sun in the ninth house brings energy and vitality to philosophy and religion. ✦ **1.** If you have the Sun in your ninth house, you're very spiritual and have strong faith. You can reach others with your faith, and make a good mentor—you don't push your beliefs on others, but inspire them to learn, as well. You enjoy studying religion and learning about different faiths. **2.** You are enthusiastic about higher education and foreign travel, and feel positive about your interactions with diverse cultures. This makes you a good teacher or educator. You can help those with divergent backgrounds get along well, and you encourage others to explore different cultures, as well.

S

⊙ **in the tenth house**   The tenth house Sun is optimistic and energetic about career. ✦ **1.** If your Sun is in the tenth house, you are enthusiastic about your career, and you make a good supervisor or leader. Others see you as a leader. **2.** You are also good at parenting, and make a good father figure—even if you're a woman. Others respect your authority.

⊙ **in the eleventh house**   The Sun in the eleventh house is energized by peer groups. ✦ If you have the Sun in your eleventh house, you are revitalized by your friends, peers, and social network. You attract lots of people to your social network—and they can help you in life. You'll attain your goals and aspirations, and your network will help you.

⊙ **in the twelfth house**   The Sun in the twelfth house is quietly energized by psychic abilities. ✦ **1.** The Sun in your twelfth house lights up the subconscious. You're energized by your psychic interactions and are highly intuitive. You're revitalized by the mysteries of life. You like to work behind the scenes, helping or accomplishing things without fanfare. You are a great observer, and your intuition helps you get beneath the surface of things, unobserved. **2.** You also feel dutiful—you have many things to finish up in this life, and you feel optimistic about this: you want to accomplish a lot, and are driven to complete things in this life.

See also *Sun, Sun in the signs, Sun retrograde.* ◯

Sun in the signs   The Sun relates to the physical self and energy. The sign the Sun is in will indicate how the native best expresses love, talent, leadership, strength, spirit, the inner child, and a sense of play and fun.

⊙ **in Aquarius**   Aquarius is an eccentric and innovative sign. ✦ If your Sun is in Aquarius, you march to the beat of your own drummer. You're an independent thinker. You believe that change is always good—and you're happy to be the one to mix things up.

⊙ **in Aries**   Aries is assertive and direct. ✦ If your Sun is in Aries, you're a go-getter. As the first sign of the zodiac, you like to start things. You don't always stick around to finish them, though. You're straightforward, sometimes brusque. Your enthusiasm is contagious.

⊙ **in Cancer**   Cancer is emotional and sensitive. ✦ Your Sun in Cancer makes you emotionally connected to family. You're nurturing and loving. You're very sensitive and can be hurt easily—for this reason, you're protective of your inner self. You sometimes hold a grudge when you're hurt, and you can be emotionally needy.

☉ **in Capricorn**   Capricorn is ambitious and practical. ✴ Your Sun in Capricorn makes you efficient and organized, and you're also very self-controlled. Sometimes you seem *too much* in control; and you won't be mistaken for a romantic. When you focus on a goal, you will persevere to make it happen, no matter how long it takes.

☉ **in Gemini**   Gemini is a thinker. ✴ When your Sun is in Gemini, you're a quick-witted intellectual. You need to communicate your thoughts, and will seek friends and partners who can keep up with your train of thought. Your cleverness can be misconstrued as flippancy—others might think you flit across the surface of things, without settling long enough to be serious.

☉ **in Leo**   1. Leo is a charismatic, generous leader. 2. The Sun is at home in Leo. ✴ Your Sun in Leo makes you bold and dramatic. You love to be the center of attention, and others like to put you there. You're generous and loyal, and are demonstrative with your affections. Appearance matters to Leo—your ego is boosted by compliments.

☉ **in Libra**   Libra is a collector of fine art, a connoisseur of balance. ✴ Your Sun in Libra gives you a need for harmony and beauty in your life. You'll have a lovely home filled with things you find beautiful. You're charming and social, and are generally popular. Your need to have everyone get along can lead you to compromise your own needs or values. You're a great listener and enjoy working with others; you don't like working alone.

☉ **in Pisces**   Pisces is intuitive and adaptable. ✴ If your Sun is in Pisces, you're imaginative, sensitive, and compassionate. You're a great listener, and you really want to help others—sometimes you sacrifice yourself to accomplish this. You're very creative, and excel in the arts. Trust your intuition.

☉ **in Sagittarius**   Sagittarius is a philosophical sign. ✴ Is your Sun in Sagittarius? You're freedom loving and enjoy exploring new cultures and learning new things. You're enthusiastic and energetic, but you sometimes lack follow-through—if you get bored, you might change your idea of commitment. Your belief system is important to you, and you like to share them with others. Be careful not to become dogmatic.

☉ **in Scorpio**   Scorpio is intense and transformational. ✴ Your Sun in Scorpio makes you intense and secretive. You like to get

S

beneath the surface of things, which can be disconcerting to those around you. You're emotional, but tend to keep your feelings under wraps until you're sure you can trust them to someone else. This makes it difficult for others to feel that they really know you.

☉ **in Taurus**   Taurus is gentle and grounded. ✳ Your Sun in Taurus makes you dedicated and dependable. You're sensual and need a comfortable, peaceful home. You're good at growing things—gardens, money, you name it. You're loyal and caring, but can sometimes be stubborn.

☉ **in Virgo**   Virgo is an analytical, orderly sign. ✳ Your Sun in Virgo makes you a perfectionist—you always want to make things better, and will look at a situation from every angle to figure out how to tackle it. You're practical and resourceful and very focused on accomplishing a goal. When you decide to do something, you do it *well*. You are a true worker bee, and have to be careful not to become a workaholic. Work isn't a negative thing for Virgo—you like to be busy, and get great satisfaction from getting things done. See also *signs, Sun*. ◯ ☼

Sun/Jupiter   See *Jupiter/Sun*.

Sun/Mars   See *Mars/Sun*.

Sun/Mercury   See *Mercury/Sun*.

Sun/Moon   See *Moon/Sun*.

Sun/Neptune   See *Neptune/Sun*.

Sun/North Node   See *North Node/Sun*.

Sun/Pluto   See *Pluto/Sun*.

Sun retrograde   As luminaries, the Moon and the Sun are always direct, never retrograde. See also *luminaries, Moon, Moon phases, Sun*. ◯ ℞

Sun/Saturn   See *Saturn/Sun*.

Sun sign   1. The astrological sign of the Sun at the time of birth. **2.** There are 12 astrological signs that comprise the 360-degree circle of the zodiac. The Sun moves 1 degree each day and stays in each sign about 30 days, transiting through the zodiac in one year.

3. Each sign is one-twelfth of the zodiac, or 30 degrees. ✦ **1.** What's your Sun sign? Your Sun sign depends on your date of birth. Because our calendar year consists of 365 and one quarter days, the beginning dates for each sign vary a day or two from year to year. **2.** A man more consciously expresses his Sun sign and learns to express his Moon sign as he integrates his feminine side into his identity. If you're a man, you will probably feel very comfortable with all the traits of your Sun sign, but you may feel that your Moon sign doesn't really describe you. You'll feel more whole and integrated as a person if you can find ways to express your Moon sign. **3.** A woman more consciously expresses her Moon sign and learns to express her Sun sign as she integrates her masculine side into her understanding of who she is. If you're a woman, you will feel more whole and creative if you can channel some of your energy into activities that match your Sun sign. See also *Aquarius, Aries, Cancer, Capricorn, Gemini, Leo, Libra, Moon sign, Pisces, Sagittarius, Scorpio, Taurus, Virgo, zodiac.* ☼◯**Z**

What's Your Sign? The Twelve Signs of the Zodiac

Sign	Dates	Keywords
Aries	March 21–April 20	Pioneer, confident, competitive, innocent
Taurus	April 20–May 21	Sensuous beauty, artistic, dependable, trusting
Gemini	May 21–June 22	Flirt, trivia master, funny, curious
Cancer	June 22–July 23	Protector, nurturing, intuitive, shy
Leo	July 23–August 22	Performer, brave, generous, loving
Virgo	August 22–September 22	Hard worker, intelligent, health-conscious, loves pets
Libra	September 22–October 23	Diplomatic, refined, fair, shares with others
Scorpio	October 23–November 22	Transformer, passionate, magnetic, powerful

S

continues

continued

Sign	Dates	Keywords
Sagittarius	November 22–December 22	Optimist, adventurous, athletic, loves big animals
Capricorn	December 22–January 21	Authoritative, responsible, serious, cautious
Aquarius	January 21–February 19	Bohemian, revolutionary, innovative, friendly
Pisces	February 19–March 21	Psychic, musical, spiritual, imaginative

Sun/South Node   See *South Node/Sun.*

Sun transits   **1.** The Sun as it moves or transits through the signs of the zodiac. **2.** The Sun transits all twelve zodiac signs in the course of a year, spending about 30 days in each sign. **3.** The Sun's transits can be compared to the placement of the Sun in a natal chart for predictive purposes. A transit shows the position of a planet at a given moment. ✨ **1.** As the Sun transits the houses of your birth chart, it brings hope and encouragement to each house, opening it up and illuminating it. When the Sun enters a house, it's a time of opportunity within the life areas of that house—you can look at it as a fresh start. As transiting Sun makes positive aspects to other key planets, those planets become energized and in turn energize the areas of your life that they rule. **2.** When transiting Sun makes negative aspect to other planets, pride, conceit, drama, or extravagance may temporarily sabotage your life. See also *progressed birth chart, Sun, transiting planets, transits.* **BC** 🏠 ◯

Sun Transiting ...	Is ...
Aries	Eager
Gemini	Confident
Taurus	Articulate
Cancer	Centered
Leo	Courageous
Virgo	Improved health
Libra	Swept off your feet in love

Sun Transiting ...	Is ...
Scorpio	Renewal
Sagittarius	Pursuit of truth
Capricorn	Success
Aquarius	Goals realized
Pisces	Visionary

What can Sun transits tell you?

- The Sun transiting your **first house** puts you and your efforts in the limelight.
- The Sun transiting your **second house** wants you to shop for your inner child.
- Want to take a road trip? Find out when the Sun enters your **third house**. Go with a sibling or neighbor.
- Wait for the Sun to enter your **fourth house** to host your open house or family reunion.
- When the Sun enters your **fifth house**, you should take time to play sports, go to the theater, or take a vacation.
- When the Sun enters your **sixth house**, work becomes more fun and creative. This is also a great time to get a cat or for healing.
- The Sun moving through your **seventh house** brings happiness into your business or life partnership. This is also a great time to find a roommate.
- The Sun transiting through your **eighth house** brings love into relationships that had been mostly sexual.
- Travel, workshops, and teaching are happier when the Sun moves through your **ninth house**.
- The Sun shines a happy spotlight on your father, boss, employer, business, or your own reputation when the Sun moves into your **tenth house**.
- Best time to throw a party for your dearest friends or children? When the Sun enters your **eleventh house**.
- Make time for dancing, painting, playing music, and making your dream messages conscious when the Sun transits your **twelfth house**.

S

Sun/Uranus   The outer planet Uranus combines with the Sun to create boundless energy. ✦ If you have the Sun in aspect to Uranus in your birth chart, you may be quite charismatic, and attract a lot of attention. You're unstoppable—you have a lot of energy. You likely have an unconventional approach to life. You're enthusiastic about life, and are always looking ahead. Once you attain a goal, you're ready to move on. You're spontaneous and self-challenging, and are also a risk-taker. You like the energy on the edge—without the Sun's influence, you might fall into the abyss. See also *aspects between planets, Sun, Uranus.* △ ☯ ○

Sun/Venus   Harmonious Venus combines effect with the luminary Sun to create an enthusiastic, loving influence. ✦ If you have the Sun in aspect to Venus in your birth chart, you are loving and kind. You enjoy the arts and are creative. You're social and get along well with others—people like you and are attracted to you. Harmony is very important to you and you tend to be romantic. You like beautiful surroundings and enjoy beautifying things. See also *aspects between planets, Sun, Venus.* △ ☯ ○

surgery   See *health/medical astrology.*

synastry   **1.** Compatibility astrology; the branch of astrology that studies relationship and compatibility. **2.** A composite chart is one that combines two people's birth charts, and is actually a chart for the relationship itself. **3.** A Davison relationship chart uses a midpoint between two people's birth information (place, date, and time) to create a chart that symbolizes the relationship between the two people.

✦ **1.** If you go to an astrologer with relationship questions, the astrologer will compare your chart with your partner's, creating a synastry grid. What will the astrology compare, exactly? For compatibility, your astrologer looks at the relationships between the Sun, Moon, Venus, and Mars in both charts. The rulers of your seventh houses are also compared. **2.** What if there are challenging aspects—such as squares or oppositions—between these planets? Your astrologer will check a bi-wheel chart to see what areas of the charts are harshly aspected. Two bi-wheel charts will be run. One has your birth chart in the center with your partner's planets surrounding your chart. The second bi-wheel chart has your partner's birth chart in the center with your planets surrounding your partner's wheel. Your astrologer can then check the synastry grid for the problematic planetary combinations and will counsel you and your partner about where difficulties are likely to arise in your relationship and how to cope with issues, when they arise. See also *compatibility, composite chart, Davison relationship chart, synastry grid.* △ BC 🌓 🐾 ○ ℞ ☼ Z

synastry grid **1.** Grid created to compare two birth charts. An aspect grid is a triangle, and a synastry grid is two triangles together, making a square. **2.** A synastry grid can help the astrologer see areas of ease and challenge in a relationship. See also *aspect grid, aspects between planets, synastry.* △ 🌓 Z

synthesis **1.** Working together or combined. **2.** Combining two or more things into something new. **3.** The astrological process of assessing all of the components in a chart. ✳ If you have planets that are opposite each other, those planets essentially have opposite agendas as they express themselves through you and in your life. Sometimes you will act out one planet and at other times, you will act out the opposing planet. In times of stress, you'll tend to behave according to the most consciously aspected planet in the more conscious part of your chart. Say you have the Sun, which rules consciousness, in your sixth house, which rules everyday life, and it's opposed by your Moon, which rules your subconscious mind, in your twelfth house, which rules parts of yourself that are hidden from you. You would *knowingly* behave according to your Sun in the sixth house and *unknowingly* behave according to your Moon in the twelfth house. Which planet would you act out during a time of crisis? This is the question answered by synthesis. See also *aspects between planets, birth chart.* △ BC 🌓

S

syzygy **1.** From the Greek word *syzygos*, meaning *union* or *conjunction*. **2.** Refers to planets—at least three—that are in a straight line. **3.** Conjunction or opposition between three or more planets within a one-degree orb. **4.** The alignment of three or more planets within the same gravitational system, such as Earth's solar system. **5.** When the Sun and the Moon are on opposite sides of the Earth or when the Sun and the Moon are conjoined with the Earth. **6.** Occurs during lunar and solar eclipses. **7.** When all of the planets are on the same side of the Sun. **8.** Dr. Carl Gustav Jung, founder of analytical psychology, used the word *syzygy* to describe the joining of a conscious and an unconscious pair of archetypes that function together harmoniously while retaining their own unique characters. The Sun and the Moon are an archetypal pair that work together as masculine and feminine polarities while still expressing their individual lunar and solar characters. See also *aspects between planets, conjunction, opposition.* △ ☯ z

tarot and astrology   Tarot is an intuitive art that uses a tarot deck—a deck of tarot cards—to provide practical information about life. There are many different tarot decks, some follow ancient paradigms while others are based on contemporary designs and modern archetypes. Astrologers often use tarot cards to complement their readings of astrological birth charts. ✦ **1.** How do tarot and astrology relate? Each of the cards in the major (karma) and minor (free will) arcanas of the tarot decks has specific astrological correspondences. Working with tarot cards can add depth to your understanding of how planets and signs work together synergistically. **2.** Astrologers and tarot readers may differ on which planets or signs specifically correlate to each card. (It's an *intuitive* art!) As you learn more and more about the qualities of each planet and sign, you'll develop your own sense of which planets or signs match the tarot deck you customarily use. See also *archetype, astrology, intuition, intuitive arts.* **BC** ◯ ☼ **Z**

tattoos   **1.** Tattoos are ruled by the planets Mars and Saturn. Mars rules sharp, pointed, metal objects, such as needles. Saturn rules ink, skin, and permanence. **2.** When Saturn transits the earth signs of Taurus, Virgo, and Capricorn, astrologers see a surge of interest in tattooing. ✦ **1.** If you have Saturn in your first, second, sixth, eighth, tenth, or eleventh houses or the Sun, Mars, or Venus in your tenth house, you have a tendency to decorate yourself with tattoos. **2.** The sign on the cusp of the tenth house in your birth chart gives you clues about what kind of tattoo is most harmonious for you, as well as the sign and house your natal Saturn is in. **3.** If you want an astrologically themed tattoo, consult a professional astrologer to help you decide on the best image, timing, and placement. Never tattoo a symbol on your body if you do not understand what that symbol signifies and what its meaning is. See also *colors, glyph*. ☯

Taurus   1. The second sign of the zodiac. **2.** Those born between April 20 and May 21 have Taurus as their Sun sign. Also called the bull, Taurus is a yin, or feminine, fixed earth sign. The ruling planet for Taurus is Venus, named for the Roman goddess of love and beauty. Venus is the planet of harmony, sensuality, and love. **3.** The glyph for Taurus is ♉, which looks a bit like a bull's head and horns, and the symbol is the bull, a steady, if stubborn, creature. **4.** Taurus is the natural ruler of the second house, the house of values, material possessions, and earning capacity. **5.** Other associations for Taurus are the color green and the emerald.

✦ **1.** The body parts associated with Taurus are the neck and throat. If you're a Taurus, you likely have a lovely speaking—or singing—voice. Take care of your throat; you're susceptible to sore throats and laryngitis when you're under stress. **2.** If your Sun sign is Taurus, you are practical, kind, and gentle. Routine and security are essential to you. Your focus is on peace, calm, and material comforts and security. You're practical and enjoy the productive process. You're hardworking and efficient, and you love it when those around you are working and achieving their goals, too. You'll put a lot of energy into making sure you have what you need—money, a house, whatever you perceive as your need. You're the person working three jobs to pay off your mortgage early. You're also the person who starts looking for a new job the minute a rumor of your company's merger hits the grapevine. If there's a possibility that you'll be downsized, you want to be prepared. If something upsets your routine or threatens your domestic tranquility, you create a plan to get things back in order, and you stick with it. Because it's what you need, you want everyone around you to be stable and secure, as well. You're also realistic about money. You find comfort in the consistency of structure and routine. If something is out of balance in your finances, home life, etc., you get upset, and when you get upset, you're likely to become stubborn, moody, and melancholy. **3.** Taurus is very good at accumulating resources. Money matters to you, but mostly for security—you need a secure home, harmonious family, and enough food and other resources. When these aren't in balance, or a crisis threatens your security, you freak out. You just don't handle disruptions to your routine very well. For this reason, you try to solve a problem before it becomes a problem. You think about possible crises, and plan for them. You might be the neighbor who's prepared to live off the grid for a few months, should some world crisis require it. **4.** As a fixed earth sign, Taurus is rock steady and dependable—but sometimes a bit inflexible. To say you don't like change is an understatement. You like all things earthy—the great outdoors is your favorite place to be, and you might be an avid gardener. If you haven't tried gardening yet, do—you have a green thumb. **5.** What subjects and careers might appeal to Taurus? In school, you're the one who's always prepared. You don't wait until the last minute to complete a project or study for a test—you have a study plan, and you stick to it. You're the same at work, focused and methodical. You're easygoing, productive, and practical in your work life. With Venus as your ruler, you have an appreciation for beauty and the arts. You enjoy art—making it and seeing it—but you like practical stuff just as much. You're very good with money— you like to make it grow. You're good at any study or job that combines a grounded sensibility with engineering precision and a nurturing touch. You are interested in progress and results, in harmony with the environment. **6.** *Watch out for:* Your loyalty and follow-through are commendable, but don't go through life with blinders on. You tend to stick to the path even when it leads you right past where you really want to go! Be willing to change direction if necessary, and readjust your plans to meet your needs, which *could* change (believe it or not!). **7.** *I'm not a Taurus, but my best friend is:* Your Taurus best friend is loyal and caring. This friend is always there with a kind word (and some baked goods) when you need a helping hand. What can you do for your out-of-sorts Taurus bff? Lift a Taurean's spirits by taking the homemade route: bake favorite cupcakes, write a poem, knit a scarf, or create something just for your friend. Taurus really appreciates the effort and originality of these one-of-a-kind gifts. See also *Taurus ascendant, Taurus descendant.* ☼

Taurus/Aquarius   See *Aquarius/Taurus.*

Taurus/Aries   See *Aries/Taurus.*

Taurus ascendant   Also called Taurus rising. The rising sign is
Taurus, so Taurus is the sign on the cusp of the first house in the
birth chart and the sign on the eastern horizon at the moment of
birth. ✦ **1.** If you're a Taurus rising, Taurus is how you present
yourself to the world and how the world sees you. **2.** If your rising
sign is Taurus, you are likely gentle and kind, with a caring, benevolent nature. Others find you affable, friendly, and charitable, and
the public likes you. You appear consistent, loyal, and responsible.
You speak pragmatically and practically. You have your feet on the
ground, and others know they can count on you to do what you say
you will. You follow through and have a strong sense of loyalty and
responsibility. You appear practical and logical. Those who know
you would call you logical, and might look to you for commonsense
advice. **3.** Taurus rising is rarely out of control. Stability is important
to you—you need order, and don't want to behave irrationally.
You're attracted to people who need help or are indecisive, and will
try to help them find the order that's so important to you. You aren't
self-serving, but rather, have a generous nature and are sensitive
with others. See also *ascendant, Taurus, Taurus descendant.* **BC** ☼

Taurus/Cancer   See *Cancer/Taurus.*

Taurus/Capricorn   See *Capricorn/Taurus.*

Taurus descendant   **1.** The descending sign is Taurus; Taurus is
the sign on the cusp of the seventh house in the birth chart. **2.** The
seventh house is the house of partnerships and marriage or significant others. ✦ **1.** Is Taurus the sign on the cusp of your seventh
house? If so, you relate to others in partnership like steady Taurus.
2. A Taurus descendant has Scorpio rising. You want to attract those
Taurus qualities of steadiness, gentleness, reliability, and practicality.
These are the kinds of partners you really need, in all areas of your
life. You attract partners who are responsible and who value security
and home life. Your partners have a strong sense of loyalty and devotion. They are steadfast and productive and enjoy working toward
financial goals. **3.** Your descending sign reveals your alter ego, or
the aspects of yourself you repressed when you were seven or eight
years old. It also describes your maternal grandmother, paternal
grandfather, third sibling, and second child. And it will tell you what
you will attract in a business partnership, roommate, spouse or life

partner, stranger, and enemy. A Taurus descendant will attract steady, loyal, reliable partners. You'll pair up with business partners who excel at accumulating resources and have a strong need for security. Your partners may also be quite sensual, and have a love for the luxuries in life. See also *descendant, Taurus, Taurus ascendant.* **BC** ☼

Taurus/Gemini   See *Gemini/Taurus.*

Taurus/Leo   See *Leo/Taurus.*

Taurus/Libra   See *Libra/Taurus.*

Taurus/Pisces   See *Pisces/Taurus.*

Taurus rising   See *Taurus ascendant.*

Taurus/Sagittarius   See *Sagittarius/Taurus.*

Taurus/Scorpio   See *Scorpio/Taurus.*

Taurus/Taurus   **1.** These two earth signs want the same things in life. **2.** Taurus is attracted to other earth signs, but will always be most attracted to fellow Taureans. This is the strongest same-sign pairing of the zodiac. Taurus/Taurus pairs may be following a karmic destiny to build and feather a nest together, or be exploring a karmic responsibility to avoid becoming too stodgy or stuck in rigid, unchallenged belief systems.

✦ **1.** These partners are both practical and sensual. They understand each other's physical as well as material and security needs. They are ruled by Venus, and share a strong need for love and loyalty. These two usually get along great and are supportive of each other's desires. **2.** Taurus and Taurus are fantastic business partners—they excel at accumulating money and material goods, and share a strong work ethic—but they really enjoy luxury, and together, they might encourage overindulgence in material goods. These partners may also encourage each other's security needs too much. They want enough of everything to keep any threat at bay, which may lead them to collect large quantities of money, food, and other resources. They can become preoccupied with material goods and money to the point that *more* is never *enough*. **3.** These two make good business

T

partners and friends and are also positive parent/child or boss/employee relationships. The fixed nature of Taurus may make this pairing difficult in marriage or domestic partnerships. It can be impossible to work through disagreements when both partners are stubborn. See also *Taurus*. ☯ ☼

Taurus/Virgo   1. The Taurus/Virgo earth and earth combination is very grounded, but includes good opportunities for each sign to grow the other. **2.** Taurus and Virgo bring out the best in each other. Taurus admires Virgo's love of sacred patterns in nature and Virgo admires Taurus's natural green thumb. ✦ **1.** Taurus and Virgo are practical and realistic. They may share similar views on money and security. Virgo is resourceful and analytical, while Taurus is extremely hardworking. Taurus brings out the sensual side of efficient Virgo and Virgo, in return, challenges Taurus's inflexible nature, helping Taurus to be more forgiving and open-minded. Virgo might be the only sign Taurus will listen to. Taurus has a tendency to plod along, never leaving their chosen path. Virgo analyzes the situation and likely outcome, and will change course to avoid disaster. Sometimes, they can convince Taurus to do this, too. **2.** Taurus and Virgo are a very compatible pair. They are compatible in friendship, in business and work relationships, as siblings, and in marriage or domestic partnerships. See also *Taurus, Virgo*. ☯ ☼

temporal houses   1. The second, sixth, and tenth houses. **2.** The houses that correspond to the earth triplicity of Taurus, Virgo, and Capricorn. **3.** The earth triplicity is ruled by Venus during the day, and the Moon by night. See also *Capricorn, second house, sixth house, Taurus, tenth house, Venus, Virgo*. ☼ 🏠 ○

tenth house   1. In astrology, the tenth house is the house of career and career calling, public service, and public reputation. **2.** The tenth house is also the house of authority figures, patriarchs, and the establishment. **3.** The tenth house also rules the skin, teeth, and skeleton.

✦ **1.** What are you called to do in your career? This isn't just how you spend your days (that's the sixth house), but really what you are meant to be doing. How you will be recognized through your career is also found in the tenth house. **2.** How will you contribute to society, to the world you live in? This is public service, and you can find out what your contribution is by what's happening in the tenth house of your birth chart. Your reputation as perceived by the public or the mainstream media is found here, too. **3.** What's your relationship with your father? With your boss? How you relate to authority figures (male and female) and patriarchs is a tenth house issue. Oh, and your mother's third sibling and your mother-in-law, too. **4.** The tenth house is naturally associated with Capricorn, and is ruled by Saturn. **5.** The planets you have in your tenth house will help define what kinds of role models you've had in your father and in your bosses. Your relationship with the police is depicted here as well. Your tenth house planets also define your *ideal* employer and boss. And they tell you what kind of home best suits your spouse. **6.** If you have irritation or infection with bones, teeth, or skin, Mars is probably transiting through your tenth house. **7.** Perhaps most importantly, the tenth house provides insight about your true career calling … and if you have no planets in your tenth house, its natural ruler, Saturn, along with the planetary ruler of the sign on the cusp on your tenth house, will give you this insight. See also *Capricorn, house, planetary ruler, Saturn, tattoos.* 🏠

terminal houses   **1.** The fourth, eighth, and twelfth houses. **2.** The fourth house is deemed terminal because it reveals circumstances of a person's death. **3.** The eighth house is called terminal because it relates to the ending of life in the physical and the beginning of life in spirit. **4.** The twelfth house is considered terminal because it rules loss. **5.** The houses that correspond to the water sign triplicity of Cancer, Scorpio, and Pisces. **6.** The water sign triplicity is ruled by Venus during the day and by Mars at night. See also *Cancer, eighth house, fourth house, Pisces, Mars, Scorpio, Venus, twelfth house.* ☼ 🏠 ◯

third house   **1.** In astrology, the third house is the house of communication and expression. **2.** The third house is also the house of siblings and early childhood relationships and experiences.

✦ **1.** Have you ever thought about *how* you think, or how your mind responds to the information it receives? The third house is all about your mental state, which was formed from your early childhood education, and your natural intellectual abilities. What is your ability to think things through, and how do you do this? In other words, what's your mental process? The third house covers how you relate to everything from thinking and speaking to writing and self-education.

T

2. If you have brothers and sisters, your relationships with siblings are found here in the third house—especially your relationship with your oldest sibling. **3.** Your spouse's first sibling's spouse (your in-law) is also ruled by the third house. **4.** The third house also rules your hands, arms, and shoulders and how you express yourself with them. **5.** Your car and trips you can make on land in a day are ruled by the third house. **6.** The third house is naturally associated with Gemini, and is ruled by Mercury. **7.** The planets you have in your third house will help define how you gather and process information, what you tend to focus on, how you speak, how you work with logic, what you tend to rationalize, how you relate to your siblings (especially your first-born sibling), and what kind of car you should drive; if you have no planets in your third house, its natural ruler, Mercury, or the ruler of the sign on the cusp of your third house, will give you clues to these insights. See also *Gemini, house, Mercury, planetary ruler.* 🏠

time zones   1. These are used to determine birth time, which is necessary for the creation of an accurate birth chart. **2.** When creating a birth chart, time of birth is based on Equivalent Greenwich Mean Time (EGMT, which is also known as Zulu Time or Universal Time). ✴ What time zone were you born in? If you weren't born along the Greenwich Meridian—in London, for example—you might need to convert the time you were born to its EGMT. Your birth time in the United States is anywhere from GMT minus 5 hours to GMT minus 10 hours. Before converting, make sure the birth time you have includes the hour and minute of your birth, and that you know if the hour was morning (A.M.) or evening (P.M.). If you're creating your birth chart using a computer program, don't worry about making the conversion—the program takes the information on your time and place of birth and converts it to EGMT for you. See also *birth place, birth time, Greenwich Mean Time.* **BC Z**

timing   1. Planning events according to astrological information to achieve the best results. **2.** Many astrologers are very concerned with the precise timing of transits, and others see the approach of a transiting planet to be as impactful as the duration of its alignment, with some residual impact until that planet has moved a good 5 degrees forward. See also *relationship astrology, retrograde planets, transiting planets, transits.* **BC** ☯ ◯ ℞ **Z**

transiting planets **1.** As a planet moves through the signs of the zodiac during the course of its orbit, it is said to be transiting. The orbit is also called a transit. **2.** Planets in their orbits around the Sun. As the planets orbit the Sun and not the Earth, they are called transiting planets. Transits are the planets' motion through the signs in the zodiac. **3.** Transiting planets are the trigger planets: they create action among the planets in the birth chart by creating aspects with them. **4.** The location of the planets at the time of a reading or on any specific date (including future dates). A birth chart records the planetary transits at a specific time.

✳ **1.** How do transiting planets affect you? As the planets travel in their orbits, or transits, they form angles to the planets in your birth chart and your progressed birth chart. Some of these aspects create strong vibrations between the planets that are transiting and your natal (birth) or your progressed planets. The energy of these connections triggers events or internal and external changes in your life. **2.** When planning events or life changes, you can consider the motion of a particular planet as it relates to your birth chart to find the best time. See also *angles between planets, planetary return, progressed birth chart.* △ **BC** ☯ ○ ☼

transits See *transiting planets.*

transpersonal planets See *outer planets.*

trine **1.** This is one of the major aspects and the most beneficial aspect in astrology. **2.** The glyph for trine is △. On a birth chart, planets are said to create a trine when they form a 120-degree angle (or the angle between them is within 10 degrees of a 120-degree angle). There may be two planets creating a trine or three. **3.** A trine is a side of an equilateral triangle. The nature of the corners of an equilateral triangle is to propel energy forward (as opposed to the corners of a square, which has 90-degree angles, where the energy tends to be more staid and stuck).

T

✳ **1.** Have any trines in your birth chart? Look for the symbol △. And then find the planets creating the trine, to find out what it means for you. **2.** Which house or houses is your trine in? This trine will tell you where the action between the planets takes place in your life. **3.** The sign or signs the trine appears in influences how this aspect affects you. **4.** Generally, a trine indicates areas of ease, comfort, and good fortune in your life. Trines indicate places where you've earned some good karma because you worked hard to learn some lessons in earlier lives. You may find that, in the areas of the trined planets in your birth chart, you have an ability to enter a beneficial flow in life. You don't need to work hard—things just move along smoothly for you. **5.** A trine doesn't mean that you'll never face any challenges in these areas. But it usually means that the outcome will be good. You are likely to make it through any troubles without great or extended difficulty. If you have a trine and find yourself in trouble in that area of your life, you may find unexpected help or guidance. You might meet someone who helps you through the crisis or provides you with something you need just at the right time. **6.** What if you have a lot of trines in your birth chart? Count your lucky stars! It's easier for you to access the talents, potential, and abilities the involved planets represent. If you also have challenging aspects in your birth chart (squares or oppositions), these trines can soften their effects. **7.** If you have mostly trines and only one challenging aspect—or no challenging aspects—in your birth chart, you may need to purposely seek out challenges for yourself so that you are prepared for tests when they are triggered by transiting planets forming squares to your natal planets. Don't take it for granted that things will always go your way effortlessly. See also *aspect grid, aspects between planets.* △ ☯ ○

tropical signs   The astrological signs of Cancer and Capricorn. See also *Cancer, Capricorn.* ☼

tropical zodiac   **1.** A tropical year is the length of time it takes for the center of the Sun to start at the vernal equinox, go all the way around its ecliptic, and return to the same point at the vernal equinox. **2.** The actual time it takes the Sun to make its full evolution is 365 days, 5 hours, 48 minutes, and 4½ seconds. See also *ecliptic, equinox, Sun.* ○

true node   See *Nodes (North, South).*

T-square   **1.** This planetary aspect places two planets in opposition, both of which are squared by a third planet. The two opposing planets form the bar of the *T* and the perpendicular planet forms the stem of the *T* as it bisects the center of the *T* bar. This T-square

pattern appears in the aspect lines in the center of the birth chart.
2. This aspect indicates a need for an adjustment in an area of life,
determined by the planets and houses involved. ✦ Oppositions and
squares can both be challenging aspects, but they also represent the
opportunity to take action and shape difficult circumstances into
more positive outcomes for you. If you have a T-square in your birth
chart, you may find yourself balancing back and forth a lot. To find
resolution, you have to look to the planet that squares the other two
in your birth chart. This will indicate the area of internal change.
This struggle may not be visible to others. It's more personal, and
relates to personal challenges, rather than karmic ones. See also
*aspect grid, aspects between planets, house, opposition, planets, Sabian
symbols, square.* △ ☯ 🏠 ○

twelfth house   1. In astrology, the twelfth house is the house of
karmic duty, karmic debt, or responsibility. **2.** Also in the twelfth
house are the unconscious mind and the hidden areas of the self.

✦ **1.** The twelfth house will tell you what you have to work on from
your past, what you have to finish up and work through in this life in
order to go toward karmic rewards or benefits. **2.** The twelfth house
is also called the house of self-undoing or self-reward. What are your
weaknesses? Whatever they are, and wherever they affect you, represents your shadow self and your unconscious mind. The hidden
areas of yourself and your mind operate in this house. **3.** The twelfth
house will show you areas you need to work on to correct imbalances
in your life. Once you work on these areas, you may find reward,
usually of an internal or spiritual nature. The purpose of your twelfth
house challenges is to help you evolve and grow into your more
complete and fulfilled self. **4.** The twelfth house also rules your
father's first sibling, your mother's first sibling's spouse, your feet,
your lymphatic system, and your father's car! **5.** The theme of your
past lives can be found in the twelfth house. **6.** The twelfth house is
naturally associated with Pisces, and is ruled by Neptune and Jupiter.
7. The planets in your twelfth house will help you define your most
recent lifetime and its unfinished business, your fantasies, your latent
talents, your hidden allies and enemies, and the nature and basis of
your addictions. Transits through this house affect your sleep, your
dreams, and your psychological state. If you have no planets in
your twelfth house, the planetary ruler of the sign on the cusp of

T

your twelfth house, and its natural rulers, Neptune and Jupiter, provide insight into your twelfth house issues. See also *house, Jupiter, Neptune, Pisces, planetary ruler.* 🏠

twelve houses of astrology   **1.** The zodiac is divided into twelve equal parts, or houses. **2.** Each house is associated with a zodiac sign, and each sign has one or more planetary rulers. **3.** In astrology, the houses tell where events and action take place. Each house relates to areas of an individual's life; the planets in the house create action in that area of life. **4.** The asteroids, with their unstable orbits, are usually not considered in aspect by astrologers, but the placement of asteroids in the birth chart will reveal insights into the energy and issues of the house they appear in. See also *asteroids, astrology, natural house ruler, planets, signs.* 🏠 **Z**

universe   **1.** Everything in existence, including all matter and energy both in macrocosm and microcosm, visible and not visible, within and without. **2.** Our solar system is located in the Milky Way galaxy, which is in turn located in the universe. **3.** The Western astrological system is based on the luminaries, planets, and other heavenly bodies in our solar system. See also *birth chart, solar system.* **BC** 🌓 **Z**

upper hemisphere   See *hemisphere.*

Uranus   **1.** Planet named for the Greek god of the sky. **2.** Uranus is the seventh planet from the Sun. Its orbit around the Sun takes 84 years; it spends 7 years in each sign of the zodiac. **3.** Uranus is the natural ruler of Aquarius and the planetary ruler of the eleventh house of goals, aspirations, and social network or peer groups. **4.** In Greek mythology, Uranus is the father of Chronos (Saturn in Roman mythology) and the grandfather of Zeus (Jupiter in Roman mythology) and Poseidon (Neptune in Roman mythology). **5.** Uranus is one of the outer, transpersonal planets, and brings the unexpected, or a radical departure from old patterns. The astrological glyph for Uranus is ♅. **6.** Uranus ℞ is more intense than the planet's direct energy. It goes beyond wanting to step to the beat of its own drummer, it wanders the Earth—or at least the country—searching for kindred spirits, a harmonious vibe, and a community where it feels embraced for its bizarre and unconventional ideas and revolutionary ways. Eventually the pain of not fitting in is so great that Uranus ℞ accepts the role of stranger in a strange land.

✦ **1.** Uranus is a planet of *change.* The location of Uranus in your birth chart can indicate areas where radical change might take place.

The change Uranus brings will not only be unexpected, it could also be revolutionary. It can portend erratic behavior, unusual circumstances, and unpredictable events. Unorthodox or unconventional ideas and behavior might land wherever Uranus rests in your birth chart. **2.** Uranus brings radical change to stir things up. After experiencing a radical shift caused by Uranus, you'll change old patterns and experience new ways of thinking about things. **3.** Where is Uranus in your birth chart? Uranus always brings surprises, but the house and sign will tell you more about the nature of the surprises and how they show up. **4.** In a daily astrological calendar, days when Uranus is in a positive aspect to the Sun are electrically charged to create a life and generate ideas that are both fun and beneficial to humanity. As Uranus and the Sun are polarities, a lot of frustration or even violence can result from difficult aspects. Both the Sun and Uranus emanate energy, which needs to be channeled into an appropriate release during stressful aspects. See also *Uranus in the houses, Uranus in the signs, Uranus retrograde.* ○ 🏠 ☼

Uranus in the houses   1. Uranus brings innovation and surprises to the areas of life relating to each of the houses. **2.** Uranus's chart placement shows areas of unexpected and original changes.
✦ **1.** Uranus is sudden change—the house Uranus appears in will tell you where that's likely to occur and the sign it is in will tell you about how to respond when it pulls the rug out from under your feet. **2.** Uranus also has to do with revolution, and the house where Uranus lives in your chart reflects the areas of your life that are ripe for an overthrow of authority.
♅ **in the first house   ** In the first house, Uranus relates to the self and the personality. ✦ **1.** In your first house, Uranus can give you an unconventional appearance. You stand out from the norm and like to make your own fashion statement. **2.** You also think outside the box. You might be unpredictable or unorthodox, but you also have a great mind for new things, and are a radical thinker—your comfort zone is where scientific or technological innovation flourishes. You know that thinking or behaving differently enriches the world with a new perspective. You encourage the unusual in others, as well. **3.** Uranus ℞ in the first house struggles to accept oddness in appearance or preferences.

♅ **in the second house**   Uranus in the second house is about what you value and what you own. ✧ **1.** In your second house, Uranus gives you an unconventional approach to money. You might also have an unusual value system—you don't value what everyone else values. You might receive a windfall at some point, or you might overextend yourself financially. Uranus brings you extremes with money and earning capacity, and you have to learn to welcome the middle ground. **2.** Uranus ℞ in the second house resists unconventional values.

♅ **in the third house**   A third house Uranus relates to communication and thought processes, as well as early childhood. ✧ **1.** With third house Uranus, you are an unconventional thinker—you process things faster and have your own point of view. You might even be a genius. You might also welcome new ways of learning—a new type of school, or a new way of communicating. **2.** You might also have an unusual relationship with your siblings, and you might stand apart from them, either mentally or physically—you might live far away from brothers and sisters. **3.** Uranus ℞ in the third house secretly thinks outside the box.

♅ **in the fourth house**   In the fourth house, Uranus is all about home and family. ✧ **1.** A fourth house Uranus brings unusual ideas about family and home. You might stand out in your family or question traditional ideas of family, as well as what your own family traditions were. Your family of origin may not understand you, or they might find your questioning nature challenging. You don't accept traditional rules about family without struggle. **2.** Uranus ℞ in the fourth house internalizes family members' eccentricities and idiosyncratic behaviors.

♅ **in the fifth house**   Uranus in the fifth house relates to creative expression and relationships with children. ✧ **1.** In your fifth house, Uranus gives you an original artistic or creative gift to be a visionary artist, writer, actor, or scientist. You bring this creative gift to whatever you pursue. **2.** You might also have unusual ideas about children, and your relationship with children could be unorthodox—you could be the parent who practices the family bed or follows nontraditional ideas about discipline, or you could be the favorite aunt to all the children you know. **3.** Uranus ℞ in the fifth house makes you worry about your children being abnormal.

u

⛢ **in the sixth house**   Sixth house Uranus will create the unexpected in areas of health and well-being, work environment, and service. ✧ **1.** Your sixth house Uranus might give you an unusual job or work environment. You might not work nine to five, or in an office. You might be an astronaut—or a freelance reporter! You might also move from job to job a lot before you accept that you need that unconventional career. **2.** You might also have an unorthodox approach to health, relying on holistic medicine or herbal remedies, for example. You might also have unusual health issues. **3.** Uranus ℞ in the sixth house feels bored by daily routine and repetitive work.

⛢ **in the seventh house**   In the seventh house, Uranus relates to partnerships and cooperation. ✧ **1.** A seventh house Uranus isn't comfortable with conventional partnerships. You need to find a partner who shares or at least understands your radical views for the partnership to last. If your relationship falls into the conventional, you'll likely get bored and jump ship. You attract unconventional partnerships—including marriage and domestic partnership. Others might not understand this, but it works for you. **2.** Uranus ℞ in the seventh house causes you to seek out a partner more strange than yourself so that you will appear less idiosyncratic.

⛢ **in the eighth house**   An eighth house Uranus is all about joint resources and new beginnings. ✧ **1.** Your eighth house Uranus can bring luck with money, and might receive a windfall in the form of an inheritance or winnings. **2.** You have a strong connection to the psychic realm and are highly intuitive. You feel the energy around you and can read other people's energy well. You're gifted at holistic or paranormal work. **3.** Uranus ℞ in the eighth house suppresses desire for outdoor or spontaneous romance.

⛢ **in the ninth house**   In the ninth house, Uranus relates to philosophy and religion, travel, higher education, and law. ✧ **1.** A ninth house Uranus placement gives you an unusual connection to foreign countries and foreign travel. You might also have an unorthodox view of education. Combine these, and you could find yourself studying abroad—and you might stay there. **2.** You have radical or extreme religious or spiritual views, even within a traditional religion. You could be a Catholic who espouses liberation theology or you might become a pagan or Wiccan. **3.** Uranus ℞ in the ninth house feigns satisfaction with traditional religion or college.

♅ **in the tenth house**   Uranus in the tenth house relates to career, public life, and authority figures. ✵ **1.** Uranus in your tenth house leads you to an unconventional career. You might change careers often, moving on to something new when your current career becomes too mundane. You could also take an unbeaten path within a traditional career, such as holistic medicine. Uranus can bring you sudden recognition within your career, as well. **2.** Uranus ℞ in the tenth house represses judgment about a superior's or employer's rules and restrictions.

♅ **in the eleventh house**   **1.** Uranus in the eleventh house relates to social networks and goals. **2.** Uranus is the natural planetary ruler of the eleventh house, and is at home there. ✵ **1.** Your friends and peer groups are important to your future with eleventh house Uranus. They will lead you to reach your goals and wishes. You likely have a very eclectic group of friends—you get along with all of them, though they might not get along with each other. You enjoy knowing very different kinds of people and learning from them. **2.** Uranus ℞ in the eleventh house joins clubs and associations that are more conservative than preferred.

♅ **in the twelfth house**   In the twelfth house, Uranus relates to psychic abilities and karma. ✵ **1.** Twelfth house Uranus looks beneath the surface of things and beyond the physical surface. You keep searching for the truth, and this makes you a good researcher, investigator, counselor, and intuitive. You could be the one to discover a cure for a rare disease. **2.** You might also want to tear down old societal structures to make way for a new way of thinking— you're trying to help society, and this might make you overlook the damage you're causing. **3.** Uranus ℞ in the twelfth house uses film or music to get in touch with feelings of angst.
See also *house, retrograde planets, Uranus, Uranus in the signs.* 🏠 ○

Uranus in the signs   **1.** Uranus is the planet of the unexpected and unusual. The sign Uranus is in will indicate how you and your generation cause social reform and revolutionary change at a grassroots level through the latest means of networking and innovative technology. **2.** Uranus ℞ in the signs generally signifies internalization of the tension of being a spiritual being in a physical body. The pressure builds and then spontaneously and erratically implodes according to the sign Uranus is in.

u

♅ **in Aquarius   1.** Aquarius is ambitious and eccentric. **2.** Uranus was in Aquarius from 1996 to 2003. ✦ **1.** The generation born during Uranus in Aquarius is radical and inventive. You will make universal change—change that benefits everyone is important to you, and you're willing to make changes to the whole system to make it better. You have a multitude of skills and are optimistic about your ability to better the world. **2.** Uranus ℞ in Aquarius can be shocking in group settings.

♅ **in Aries   1.** Aries is all about action. **2.** Uranus enters Aries in 2010 (Uranus was last in Aries from 1928 to 1935). ✦ **1.** Those born with this Uranus placement want to make a quick break from the conventional. There's a pioneering spirit here—the old ways aren't working, and you want to change things *now*. You aren't happy to sit around waiting for things to change. Instead, you have to make it happen. **2.** Uranus ℞ in Aries rashly seeks attention through violent behavior.

♅ **in Cancer   1.** Cancer is emotionally connected to home and family. **2.** Uranus was in Cancer from 1949 to 1956. ✦ **1.** If you were born when Uranus was in Cancer, you need to break apart the old values around family and home, creating a new ideal of family. This generation came of age during the 1960s and 1970s—the era of free love and women's lib. **2.** Uranus ℞ in Cancer may suddenly distrust the familiar.

♅ **in Capricorn   1.** Capricorn is practical and disciplined. **2.** Uranus was in Capricorn from 1988 to 1996. ✦ **1.** Are you part of the Uranus in Capricorn generation? You were born during a decade of greed for material goods, and as you grow into adulthood, you'll want to tear down old structures and methods to rebuild new ones that work better for the world we live in now. **2.** Uranus ℞ in Capricorn can burst into blame at the system.

♅ **in Gemini   1.** Gemini is an innovative thinker. **2.** Uranus was in Gemini from 1942 to 1949. ✦ **1.** This is a generation of inventive and original thinkers responsible for innovation in areas of science, technology, and communication. Expanding education is important to you, as a way of creating advancement. **2.** Uranus ℞ in Gemini rarely speaks and then suddenly starts nonstop babbling.

♅ **in Leo   1.** Leo is a charismatic leader. **2.** Uranus was in Leo from 1955 to 1962. ✦ **1.** Were you born during this time period? This generation is determined and generous, and believes in educating everyone for a better and liberated future. You can be very inspirational, and motivate others toward action. This is a generation of leaders interested in new areas of self-expression. **2.** Uranus ℞ in Leo surprises everyone with a sudden demand to be the center of attention.

♅ **in Libra   1.** Libra is all about balance and beauty. **2.** Uranus was in Libra from 1968 to 1975. ✦ **1.** If you were born in this generation, you believe in liberation through justice and legal fairness. You're socially conscious and have new ideas about social traditions, including marriage and domestic partnership. **2.** The arts are also important to you, and you innovate new artistic methods. **3.** Uranus ℞ in Libra decides out of nowhere that a partner is an embarrassment.

♅ **in Pisces   1.** Pisces is the sensitive dreamer of the zodiac. **2.** Uranus was in Pisces from 2003 to 2010 (Uranus was last in Pisces from 1912 to 1919). ✦ **1.** Uranus in Pisces will produce a creative and intuitive generation. You are spiritually inclined and love the mysteries of life. This generation is compassionate and will sacrifice for humanity. They have a universal view of the world, and will fight for the rights of all creatures. **2.** Uranus ℞ in Pisces vacillates between realities like a mad thing.

♅ **in Sagittarius   1.** Sagittarius is the zodiac's optimistic philosopher. **2.** Uranus was in Sagittarius from 1981 to 1988. ✦ **1.** Were you born when Uranus was in Sagittarius? You have new ideas about religion—you're progressive and have a global perspective about religion and the spiritual. You are an original thinker, and you make and follow your own path. **2.** Uranus ℞ in Sagittarius, normally very cautious about trying new things, suddenly wants to book a trip to a third world country.

♅ **in Scorpio   1.** Scorpio is intense and passionate. **2.** Uranus was in Scorpio from 1974 to 1981. ✦ **1.** If you were born when Uranus was in Scorpio, you are powerful and intuitive. You see the dark, intense side of the world and of people in general. You might be responsible for revolutionary or radical change—be careful about your methods, and be sure they aren't destructive. **2.** Uranus ℞ in Scorpio sporadically shifts from easygoing and cooperative to power hungry.

♅ **in Taurus   1.** Taurus is steady and dependable. **2.** Uranus was in Taurus from 1934 to 1942. ✦ **1.** This generation is very determined and focused on security, as well as accumulating material wealth and prosperity. You also want others to realize that prosperity is all

U

around you—it just might not be what you expected. **2.** Uranus ℞ in Taurus suddenly loses control and goes on a spending spree.

♅ **in Virgo** **1.** Virgo is analytical and orderly. **2.** Uranus was in Virgo from 1962 to 1969. ✴ **1.** If you were born with Uranus in Virgo, you're concerned about health and well-being and bring new ideas about these topics as well as environmental health to the public. Breakthroughs in health and changing the health-care system are important to you. You also analyze the work environment and want to liberate yourself and others from stress and difficulty in the work environment. This generation brought new technology to the workplace. **2.** Uranus ℞ in Virgo surprises everyone by ditching work and taking an unplanned vacation. See also *Uranus, signs*. ◯ ☿

Uranus/Jupiter See *Jupiter/Uranus*.

Uranus/Mars See *Mars/Uranus*.

Uranus/Mercury See *Mercury/Uranus*.

Uranus/Moon See *Moon/Uranus*.

Uranus/Neptune See *Neptune/Uranus*.

Uranus/North Node See *North Node/Uranus*.

Uranus/Pluto See *Pluto/Uranus*.

Uranus retrograde, personal **1.** Uranus is retrograde in the birth chart, creating a personal effect in the birth chart of the native. **2.** Uranus is retrograde for 150 days each year. Those born during these 150 days have Mars ℞ in the natal chart. **3.** Personal retrogrades have varying influence depending on the activity of other planets in the birth chart. ✴ **1.** If you have Uranus ℞ in your birth chart, you'll notice that you feel kind of low key most of the time and then you suddenly start acting manic. If you tune in to your feelings more often, you will notice when stress is starting to build up and you can relieve it before the retrograde energy bursts forth, spewing like a live volcano. **2.** Uranus ℞ presents an opportunity to discover balance in all things, to reach a harmony between yang and yin, giving and receiving energies. See also *Uranus; Uranus retrograde, transiting; retrograde, personal*. ◯ ℞

Look to the astrological sign of your personal Uranus retrograde for advice on the best course of action:

- ♅℞ **in Aries:** Look for ways to establish your independence and dress like a teenager.

- ♅℞ **in Taurus:** Seek unusual money-making opportunities.

- ♅℞ **in Gemini:** Drive a green (environment-friendly) car.

- ♅℞ **in Cancer:** Choose a home that has an air of eccentricity or unconventional design.

- ♅℞ **in Leo:** Support your children in their nonconventional pursuits.

- ♅℞ **in Virgo:** Balance your body with vibrational medicine.

- ♅℞ **in Libra:** Marry a friend rather than society's ideal.

- ♅℞ **in Scorpio:** Openly share your brilliant insights about sex and death.

- ♅℞ **in Sagittarius:** Adopt an optimistic philosophy.

- ♅℞ **in Capricorn:** Consider how discipline gives you more freedom.

- ♅℞ **in Aquarius:** Start a collective whose members inspire each other.

- ♅℞ **in Pisces:** Dance around your living room, letting the music move you.

Uranus retrograde, transiting   1. Uranus's transiting retrograde lasts 150 days; that's five months. **2.** Finding ways to channel Uranus's radical energy can seem difficult during retrograde periods. ✧ **1.** When you're moving through a transiting Uranus ℞, the astrological cliché would be to "expect the unexpected." But how can you *really* do that? Uranus is all about what's sudden and unknown. Astrologers now believe that Uranus ℞ is really all about authenticity. For you, this means being your authentic self, no matter the stresses to the system that life can bring to you, or what other people or institutions might want you (even push you) to be. **2.** For humanity, Uranus ℞ means respecting the truth and holding everyone to that high standard. The truth can be hard to discern, though, and Uranus is willing to rock the boat a bit to see what happens. If you are able to remain authentic when put to the test, you stay original, pure. If you're faking it when Uranus is in retrograde (or worse, if you're cheating), it will be hard to persuade people or draw them to you or

U

any of your causes. Uranus ℞ separates fact from fiction and pushes you to be true to your highest ideals. See also *Uranus; Uranus retrograde, personal; retrograde, transiting.* ◯ ℞

If transiting Uranus retrograde throws too many shocks your way, look to the astrological sign to shine some light on the situation:

- **In Aries:** Make your own path if need be.
- **In Taurus:** Examine the laws of attraction.
- **In Gemini:** Recognize yin and yang are opposites, not twins.
- **In Cancer:** Determine what you can stomach.
- **In Leo:** Roar, and see what happens next.
- **In Virgo:** Understand your idea of perfection may not be the same as someone else's.
- **In Libra:** Put on the blindfold and see the truth.
- **In Scorpio:** Try once more, with *extra* intensity (just in case you didn't feel it the first time …).
- **In Sagittarius:** Avoid hyperbole.
- **In Capricorn:** Be prepared for your GPS to send you down a dead-end road that's not on the map.
- **In Aquarius:** Know it is possible to think too much.
- **In Pisces:** Forget about being practical.

Uranus return   **1.** Point at which Uranus returns to the position it held in a person's birth chart. **2.** Uranus is in each sign for about 7 years, and has a total orbit time of 84 years. Therefore, it would take 84 years for Uranus to return to an exact place in its orbit. ✴ **1.** Unlike your ancestors, you will probably be here to experience your Uranian return; living to 100 (or nearly so) isn't as shocking as it used to be! **2.** Your Uranian return encourages you to find even more freedom in your life, especially freedom from old guilt and shame imposed upon you by family, friends, and society. See also *planetary return, Uranus.* ◯

Uranus/Saturn   See *Saturn/Uranus.*

Uranus/South Node   See *South Node/Uranus.*

Uranus/Sun   See *Sun/Uranus.*

Uranus transits   1. Uranus as it transits or moves through the signs of the zodiac. **2.** Uranus takes 84 years to orbit the Sun, and it transits all twelve zodiac signs in that time, spending about 7 years in each sign. **3.** Uranus transits can be compared to the placement of Uranus in a birth chart for predictive purposes. A transit shows the position of a planet at a given moment. **4.** Transiting Uranus activates and awakens other heavenly bodies as it enters a new sign or a new house, and as it forms aspects with other transiting planets or planets in both birth and progressed charts. Uranus is used by professional astrologers to predict events that shake the native out of denial and free restraints. ✴ **1.** Transiting Uranus will wake you up and force you to change course. You'll likely experience some change in awareness—a very big ah-ha moment. **2.** Uranus transits are times of kundalini release and visions of the future. See also *chakras and astrology, progressed birth chart, transiting planets, transits, Uranus.*

△ BC 🏠 ○

What can Uranus transits tell you?

- Uranus transiting your **first house** wants you to break free of old roles.
- Uranus transiting your **second house** brings financial windfalls and unexpected expenses.
- Uranus entering your **third house** manifests through unconventional neighbors.
- When Uranus enters your **fourth house,** you'll have electrical issues in your home.
- When Uranus enters your **fifth house,** it's time to take a once-in-a-lifetime vacation.
- When Uranus enters your **sixth house**, a healing crisis focuses your attention on vibrational healing.
- Uranus moving through your **seventh house** brings a surprise lawsuit or marriage.
- Uranus transiting through your **eighth house** unleashes kundalini energy and frees you from your fear of death.
- When Uranus moves through your **ninth house**, a life-changing mentor or guru appears.
- When Uranus moves into your **tenth house**, there is an unexpected changing of the guard with your employer or in your industry.

u

- Uranus transiting your **eleventh house** awakens your global consciousness.
- When Uranus transits your **twelfth house**, psychic ability takes off and real moments of enlightenment occur.

Uranus/Venus   Uranus brings the unexpected to Venus's love of beauty. Uranus seeks freedom and tends to resist commitment, whereas Venus seeks emotional attachment. ✳ Uranus and Venus connect in your birth chart to attract unusual friends and lovers. You might attract or be attracted to those who aren't the most compatible with you. The frolicking nature of Uranus gets giddy in the presence of sensuous Venus. When these two planets come together in your chart, expect sudden windfalls to come as easily as sudden shortfalls; expect to fall in love fast and hard and to fall out of love just as quickly and completely. See also *aspects between planets, Uranus, Venus.*

△ ☯ ○

V

Vedic astrology   See *Hindu astrology, sidereal zodiac.*

Venus   **1.** Planet named for the Roman goddess of love. **2.** Venus is the second planet from the Sun. Its orbit around the Sun takes 225 days; it spends about 19 days in each sign of the zodiac. **3.** Venus is the natural ruler of Taurus and Libra and the planetary ruler of the second and seventh houses of the zodiac. **4.** In Roman mythology, Venus is the goddess of love and beauty. Her Greek equivalent is Aphrodite. **5.** Venus is one of the personal or inner planets, and brings harmony and balance. The astrological glyph for Venus is ♀. **6.** Venus ℞ has self-esteem issues and fears manipulation is behind offers of love, compliments, and gifts. It chooses objects of affection that are less desirable to feel *more* desirable, but the relationship lowers self-esteem even more instead of raising it.

✦ **1.** Venus is a planet of balance. Venus brings love, affection, harmony, and abundance wherever it lands in your chart. Venus in your birth chart will tell you how you love. It's considered a beneficial planet, and brings good things to the house of your birth chart it is in (and when transiting through your chart as well). Venus also relates to fertility and abundance. If you're trying to have a baby—or grow a garden—look at Venus in your birth chart. **2.** Venus also relates to art, music, beauty, and aesthetics. Venus's placement in your chart can tell you where and how beauty is important to you. Venus also likes sweets—if you're a Taurus or Libra, you might have a sweet tooth! **3.** Where is Venus in your birth chart? Venus brings abundance and harmony, but the house and sign will tell you more about Venus's personal meaning for you. **4.** In a daily astrological calendar, days and times when Venus is in a positive aspect to the Sun (such as conjunct, trine, or sextile) are usually good times for making jewelry, aromatherapy, flirtation and romance, being with children, seeing a live performance, and celebrating life. Days when Venus is in a more challenging aspect to the Sun (such as opposition or square) can be times when sexual feelings do not lead to a loving relationship, money gets spent on unhappy vacations, fashion and jewelry or toys bought to placate a child never get worn or used. See also *retrograde planets, Venus in the houses, Venus in the signs.* △ ○ ℞

Venus in the houses **1.** Venus brings harmony and abundance to the areas of life relating to each of the houses. **2.** Venus's chart placement shows where you will have love and abundance in your life. ✧ Venus is peace and harmony—the house Venus appears in will tell you about what you value and love in your life, as well as where you'll *find* love.

♀ in the first house Venus in the first house has self-love and a love of beauty. ✧ **1.** If you have Venus in your first house, you are likely kind and affable. You love beauty and like to have beautiful things around you. You may be quite attractive and charismatic. You also have a beautiful soul. You bounce back from struggle—people like to help you. You attract love and affection. **2.** You can also be somewhat overindulgent or have a desire for glamour and decadence. **3.** Venus ℞ in the first house gives you difficulty seeing your own beauty.

♀ in the second house Venus in the second house means that you value pleasure and beauty. ✧ **1.** If you have Venus in your second house, you have an ease with money—you like working and never have difficulty finding work. You also collect things that are both valuable and beautiful—paintings, for example, or jewelry. You value harmony and comfort in life. You want others around you to get along—and you'll sacrifice to make this happen. **2.** You are very generous, and sometimes give away more than you should—you might not keep enough for yourself. **3.** Venus ℞ in the second house struggles to feel valuable.

♀ in the third house Venus in the third house is a loving communicator. ✧ **1.** If you have Venus in your third house, you love your siblings and likely had an affectionate childhood, and retain pleasant memories of childhood and education. You're optimistic and you always hope for the best for you and for those around you. You're a good communicator, and are a constructive and thoughtful speaker and thinker. You're also respectful of others' ideas. **2.** You enjoy travel and are open to other cultures. Your kindness helps you when you travel—others want to help you, and you're openly appreciative of assistance. **3.** Venus ℞ in the third house fears telling others their desires.

♀ **in the fourth house**   In the fourth house, Venus values home and family. ✻ **1.** Having Venus in your fourth house may mean that the people who raised you surrounded you with love. Even if there were problems, you felt blessed with your family and home life. Your home is important to you, and you want it to be beautiful and comfortable. You also want to help others develop a better life, and are generous with your aid. **2.** Venus ℞ in the fourth house feels undeserving because of early relationships within the family of origin.

♀ **in the fifth house**   Venus in the fifth house is an artist. ✻ **1.** If you have Venus in your fifth house, you're creative. You might have a talent for acting or writing poetry, painting or interior design. You might be an architect—or have your own design show! **2.** You have a strong affinity with children, and are genuinely concerned for the welfare of all children. **3.** You're also very attractive—you'll likely have a large group of friends, lovers, and admirers—and you like to hold on to your former lovers as friends once your romantic relationship ends. **4.** Venus ℞ in the fifth house gives you little faith in your own creative abilities.

♀ **in the sixth house**   Venus in the sixth house loves the workplace and is lucky there. ✻ **1.** If you have Venus in your sixth house, you are devoted to work and probably love your job. You are fortunate with work, also. You're likely very good at your chosen career. You get along well with co-workers, and form close friendships with them. Your work environment is important—you need to beautify it, and you also need your co-workers to get along. **2.** You usually enjoy good health and tend to be fortunate with health care when you have a medical issue. **3.** Venus ℞ in the sixth house settles for unfulfilling work.

♀ **in the seventh house**   **1.** Venus in the seventh house is a cooperative and affectionate partner. **2.** Venus rules the seventh house and is comfortable here. ✻ **1.** If you have Venus in your seventh house, partnerships of all kinds are very important to you. You are a devoted and affectionate spouse or domestic partner. You put a

V

lot of energy into your partnerships, and want them to be peaceful and long-lasting. **2.** You attract lots of partners, which can create problems—you can't make everyone happy, and it's difficult to maintain harmony among your many partners. You make friends out of your business and work partners, and you might have many romantic partners during your life. (We hope not all at the same time!) Trust your heart when picking a romantic partner—choose the partner you *love*. **3.** Venus ℞ in the seventh house marries beneath standards in hope of being adored.

♀ **in the eighth house**   Venus in the eighth house has a gift with resources, including money. ✦ **1.** If you have Venus in your eighth house, you're good with resources and investing. You manage your own and others' money well and usually come out ahead in investments. Your needs are always met. **2.** You're charismatic and others are attracted to your spirit. You're protected by good karma with this placement, and you might receive gifts in this lifetime—those are your karmic rewards! **3.** Venus ℞ in the eighth house attracts manipulation because of *fear* of it.

♀ **in the ninth house**   Venus in the ninth house has powerful spiritual or religious beliefs. ✦ **1.** If you have Venus in your ninth house, you are spiritually devoted. You can be a charismatic spiritual leader, a guru, pastor, or nun. Education is important to you, and you make a generous, compassionate teacher or counselor. You want to help others grow and reach a higher level, mentally and spiritually. **2.** You're open-minded and enjoy travel and foreign cultures, and benefit from time spent traveling. **3.** Venus ℞ in the ninth house seeks self-esteem through attachment to religious leaders or scholars.

♀ **in the tenth house**   Venus in the tenth house loves work and career. ✦ **1.** If you have Venus in your tenth house, you love your job and are devoted to your career. You make an inspiring leader, and are generally well-respected and liked by your co-workers and employees. Community work is also important to you—you want to improve your neighborhood and have a positive impact on your society. You're generous with your neighbors, and part of your career calling is to improve where you live. **2.** Venus ℞ in the tenth house longs for approval and credibility from the establishment.

♀ **in the eleventh house**   Venus in the eleventh house finds love through friendship. ✦ **1.** If you have Venus in your eleventh house, you're a devoted friend, and your friends and peer groups are very important to you. Your friends are also devoted to you and they are beneficial to your life and career. You are likely to find romantic love through your social network. You're a team player—cooperating with others is a gift, and you benefit from the power of your network. **2.** Venus ℞ in the eleventh house feels too different from others to be loved and valued.

♀ **in the twelfth house**   Venus in the twelfth house is idealistic in love. ✵ **1.** If you have Venus in your twelfth house, you enjoy your alone time, but you have a strong desire to find a soul mate. You don't need to be in a relationship—you want something bigger than just a partner, and you have an ideal vision of this mate that may not actually exist in the real world. You sometimes like to be taken care of. You're extremely compassionate and giving and want to help others. You're psychically attuned and can often sense when something is wrong with someone you know—a mental or emotional need or a physical problem. Your intuition makes you a good problem solver. You're loyal and can keep a secret. **2.** There's a danger in seeking attention outside your relationship when you aren't happy with your partner. You might engage in illicit affairs when you just need affection from your partner or friends. **3.** Venus ℞ in the twelfth house tries to escape loneliness through addictive pursuits.

See also *house, retrograde planets, Venus, Venus in the signs.* 🏠 ◯

Venus in the signs   **1.** Venus is the planet of harmony and beauty. The sign Venus is in will indicate how beauty, self-esteem, money, and justice are experienced. **2.** Venus ℞ in the signs generally indicates resistance to receiving and experiencing wealth, harmony, and appreciation.

♀ **in Aquarius**   Aquarius is an inventive, communicative sign. ✵ **1.** With Venus in Aquarius, you can seem aloof or standoffish. You seem detached, because you're thinking about things, and don't express your deepest feelings. You need an intelligent partner who's your intellectual equal. You're a thinker, and are interested in problem solving in relationships. You don't want a dramatic partner, and you aren't possessive. You're loyal, though. You're philanthropic, and want to contribute to society by helping others. **2.** Venus ℞ in Aquarius fears humiliation about feelings of attraction and desire.

♀ **in Aries**   Aries is an extroverted go-getter. ✵ **1.** Your Venus in Aries makes you independent. You don't like to be told who you should love. You're very demonstrative and affectionate. You're also

V

intense in your relationships, but if the passion wanes and you get bored, you'll move on. **2.** Venus ℞ in Aries lives out desires vicariously.

♀ **in Cancer**   Cancer is emotional and family-focused. ✵ **1.** Your Venus in Cancer gives you devotion to family. Your parents, spouse, partner, and children are the center of your life. You're nurturing and compassionate, and are known for your generosity—you share your time, money, spirit, and love. You notice when others are in need, and you step in to help. **2.** You're very creative. **2.** Venus ℞ in Cancer puts everyone else's needs first.

♀ **in Capricorn**   Capricorn is an organized, practical sign. ✵ **1.** If you have Venus in Capricorn, you take love seriously. You scrutinize a potential partner, and don't enter into commitment lightly. You're loyal and devoted once you do commit, though. You realize that romance can fade, and are willing to do the work required to maintain the relationship after the initial infatuation has passed. The romance isn't the most important part of the relationship to you—you want a long-term partner. **2.** You're skillful in business, and you like to help others—including your romantic partners—be successful and prosperous. **3.** Venus ℞ in Capricorn wants to be a big success to feel worthy of the love they desire.

♀ **in Gemini**   Gemini is an intellectual, communicative sign. ✵ **1.** If you have Venus in Gemini, you need a love interest who's your intellectual equal. You need to communicate with your partner, and are attracted to your partner's mind. You can be particular about your romantic partner, because you need to find a partner on your level. You might flit around a bit, looking for a good match. **2.** You're a good traveler, and enjoy spontaneous trips. **3.** Venus ℞ in Gemini is hesitant to express feelings of love and resists compliments.

♀ **in Leo**   Leo is magnetic and generous. ✵ **1.** Your Venus in Leo is a generous, passionate romantic partner. You are in love with love—and maybe also in love with yourself. You're openly affectionate and demonstrative, and you need an equally affectionate partner. You're loyal and passionate and you require loyalty in your partner. You like the good things in life, and can be showy, owning a beautiful house and designer clothes. **2.** Venus ℞ in Leo resists seeking and receiving attention and admiration.

♀ **in Libra**   **1.** Libra is a charming, active sign. **2.** Venus is the planetary ruler of Libra. ✨ **1.** Your Venus in Libra is easygoing and understanding. You communicate your feelings well. You're generally well liked and are good at putting others at ease. You have a love of beauty that might express itself in your personal style or your home. You enjoy romance—chocolate, flowers! Fairness is important in a relationship, and so is harmony—you'll work and sacrifice to keep harmony in your romantic or family relationships. **2.** You're creative and artistic, and you appreciate a beautiful environment. You like to beautify the world you live in. **3.** Venus ℞ in Libra tends to marry or partner outside their social or economic class.

♀ **in Pisces**   Pisces is compassionate and intuitive. ✨ **1.** Your Venus in Pisces is very emotional and intuitive. You're affectionate and loyal, and are connected and devoted to your loved ones. You're idealistic about love, and try to see the best in everyone—sometimes you'll see what's not there. You feel your loved ones' emotional pain. You can be persistent in a relationship, and will pursue a partner, which can lead to an unequal relationship. You need to find partners who are what you believe them to be so you don't become disenchanted in the relationships. Generally, you believe that love triumphs in the end. **2.** Venus ℞ in Pisces often settles for (even prefers) fantasy in place of reality, especially if the truth will hurt.

♀ **in Sagittarius**   Sagittarius seeks truth and adventure. ✨ **1.** Your Venus in Sagittarius, you are gregarious and adventurous in love. You like to *do* things. You need open-minded partners who speak their minds, and prove spontaneous—like you. You have no problem with honesty in a relationship, and will speak the truth, even if the truth hurts your partner. You might not go for traditional routes of commitment, and will explore other kinds of relationships. **2.** Venus ℞ in Sagittarius may replace desire with religious fervor.

♀ **in Scorpio**   Scorpio is an intense sign of transformation. ✨ **1.** Your Venus in Scorpio makes you intense, sensual, and passionate. You might keep this side of yourself private, though, sharing it only with your chosen partner. You're physically demonstrative, but might have difficulty with verbal expression of your feelings. This can cause misreading of your feelings or intentions. You're a loyal and devoted partner. You're insightful, and know immediately when something is wrong in your partner or your

V

relationship. **2.** You can be secretive, and you don't like public exposure of what you consider private. You need a partner who can respect this. **3.** Venus ℞ in Scorpio has trouble revealing what they really want in intimate relationships.

♀ **in Taurus** **1.** Taurus is generous and sensual. **2.** Venus is the planetary ruler of Taurus. ✴ **1.** Venus in Taurus is steadfast, loyal, loving, and kind. You're focused on security, and might equate love with possessions. You're generous and devoted with your partner, and you need reciprocation. Your partner has to demonstrate devotion. A happy home is essential to you. You see natural beauty all around you, and you enjoy comfort. **2.** Venus ℞ in Taurus only feels comfortable receiving what they have earned.

♀ **in Virgo** Virgo is an orderly perfectionist. ✴ **1.** If you have Venus in Virgo, you are cautious and nitpicky. You might analyze a partner until there's no joy left in the partnership, no romance in the love. But you need to ferret out all of the facts and nuances of the relationship before you can commit. It's how you live—you scrutinize *everything*. You need an intellectual equal, and if you can't find someone you can really communicate with, you're happier alone. **2.** Don't be so particular that you rule out every possible partner— you can be happy if you allow yourself and your partner a few flaws. **3.** Venus ℞ in Virgo resists believing they are attractive and desirable. See also *Venus, signs.* ◯ ☼

Venus/Jupiter See *Jupiter/Venus.*

Venus/Mars See *Mars/Venus.*

Venus/Mercury See *Mercury/Venus.*

Venus/Moon See *Moon/Venus.*

Venus/Neptune See *Neptune/Venus.*

Venus/North Node See *North Node/Venus.*

Venus/Pluto See *Pluto/Venus.*

Venus retrograde, personal **1.** Venus is retrograde in the birth chart, creating a personal effect in the birth chart of the native. **2.** Venus is retrograde for 42 days every 18 months. Those born during these 42 days have Venus ℞ in the birth chart. **3.** Personal retrogrades have varying influence depending on the activity of other planets in the birth chart. ✦ **1.** If you have Venus ℞ in your birth chart, you might feel that you are not deserving of love unless you help others or contribute time, effort, and resources. Your Venus needs you to know that you have worth whether you help or not. **2.** The sign and house that your Venus ℞ is in will help you acknowledge how you are especially valuable and in what areas of life. See also *Venus; Venus retrograde, transiting; retrograde, personal.* ◯ ℞

Look to the astrological sign of your personal Venus retrograde for advice on the best course of action:

- ♀℞ **in Aries:** Learn martial arts to help you learn to receive energy.
- ♀℞ **in Taurus:** Buy yourself flowers, as they reflect your beauty back to you.
- ♀℞ **in Gemini:** Give yourself compliments … out loud.
- ♀℞ **in Cancer:** Be a good mother to yourself and feed yourself delicious, nutritious meals.
- ♀℞ **in Leo:** Ask a friend to listen. You wouldn't expect your pet to thrive without attention.
- ♀℞ **in Virgo:** Care for your health—it builds your self-esteem.
- ♀℞ **in Libra:** Say no to those who don't appreciate you—no matter how amazing they may seem.
- ♀℞ **in Scorpio:** Take steps to end relationships and situations that are negative.
- ♀℞ **in Sagittarius:** Find a way to travel to foreign lands as soon as possible.
- ♀℞ **in Capricorn:** Ask your boss what you should do to be considered for a promotion.
- ♀℞ **in Aquarius:** Host a party with an unusual theme, such as dress as your favorite TV character.
- ♀℞ **in Pisces:** Schedule a photo shoot so that you'll have a really flattering picture of yourself for your webpage

Venus retrograde, transiting **1.** Venus's transiting retrograde lasts 42 days; that's six weeks. **2.** Finding ways to channel Venus's harmonious energy can seem difficult during retrograde periods. ✦ **1.** The average person may equate Venus with love, love, love, but people in the know about astrology understand there's more to Venus: Venus is about achieving abundance and Venus ℞ is about

V

being resourceful. Some astrologers will tell you that a transiting retrograde Venus has as much to do with money as with love! During these retrograde times, whatever you've got, you want more. How you go about getting it says everything about how successfully you will live in harmony with Venus ℞ energy. **2.** This may be a great time to write poetry, create an avatar, or even—*gasp*—to get married. Partnerships formed with care and intent during a Venus ℞, especially pairings that involve being reunited with a loved one, gain extra strength and durability for commitments made now. See also *retrograde, transiting; Venus; Venus retrograde, personal.* ◯ ℞

If transiting Venus retrograde leaves you unfriended, look to the astrological sign to throw some light on the situation:

- **In Aries:** Going it alone is antithetical to being a good partner.
- **In Taurus:** Make sure the bank is safe.
- **In Gemini:** Recognize that sometimes sisters and brothers are good friends, and sometimes they are not.
- **In Cancer:** Embrace the notion that things will get better.
- **In Leo:** Introduce your right brain to your left brain.
- **In Virgo:** Be like a virgin, touched for the very first time.
- **In Libra:** Determine when things are too light or too heavy.
- **In Scorpio:** Who is being obsessive or compulsive?
- **In Sagittarius:** Tell the one you love the best.
- **In Capricorn:** Pull an all-nighter to count the ways.
- **In Aquarius:** You don't need to be aloof and skeptical.
- **In Pisces:** You have visions while the rest of the world wears bifocals.

Venus return　1. Point at which Venus returns to the position it held in the native's birth chart. **2.** Venus is in each sign for about 19 days, and has a total orbit time of 225 days. Therefore, it would take Venus 225 days to return to an exact place in its orbit. ✲ You'll have at least one Venus return every year—what will these dates means to you? Your Venus return offers a great opportunity for shopping, especially for fashion, precious gems, gourmet food, art, cosmetics, musical instruments, and party gifts. If you sing, a Venus return is perfect for a concert. If you have been in therapy working on your self-esteem, you'll feel the results on your Venus return.

This is also a great time for a facial, a makeover, aromatherapy, an art installation or show, society functions, engagements, or weddings. See also *planetary return, Venus*. ◯

Venus/Saturn   See *Saturn/Venus*.

Venus/South Node   See *South Node/Venus*.

Venus/Sun   See *Sun/Venus*.

Venus transits   **1.** Venus as it transits or moves through the signs of the zodiac. **2.** Venus takes 225 days to orbit the Sun, and it transits all twelve zodiac signs in that time, spending about 19 days in each sign. **3.** Venus transits can be compared to the placement of Venus in a natal chart for predictive purposes. A transit shows the position of a planet at a given moment. **4.** Transiting Venus activates the energy of other heavenly bodies as it enters a new sign or a new house, and as it forms aspects with other transiting planets or planets in both natal and progressed charts. **5.** Venus is used by professional astrologers to predict the arrival of money, an engagement proposal or outcome, success of a fundraiser, or when a woman will show up. ✦ Venus brings money, love, luck, and happiness as it transits your chart, especially in the signs it rules, Taurus and Libra, and in its sign of exaltation, Pisces. See also *progressed birth chart, transiting planets, transits, Venus*. △ BC 🏠 ◯

> **What can Venus transits tell you?**
> - Venus transiting your **first house** enhances your attractiveness.
> - Venus transiting your **second house** brings money.
> - Venus entering your **third house** is an excellent time to buy or lease a car.
> - When Venus enters your **fourth house**, consider buying real estate.
> - When Venus enters your **fifth house**, get your oil pastels out.
> - When Venus enters your **sixth house**, you should ask for a raise or promotion.
> - Venus moving through your **seventh house** may bring a proposal or wedding invitation.
> - Venus transiting through your **eighth house** is a good time to do taxes, buy insurance, or think about setting beneficiaries.

V

- When Venus moves through your **ninth house**, plan a spa vacation in a foreign country.
- When Venus moves into your **tenth house**, start a side business.
- Venus transiting your **eleventh house** means your party or fundraiser will be a hit.
- When Venus transits your **twelfth house**, you'll get quality rest and have sweet dreams.

Venus/Uranus   See *Uranus/Venus*.

Vesta   1. An asteroid discovered in 1807 by Heinrich Olbers. Vesta is named for the Roman virgin goddess of the hearth and home. Her Greek counterpart is Hestia. **2.** The glyph for Vesta's astrological symbol is ⚶. **3.** In Roman myth, Vesta is the patron of the home and family. She is seen as the protector of children and family. **4.** Physically, Vesta has similarities to the Earth and Moon. **5.** In astrology, Vesta can give insight into areas of life relating to morality, ancient spiritual rituals, commitment to work, and domesticity (family, spouse, children, home). Vesta corresponds to the signs of Virgo and Scorpio. Computer astrology programs generally include Vesta when casting basic birth charts, and most astrologers include Vesta in astrological readings. ✦ **1.** In what house and sign does Vesta appear in your birth chart? Vesta's house placement is where you'll have her protection: the house indicates the areas of life where she will protect you, and it's also where *you* feel protective. You will be very concerned about this area of your life. You might feel that this area of life is sacred to you, and you feel a spiritual connection and devotion there. **2.** The sign Vesta is in tells you about your sexual attitudes, your contribution of protection to others, your ability to work with kundalini energy, your relationship to your body as a sacred vessel, and your level of devotion to spiritual principles. See also *asteroids, planets*. ○

In what sign do you have Vesta in your birth chart?

- **Vesta in Aries** pursues ideals with courage and, if necessary, violence.
- **Vesta in Taurus** commits to love as a sacred contract.
- **Vesta in Gemini** insists on contracts in writing.
- **Vesta in Cancer** waits patiently at home with open arms and a meal in the oven.

- **Vesta in Leo** is a student of sacred sex during youth and becomes an avid teacher with maturity.
- **Vesta in Virgo** understands the importance of daily ritual.
- **Vesta in Libra** demands spiritual integrity in marriage.
- **Vesta in Scorpio** understands the power of sex as a unifying and transformative act.
- **Vesta in Sagittarius** offers wise and protective counsel while traveling foreign lands.
- **Vesta in Capricorn** reorganizes a failing business into a determined and committed team.
- **Vesta in Aquarius** employs unusual and unorthodox means to raise awareness about child abuse.
- **Vesta in Pisces** connects people through sacred music that inspires dance.

In what house do you have Vesta in your birth chart?

Vesta ⚶	Keywords
First house Vesta	Special knowledge grants privilege and prestige
Second house Vesta	Spiritual work generates income
Third house Vesta	Writer who inspires spiritual learning
Fourth house Vesta	Creator of a warm, protective home that welcomes family, friends, and strangers
Fifth house Vesta	Spiritual leader
Sixth house Vesta	Devotion to highest expression of healing
Seventh house Vesta	Find wholeness through purification
Eighth house Vesta	Born to co-create with a soul mate
Ninth house Vesta	Connected to past life as a priest or priestess
Tenth house Vesta	Fulfills karmic obligation through dedication to business ethics

continues

continued

Vesta ⚶	Keywords
Eleventh house Vesta	Gathers people together to form a spiritual community
Twelfth house Vesta	Provides charitable care to those confined in institutions

Virgo **1.** The sixth sign of the zodiac. **2.** Those born between August 22 and September 22 have Virgo as their Sun sign. Also called the Virgin, Virgo is a yin, or feminine, mutable earth sign. The ruling planet for Virgo is Mercury, named for the Roman god of communication. Mercury was the only god who could travel unharmed from Olympus to Earth to the Underworld and back. With Mercury as its ruler, Virgo is able to humbly relate to individuals from the highest to the lowest ranks of society. **3.** The glyph for Virgo is ♍, and the symbol is the virgin, a symbol of purity and sacrifice. **4.** Virgo is the natural ruler of the sixth house, the house of health and well-being, work environment, and service. **5.** Other associations for Virgo are the colors yellow-green, navy blue and gray, and the sapphire.

✳ **1.** The body parts associated with Virgo are the nervous system and intestines. If you're a Virgo, you likely have a sensitive stomach. When you're anxious or stressed-out, you tend to get stomach or intestinal ailments. Watch what you eat—a balanced diet is essential to your good health. **2.** If your Sun sign is Virgo, you are analytical and orderly. You see perfection where others see chaos, and at the same time, you're always working to improve things. Virgo is the worker bee—and the potential workaholic—of the zodiac. You are also a healer—you want to make things better to help others. You make a good mentor. Some Virgos are very neat, and this is obvious by their appearance and the appearance of their home or office. Others hide their anal retentive tendencies, and may appear quite messy, while living within their own mental order. If you shift their piles of stuff around, you'll mess up that order—and you'll have an angry Virgo on your hands. **3.** Virgo is the time of the harvest, and Virgo natives are very good at maximizing resources. **4.** As a mutable earth sign, Virgo is both flexible and orderly. Virgos are gifted communicators, and tend to express their need for perfection and order—either throughout their lives or within one specific area. (Virgos are the ultimate vacation packers, and can fit two weeks' clothing into a small carry-on.) **5.** In school, everyone wants to borrow your class notes before the big test. Virgos are orderly and organized and include every detail of every lecture. Virgos do well in public service careers, as a teacher, nurse, therapist, or social worker. You can use your focus on detail and your analytical skills in fields of science (research or human behavioral) or the food industry. You enjoy working with people and are highly organized, a skill you bring to whatever you do. You're also good at business. **6.** *Watch out for:* You're a worrier, and this can affect your health. You also tend to live in your head, and should try to get some air once in a while. Take a walk or try a new outdoor sport. You can be overly analytical or obsessive, as well as critical, and you tend to be hardest on yourself. Loosen up—others think you're great. Don't be too self-deprecating. **7.** *I'm not a Virgo, but my best friend is:* Your Virgo best friend might often be quiet—this friend is probably thinking about how to improve something. A Virgo bff might seem critical, but really is trying to help. It will make these friends happy if you show your appreciation for their painstaking efforts. Virgo is a devoted and loyal friend. See also *Virgo ascendant, Virgo descendant.* ◯ 🏠 ☼

Virgo/Aquarius   See *Aquarius/Virgo.*

Virgo/Aries   See *Aries/Virgo.*

Virgo ascendant   Also called Virgo rising. The rising sign is Virgo, so Virgo is the sign on the cusp of the first house in the birth chart and the sign on the eastern horizon at the moment of birth. ✧ **1.** If you're a Virgo rising, you present yourself to the world as a Virgo, and that's how the world sees you. **2.** If your rising sign is Virgo, you appear orderly and efficient, as well as quiet and shy. You likely have a neat appearance, and are usually well groomed. Virgo rising is meticulous and reliable. You're likely organized, and you are more effective in an organized environment. You're very communicative and also cordial. Virgo rising can be self-critical and self-effacing. Don't be too hard on yourself. Realize that you can improve yourself, and appreciate your abilities. **3.** Virgo is a sign of service. Virgo rising

V

is here to learn public service, and they often work in jobs that contribute to making a better world. See also *ascendant*, *Virgo*, *Virgo descendant*. **BC** ☼

Virgo/Cancer   See *Cancer/Virgo*.

Virgo/Capricorn   See *Capricorn/Virgo*.

Virgo descendant   **1.** The descending sign is Virgo; Virgo is the sign on the cusp of the seventh house in the birth chart. **2.** The seventh house is the house of partnerships and marriage or significant others. ✦ **1.** Do you have Virgo on the cusp of your seventh house? If so, you relate to others in partnership like analytical Virgo. **2.** A Virgo descendant has Pisces rising. You attract a meticulous, practical, hardworking partner. Your partners will be logical, and they will keep you grounded in reality. They are pragmatic and sometimes critical. You need to learn practicality and discipline from your partners, and you need to help them lighten up and be less serious. You might have high expectations of your partners, and may scare potential partners away with your scrutiny. You're looking for an ideal, perfect mate—you'll have to learn to settle for reality. **3.** Your descending sign reveals your alter ego, or the aspects of yourself you repressed when you were seven or eight years old. It also describes your maternal grandmother, paternal grandfather, third sibling, and second child. Virgo descendant needs a partner who will apply practical know-how and diligent effort to make their dreams a reality. Virgo descendant tends to worry, so it helps to have someone around to remind them of all the things that are actually going well. See also *descendant*, *Virgo*, *Virgo ascendant*. **BC** ☼

Virgo/Gemini   See *Gemini/Virgo*.

Virgo/Leo   See *Leo/Virgo*.

Virgo/Libra   See *Libra/Virgo*.

Virgo/Pisces   See *Pisces/Virgo*.

Virgo rising   See *Virgo ascendant*.

Virgo/Sagittarius   See *Sagittarius/Virgo*.

Virgo/Scorpio   See *Scorpio/Virgo*.

Virgo/Taurus   See *Taurus/Virgo.*

Virgo/Virgo   **1.** Virgo, an earth sign, is intelligent and analytical.
2. Virgo/Virgo pairings may be following a karmic destiny to seek
order, but must work to avoid the tendency to love detail more than
each other. ✳ **1.** If both Virgos in this pair are neatniks, or if neither is, they'll get along great. But this pair is bad news if they don't
agree on structure or organization. These two really need to think
alike to get along well in a close relationship. Virgo is very affected
by their environment, and order and structure—of some kind—is
important to them. Mercury rules Virgo, so they communicate well
together, and can talk and talk. But two Virgos in the same household can be disastrous. **2.** These two are well paired as friends or in
a parent/child, teacher/student, employer/employee, or co-worker
relationship. This is a more difficult combination for cohabitation,
and Virgos can conflict in marriage or domestic partnership. Virgo/
Virgo needs to remember that love is not only in the fine print, but
in your lover's eyes. See also *Virgo.* ☯ ☼

VOC   See *void of course Moon.*

vocal signs   **1.** The astrological signs Gemini, Libra, and Aquarius.
2. The air sign triplicity ruled by Saturn during the day and Mercury
during the night. See also *Aquarius, Gemini, Libra, Mercury, Saturn.*
☼ ◯ **Z**

void of course Moon   **1.** Refers to the Moon in any given sign
at the point just after it was in aspect to another planet, but before
it moves into the next zodiac sign. **2.** The Moon when it is not
in aspect to any planet. **3.** Traditional astrology views the void of
course Moon (abbreviated VOC) as "no aspects, no events." In
other words, if the Moon isn't in aspect with another planet, it has
no power. Once the Moon is in aspect with another planet again, it
will have the power to manifest an event or condition. ✳ **1.** A void
of course Moon can be seen as a time when the Moon has no power,
but it's also an incubation period. The Moon void of course gives
you the chance to take a breather, and wait before pursuing or completing something. **2.** Activities begun and contracts signed during
the void of course Moon sometimes don't have lasting power; maybe
there's no follow-through by one of the parties, or there could be a

V

technical reason that the contract is voided. If this happens, you'll likely be glad it did—and you may be given another opportunity to revisit the contract at a later date and better aspected time. **3.** The time the Moon is void of course can be anywhere from a few minutes to two and a half days, but it usually lasts a couple of hours. See also *Moon, Moon phases.* ◯

waning Moon See *last quarter Moon*.

water, element **1.** One of the four astrological elements. The other elements are earth, air, and fire. A feminine (yin) element, water stands for emotions. **2.** The twelve astrological signs are divided equally among the four elements. The three water signs are Cancer, Scorpio, and Pisces. **3.** The twelve houses are also equally divided among the elements. The three water houses are those that correspond with the water signs: the fourth, eighth, and twelfth. These houses relate to home and family; joint resources, sex, death, and rebirth; and karmic duty and the collective unconscious. Planets found in these houses/signs are known as water planets.

✦ **1.** To find out whether you have water planets in your birth chart, you need to figure out what signs the planets in your chart are in. See how many planets are in the water signs of Cancer, Scorpio, and Pisces, which correspond with the fourth, eighth, and twelfth houses. **2.** People ruled by water signs are often highly intuitive and emotional. Water will find its way, and water signs use flow states to achieve balance. **3.** If you have lots of water planets in your birth chart, you are likely to possess an incredible memory and approach things from a multifaceted point of view—other than straight on. **4.** What if you have a shortage of the water element in your birth chart? If you have few water planets in your birth chart—or even none at all—you may lack some of the qualities of the water element. You may not be very sensitive to other people's feelings, or you may have difficulty expressing your own feelings. You may also be selfish. On the other hand, the absence of planets in the water houses (fourth, eighth, and twelfth) may indicate that you are simply not focused on these areas in this lifetime. **5.** If you have no water planets anywhere in your birth chart, you are likely a water adept: you've mastered the water element in a past lifetime. In this lifetime, you'll have to learn about and master the other elements, without continuously relying on your abilities with water. See also *adept, air sign, Cancer, earth sign, eighth house, elements, fire sign, fourth house, Pisces, Scorpio, twelfth house, water sign.* **BC** 🌑 🏠 ◯ ☼

water sign   **1.** Cancer, Scorpio, and Pisces are the three water signs, or the *water triplicity*. Water signs are emotional and intuitive. **2.** Water signs are empathic and creative. They rule receptive states and consciousness.

✦ **1.** If your Sun sign is Cancer, Scorpio, or Pisces, emotions and feelings—your own and those of the people around you—are your main focus. If you're a water sign, you're (seemingly) more emotional than logical. If you're a Cancer, you were born with antennae that pick up on upcoming trends, cycles, and themes. You find peace and calm in knowing that what is lost will eventually return. If you're a Scorpio, you help others get in touch with their darker feelings so that they can face them and free themselves. Scorpios are amazingly helpful with victims of violent crimes and in hospice work. If you're a Pisces, you have the ability to step back or zoom out and take in the bigger picture to see how everything can work together. For this reason, Pisces people make great film directors, music conductors, editors, and mural painters. **2.** All the water signs have feminine or *yin* energy. Like water itself, water signs are sometimes turbulent, sometimes placid. If you're a water sign—Cancer, Scorpio, or Pisces—your energy is fairly even as long as you *feel* your feelings. When you deny your feelings, addictions or compulsions can kick in, making you miserable. Water signs need heat to help get the stagnant dampness out. Heat from exercise, spicy food, or getting in touch with anger will all work. Water signs typically repress anger and just feel sad instead. Fortunately, water signs respond well to therapy, but they do need a sensitive soul they can trust to supervise their surrender into vulnerability. **3.** If you're a water sign, how do you mix with the other elements? Briefly, here's a look at your elemental compatibility: a water and earth combination makes things grow—it's very nurturing. Earth lends water the support water needs to feel safe; water provides the versatility that keeps Earth feeling young. When water and fire combine, there's sure to be steam: fire might be too strong-willed for sensitive water. Water and fire signs are adjacent in the zodiac, but that doesn't mean they're *happy* neighbors. The water person wants the fire person to turn down the music, send home their guests, and go to bed at a decent hour. The fire person wants the water person to come out of hiding, join the party, and stop being so sensitive. In two more settled individuals, this combination can bring some welcome steam to an otherwise dull sex life. Water and air is a carbonated mix—think effervescent bubbles. These neighbors are also friends. Water feels lighter about life and revived by air, and air feels refreshed by water. Water and water: this is a very emotional mix, but water flows, and these two get along swimmingly. They easily sympathize with each other's issues because they have the *same* issues. See also *Cancer*; *elements*; *Pisces*; *Scorpio*; *water*, *element*; *yin*. ☼

waxing Moon   See *first quarter Moon*.

Western astrology   **1.** Astrology as practiced in the Western world. **2.** Astrology as different from eastern Hindu or Vedic astrology. **3.** Western astrology relies on the zodiac that was in place when the Babylonians first developed a system of astrology. This is known as the *tropical zodiac*. The Babylonians were probably influenced by the astrological systems already being used in India and Egypt. Western astrology is more a symbolic than actual representation of the heavens, whereas Eastern astrology works with the actual astronomical positions of the planets, where they appear now. **4.** Eastern astrology connects the signs to the actual constellations, the *sidereal zodiac*. Western astrology's birth chart is the tropical zodiac. Eastern astrologers, Vedic astrologers, prefer their zodiac because it is an accurate depiction of the heavens now. Amazingly, both systems seem to work equally well, and perhaps they are also the yin and yang of each other. **5.** Western astrology includes the outer planets of Uranus, Neptune, and Pluto, as well as the asteroids, whereas Eastern astrology does not. **6.** Western astrology is based on a zodiac with twelve Sun signs that are described by the four elements, two energies (yin and yang), and three qualities (cardinal, fixed, and mutable).

W
X
Y
Z

✦ **1.** Why use Western astrology? Some Western astrologers practice both Western and Vedic astrology, but it's difficult to give up Western astrology once you've encountered the depth made possible through the interpretations of the outer planets and the asteroids. The original twelve constellations may no longer be in the same place, but the energy of where they were when astrology took its first breath in the Western world remains potent. **2.** Western astrology is richly influenced by Greek mythology, letting you easily identify archetypal patterns and life themes occurring in a birth chart and in progressed charts and transits. **3.** Eastern astrology uses the more astronomic zodiac and Western astrology uses the more archetypal zodiac. Like the Taijitu, the Taoist symbol for the divided circle of yin and yang dynamics, tropical zodiac and Western astrology balance out the sidereal zodiac and Eastern astrology. You may decide to use both. See also *astrology, Babylon, Hindu astrology, sidereal zodiac, Vedic astrology, yang, yin, zodiac.* **BC** ☯ **Z**

western hemisphere   See *hemisphere.*

work   1. Astrology can help determine not only whether to take a new job, but also what kind of work a person is best suited for. Look to the second house of income and find any planets posited there, as well as the second house's natural planetary ruler—Venus—to determine which planets bring in resources and how those resources come in. Remember, the planet is like a noun in that it tells you *what* sources the money. The sign is like a verb in that it tells you *how* the money comes in. **2.** The sixth house provides information about what kind of day-to-day duties and co-workers are best. Look at what planets are in this house and how they are aspected. Also consider the sixth house's natural planetary ruler, Mercury. The sign on the cusp of the sixth house reveals how a person functions best at work. **3.** The tenth house provides information on what type of industry, employer, and boss is best. Look for planets in the tenth house, and also remember that Saturn is its natural planetary ruler.

✦ **1.** After you have studied the houses and their respective planets, learn what you can about your chart placements of Venus, the planet of income, Mercury, the planet that rules the actual job, and Saturn, the planet of career and success. **2.** Look at your solar progressed chart to see where Mercury, Venus, and Saturn are now. Saturn may not have moved much, but Mercury and Venus will most likely be in different signs and houses than those they occupied in your birth chart. This gives you another layer of meaning to areas of work in your life, and it can help you understand what you are likely to attract *now*, at this point in your life. See also *business astrology, Mercury, Saturn, second house, sixth house, solar progressed chart, tenth house, Venus.* **BC** ☯ 🏠 ◯ **Z**

xenophile/phobe   **1.** When Jupiter is in Sagittarius, the sign it rules, or in Cancer, its sign of exaltation, the native is very attracted to everything foreign, including people, things, knowledge, culture, and experiences, particularly when Jupiter is in the first, fourth, fifth, seventh, or ninth house. **2.** If Jupiter is on a chart angle (the ascendant, nadir, descendant, or midheaven), the native tends to achieve a high position in some area of foreign relations. **3.** If Jupiter is in detriment or fall—in the signs of Gemini and Capricorn—the native tends to resist or even fear foreign people, their cultures, and even things made in foreign countries. See also *ascendant, Cancer, Capricorn, descendant, detriment, exalted, fall, fifth house, first house, fourth house, Gemini, Jupiter, midheaven (Medium Coeli), nadir (Imum Coeli), ninth house, Sagittarius, seventh house.* ☼ 🏠

yang   **1.** A name for direct or masculine energy; this energy is a giving, penetrating energy. **2.** Air and fire signs have yang energy: Aries, Gemini, Leo, Libra, Sagittarius, and Aquarius. **3.** Yang energy is both mental and spiritual. It is an active, hot energy, and tends to be literal, sequential, and linear. Yang signs are external and expressive. **4.** The Western half of the birth chart, the right side comprised of houses four through nine, is the yang side of the chart. ✧ **1.** Are you more masculine if your Sun sign is a yang sign, such as Gemini? You have to remember that you're everything in your birth chart— all of your planets in their various signs—not just your Sun sign. When your Sun is posited in a yang sign, it means you tend to think creatively and initiate activity. You're the person who gets something started—you energize and excite other people. Others react, respond, accommodate, and reflect your ideas back to you. You excel at start-ups, but may lose interest once the initial excitement dies down. **2.** If you have the majority of your planets in yang signs, you tend to express yourself in a more masculine manner. This is not so much about *gender* as it is about *mode*. More planets in yang signs

W
X
Y
Z

mean a greater emphasis on mental or spiritual expression, an inclination toward logic rather than intuition, and a more extroverted than introverted personality. See also *masculine principle*. **BC** ☯ **Z**

yin   **1.** A name for indirect or feminine energy; this is a receiving energy. **2.** Water and earth signs have yin energy: Taurus, Cancer, Virgo, Scorpio, Capricorn, and Pisces. **3.** Yin energy is physical and emotional. It reciprocates and is cool in nature. Yin signs tend to internalize and ponder. **4.** The Eastern half of the birth chart, the left side comprised of houses ten through three, is the yin side of the chart. ✦ **1.** What does it mean if your Sun sign has yin energy, or you have a lot of yin energy in your birth chart? You see creativity as a co-production. You may be very creative, but you like to share the leadership role, the process, and the credit for any endeavor. You can stick with a creative project for a long time—your Sun's fire burns slowly in its yin sign. **2.** If you have a majority of planets in yin signs, you put more emphasis on expressing yourself in a physical or emotional manner. You're more comfortable following your instincts and trusting your intuitive hunches, and are inclined to be more reflective and introspective. You also need your hermit time. See also *feminine principle*. **BC** ☯ **Z**

yod   **1.** A rare aspect between planets, also called the *hand of God* or the *finger of God*. When viewing the aspect lines in the center of a birth chart, a yod looks like a very long triangle. **2.** A yod occurs when one planet is flanked by two other planets that are each 150 degrees away on opposite sides of the finger planet. The two planets that are inconjunct (quincunx) the finger planet form a sextile between them. **3.** A yod is composed of the two inconjuncts and the finger planet at the apex of the triangle that is being pushed by the inconjuncts to make adjustments for the other two planets. **4.** Each of the planets in a yod configuration is in a different element, so each planet has a different temperament from the others. **5.** The finger planet has a different polarity than the sextile planets. For instance, if the finger planet is yang, the sextile planets are yin. This tends to create opposing energy between the finger planet and the sextiled planets.

✦ If you have a yod in your chart, don't be intimidated or afraid of its energy; even though each of the planets forming the yod seem to have disparate agendas, you can create something of genius when

you find a way for these three planets with nothing in common to unite with a common goal or purpose. The results may be beyond your expectation, though at first glance the situation could seem futile. Persevere! See also *aspects between planets, inconjunct, sextile.*
△○

young soul   **1.** Some astrologers interpret birth charts that are first quadrant-dominant with only personal planets (Mercury, Venus, and Mars) in the eighth, tenth, and twelfth houses (relating to karma) as charts of young souls. **2.** All of the planets are typically at different numbers of degrees, and the outer planets are more than 15 degrees away from the outer planets of Saturn, Uranus, Neptune, and Pluto. **3.** Young souls are souls that have had very few incarnations. The astrologer's job is to assist the young soul in accepting this life path with its flaws and challenges.

✦ **1.** Are you a young soul, according to this interpretation of your birth chart? Astrology considers all souls to be the same age in terms of existence, but young souls have had few other, if any, incarnations on Earth. Some astrologers might say you were recently an angel if you're a young soul. The Earth can be a very frightening place to be when it is new to you. You may have achieved a lot in other dimensions, but here on Earth you could feel frustrated by your newbie status. Young souls aren't accustomed to the lag time between getting an idea and making it real. Lots of type A personalities are simply young souls who are frustrated by how long it takes to make things happen here—they try pushing harder to make things happen faster. **2.** The ascendant and its ruler can provide you with guidance about what to focus on in this life when you are a young soul. See also *birth chart, eighth house, karma, old soul, personal planets, tenth house, twelfth house.* **BC** 🏠 **Z**

zodiac   **1.** The path of the Earth in its orbit around the Sun. **2.** The band of sky in which the planets and their motion is seen throughout the year, or the band showing the Sun's imagined path in the sky during the year. **3.** The area of the ecliptic (and beyond it by 8 or 9 degrees), creating a circle. This is divided into twelve equal sections (of 30 degrees each), and each section is named for a constellation originally within it. **4.** The twelve parts of the zodiac are the twelve astrological signs, or signs of the zodiac, named for

W
X
Y
Z

the twelve constellations. **5.** The twelve Sun signs are: Aries, Taurus, Gemini, Cancer, Leo, Virgo, Libra, Scorpio, Sagittarius, Capricorn, Aquarius, and Pisces. **6.** The word *zodiac* comes from the Greek words *zoion* meaning "animal" and *diac* meaning "dial." Zodiac literally means animal dial or animal circle. **7.** Imagine a circle that goes along the outside of the solar system that is divided into twelve equal sections. These sections are imaginary, but are also energetic. Each section holds a specific primal or archetypal energy. See also *archetype, astrology, constellation, ecliptic, Sun sign, Western astrology.* ☼ **Z**

zodiac order   This is the order in which the astrological signs circle the zodiac wheel, based on their calendar position. The zodiac order of the signs is: Aries (March 21–April 20), Taurus (April 20–May 21), Gemini (May 21–June 22), Cancer (June 22–July 23), Leo (July 23–August 22), Virgo (August 22–September 22), Libra (September 22–October 23), Scorpio (October 23–November 22), Sagittarius (November 22–December 22), Capricorn (December 22–January 21), Aquarius (January 21–February 19), and Pisces (February 19–March 21). See also *Sun sign.* ☼ **Z**

Astrology at a Glance

This appendix contains key astrology graphics to help you in your study of astrology. Use everything you see here to deepen your understanding as you read the astrology dictionary and learn about astrology's houses, planets, and signs.

The Zodiac Wheel

Keywords for Astrology's Houses

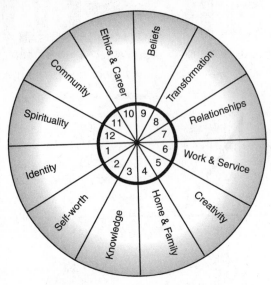

Natural Planets and Natural Signs in Their Houses

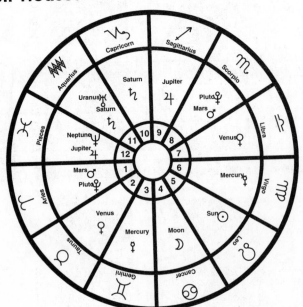

CHECK OUT THESE
BEST-SELLERS

More than 450 titles available at booksellers and online retailers everywhere!

Grammar and Style SECOND EDITION
978-1-59257-115-4

Word Search Puzzles
978-1-59257-900-6

Glycemic Index Weight Loss SECOND EDITION
978-1-59257-855-9

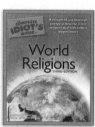
World Religions THIRD EDITION
978-1-59257-222-9

U.S. HISTORY GRAPHIC ILLUSTRATED
978-1-59257-785-9

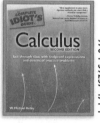
Calculus SECOND EDITION
978-1-59257-471-1

Positive Dog Training SECOND EDITION
978-1-59257-483-4

Personal Finance in Your 20s & 30s FOURTH EDITION
978-1-59257-883-2

CD INCLUDED!
Learning Spanish FIFTH EDITION
978-1-59257-908-2

Wine Basics SECOND EDITION
978-1-59257-786-6

Microsoft Windows 7
978-1-59257-954-9

CD INCLUDED!
Music Theory SECOND EDITION
978-1-59257-437-7

The Perfect Resume FIFTH EDITION
978-1-59257-957-0

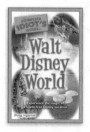
Organizing Your Life FIFTH EDITION
978-1-59257-966-2

Walt Disney World
978-1-59257-888-7

ALPHA idiotsguides.com

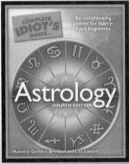

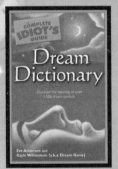